WORKING AGAINST THE GRAIN

Cross Cultural Theologies

Series Editors: Jione Havea and Clive Pearson, both at United Theological College, Sydney, and Charles Sturt University, Australia, and Anthony G. Reddie, Queen's Foundation for Ecumenical Theological Education, Birmingham

This series focuses on how the "cultural turn" in interdisciplinary studies has informed theology and biblical studies. It takes its leave from the experience of the flow of people from one part of the world to another. It moves beyond the crossing of cultures in a narrow diasporic sense. It entertains perspectives that arise out of generational criticism, gender, sexual orientation, and the relationship of film to theology. It explores the sometimes competing rhetoric of multiculturalism and cross-culturalism and demonstrates a concern for the intersection of globalization and how those global flows of peoples and ideas are received and interpreted in localized settings. The series seeks to make use of a range of disciplines including the study of cross-cultural liturgy, travel, the practice of ministry and worship in multi-ethnic locations and how theologies that have arisen in one part of the world have migrated to a new location. It looks at the public nature of faith in complex, multicultural, multireligious societies and compares how diverse faiths and their theologies have responded to the same issues.

The series welcomes contributions by scholars from around the world. It will include both single authored and multi-authored volumes.

Published

Global Civilization
Leonardo Boff

Dramatizing Theologies: A Participative Approach to Black God-Talk
Anthony G. Reddie

Art as Theology: The Religious Transformation of Art from the Postmodern to the Medieval
Andreas Andreopoulos

Black Theology in Britain: A Reader
Edited by Michael N. Jagessar and Anthony G. Reddie

Bibles and Baedekers: Tourism, Travel, Exile and God
Michael Grimshaw

Home Away from Home: The Caribbean Diasporan Church in the Black Atlantic Tradition
Delroy A. Reid-Salmon

Forthcoming

Another World is Possible: Spiritualities and Religions of Global Darker Peoples
Edited by Dwight N. Hopkins and Marjorie Lewis

The Non-Western Jesus: Jesus as Bodhisattva, Avatara, Guru, Prophet, Ancestor and Healer
Martien Brinkman

WORKING AGAINST THE GRAIN

RE-IMAGING BLACK THEOLOGY IN THE 21ST CENTURY

Anthony G. Reddie

LONDON   OAKVILLE

Published by Equinox Publishing Ltd.
UK: Unit 6, The Village, 101 Amies St., London SW11 2JW
USA: DBBC, 28 Main Street, Oakville, CT 06779

www.equinoxpub.com

First published 2008

British Library Cataloguing-in-Publication Data

A catalogue record for this book is available from the British Library.

ISBN-13   978 1 84553 385 4 (hardback)
          978 1 84553 386 1 (paperback)

Library of Congress Cataloging-in-Publication Data

Reddie, Anthony.
Working against the grain: Re-imaging theology in the 21st century /
Anthony G. Reddie.
      p. cm.—(Cross cultural theologies)
   Includes bibliographical references and index.
   ISBN 978-1-84553-385-4 (hb) — ISBN 978-1-84553-386-1 (pb) 1. Black theology.
I. Title.
   BT82.7.R46 2008
   230.089'96—dc22
                                   2008004698

Typeset by S.J.I. Services, New Delhi
Printed and bound in Great Britain by Lightning Source, Milton Keynes, UK.

Contents

This book is dedicated to my family, particularly my parents Lucille and Noel Reddie. You have all inspired me beyond belief and have enabled me to see the essential wisdom and fortitude that lies deep in the heart of ordinary Black people. God bless you all. Peace.

Preface

This text is a re-affirmation of the radical intent and practice of Black theology. I have described this work as one of re-imaging Black theology in the twenty-first century for it seeks to offer a new model of and methodological approach to undertaking this discipline. This "new" model and approach is one that seeks to combine participative methodologies of Christian education and discipleship with Black constructive and systematic theologies.

Working against the Grain represents the distillation of an ongoing process of seeking to combine Christian education – with its emphasis upon participative learning for ordinary people and Black liberation theology – and its structured approach to re-articulating the meaning of God and faith. This convergence of transformative education and Black theological content has been undertaken in much of my previous writing, but this text is a notable departure, in that the scale and methodological intent of this work represents a more comprehensive appraisal of this approach to doing Black theology.

Working against the Grain is offered as a radical commitment to a re-imagined form of deconstructionist thought which, like the plane that works against the grain of the wood, seeks to disrupt, complicate and, in Jamaican speak, "to mash up" the settled pattern of that which presently exists. In a world of studious conformity, where the "victory" of neo-liberal economics and globalized capitalism, White conservative politics and charismatic, prosperity-led models of Christianity seems somewhat complete, *Working against the Grain* offers an unapologetic theo-educational polemic for a new model of Black theology that is combative, argumentative, challenging, protesting, but importantly of all, committed to the cause of Black liberation.

I hope you enjoy reading the book.

Acknowledgements

My initial thanks are reserved for all the seemingly nameless and faceless "ordinary Black people" (in truth, none of us are simply ordinary, but extraordinary) whose fearless contributions to the many workshops I facilitated across the length and breadth of Britain assisted in making this book possible. I am not only grateful to your input, but consider it a blessing and joy to have had the honour of engaging with you.

I remain profoundly grateful to the Methodist Church (of Great Britain) for her continued support, financially and spiritually, in enabling me to do this work over the past number of years. I am, I believe (to the best of my knowledge), the only person funded by their church to operate as a self-identified Black theologian.

Most churches will eschew all contact with this seemingly dangerous entity named "Black Theology," let alone identifying and supporting "one of their own" to undertake it. If at times I have been rather trenchant and somewhat less than polite to my Church, it is due to the lifelong affection I hold for it, not because I don't care.

Special thanks are reserved for the "Formation in Ministry" office of the Methodist church for providing the infrastructure and moral and financial support that has enabled me to function as a church-sponsored Black theologian. Additional thanks are offered to the "Racial Justice Office" of the Connexional Team of the Methodist Church.

I am also deeply grateful to The Queen's Foundation for Ecumenical Theological Education, particularly the Research Centre, which has provided a convivial and highly creative space in which I have been able to reflect and write. Queen's is an exciting and challenging place to be and I have enjoyed all my years there! My thanks are also extended to all my colleagues at Queen's, particularly those who share with me the passion for and commitment to Black and Liberation theologies; I am thinking especially of Mukti Barton, Michael Jagessar, Carol Troupe and George Wauchope.

Thanks are also extended to the monthly Black Theology in Britain Forum, which meets at the Queen's Foundation for Ecumenical Theological Education, in Edgbaston, Birmingham (UK) on the last Thursday of every month. This forum has been in existence since the early 1990s and has proved an invaluable space for the nurturing of Black theological scholarship and talent. When I first came to the forum in the early to mid 1990s, I was a fledgling doctoral student, with greater hopes than ability at that time. Now some fifteen years on, I have the great honour and privilege of chairing the forum. I grateful to this body for the lively conversation that always ensues on the last Thursday of the month!

Then of course, I have to acknowledge the visionary figure of Janet Joyce, the Managing Director of Equinox Publishing. Janet and her company have been and remain a stellar operation in the support and development of Black theology in Britain. Through the publishing of *Black Theology: An International Journal*, to the development of the "Cross Cultural Theologies" book series, Equinox have shown themselves to be a company of integrity and vision, and I am proud to be associated with them. This is the third project I have undertaken with them and they remain my intellectual home in which much of my scholarship is housed.

I would like to thank my family, particularly my parents, Lucille and Noel Reddie, but not forgetting my siblings, Richard, Christopher and Sandra, plus Uncle Mervin and Auntie Lynette, and best of all, my little nephew Noah and niece Sasha – the next generation of my family. You are all special people in my life, and without you I would be a lesser human being.

Finally, of course, there is God. Through whom all things are possible; often making a way out of no way. My gratitude knows no bounds and cannot be expressed in words.

Thank you all.

Prologue: A Personal Manifesto

My Commitment to Black Theology

This text is written as a plain, unambiguous, unequivocal contribution to the cause of Black Liberation theology, or as is my preferred term, simply Black theology. I believe that the insertion of the term "liberation" is there for emphasis, or as a rhetorical device, rather than posing any substantive purpose, for in many respects its usage is tautological. Black theology's "dominant reason" for being is to espouse the theme of liberation.[1]

This book is conceived as a robust defence for a continuing commitment to Black theology that is prophetic, liberationist, angry, polemical and passionate. This book is written in that vein. It is not intended as an objective, calm and reasoned cry for Black theology as the substantive underscoring for Black liberation. It an angry polemic, pure and simple!

As I will outline at a later juncture, particularly in the next chapter, my approach to the "doing" of Black theology is built on the nexus of "church" and "academy," and "Christian education" and "systematic theology." In terms of the former, I have written this book in the same vein as all my longer published work, namely, as a means of trying to bring the church and academy into closer proximity. Since my days as a doctoral student in the 1990s, I have attempted to undertake Black theology as a means of formation and conscientization of ordinary Black people[2] in order to build faithful communities of resistance from the grassroots.[3] Whilst Black theology has been dominated by systematic theologians, and has drawn extensively from that tradition, the failure to connect with ordinary Black people has not been due to any lack of intent, but rather, failure in theological (and educational) method.

From the outset, I have attempted, through the use of personal narratives, experiential exercises and drama; sought to create more accessible ways of presenting Black theological material in order to challenge, inspire, affirm and empower ordinary Black people. This intent has led me to write in a more accessible and immediate fashion. The use and inclusion of interactive and participative methods in my published work as a means of doing Black theology has been to seek to engage ordinary Black people and to demonstrate a level of consistency between the method for undertaking research and the ways in which that body of knowledge is then presented.

In terms of the latter point, I have noted the disparity between the working methods of some scholars, in their engagement with ordinary people and the resultant published work. My criticism of some of these scholars is that the final published work does not cohere with or do justice to the interactive and accessible methods by which their scholarly material was gathered. I have sought to close that methodological and semantic gap.

Whilst I cannot claim to know, as a matter of fact, whether many (if any) of my books have exerted a significant impact on the consciousness and contemporary Christian praxis of ordinary Black people, at least my research respondents cannot say that I did not attempt to keep them in mind when I was seeking to document my reflections and collaborative insights. All my work, including this one, has been developed from my ongoing predilection for engaging in face-to-face participative work (I would best describe myself as a "participative Black theologian") through workshops undertaken in Black communities across the length and breadth of Britain.

The desire to undertake my work as a Black theologian through a participative framework in workshops and other informal learning contexts has been shaped by a lifelong interest in issues pertaining to pedagogy. My approach to Black theology has always been informed by the interactive and dialogical practices of Christian education. From my first two books[4] onwards, it has never been my intention as a Christian educator to teach people about and induct them into "normative Christianity."

Rather, my passion for Black theology has resulted in a wide variety of participative exercises that have been created in order to (a) help learners to gain a greater sense of the nature, meaning and intent of Black theology and (b) for me to gain insights from these encounters as a means of generating new knowledge about Black theology. I have termed this form of knowledge construction as theology from the "bottom up."[5]

The bringing together of Practical theology (Christian education) with Systematic theology in my work as a participative Black theologian has been the central narrative thread of my scholarly work since its inception. This nexus is intended to both propagate the central ideas of Black theology in addition to locating an interactive and dialogical means by which it can be undertaken.

I suspect that in the eyes of some, if not many, I am to be perceived as a relatively shallow scholar lacking in the necessary sophistry and cerebral forms of argument to be considered a serious or major scholar. If that is "to be my fate" for attempting this mission for undertaking Black theology, then so be it. Not all of us can aspire to greatness!

Black Theology that Addresses the Whole of Life

Having grown up within a Christian family in Britain, there is a real sense that my Christian faith did not come alive until the early 1990s. Prior to that period in my life, I think it is true to say that my Christian faith was somewhat moribund. The arid nature of my so-called Christian discipleship, the sense of trying to follow and give "my all" to the person of Jesus, made some kind of intellectual sense but did not challenge me emotionally. I have written about my sense of detachment from the corporate dimension of Christian traditional teachings in previous pieces of work.[6]

The discovery of Black theology in the early 1990s brought my desultory Christian faith back to life. At that moment, I caught a glimpse of the means by which I could breach the gap between the left-of-centre socio-political frameworks I had imbibed from childhood and the more conservative Christian faith into which I had been socialized from birth.

On the one hand, the former had given me a pronounced sense of the need to commit oneself to the ideas and practices of social justice. In the secondary school I attended, a kind of incipient quasi-Marxism was always buried deep in the subtext of the modus operandi of the teaching and learning process. Long before I came across the work of one of my later heroes, Paulo Freire, I had been schooled in the notion that education should be best understood as the practice of freedom. That to be educated meant being able to challenge authority and received wisdom and, most crucially of all, to ask "the why question."[7]

From very young I became enamoured by and excited at the possibilities that emerged from the processes of education. I noticed how "knowing something" could change one's whole outlook on the world. Long before the language of critical consciousness and conscientization became a part of my lexicon, I was captivated by the excitement of learning new things and seeing my world expanded beyond any reasonable conception, given the limitations placed on me by the expectations of wider society in terms of my working-class background and ethnicity.

But this educative process was not value-free, as is the case with any form of pedagogy.[8] Whilst it was undoubtedly progressive in its realization of the pursuit and intent of education, it was resolutely opposed to the idea of revealed truth within the repository of organized religion. Habitually, in some of my science and history classes, one would hear school teachers opining on the negative consequences of the Christian faith.

Whilst I was not inclined to defend Christianity (I had experienced too much racism from so-called good White Christians and other forms of prejudice from conservatively minded Black ones to do that), I nevertheless still believed in a God that had been revealed in Jesus Christ.

The sharpness of this divide became all the more apparent when I attended church on Sunday morning. Despite its former genealogy of social radicalism, the Methodism into which I was inducted in the 1970s was decidedly conservative in its social mores and political outlook. Whereas school was a haven for progressive and deconstructionist thought, church seemed intent on reinforcing the status quo. The value judgements that were replete within this particular religious code were myriad. Growing up in this context was to align oneself with the "righteous" against those who were not like us and were most definitely not of the "right stuff" in social, religious or theological terms. Across the years in which I attempted to make sense of this dichotomous struggle, it seem to me that one could characterize this phenomenon in figurative terms as an "inside" or interior versus "outside" or external battle for truth.

In terms of the socialist inspired education I received from a progressive comprehensive secondary school (that had been converted from an elite grammar school in the 1960s), this taught us to question the world; with special emphasis placed on the changes the process of learning could exert on the material fabric of the individual person and wider society. This is not to suggest that the overall curriculum or the pedagogy within it were not cognizant of the inner fabric of the human person and the need to change hearts and minds.

In classically pragmatic terms, however, the school was intent on serving its predominantly working-class neighbourhood and changing the life chances of those for whom education was often perceived as being either beyond them or of no particular relevance at all. The process of social and geographical mobility was enshrined into the very fabric of the ontology of ideology in the school.

I do not recall at any point there being any talk (much more fashionable in the present epoch) of the school attending to the spiritual awareness or promoting some sense of spirituality in the identities of its pupils. In many respect, this was a kind of Ruskin[9] inspired utilitarian approach to the products of accessible and affordable education for all. I, for one, remain grateful for the vision of the 1944 education act and its inspired model for enhancing the educational opportunities of working-class communities in Britain. The progressiveness of my secular education from the British state was counterpoised with the conservatism of the practice of the religious tradition into which I had been socialized.

The inside battle for truth was undertaken by the church I attended and the religious nurture I experienced in that communitarian setting, in Bradford, West Yorkshire. Whilst my secular education stressed the importance of external, material change, my religious instruction emphasized the inner dynamics of change. The ability to be changed from the inside-out was emphasized with some regularity within the life of the church.[10] This process of change occurred in the power of the Holy Spirit working through the believer in the ongoing process of "Entire Sanctification," leading inexorably, towards Holiness.[11]

The implications for social change by means of this religious code were implicit rather than explicit. Whilst many of my Sunday school teachers and Youth leaders were kind and dutiful people (mostly, if not exclusively, White), their sense that the Christianity that we all were imbibing might be the conduit for radical social change, was rarely, if ever, acknowledged. In many respects, "studious conformity" was the essential marker of this religious tradition.

Whilst I have acknowledged the importance of each paradigm in my formative, developmental growth in a previous book,[12] this should not disguise the inherent tensions in this experiential, psycho-social dialectic. The struggle for truth between the outside and inside dynamics of truth was to continue throughout my adolescence and into my early twenties.

In many respects, the challenge between these two opposing codes could be summed up in the often used ethical dialectic posed to students in theological education (seminarians in the US), namely, which is more important, "To believe Jesus but not to put in his actions in practice, or to be seen to put his actions into practice, but not necessarily to believe in him?" This dilemma, in effect, defined the social and theological dialectic in my formative years.

On the one hand, my attraction (and continued commitment) to left-wing politics and activism[13] was fostered through an explicitly egalitarian world view that was the product of my public education. My interaction with school teachers engendered within me a committed sense that Black and working-class peoples' best interests were always contained within left-of-centre policies and their concomitant political activism. I remain sceptical about the forces of Conservatism, particularly in the realms of party politics – especially those who want to convince working-class people of the merits of "caring Conservatism." In the salient words of the political left (I attribute them to the famous left-wing Labour politician Tony Benn), "show me a caring conservative and I'll show you a vegetarian wolf."

From my reading of British history, the machinations of the political right have always given rise to manifest suspicion in the minds of many Black people. Whilst I have no doubt all *political parties* run by White people are to be held in suspicion I am equally sanguine that those on the left have traditionally proven themselves to be happier bed fellows for Black and other minority ethnic peoples. I still remember the deleterious effect of right-wing Thatcherite policies on Black working-class communities in 1980s Britain in order not to be persuaded of the efficacy of "hitching my wagon" to the pioneering trail being led by political conservatives.

I have written this text, in part, to try and tease out an agenda and ideological intent for Black theology that remains committed to a left-of-centre model of social transformation and socio-economic change. At the time of writing, it is interesting to note the extent to which so-called, former left-wing firebrand and former Lord Mayor of London, Ken Livingstone, has gone further than any other politician in Britain in his apology for the slave trade and engaging in much needed debate around a reparations fund for assisting in the development of Black communities in London.[14] No Conservative politician has yet to make any comparative kind of public gesture or socio-economic commitment, at the time of writing.

I make these trenchant, political remarks, for I remain convinced that the vision for Black theology, as outlined in this text, must align itself with left-of-centre perspectives on societal change and transformation. The blandishments of so-called free trade and the market, bolstered by neo-liberal economics, the hyper-focus on the individual and the discourse of Victorian "family values" are the rhetoric of the right that is intended to "herd" Black people into a constricted space that represents the "we know best"[15] mentality of White corporate power. If such strictures are ever "successful" for Black people, then it is usually no more than a minority of us who experience the benefits of such doubtful largesse or generosity, which tends to be usual mode of operation of the Conservative right in their dealings with Black people.

As I will demonstrate in the next chapter, Black theology, as a branch of the wider family that is "Theologies of Liberation," draws sustenance from Marxist forms of analysis and an accompanying emphasis upon structural and materialist change for all, especially those who are deprived "full life" on the grounds of pernicious economics, patriarchal practices and racist ideologies. I cannot countenance how the rhetoric of the right can be seen to be compatible with the thematic and methodological intent of Black theology, which represents the faithful, theological framework for envisioning and working towards the "Beloved Community."[16]

But Black theology has always been more than a mere cipher for the inculcation of Marxist tools of analysis and an overarching focus on systemic oppression and structural and societal change. The personalism of God as understood within Evangelical Protestant theology has remained, albeit a distant theme, within Black theology. The liberative praxis of Black spirituality evident in the lives of marginalized and oppressed Black people and to which Black theology bears witness has been addressed in more recent times by the renowned African American scholar Gayraud Wilmore.[17] Wilmore states:

> I call Africentric spirituality *pragmatic* because it is not particularly interested in mystical experiences, speculative theologizing, or idealizations of what it means to exist in the eternal presence of a Supreme Being who mainly deals with us in a nonmaterial, spiritual realm… The pragmatic character of this spirituality is rooted in its human direction and goal, its propensity for loving service to others as an emulation of God's love for humankind that is manifested primarily in the biblical picture of Jesus' earthly ministry to "the least" of his sisters and brothers.[18]

The historic Afrocentric pragmatic spirituality of which Wilmore speaks is not abstract, other-worldly, disconnected, individualistic, pietistic, constrained by the limitations of false-consciousness and a retreat from the messy realities of human life and context. All of the aforementioned characteristics are seen as the antithesis of popular human struggle as advocated by the political left and to which the worst excesses of late 20th/early 21st century neo-Pentecostal hyper-spirituality is seen as in opposition.

Indeed, one need only point to the global success of some neo-Pentecostals, particularly in the US and their support of the Presidency of George W. Bush, to see the truth of claims from some critics on the left, towards organized religion and aspects of Black Christian faith in the 21st century.

My education and socialization by means of left-of-centre thinking enabled me to see the world in a particular fashion and to believe in the need for radical action for societal and indeed global change. What it lacked was any sense of transcendence or the numinous quality of the inner dynamics of spirituality that would inspire people to want to commit themselves to that sort of activism.

I know from personal experience that prolonged exposure to the sometimes arid rhetoric of Karl Marx or the sermonistic pronouncements of our student leaders in the Socialist Workers' Party at the University of Birmingham did not charge us for action. Rather, as Allan Boesak and Charles Villa-Vicencio outline in their important work documenting the Black Liberation struggle in South Africa,[19] prayer and spirituality are essential components of the faithful struggle for justice. Boesak states most poignantly:

> If the rulers will not hear the cries of the people, if they will not change, if they continue to prevent justice, let us pray them out of existence. God will hear our cry… We do not believe in the power of violence, but we do believe in the power of prayer. (South African Conference of Churches, National Conference, June 1984)[20]

On the face of it, Boesak's words appear to carry the very strains of the kind of political disengagement and social conservatism that is characteristic of Black religion in the eyes of political activists from the left. I remember having to defend my Christian faith whilst I was a member of the SWP as an undergraduate student in the 1980s.

And yet one only has to reflect upon the activism of Black people of faith in several parts of the world and across vast stretches of space and time to see that there is another story to be told about Afrocentric or Black spirituality. One can turn to South Africa during the epoch of apartheid, or the Civil Rights Movement in the US in the 1950s and 60s, or the activism of Sam Sharpe, a Baptist Deacon in Jamaica, and his initiation of one of the large rebellions against slavery in 1831, for inspiring examples. In these events one sees the subversive nature and liberative praxis of Black spirituality when harnessed to a passionate commitment for social change.

Robert Beckford, a leading Black British religious scholar and celebrated broadcaster, outlines a model of Black British political theology that is grounded on a form of liberative praxis that emerges from an embodied and committed spirituality that is attuned to the desire for radical social change.[21] Beckford writes:

> Congregations participate in a worshipping community that is constantly striving for the transformation of the individual and the community... All levels of the human being are involved in this worshipping community, both conscious and unconsciousness. The Black Pentecostal experience is fundamentally an experience of community. Therefore, any meaningful political theology for Black Pentecostals in Britain must be communal theology: it must place the individual firmly within the community of faith as well as the Black community.[22]

Beckford's words are a clarion call for a dynamic form of Black spirituality in Britain that disproves the stereotypical views of the ineffectual nature of Black religion often held by the political left. This text seeks to amplify Beckford's call without being wedded to his own particular brand of Black religio-cultural myopia that refuses to acknowledge the activism and contributions to Black faithful struggle for justice in Britain by those beyond Black Pentecostalism.

This work is committed to re-affirming the movement of Black theology with the social activism of the left, without being either subservient to all its rhetorical Marxist formulations or the negation of matters spiritual or religious.

On a final, personal note, I have found in Black theology a means of uniting my political commitment to the left whilst holding onto the personal faith and piety of my forbears, particularly my mother. Black theology, to my mind, remains the only viable form of Christian praxis that is worth its name and to which Black people should give their allegiance. In the forthcoming chapters, I outline what I mean by Black theology and demonstrate how this particular understanding of God can address issues of reconciliation, the church, slavery and reparations, violence against Black people, how we understand the person of Jesus, Christian education, engaging with social justice and the scourge of HIV/AIDS.

1 Defending Black Theology from Homogeneity

This book is a collection of themed essays. It has been undertaken by an embodied, self-conscious individual who is alive to the fact that as a subject in history, his life has been informed by the ebbs and flows of historical processes that have shaped his own existence and those of many others. I do not write, think, love, sometimes hate or simply exist in a vacuum. So who is the "I" at the centre of this work, which is attempting to work against the grain?

These essays are linked in their attempt to outline a new vision for a liberative model of Christianity built upon the insights of Black theology. The various pieces offer a series of vignettes for the promulgation of Black theology.

The work has emerged from the development of my eclectic teaching and workshop programmes (principally in theological education and local church contexts), where I have continued in my pioneering work of linking Black theological content with transformative pedagogy. The use of experiential models of learning, coupled with my developing thinking around Black theology, has led to a growing body of reflections that has been used to raise the critical consciousness of participants within formal and informal learning environments.

Locating Myself

As a contextual theologian I am always wary of the people who do not locate either themselves or their work within any particular social or cultural milieu when they begin to explicate their ideas. I shall not make that elemental mistake.

I am an African Caribbean male Christian. I was born in Bradford West Yorkshire in 1964. My parents arrived in Britain in the late 1950s from the Caribbean island of Jamaica as part of the mass migratory movement of predominantly Black people from the so-called "New Commonwealth."[1]

Alongside my cultural and ethnic identities (I am at once informed by West Yorkshire sensibilities, the Caribbean and being Black), there also my religious, denominational and spiritual heritages to be considered in the complex hybridity that is a generic part of what it is to be human.[2] My religious and denominational heritage is located within the Wesleyan Methodist tradition. I was baptized in the Christian Church in the spring of 1965 at Prospect Hall Methodist Church in Bradford. When this church closed, my family and many others decamped to Eastbrook Hall Methodist Central Mission in Bradford town centre. There I spent the next fifteen years of my life before I left Bradford in 1984 to read History at the University of Birmingham. In a previous piece of work I have stated that I am much more Methodist than I care to admit and rather too Methodist than is really good for me.[3] My work as a Black British theologian and Christian educator has been and continues to be informed by the denominational and religious tradition into which I have been socialized. This can be seen in my previous work, such as *Growing into Hope*, just as Robert Beckford's work is influenced greatly by his Pentecostal roots.[4] My own roots and identity have been shaped by Methodism. I was nurtured into and have imbibed Methodist values in my understanding of self, God, education, notions of social progress or advancement and, of course, how one "does theology."[5]

What to Call Ourselves?

In line with my own positionality and the sense of subjectivities that I inhabit and with which I identify, I have used my preferred nomenclature of "Black" in order to describe myself and the subjects at the heart of this book. I am aware of the myriad complexities in the self-naming processes of Black people of African descent. Hence, my struggle in trying to decide what naming strategies I will employ when seeking to name the people at the heart of this study. For some, "Caribbean British" is their nomenclature of choice.[6] For many others, a variety of terms could be employed in their attempts to name their existential self.[7] Elsewhere, I have argued that self-definition and self-naming is essentially an existential act of being human and the exercising of free will.[8]

Throughout this text I have used the nomenclature of "Black" with which to name myself and other people of African descent, whose subjectivities are the major cause for this text to be written. In using this term, I am not seeking to impose my preferential subjectivity onto others. I respect the naming strategies employed by persons of African descent, irrespective of whether it is a designation I like or is one that I might use.

Naming is an existential act and, as such, should be beyond the strictures or the "thought-policing" tendencies of others. But in using this term "Black," I want to suggest a very particular positionality for the people whose lives and experiences have assisted in shaping this book. As I will argue shortly, not everything that is done in the name of and by people of African descent can be named "Black theology." In much of my early work as a Christian educator, my concern was to create resources that would assist Black people in the formation of a version of Christianity that was consonant with the central tenets of Black theology.[9] Even at that early juncture, I was not interested in educating people about and inducting them into normative Christianity. Rather, the specific intentionality of Black theology was the preferred medium in which the articulation of Christian faith was to be explored and expressed.

The intentionality of the term "Black" as a subversive and thematic challenge to the notion of "White" and Whiteness has been explored by a plethora of Black theologians. Using such nomenclatures as "Caribbean" or "African," whilst very suggestive, do not necessarily outline a specific, unambiguous positionality vis-à-vis the individual or the groups who deploy these terms. To put it bluntly, tyrants can be "African" and "Caribbean." They can claim identity with the context, the history and the experience, alongside the many others with whom they share that particular designation.

I am sure that others would say the same for the term "Black." I have no doubt that one could argue that Black is no more immune from contamination and mis-representation as are the other terms employed by people of African descent in Britain. What has always drawn me to the term Black is its iconoclastic status, particularly when applied to the word theology. As has been argued elsewhere, Black can function as a political signifier, encompassing all peoples who might describe themselves as the socially-constructed other in "Postcolonial Britain."[10] Yet, on other occasions, Black simply denotes people of African descent. These terms are often used interchangeably.

In my own work, I often use the more politicized and global meaning, as witnessed in my co-edited work with Michael Jagessar entitled *Postcolonial Black British Theology*,[11] and in the monthly "Black Theology in Britain Forum," which meets monthly at Queen's and is chaired by myself.[12] Conversely, in my own solely authored work and also in the co-edited (again with Michael Jagessar) *Black Theology in Britain: A Reader*[13] I have used Black to denote people of primarily African descent, whether on the continent or in the Diaspora. My personal preference for the term Black is that it is specific and yet inclusive of others. It suggests coalition building and solidarity in struggle with others, and yet has a specificity for identifying themes that are central to the collective experience of being "African."

For many, particularly when juxtaposed with the words "theology" and "Church," it remains controversial. I hold to the view that, such has been the scandal of Black suffering and oppression, we are called to be nothing less than controversial and iconoclastic. This view is amplified in the chapter on the Black church, which follows at a later juncture in the book.[14] In the words of my deceased friend, Jil Brown:[15] "When we are silent we are still afraid. So it is better to speak, remembering that we were never meant to survive."[16]

The fact that we were never meant to survive as a people seems reason enough for us to adopt terms that are, in themselves, deeply political and uncomfortable. Our presence should never be one that makes others, particularly White hegemony, feel comfortable. In using the term "Black" I know that I am also bound to make many Black people feel uncomfortable, let alone White hegemony. For many Black people, juxtaposing "Black" with "Christian" and "theology" is to commit heresy. Such has been our socialization into and the concomitant imbibing of the overarching negative world view of self-negation; many Black people are unable to accept that their sacred talk of God should incorporate and indeed be informed by the notion of being "Black."[17]

Black People and Christianity

Christianity has long remained something of a conundrum for Black and other oppressed peoples of the world. This global phenomenon has been, in part, both the cause of violence and oppression on the subjugated, dispossessed and marginalized peoples of the world, whilst conversely, being a source for counter-oppressive struggle. Black Christianity has sought to respond to the vicissitudes of life by seeking solace in the redemptive figure of the Christ who has accompanied Black people in their ongoing struggles for human dignity and liberation.

Black theology, working from within a largely (although not exclusively) Christian framework, has sought to offer the much needed tools for this process of re-imaging human life, death and possibilities for a new world. Of late this radical challenge has appeared to have "run into the sand" as the continued rise of charismatic, conservative neo-Pentecostalism seems to have displaced whatever foothold Black theology once had in the theology and working practices of predominantly Diasporan African churches and faith communities.

This text argues that a re-imagined Black theology can enable Christianity in particular and Black Christian faith in general, to recapture the radical intent of this globalized religious framework. The roots of Black faith, for example, lie in a radical appropriation of the Gospel in order that those who are the "least of these" (Matthew 25:31–46) might live, and have that life in all its fullness (John 10:10). That work was a praxis orientated one and was not mindful of either doctrinal purity or biblical literalism.

Black Christian faith has for far too long drunk rather too deeply from the well of "Protestant Post-Reformation Evangelical theology" that has largely muted Black Christianity of its embodied radical intent.

I was first introduced to Black theology in the early 1990s. My first reaction upon reading the likes of James Cone and Gayraud Wilmore was to exclaim "So this is the missing link!" Whilst many of my peers have found the central tenets of Black theology troubling or even controversial, I can honestly attest to a sense of relief and excitement upon reading the early work of James Cone et al.

The truth was that my nurture and discipleship in the Christian faith had always been a struggle. This struggle was with the orthodoxy of classical Christian teaching. There were many instances when I found myself secretly railing against the creedal norms of Christianity, aware that as I was doing so, I was at a variance from the central tenets of the faith as understood by history and tradition.

I remember attending a well-to-do church and seeing on display a whole host of well-meaning individuals who would exclaim to being saved and yet seeing within their behaviour all the conspicuous traits of social superiority and racial intolerance. And yet, within the broader contexts of my life in working-class Bradford I met individuals who would never have described themselves as "saved" or being Christian, but whose praxis of life was exemplary. In the teaching I imbibed from my church it was made clear to me that "Only godly people would go to heaven, not good ones." Yet the truth of my life experience was that I felt more assured and in safer company with the good people than the so-called godly ones.

In more recent times, as I have plied my trade as a Black theologian and religious educator, I have assisted in the development of Black theology as an academic discipline in Britain. At the time of writing, I am the editor of the only international Black theology journal in the world and also the convener of the national Black theology forum in Britain, which meets at the Queen's Foundation in Birmingham. I am also the only Black British scholar who in the position as a (co)editor of a book series, who can assist in the commissioning of work for publication by Black British scholars. These roles have afforded me the great privilege of being actively involved in what I take to be one of the most dynamic academic movements in Britain.

Again, at the time of writing I am the longest continuous presence at the national Black theology forum, having first attended the forum in the autumn of 1994, some eighteen months after it had first met. I have been an ever present attendee of this forum since that time. I have been the chair of the forum since the autumn of 2003.

In that time, I have seen the development of Black theology grow impressively. There are currently approaching 30 postgraduate students undertaking some form of work in Black theology, linked mainly to the theology and religion department of the University of Birmingham and the Queen's Foundation where I work.

This book has been written in order to assist in re-invigorating the ongoing development of Black theology in my context and to offer these reflections for comparative analysis with the other major geographical centres where Black theology is undertaken.

This text has been entitled *Working against the Grain?*, in order to demonstrate the manner in which Black theology at its radical and iconoclastic best has never been afraid to move way beyond the confines of the doctrinal mainstream of Christianity in order to refashion a new notion of faith for the explicit purposes of Black liberation and social transformation.

It is my belief that Black theology can only be understood in this light. Namely, that without a commitment to liberative praxis and social transformation, one may be undertaking a form of important and necessary work, but to describe that enterprise as Black theology is a misnomer. Black theology has a specific identity and methodological intent that is not the preserve of all Black people who undertake the task of doing theology.

I have termed this work *Working against the Grain* because Black theology is not concerned with "natural flow of things," such as doctrinal niceties or orthodoxy for its own sake. Rather, Black theology is committed to liberative praxis and social transformation. Doctrine and dogmas may assist us in clarifying what can be described as being "of God" and being in sympathy with and consonant with God's reign or rule. I am not arguing for a doctrine free approach to religion or the Christian faith. By definition Christianity believes certain things to be true and others to be less true or not true at all. But I am clear, however, that whilst doctrine assists us in discerning this all-embracing and often elusive being named God, in order that we can better serve God for the needs of all those who are the "least of these" (Matthew 25:31–46); it is not an essential factor in and of itself. In short, I am saying that doctrine and dogma assist us, but we should never surrender the praxiological needs of ordinary oppressed and marginalized people for the sake of it.

As I will demonstrate at a later juncture in this book, I know from first hand what it means to be discriminated against by good Christian folk who believed all the right things and used all the right words, but whose notion of empathetic Christian praxis was non-existent.

So in this text, I am undertaking an exploration of the meaning, intent and praxis of Christianity through the focusing lens of Black theology. By attempting to re-imagine Black theology, this text begins to sketch a tentative terrain for the mapping of a new form of Christianity for the 21st century. A form of Christian faith built upon the insights of Black theology. The pre-modern dream of Christendom has died – long live a new Christianity!

Christianity and the Black Experience: A Critical Re-assessment?

When leading workshops in local churches and in more formal learning contexts, I have often commented that for the most part,[18] Black people can be trusted to do two things – namely, "we"[19] will read the Bible and will also go to church. In a previous piece of work, I argued, along with my colleague Michael Jagessar, that the ethnocentric complexion of religious discourse in Britain was such that no mention was ever made of the burgeoning growth of Black Christianity in Britain. So long as traditionally conceived White notions of Christianity held sway, there is little or no attempts to acknowledge the vibrancy of Black Christianity in Britain or what insights one might learn from this growing phenomenon.[20]

Black Christianity in Britain is indeed booming.[21] In addition to its all-pervasive growth in Britain, there is the question of its character and identity. Whilst scholars such as Aldred[22] and Sturge[23] have made important studies into the nature and identity of Black Christianity in Britain, their work has not explored the growing phenomenon in light of the challenges posed by Black theology. As I will outline at a later juncture in this chapter, Aldred and Sturges' work fails the "Black theology test" for they appear more concerned with accommodating Black experience within the broader frameworks of doctrinal Evangelical Christianity rather than re-thinking or even deconstructing the traditional hinterland of Christian tradition.

In attempting to "work against the grain" I am arguing that the existential realities of the Black experience cannot be constrained by the orthodoxies of Greek-derived thought. In the still apposite words of Robert Hood, "Must God Remain Greek?"[24] Hood looks at a plethora of African derived religious cosmologies and argues for their legitimacy as theistic constructs that are often no less syncretistic or lacking theological coherence than Christian inspired thought. In arguing that we should be working against the grain, I am not suggesting that the Christian-influenced version of Black theology[25] should totally divorce itself from the historical, biblical and doctrinal frameworks provided by normative Christianity.

At the heart of this work is a crucial dialectic. It is a delicate balancing act between the theological conservatism of many ordinary Black Christian people and the need to go beyond these strictures in order to outline a radical and non-restrictive framework for detailing the nature of Black humanity in a world of rampant and unapologetic White power.

In using the term "working against the grain," I want to play with the notion of what it means to belong to a tradition that has both been the cause of oppression and a tool for liberation. In whose direction are we moving when we say the creeds, say that we believe in Jesus as the Christ, sing our hymns, both ancient and modern, take up offices such as Deacon or Steward, or for some, even seek ordination? When some of us say that we are Christians (some might even say Black Christians) or others, that we are followers of the "Jesus Way," are we sure how these terms and the ideas that underpin them really impinge upon the material reality of our Blackness?

In using this term "working against the grain" I would like to both problematize and hold out renewed hope for a version of the Christian faith that is fully life giving and not life-denying or some kind of unreflective compromise that sits somewhere in the middle of the aforementioned poles. This term adopts some of the ambiguity and hybridity of that found in the nomenclature "Postcolonial." Elsewhere, my colleagues, Michael Jagessar and I describe postcolonialism as being

> not about the demise of colonialism as "post" since it embodies both "after" and "beyond." It is not historical chronologies, but more about a critical stance, oppositional tactic or subversive reading strategy... This new mode of imaging or counter-discourse to Eurocentric monologic has been at the heart of Black British theology from its inception.[26]

In using term "working against the grain" I am offering a subversive critique of traditional, missionary Eurocentric, historical, doctrinal Christianity into which the bulk of Black peoples across the world have been inducted and baptized. I want to challenge the existing frameworks of this religious tradition in much the same way that my scholarly hero James H. Cone did back in the 1960s and early 70s. I make no pretence to be the scholar that he was and is. In many respects, this text is a re-stating of the socially conscious and challenging work previously undertaken by systematic theologians, ethicists and biblical scholars over the past forty or so years. This text, written by a Practical Black British Liberation theologian is an attempt to argue once again for the radical and subversive agenda of the Black and Womanist theologians who first inspired me to undertake postgraduate work back in the mid 1990s.

The reality and experience of most Black people in the world in the 21st century is such that there is more need for a radical re-appraisal and articulation of Christianity by means of Black theology than ever before. This text is quite modest in its proposals. I am not a systematic or constructive theologian. This text does not offer any radically new doctrines or metaphysical thought forms by which Black thinking and life might be conceived. Rather, in its simple re-statement of the central tenets of Black theology, it offers a practiced-based approach to the articulation and praxis of Christianity for the *sole purpose* of Black existential liberation and the ultimate fullness of life as promised by Jesus.

What Is and What is Not Black Theology?

When speaking of Black theology, I am referring to the specific self-named discipline of re-interpreting Christian traditions and practices in light of liberationist themes and concepts, which arise out of Black experiences. This approach is one that makes Blackness and Black experience the initial point of departure (in partnership with Scripture and not the Bible alone, as sole authority) and uses these sources as the primary hermeneutical lens by which the truth of God's liberating agency is discerned. In effect, Blackness becomes the prime interpretative framework of re-interpreting and re-imaging God and the Christian faith.

In speaking of Black faith from within the framework of Christianity, it is not my intention to presuppose a Christian imperialistic or triumphant assertion over and against other religious traditions (or none for that matter!). I take seriously the work of Anthony Pinn, for example, and his assertion that Black people (predominantly African Americans for the most part in his writing) have spiritualities and religious traditions that stand outside the seeming normativity of Christianity and the Black Church.[27]

As I outline at several points, in a number of the essays, I have chosen to work within the confessional confines of Christianity not through any sense of closed or imperialistic forms of Evangelicalism; but rather, out of a sense of pragmatism. In using this phrase, I simply mean that the majority of Black people of faith will self-identify as "Bible-believing Christians" (hence the number of chapters that address the Bible, even though I am not a biblical specialist). So my version of Black theology falls within the "hermeneutical school" as identified by Ware.[28] I make no apologies for it and but neither do I want to suggest that it is superior to alternative forms of conceptualizing Black theology as outlined by other scholars.[29]

One of the central problems that have afflicted Black theology in more recent times in the UK is the difficulty of defining what is, and what is not, Black theology. As I will demonstrate shortly, there has been the presumption in the UK, where Black theology is still very much in its infancy, that Black theology is a discipline undertaken by all Black people who might describe themselves as theologians. The co-edited *Black Theology in Britain: A Reader*[30] has gone some way into delineating the basic folly of this contention. In this text I want to press the case even further in terms of what is Black theology and, as a corollary, to ask what is a Black theologian? This analysis will be juxtaposed alongside the need to articulate what are the alternative approaches to detailing the Black Christian religious experience.

In order to undertake this analysis I have decided to construct a three-part typology for outlining the differing ways in which Black religious scholars have approached the task of interpreting the meaning of the Christian faith and the role of theology in that ongoing enterprise.

The First Typology: the Colour Blind Approach

The first of the three typologies to which mention should be made is what I will term the "colour blind" approach to Black Christian faith. Adherents to this approach do not see colour in their hermeneutical engagement with the Christian faith. This particular typology works from the basis that God is spirit and that "in Christ" there is no discernible physical differences in terms of identity and materiality (Galatians 3:28). As African American theologians Pinn and Hopkins[31] have demonstrated, and more latterly, Womanist theologian Kelly Brown Douglas, Black Christianity drawing on the dualistic modes of thinking developed by Greek antiquity and largely propagated through Pauline theology has encouraged many Black people to downplay or even despise the materiality of the Black body. In short, the finite nature of Black bodies does not matter as much as that of the infinite and transcendent soul that resides within.

By drawing upon notions of abstract and non-physical or material reality of the self within the body of Christ, many conservative Black Christians are able to ignore the reality of their Blackness by alluding to a transcendent centre that is beyond the immediate materiality of their Black bodies.

This colour blind notion remains one of the most potent, and in my opinion, corrosive attempts to deal with the reality of Blackness as it relates to the lived experiences of people of African descent in the Diaspora. The basic premise behind notions of colour blind theologies is the sense that it is our very Blackness or the more generic realities of physical difference (based on skin pigmentation and phenotypes) that are the cause of ructions and disruptions in the body Christ.[32] That is, if we can only move beyond the immediacies of our restricted and sinful bodies towards the transcendent spirit and the soul that are the true essence of what it is to be human, then we will be better able to deal with racism and other forms of discrimination and prejudice. It is important to note, of course, that I am not asserting that only conservative Black Christians adhere to this particular form of theological construction. Many liberal and conservative White people will also make recourse to this form of thinking, but as this text is largely concerned with Black theological discourse as it emanates from Black people, the latter is not my primary concern in this work.

Colour blind approaches of Black Christians to my mind fail because they are both unrealistic and theologically flawed. In the first instance, they fail because people can be no more colour blind in how they deal with others as they can be non-human in their daily operations in the world. All of us live within a particular skin and are influenced by specific factors and contexts that affect and influence what it means to be human.[33] I am not asserting a belief in a crude notion of biological determinism, but I am arguing that none of us lives in an abstract, non-material world that is entirely spirit. Clearly as Black Christians, I want to acknowledge that there is more to life than mere matter; but I also recognize that matter matters – our enfleshed self is a God-given gift from the Creator and is not be overlooked or disparaged as a mere encumbrance of what it means to be human.[34]

Such approaches are also theologically incorrect as they do not pay due cognizance to the Incarnation or the pneumatological inspired difference of Pentecost. In terms of the former, the Incarnation of the "Word" that is Jesus demonstrates the importance of human flesh. God became one of us – a human being, enfleshed within a fallible and limited skin just as we are. I am not suggesting that his human-ness exhausts all that can be said about Jesus, but I am equally sure that his historical, situated, material identity as a human being should not be overlooked either. It is interesting to note that engagement with humankind operates through God's own self becoming human and entering into human history; into our reality and living and dying our death. God did not choose a long-ranged, distanced approach, via the realms of abstracted metaphysics as God's way of engaging with humankind. Rather, it is through the flesh of human being that God seeks to offer us a new paradigm for what it means to be human and to follow the way of "Christ" in the form of Jesus, who lived our life within history.

In terms of Pentecost, which remains an important theological paradigm for Black Christians and Black theology,[35] notions of difference and particularity are emphasized by *any* materialist reading of the Acts chapter 2 narrative.[36] If God, as supreme creator, is the author of all humanity then it stands to reason that God is also the originator of the very material, physical difference that is often perceived as "the problem" in our handling of difference. So if the very physical differences in terms of "race" are essentially the problem, and God as author of humanity created those very differences; then ultimately, is God to blame for the physical, materiality that ails us? In effect, it is all God's fault!

I would assert that difference itself is not the "problem," but rather, the value judgments and meanings attributed to notions of "race" and ethnicity (plus gender, class and sexuality for good measure) that have always been the fault line that has divided people. Making recourse to a colour blind approach to handle the realities of our Blackness is, in my mind, unfortunate and ill conceived. In the Pentecost narrative, we see that difference itself is not the problem. The believers at that epoch-making event in Jerusalem are united in faith and adherence to God and not through a sublimation of their material differences. Colour blind approaches are theologically flawed and do not serve the purpose of attempting to affirm the humanity of Black people. The notion that one affirms Blackness by ignoring it seems a most incongruous idea!

The Second Typology: Black Christian Religious Experience

The second typology is that which falls within the realms of "Black Christian religious experience." When speaking of Black Christian religious experience, this term refers to the "folk" orientated approach to Christian traditions which arise out of Black experiences, but which do *not necessarily* have a political or explicitly progressive and transformative agenda. Neither does this approach necessarily see Blackness as being a primary hermeneutical lens for re-interpreting the Christian faith, nor is it the case that one necessarily begins with Black experience as the normative source for doing theology.

This particular approach is more radical than the colour blind formulation as it recognizes the material reality of ethnicity and "race" in our understanding of what it means to be human. Whereas the colour blind approach has made no substantive contribution to the development of Black theology (by definition, if one is reluctant to acknowledge Blackness, then it would stand to reason that Black theology will be an anathema to those in this typology), those in the Black Christian religious experience camp have offered some important insights to the movement, certainly as it has developed in Britain.

There is a wealth of material written and edited by Black authors who have expressed the important insights into the experiential articulation of Black Christian faith in Britain. Emmanuel Lartey delineates many of the salient texts in two critically important contributions in *Black Theology: A Journal of Contextual Praxis.*[37] More recent work by the likes of Mark Sturge[38] and Joe Aldred[39] have also added to the sum of knowledge regarding the Black Christian religious experience in Britain, for example, and, as such, have made an important contribution to the broader development of Black theology. These texts, as fine as they are, cannot, in my mind, be considered as Black theology texts.

My reasons for making this critical assessment are twofold. First, those in the Black Christian religious experience typology have often failed to engage with the structural and systemic realities of Blackness and what that means, not only to the articulation and expression of Christianity, but secondly, and of greater import, in terms of what this connotes for the very meaning of the Christian faith itself. In short, how does Blackness re-configure the very nature of Christianity in light of Black experience?

Whilst not wishing to be judgmental on this second typology, it is important to note that my critique of this perspective is in light of Black theology rather than any substantive and overarching assessment of that position in and of itself.

In terms of its relationship with Black theology, the Black Christian religious experience typology is deficient due to its inability to engage in any substantive systemic, situational analysis. Two examples, I believe, will suffice at this juncture. Joe Aldred's *Respect* and Mark Sturge's *Look What The Lord Has Done!* are very important and much needed pieces of work within the British context. Both texts outline, in differing ways, the development and nature of Black Christian faith in Britain. It is not my contention to mount any substantive critique of either text in themselves. In highlighting these texts, I simply want to differentiate between Black Christian religious experience and Black theology. Both of these important texts fall into the former category. Neither can be understood as Black theology texts. As I will demonstrate shortly, there are, to my mind, a number of immutable "givens" within the discipline of Black theology that help to give this theological enterprise its character, distinctiveness and overarching modus operandi. Simply arguing that Black theology is God-talk undertaken by Black people is to misunderstand the nature and methodological intent of Black theology.

To suggest, for example, that all theology undertaken by Black people is Black theology is to then rob this discipline and practice of any specificity. In that case, then *all* theology done by Black people is Black theology. If Black theology is so generic, it, in effect, ceases to exist. The best analogy I would make in order to shed light on this contention is to point to the parallel discipline of Womanist theology. Not all Black women who do theology are necessarily Womanists![40]

Womanist theology is not simply theology that arises from the experiences of Black women; for this approach and movement is redolent of a particular consciousness, vis-à-vis the relationship of women's experience to the historical phenomenon of Christianity and the androcentric doctrines and epistemologies that have stymied the existential realities of women.[41] There are conservative Black women who will prioritize the religious tradition, particularly the divinely inspired canon, over and against their own material interests; often in a manner that is at variance with their own experiences. Such women may have important insights to offer the larger collective whole of humanity in terms of any resultant God talk, but that God talk is not automatically Womanist simply because a Black woman is undertaking that talk. In short, I am arguing that there is a particular consciousness, experiential intent and an understanding of the self in relationship to religious tradition that differentiates Womanist theology from theology done by Black women. Similarly, one can see this form of differentiation in terms of Black theology versus Black Christian religious experience. Womanist theology makes particular claims for the experiences of women as a source and a norm for doing theology. It privileges women's experiences and the female body as a site for divine revelation. Clearly, not all women will subscribe to this potentially radical and iconoclastic agenda.

If this argument is true for Black women, I believe it is no less true for all Black people. Not all Black people doing theology are engaged in Black theology. This is not to suggest that those, such as Aldred or Sturge, who I perceive as belonging to the Black Christian religious experience camp, are not engaged in valuable theological enterprises; for clearly they are, and I affirm their work, in so far as it is making an important contribution to Black religious scholarship in Britain; but crucially, it is not, to my mind, Black theology.

It is equally not the case that either writer is embarrassed about engaging with the issue of Blackness. In both texts, the authors are pains to outline the Black expressive quality of Christianity as it has emerged from within Black cultures across the African Diaspora, particularly the Caribbean. Whereas those in the first typology will hold to a colour blind doctrine, this cannot be said of either Aldred or Sturge of others in this typology for that matter. Neither of these important figures in Black British Christianity has sought to ignore the qualitative issues of Black Christian faith in Britain and how that concomitant cultural expression has given rise to a distinctive practice of Christianity in Britain.

What separates these texts from Black theology per se, however, are two important factors. First, neither text engages in substantive systemic, situational analysis of the Black experience in Britain in terms of power and epistemology. Right from the outset, Black and other Liberation theologies have engaged the challenging insights of situational analysis, drawing from neo-Marxist thought. They have also aligned themselves with the work of the social gospel movements of the early part of the twentieth century, plus the ideas emerging from the social scientific approaches to critical studies of the Frankfurt school in Germany. The work of Raushenbusch[42] and Feuerbach[43] has been supplemented by later scholars of the ilk of Paulo Freire[44] and Gustavo Gutteriez.[45]

Neither Aldred nor Sturge significantly draws from sources external to Christianity in order to critique Christian faith in light of Black social existence. It is interesting to note that both authors, plus a companion in this typology, Joel Edwards,[46] would all self-identify as Black evangelicals. In effect, their engagement with Blackness leads to an acknowledgement of the differing ways in which Black people might express the Christian faith, but will not easily countenance the ways in which Blackness reinterprets the very faith itself; often concluding with dramatically alternative forms of hermeneutics and doctrines than that which was fashioned during the Reformation (often the cultural and philosophical basis for White Evangelicalism from which Diasporan Black Christianity emerged). I have termed this process the "colourization" approach, in a previous piece of work.[47] The process of "colourization" is one where the essential marker between European derived notions of Christianity and African ones is the notion that the latter adds "colour" to the basic inviolate template that is Christianity. To assert an adherence to Evangelicalism is to place greater emphasis on the so-called historic truths of the faith as opposed to the contextual and liberationist re-thinking of any such ideas in light of the contingency and exigency of Black experiences over the past five hundred years.

Whereas Robert Beckford and myself, for example, offer radical alternatives to Christology[48] and the doctrine of God,[49] Sturge, in particular, affirms traditional androcentric Christian teachings in a manner that views them as largely unproblematic.[50]

The second point is an amplification of the last remark, namely that Black theology, like all liberation theologies, is governed by the necessity of ortho-praxis rather than orthodoxy. It is important to note that those in the Christian religious experience camp, when (in Jamaican speak) "Push come to shove,"[51] they will tend to emphasize traditional Christian teaching as opposed to the exigencies of the Black experience.

As I will demonstrate in a later chapter on biblical hermeneutics, it is interesting to note that Aldred, Sturge and Edwards all adhere to the traditional teachings of Christianity around the prohibition on homosexuality. This adherence accords with the biblical text and the sharp discourses against homosexual practice. Unlike the many authors in the influential African American text, *Loving the Body*,[52] there is no "hermeneutic of suspicion" regarding the conflation of societal norms, socio-political imposition and authorial collusion with oppressive normative structures in terms of the construction of and any resultant reading of biblical texts. In terms of the issue of homosexuality, all three authors display no difference in hermeneutical approach to Christianity than what might be expected from White Evangelicals. In short, the framework of church dogmatics triumphs over contextual experience.

In making this observation, I am not suggesting that any of these three writers should "embrace" homosexuality. But to mind, seeking to remain within the framework of Evangelical faith is inimical to any sense that they might describe themselves as Black theologians or that their work falls within the paradigm set by Black theology.

Whether in the work of James Cone,[53] Delores Williams[54] or Robert Beckford,[55] Black and Womanist theologians have not been afraid to jettison traditional Christian teachings in order to affirm the new revelation that arises from Black experience. In the case of Cone, sin becomes a systemic material evil emanating from the in-human practices of oppressors and is not a cosmic metaphysical phenomenon that emerges from early Christian mythology.[56]

Similarly, Williams completely re-orientates atonement theories in light of the suffering and oppression of Black women.[57] For Williams, the cross can never be salvific! Black Christian religious experience is simply unwilling to engage in this form of deconstructionist and reconstruction work in order to refashion Christian teaching in a way that is commensurate with the realities of Black negation and struggle.

I still remember engaging with another well-known Black Christian religious experience scholar in the UK, at one of the monthly Black theology forum meetings in Birmingham, where I was the designated speaker. His retort to my invoking the work of James Cone as central to my own understanding of Black theology was to ask the question, "But tell me this, is James Cone saved?" I did not answer (it was not my place to make any such experiential declarations on behalf of another), but it did occur to me that in light of my talk on the nature and intent of Black theology, this was an entirely irrelevant question to ask.

Having spoken for almost an hour on the horrors of the slave trade and the oppression of Black people in the Americas, the Caribbean and Britain, the best question this man could mount was "Is Cone saved?" My retort was one of "saved from and for what?" Such are the strictures of aspects of Black evangelicalism that continue to be constrained within the maze of doctrinal and dogmatic certitudes as opposed to engaging with Black existential experience.

For many in this camp, salvation remains that which is conceived *solely* in terms of adherence to the belief in Jesus Christ as Lord and Saviour and is expressed within the context of individual experience and personal salvation. Salvation as understood in terms of liberation, social transformation and societal reconfiguration are given less emphasis, or in some cases, are rejected altogether.

It should be noted, however, that Aldred, although identified (to my mind) with the Black Christian religious experience typology, has, nevertheless, made an important contribution to the development of Black theology through his early writing in *Black Theology*[58] and his organizational work that enabled the *Black Theology in Britain* journal to come to fruition in 1998.[59] It is my hope that the conservatism (Aldred describes himself as being a "radical" but radicals can also be conservative – one only has to note the practices of Margaret Thatcher to see this in evidence) that has become more evident in later times will be dissipated and challenged, as his work continues to develop.

I am at pains to reiterate that my assessment of those in both the previous typologies has been made on the basis of a comparative analysis with the nature and intent of Black theology, rather than any substantive critique of the work and the people in these categories in and of themselves. Those in the second typology, in particular, have made immense and invaluable contributions to the development of Black Christianity in Britain and they are to be saluted for that investment of time and energy.

I would acknowledge that the lines of demarcation between these differing perspectives are blurred. There are many commonalities between these differing forms of Black religious scholarship. For example, all Black Christian religious experience is implicitly liberationist, even when constrained by conservative doctrines and neo-conservative ethics.

The Third Typology: Black Theology

Black theology in Britain is a plural term for a broad range of theological practices and methodologies that whilst quite eclectic, are nonetheless informed by a series of constructive and generative themes. In terms of the latter, these themes can be summarized in the following way.

First, Black theology gives priority to the reality of the Black experience. The existential point of departure is the reality of what Black people have known and felt to be true. This truth is often attested to and affirmed by making recourse to other foundational sources for doing theology; most often scripture. Whilst there is a dialectical tension between the normativity of the holy text and the contingency of the human context, there is nonetheless a contested reality between the horizon of the historical narratives and the encounter with the divine that operates in front of the written page, emanating from the lived experiences of the reader. As I have asserted in a workshop with grassroots Christians in Birmingham, "There is no proof that when these Biblical texts were being written the authors had the realities of Black experience in mind. They wrote for their time and space, and we cannot be limited to their truth assertions, given the alternative realities in which we presently exist!" In the words of one of the stalwarts of the Black Theology in Britain movement, when asked "what does the Bible say on a particular matter," he has been known to reply, "Well the Bible doesn't say anything until we open it and read it."[60]

I would affirm the words of my colleague and would reiterate that there exists a dialogical relationship between the Bible and the human reader. Yes, the Bible will judge the human being, but the hermeneutical frameworks that arise out of the human encounter with the wider context lead to particular experiences and social realities that can be used to *read* and *judge* scripture.

The examples of Black people re-reading Paul's defence of the status quo in terms of political power and slavery are prime examples of utilizing a "hermeneutic of suspicion" to work against the apparent literal meaning of the text in light of human experience. In effect, whatever the holy text *may have* stated as true, human experience, which becomes the site for an alternative and ongoing form of revelation, can lead us to new insights that may radically critique the accepted norms.

Second, Black theology affirms Black history and story as another source for talking about God's agency in human affairs. In effect, what have we seen, felt and known to be true over the past five centuries since our forced removal from Africa?[61]

Third, Black theology emphasizes a Black re-interpretation of the Bible.[62] In light of the collective well-spring of Black human experience, how do we read and engage with the scriptures? What new insights will our own experience provide and how will they enable us to unlock the scriptures? It is my belief that one of the most challenging examples of the use of a Black hermeneutic can be found in an essay by Valentina Alexander, where she inhabits the psyche of the runaway slave Onesimus (who does not have a voice in the biblical narrative) and seeks to write an imaginative response to his master Philemon in light of Paul's pastoral letter to the latter. Alexander writes on behalf of Onesimus:

> Paul has suggested that my new-found faith in the Lord should make me more useful to you as a brother and as a slave. Yet as much as I admire, respect and am grateful to him I cannot agree with his opinions in this matter. When I ran away from you all

those weeks ago, I felt tired, embittered and a resentful man. It was not that you worked me too hard, or chastened me too harshly, for as masters come you have been a kind one to me. Yet in spite of your kindness I was unhappy and no matter what I tried to do to ignore my unhappiness or come to terms with it, nothing would make it depart from me.[63]

Alexander, utilizing a Black hermeneutic, dares to re-imagine the biblical text in light of Black existential experiences. Black, Diasporan Africans who were once slaves, continue to feel the reality of structural poverty, life in prison, immigration detention and being overdosed on medication for mental ill health; we know what it is like to feel entrapped, desperate and unhappy like Onesimus. And whilst not wishing to discount the necessity of spiritual resources for surviving and thriving, we also know the importance of material, structural and systemic change.

Fourth, Black theology recognizes the importance of both analysing and deploying our cultural resources for effecting liberation. By analysing Black culture(s) and their various material forms for an indication of Black selfhood, identity and the substance and reality of being human, Black theology has sought to locate divine agency not only in the historic texts of the tradition but also within the matrices for human living, in which there is an ongoing encounter with the Divine reality.[64]

Black British theologian, Robert Beckford in particular, has been at the forefront of discerning within Black African Caribbean popular cultures, and the accompanying expressive practices, a site for the continuing revelation of God that can enable Black people to develop a level of critical consciousness that leads, as a corollary, to new ways of seeing and doing. Renewed praxis cannot emerge without their being some preliminary change in one's understanding and perception of the world.[65]

The analysis of Black expressive cultures and contemporary Black ecclesial practice can be undertaken in a variety of forms. In my previous research, working from within the context of education methodologies, I have argued for a process I define as "redefining the norm."[66] This process is one where ordinary Christians at the grassroots of society and the church are enabled by means of a worked, experiential model of Christian learning to analyse cultural frameworks and norms in order to discern the ways in which these structures restrict their thinking and consequent action.[67] I argue that ordinary Black people, working together in "base ecclesial communities," often in the context of worship and learning are enabled to rethink and re-imagine their world in order to effect change, and so develop renewed forms of praxis from the bottom up.[68] I state that

> The process of redefining the norm was effected through the medium of these all age acts of worship… Redefining the norm offers an important tool for the liberation of all marginalized people in faith communities in Britain.[69]

Underpinning these varying sources for undertaking Black theology is the central normative thread that is the concept of liberation. The reality that Black people are more likely to be excluded from school, incarcerated in prison, detained on a mental health ward, refused leave to enter the country, become the victim of an unsolved "racial attack" or spat at simply for having Black skin challenges the conservative and liberal discourse that Black people are not living in an oppressive state in postcolonial Britain or in any other White dominated context in the world. Beckford, in particular, has highlighted these realities in one of his seminal texts, *God of the Rahtid*.[70]

Black theology seeks to challenge the structural and systemic ills that have plagued Black people for as long as we have existed in this contested space that is the post Enlightenment Euro-America world order! Black theology is related to, but is somewhat different from, the "colour blind" approaches to Black Christian faith in the first typology and the "Black Christian religious experience" of the second typology. The praxis of Black theology is not based upon the notion of merely providing information, which often seems to be the main modus operandi of the second typology. The work of social theorists has shown that increased information that is not allied to systemic or structural change simply leads to the provision of "better educated racists."[71]

Contentiously, I have arrived at a formulation for the definition of Black theology that argues for specific intentionality to the articulation and the doing of Black theology, i.e. Black theology is not that which is done by any Black person of faith or no faith for that matter. It is certainly not undertaken by those Black people who refuse to "see colour." Neither is it necessarily done by those who will not submit the tradition and the normative status of the Bible to scrutiny under the lens of the ongoing realities of Black experience.

Black theology is, in my mind, is a minority enterprise amongst Black Christian folk in Britain, if not the world. It is risky business and not for the faint hearted or those whose primary aim is to be acceptable or respectable in the eyes of the British or any other White dominated establishment. Black theology is protesting in the best traditions of Jesus of Nazareth,[72] who was not concerned with strictures of acceptability, hierarchical power or respectability. Black theology, like her counterparts in other parts of the world (primarily North America, the Caribbean and South Africa), is concerned with waging war against structural poverty and injustice in order that freedom and the wholeness of life may accrue for those who are deemed the least of these (Matthew 25:31–46), at whatever the cost – even the scandal of the cross! The cross stands not as symbol of a spiritualized and generic failing of all people in their relationship to God, but rather, is the sign of the price to be paid for fighting injustice and living the Jesus way of love and peace for all people, especially those who are oppressed.[73] Black theology remains committed to the "Beloved Community" so eloquently expressed by Martin Luther King Jr., who himself paid the ultimate price in his struggle to proclaim the reign of God.[74]

A Pragmatic and Practical Approach to Doing Black Theology

This study is undertaken by a practical[75] Black theologian in Britain. In using this term, I am drawing attention to the need to hold in dialectical tension the competing claims of theory and practice in terms of the practical expression of Christian theology and praxis. This approach is one that pays particular attention to Christian action and how and in what ways are these forms of "performance" resourced, nourished and even impeded by Christian traditions and reflections that have emerged from the latter.

In using the term "pragmatic" I am in debt to the great African American religious historian Gayraud Wilmore who claims that Black Christianity is essentially pragmatic in quality.[76] In using this term I am not subscribing to the Joseph Washington's reductive and purely utilitarian perspective on Black Christianity, particularly in the US context.[77] This work is a pragmatic polemic. By pragmatic, I am working within the framework of my own practice as a Practical Black theologian, who in using the methodological approaches of Christian education, is attempting to create a model of Black theology that is concerned with issues of conscientization, formation and social transformation. I am working from the standpoint that ecclesial settings remain potent symbols for creative and constructive change, and that transformative ministry can be a conduit for the working out and working through of Martin Luther King Jr.'s notion of the beloved community.[78] I have termed this approach as one that is pragmatic because I recognize the inherent conservatism of ordinary Black Christians. This approach is one that attempts to engage in direct fashion with the religious positionality of ordinary Black people of Christian faith in Britain.

Whilst I have no epistemological or procedural difficulty with systematic and constructive theologies as academic disciplines and the Black theological engagement with them, the truth is, the relationship between most ordinary Black people and these various thought forms can be likened to the distance between the earth and the moon. For many ordinary Black Christians, Christian theology begins and ends with the Bible and our love for Jesus. Going to church is the tangible expression of the former. As a Practical Black theologian, working through the frameworks provided by Christian education as a means of disseminating and conscientizing (predominantly) ordinary Black people, by means of Black theology, I want to attend to those aspects of Christian practice that directly confront and impinge on the lives of Black folk.

This text is concerned with addressing the hinterland of Black Christian expression with a view to challenging and enabling ordinary Black people to re-think, interrogate and re-assess the nature of their Christian faith and expression in light of their historical materiality. To what extent has Black Christianity seriously engaged with the nature of the Black experience with a view to both transforming that experience, but perhaps of greater import, to transform the wider contexts and societal frameworks in which those experiences are housed? To what extent has Black Christian thought simply re-affirmed and even colluded with the Greco-Roman epistemological underpinning of much that can be construed as "traditional Christianity"?

If this text is seeking to engage with ordinary Black Christians and their normative points of departure, then it is also the case that I am working within a self-confessed Christian framework as the basis for my construction of Black theology. In doing so, I am aware of the dangers of Christian myopia and supremacy that stalk this seemingly innocent undertaking like a ravenous wild animal. In terms of Christian myopia, Anthony Pinn in his very influential *Varieties of African American Religious Experience*[79] has argued against the short-sightedness of many Black religious scholars in addressing their gaze towards Christianity alone as they seek to determine the contours of Diasporan African religious sensibilities.[80]

The sense of supremacist leanings within Christianity has been expertly recounted by Kelly Brown Douglas,[81] and recounted in brief, in a later chapter in this book.[82] In both cases, particularly within Douglas's work, we can be in no doubt that Christianity, taking her cue from the "Jealous God"[83] at the heart of this religious framework, is one that does not take too kindly to rivals or competition.

The presumption in much Black religious literature that all Black people are Christians is one that needs to be challenged. I am aware that I may be guilty of this kind of myopia and supremacist leanings in this work. In my defence, I would argue that as a Practical Black theologian, my point of departure is the positionality that lies in the conservative religious hinterland where the greater majority of Black peoples locate themselves. Namely, that whilst there is an undoubted variety of religious expression in the African Diaspora and I for one would not wish that to be anything but the case, nonetheless, the majority of religious expression amongst Black people is undoubtedly Christian.

In making this declaration, I am not wishing to suggest that this state of affairs is normative or preferable. It is simply the way it is. My position is not that of a conservative Evangelical.[84] I do not hold to a literal interpretation of John 14:6 and the notion that salvation is achieved through Jesus Christ alone.[85] Like Dianne Stewart, whose interest lies in exploring the religious sensibilities of predominantly Caribbean peoples,[86] I am aware of the myriad religious dimensions of Black people of African and Caribbean roots.

This text is a pragmatic one for it seeks to engage with the positionality of most ordinary Black religious believers, namely Christians, and seeks to work within the paradigms this religious tradition provides, in order to re-define and re-assess its central meaning and intent. In many respects, this work is undoubtedly a conservative one, for it seeks to work within the established paradigm that is traditional Christianity, albeit with the aim of re-defining the meaning of this religious framework. Many might ask, legitimately, why not look at Islam or Rasta as alternative frameworks for Black religiosity? And in all truth, they have a very valid point. But knowing ordinary Black people as I do, from my peripatetic work as a Practical Black theologian in Britain, one simply has to engage with these people from their own points of departure and not where others think they should be!

Knowing that many Black people will read the Bible, give their total allegiance to Jesus who is the Christ, and will work out the aforementioned through their attendance at church, it is incumbent on me, therefore, to address these significant and formative points of departure.

It is for these reasons that I have addressed a good deal of my scholarly thinking in this text around such core issues as Christology, the reading and interpreting of the Bible and articulating the nature and intent of the church. These are all core issues for many Black Christians. I have attempted to address much of the myopic and constricted thinking that takes place within Black Christian communities and the forces of conservatism that have limited the radical praxis of Black Christian faith, both in Britain and further afield.

The Shape and Content of the Book

As I have stated previously, this book is a collection of themed essays. The essays are linked in their attempt to outline a new vision for a liberative model of Christianity built upon the insights of Black theology. The various pieces offer a series of vignettes for the promulgation of Black theology.

Chapter 2 is a theological exploration of the frameworks that both gave rise to and provided comfort for the development of chattel slavery across the Black Atlantic. The chapter argues that an abstracted spiritualization of the central tenets of the Christian faith enabled White Evangelical slave owners to be assured of their own salvation whilst being able to abase and abuse Black flesh. This essay was previously, published in *Black Theology: An International Journal* 5, no. 3, 2007.]

Chapter 3 draws on some of my previous work and research in the areas of Christian education and Practical theology and argues that there are deep religio-cultural factors that underpin the varied ways in which many communities read and interpret the Bible. My argument in this chapter is twofold. The more minimalist assertion is that using a hermeneutical tool of "a Black religio-cultural approach" to reading the biblical text, one can assist faith communities – in this case, African and African Caribbean communities in Britain – to have greater cognizance of the reasons why they interpret the Bible and particular sections of it in certain, distinctive ways. My more expansive and, dare I say, radical or polemical assertion is this: That in all truth, the Bible does not give human faithful communities authority, for the Bible has no authority other than that which the church, as the main faithful community, has given it. That in effect, we give the Bible authority and not the other way around.

Chapter 4 looks at Jesus. In our traditional understanding of Christianity, the figure of Jesus Christ is seen as central. Jesus, who is believed to be God Incarnated – God who takes the form of human flesh and becomes one of us – remains the basis on which Christianity conceives of itself as offering a unique vision of the world as it is and as it will be.

This chapter seeks to re-image Jesus and asks the question, "what really happens to Black folk when we seriously envisage Jesus as one of us?" I know that there are many Black Evangelical Christians who will assert that, courtesy of the notion of the "Jesus of Faith," the one who is present where two or three are gathered, this same Jesus can no doubt be Black when in the presence of two or three Black people – but my critical question remains: Does this Black Jesus still do the same kind of work as the traditional universalizing White one?

Chapter 5 outlines a Black theological approach to re-reading biblical texts. This interactive process – working alongside ordinary Black Christians – is one that attempts to create an *accessible* and *creative* method for bringing the insights of Black theology into conversation with sacred texts. This chapter highlights the accessible and creative approach to attempting to bring the academy into conversation with the church.

Chapter 6 is a Black theological reading of the development, intent and characteristics of Black churches across the African Diaspora. It is based upon a clear theological rationale for the ideological and intentional collective agency of Black people in Black ecclesial spaces. My notion of Black church is predicated on the notion of a politicized ecclesial collectivity of Black people in the African Diaspora. I am writing on the firm premise that there are a number of distinctive cultural and theological markers for Black churches in the African Diaspora. Not all Black churches in the African Diaspora will either wish to be identified as being Black or perceived as being related to the liberative theological agenda within which this essay is constructed. Despite such sensitivities and blandishments, I remain convinced that the substance of Black Diasporan history gives weight and credence to my liberative contentions for the nature, purpose and intent of Black churches across the past four centuries and into the present day.

Chapter 7 outlines a Black theological exploration of the relationship between Christianity, violence and the "other" in postcolonial Britain. The chapter argues that notions of "in" and "out" and the propensity within such frameworks for harbouring suspicion, prejudice and even violence against those who are not deemed to be "one of us" has potentially dangerous consequences for Black people living in Britain. So what happens when, as Black Christians, we find ourselves on the inside as the "one of us" – alongside White hegemony, within a racist, classist, paternalistic and patrician construct that is Judeo-Christian Britain?

Chapter 8 consists of some preliminary thoughts and reflections on the biblical and theological case for reparations in the wake of the terrible legacy of the Atlantic slave trade, in which Britain was a notable contributor and chief custodian of economic benefit and profit. This essay will argue for a distinctively Judeo-Christian framework and rationale for the monetary and economic restitution to people of African descent for the horrors and the unbridled profit of the slave trade from which Britain benefited.

Chapter 9 follows on from the work in Chapter 8, in that it is concerned with the legacies of slavery and the different ways in which Black people have handled this issue in their contemporary reflections and reactions in Britain. In the previous chapter I outlined a tentative proposal for reparations based upon a postcolonial-inspired Black theological reading of the Bible and Christian tradition. In this chapter, I want to move from more theoretical considerations to those that arise from the need for praxis in the lived experiences of Black people in terms of how we engage theologically with the legacy of slavery, which so shapes the macro and micro dimensions of life in the African Diaspora. The impetus to write this chapter arose from my engagements, last year, across the length and breadth of Britain, as we marked the bicentenary of the abolition of the slave trade.

Chapter 10 is a republished essay from *Black Theology in Britain: A Journal of Contextual Praxis* (issue 6, 2001). In this essay, I argue for a radical approach to Black Christian education, which I define as the practical arm of Black theology. I argue that this model of education can be an important transformative pedagogy for educating Black people to live and work for the coming of God's Kingdom. This essay has been re-published, for whilst some time has passed since it was first written, the challenges for Black Christians (and others of course) are to continue in the quest to seek to give meaning to their lives in a world that remains oblivious to Black suffering and death. I remain adamant in the belief that if a fraction of 30,000 people who will die everyday on the continent of Africa were White people, we would have solved the scandal of world hunger yesterday, let alone tomorrow.

Chapter 11 addresses the social mores and theological frameworks that have influenced the reaction of Black, African Caribbean peoples in Britain to the growing incidences of HIV/AIDS within their communities. This chapter uses Liberative models of Christian education and formation that are cognizant of Black cultures and histories in order to offer a brief snapshot of how and for what reasons many African Caribbean Christian communities in Britain perhaps have been unwilling to either confront or offer any meaningful support and pastoral care to those suffering from HIV/AIDS from within their ranks. I am not, I hasten to add, either a health specialist nor have I undertaken specialist work in HIV/AIDS.

Chapter 12 is an attempt to sketch some nascent thoughts around how a re-imagined Black theology, approached through the lens of Practical Christian theology, might begin to be "cashed out" in the messy and grossly un-equal world in which we presently live. This chapter uses five case studies as ways of posing critical questions around how a Black theology of practice – one which is not afraid to challenge and work on the margins of traditional, Judeo-Christian thinking – can become a resource for personal and systemic change during this century. I have termed this chapter "Making the Difference" because at the very heart of this exploration of Black theology, it is essentially about just that – how do we make the difference?

In summing up this work, then, I can report that it is written by a Practical Black theologian living and working in Britain and it is a polemic. In this text I am making no apologies for the tendentious and bombastic approach to my writing. In effect, I am ignoring the spurious claims to objectivity and neutrality that seem to be the polite and conventional mode of scholarly theologizing within the academy. As James Cone, the "Founding Father" of Black theology has argued, notions of balance and studious objectivity are not facets one can find in the God of the Judeo-Christian tradition.[87] This work makes no attempt to be balanced or objective in its analysis. The writer is being unashamedly subjective and personal in his reflections upon the nature of being a Black body in an all enveloping sea of normalized Whiteness.[88] I hope it challenges you; but I also hope it helps you to engage with realities of the 21st century from the perspective of a Black British body!

2　A Black Theological Approach to Reconciliation

My Contextual Background

I was nurtured and socialized within a conservative evangelical Methodist Central Mission in Bradford, West Yorkshire.[1] The spirituality of this church fell within the framework of classical Wesleyan sensibilities in which the quest for holiness and moral rectitude were at the forefront of the heightened consciousness of this community of faith.[2]

As I became increasingly knowledgeable about the tradition into which I was being nurtured, it soon became increasingly clear that my church was absorbed by one major preoccupation. This preoccupation was the acute consciousness of the reality of sin and the power of Jesus' blood to blot out our transgressions. The emphasis in Christian discipleship was on gratitude and fidelity to God in Christ, expressed in terms of using the appropriate Christian language of piety and religious observance.[3]

Two texts have defined that formative period in my life as prime exemplars for the determining framework of theological reflection and Christian discipleship that dominated mine and the lives of countless others. These are, first, the classic Charles Wesley hymn *And Can It Be?*, and second, the *Apostles' Creed*. Both texts were sung and read with what appeared to be constant regularity in that gathered assembly within the Wesleyan tradition.[4]

And Can It Be?

And can it be that I should gain
An interest in the Saviour's blood?
Died he for me, who caused his pain?
For me, who him to death pursued?
Amazing Love! How can it be
That thou, my God, shouldst die for me?

'Tis mystery all: the immortal dies!
Who can explore this strange design?
In vain the first-born seraph tries
To sound the depths of love divine.
'Tis mercy all! Let Earth adore,
Let Angel minds inquire no more.

He left his father's throne above –
So free, so infinite his grace –
Emptied himself of all but love,
And bled for Adam's helpless race.
'Tis mercy all, immense and free;
For O, my God, it found out me!

Long my imprisoned spirit lay
Fast bound in sin and nature's night;
Thine eye diffused a quickening ray–
I woke, the dungeon flamed with light,
My chains fell off, my heart was free,
I rose, went forth, and followed thee.

No Condemnation now I dread;
Jesus, and all in him, is mine!
Alive in him, my living Head,
And clothed in righteousness divine,
Bold I approach the eternal throne,
And claim the crown, through Christ my own.
(Charles Wesley 1707–88)

Apostles' Creed

I believe in God, the almighty,
Creator of heaven and earth.

I believe in Jesus Christ,
God's only son, our Lord,
who was conceived by the Holy Spirit
born of the Virgin Mary, suffered under Pontius Pilate,
was crucified, died, and was buried;
he descended to the dead.
On the third day he rose again,
He ascended into heaven,

He is seated at the right hand of the Father,
and will come to judge the living and the dead.

I believe in the Holy Spirit
The holy catholic Church,
the communion of saints,
the forgiveness of sins,
the resurrection of the body,
and the life everlasting. Amen.

My decision to look at the hymnody of Charles Wesley and words of the
Apostles' Creed will become apparent at a later juncture in this essay.
These two texts exerted a significant impact upon my life for many years
for they provided the macro-theory for the essential inviolate meaning of

Christianity. In short, this classical evangelical version of Christianity is primarily, if not solely, concerned with Jesus' death and resurrection, and the acknowledgment that this is the basis on which full life as conceived in terms of Christian faith is understood. This has been the historic, evangelical faith into which the bulk of Black peoples across the world have been inducted.[5]

For the majority of Black people of the African Diaspora, our engagement with Western societies and with Christianity has emerged from beneath the choking evils of the Atlantic slave trade. Black people, Christians in particular, have to deal with the dialectical struggle between living within a religious code that asserts freedom and the realization that this very identity brought with it servitude and oppression. White people exported a racist, White supremacist inspired version of Christianity onto the oppressed body and mind of the Black slave.[6]

Black and White have co-existed within the one global entity that is Christianity on very unequal terms. In many churches in Britain and across the world, descendents of former enslaved Africans and former slave owners all give their lives to and claim to follow the one universal Christ figure. The Christ who died for all! In light of the 200-year legacy of slavery, and the need for all Christian people to be united in Christ, the crucial question to be asked, therefore, is how can we be one?

What does it mean to be together as one people? How can our unity in Christ deal with the legacies of the past, which can and do affect what it means to be "together as one people"?[7] What does it mean to be reconciled to one another and to God as brothers and sisters in Christ? What does it mean to be reconciled?

Going Back in Order to Go Forwards

The act to abolish the slave trade was passed in Britain in 1807. This date is no doubt, hugely significant to some, but largely ignored and considered irrelevant by many. Why are some of us bothering about remembering something that happened all those years ago? I am sure that some will see this as yet another pointless and tiresome act of "political correctness" on behalf of the "whining brigade" who want to make all of us feel bad and guilty.

Given that the slave trade ended 200 years ago, the question that faces us all is, namely, what are we to make of that evil institution in our present time? How do we move forward as a nation, as a world, in the knowledge that the legacies of slavery have not gone away, nor, indeed, have the realities of human trafficking and exploitation?

One way of dealing with the past is to affect some form of reconciliation between Black and White as a means of ensuring that the past is dealt with and that its impact does not infiltrate or infect our future. In this brief chapter, I want to suggest a way of handling the notion of reconciliation that moves beyond the classical approach often seen within Christian theology, to one that explores the radical model to be found within Black theology. This latter model is one that takes the social and systemic realities of sin seriously and does not fall into abstract, spiritual ideals that often end up sanctioning the status quo, thereby leaving White people in the "box-seat" as the masters.

I make no apologies for offering a radical approach to reconciliation, for I feel that the classic model given us by Christendom is naïve and best suited to the cause of placated White people rather than dealing with the need for justice, repentance, penitence and reparations.

Exploring the Tradition

In traditional terms, Christian theology has sought to locate notions of reconciliation within the restorative work of Jesus' passion and subsequent death on the cross. The sinful nature of humankind led to a breach between the holiness that is God and the "fallen" state in which men and women exist. Jesus' death on the cross serves as the link between a holy God and sinful humanity.

One can trace a trajectory from the apostle Paul, through to St. Anselm and then Martin Luther, for the development of a form of atonement theory, in which the central importance in the formula for effecting reconciliation is Jesus' saving work on the cross.[8] Paul's writings, which form the earliest documented texts in the New Testament canon, are replete with references to God's reconciling work in Christ on the cross. One can point to such texts as Rom. 5:10, 1 Cor. 5:14–21, 2 Cor. 5: 18–20, and Col. 1:18–23.

For Paul, the love of God in Christ, demonstrated on the cross, not only reconciles us to God, but that love, transmitted through the transforming work of the Holy Spirit, reconciles us to one another. In the classic imagery of Christian theology, reconciliation within the purposes of God is represented in the shape of the cross. The vertical axis represents the reconciliation between God and humans and the horizontal between humans and the "other" – those who are not us, i.e. other human beings.

The image of the united body of Christ (1 Cor. 12:12–31) is one in which all are unified through the one baptism to live a life worthy of our calling as the saints of God (Eph. 4:1–7).

The nature of Paul's spiritualization of the salvific work of Jesus finds expression in his downplaying of the physical in favour of the spiritual (1 Cor. 15:35–50). Paul's injunctions against the weakness of the flesh leads to a diminution in the importance of the Incarnation and Jesus' physical reality in favour of his spirit presence.[9]

The downplaying of the contextual nature of the person of Jesus (a first-century Judean Jew) in favour of his spiritual reality enables the Jesus of History to become the universal salvific Christ whose death saves all people for all time. By downplaying the body and the Incarnation, Paul creates opportunities for later followers of Christ to punish and persecute the body of Black people, safe in the knowledge that it is their souls that ultimately matter, not their bodies.[10] After all, if Jesus' own body is of limited importance then the bodies of Black folk are largely irrelevant in how their humanity is construed.[11]

A Theology of Homogeneity and Unity

One of the things you may have noticed from the outset in the brief, cursory summary of the classical doctrinal position regarding reconciliation in Christian theology is the wholesale lack of specificity or particularity in its formulations. The theology of homogeneity runs deep within Christianity. The injunction of the writer to the Galatians (3:28) that in Christ there is no Jew or Greek, or slave or free, remains a powerful theological and societal ideal of which we all dare to dream.[12] The spiritualization of Christianity led to a diminution of the contextuality and particularity of difference. Biblical scholars such as Esler have investigated the attempts of the early Christian communities to surmount the seemingly endemic differences of ethnic and cultural particularity that would have faced the author of the book of the Galatians.[13]

Inderjit Bhogal, the first Black President of the British Methodist Conference, drawing upon the work of Balasuriya,[14] constructs an inclusive ideal for human interdependence based upon the notion of a "table for all" that is the embodied ideal of the Eucharist or The Lord's Supper.[15] Bhogal sees within Christ's invitation to come to his table to be fed, a model for a radical form of inclusivity that transcends all ethnic, religious, cultural, ideological, gender and class based differences.

It is my suspicion that many White, largely evangelical theologians, albeit in a sub-conscious, pragmatic vein, have drawn upon the language and theology of homogeneity in Christ in order to do their theology in a somewhat abstract and context-less manner.

By sublimating the reality of contextual particularity, whether in terms of class, gender, ethnicity, sexuality or economics, many White evangelical scholars are able to address seemingly more generic, spiritual and theological concerns that would appear to transcend the differences I cited a few moments previously.

This form of sublimation is not new of course. Despite the deeply conscious embodied and contextual reality that was and is the Incarnation, Christianity quickly jettisoned the desire to locate its concerns amongst the material and physical in favour of the abstract and the spiritual.[16] The Church has learned to ignore the material needs and the embodied nature of human subjectivity, particularly if those human subjects are Black or people of colour.[17]

Problematic Sameness

There are a number of problems with this commitment to transcending cultural, ethnic, gender and class differences. My chief problem with this theological construct and, as a corollary, the creative manifestation of generic universalism is its spectacular failure when scrutinized through the lens of Black historicity. A Black hermeneutical reading of many of the standard classical, normative theological texts simply reminds us of the hypocrisy of White supremacy.

Black theology came into existence as a response to the failure of White power to live out the very theology it had so carefully constructed from the later medieval period. Whether in its self-conscious political form from the 1960s onwards,[18] or in its more implicit folk religion incarnation through the lives of Black enslaved Africans and subjugated Africans living under the yolk of colonialism and segregation,[19] Black theology continues, for the most part, to be a response to the de-humanizing tendencies of White hegemony.

One would be hard pressed to find much evidence for the transcending of difference as evidenced in the practice of White power when it collided with the existential experiences of Black people. So how can we ignore difference? How can we say that it should be ignored, for we are all one? In theory yes, but in practice, most definitely no.

W.E.B. Dubois in his groundbreaking book *The Souls of Black Folk* argued that the problem of the twentieth century would be the "color line."[20] The twentieth century came and went, and we, the collective mass that is humanity, are no nearer dealing with the "color line," over a century since Dubois wrote those prescient words.

The Problematic Nature of this Formulation

The problem with this classic notion of reconciliation was the narrow limits it placed upon what constituted the "saving work of Christ." Paul, who is the architect of much of the initial development of Jesus' death as possessing saving qualities, which through justification and redemption, leads to the salvation of people (Soteriology), constructed his notion of Jesus' saving work based purely on Jesus' death. Given that Paul's writings predate the earliest Gospels by a generation, Paul makes little attempt to "tell the story of Jesus." Rather, he is content, some might even say determined, to concentrate his creative theological genius on Jesus' passion and death and resurrection. By ignoring Jesus' life, Paul set in motion a dangerous set of events that would lead, some sixteen centuries later, to the wholesale exploitation and oppression of several million Black people. I am at pains to add, of course, that the Apostle Paul cannot be blamed directly for the incarceration, oppression and genocide of millions of African people under the yoke of slavery. But what I am suggesting, however, is that his theological myopia enabled successive generations of White Christians to use his abstracted and hyper-spiritualized Christology as an opportunity to oppress darker skinned people, with no significant impact on their own religious convictions or sense of righteous well-being.

So how did this happen? By concentrating upon the vertical axis of reconciliation, by means of Jesus' death, Christian theology soon found convenient ways to ignore the claims of those who were different from them, whether on grounds of ethnicity or nationality.[21] As early as the sixth century there were already signs that Christian communities were beginning to exhibit prejudicial notions about Black people.[22] But given that Jesus' two great commandments indicate the centrality of this cross shaped formula for love and reconciliation (Matt. 22:37–39), namely, loving God and your neighbour as yourself, how did Christianity manage to exploit and enslave Black people?

The answer lies in the wholesale way in which the concrete nature of Jesus' life was ignored. Jesus' life as depicted in the gospels totally undercuts any notion of ethnic, cultural or national prejudice. In his dealings with women, as seen in his encounter with the Samarian woman (John 4:1–45) or the Syrophenician woman (Mark 7:24–30) these texts display the manner in which Jesus went beyond the gender, cultural, ethnic and national boundaries that had traditionally defined the covenant between God and Israel.

With the rise of slavery, Christian apologists for Black chattel exploitation could rest assured in their individual salvation, by grace through faith (the vertical axis), but could completely ignore the humanity of Black people, and therefore their claims as neighbours who should be loved as themselves (the horizontal dimension). By downplaying the concrete reality of Jesus' life, Christian theology could focus upon the spirit and the abstract notion of the atoning work of God's son, which reconciles us to God and makes possible salvation for all people.

In effect, despite the reality of Jesus being a human, born within a specific setting (this can be seen in the Incarnation), Christianity quickly jettisoned the desire to locate its concerns amongst the material and physical in favour of the abstract and the spiritual.[23]

In this spiritualized and abstract state of affairs, Jesus is the fair, decent and "kind sort of chap" who loves everyone and does not take sides. This is the kind of Jesus who will not get his hands dirty nor involve himself in the nasty, unfortunate and "can't be helped" forms of racism that have stalked the world and blighted the life experiences of Black people for the past half millennia.

In order to affect this form of myopic theological construction, classical White evangelicalism has resorted to a wholesale spiritualization of the central tenets of Christianity.[24] One only has to look at the central heart of the Nicene and the Apostles' Creeds to see the truths of this contention. The creeds tell us everything about what Jesus stands for in terms of his symbolic, universalizing work of atonement and salvation, but nothing about his liberating actions as exemplified in his life.[25] In the words of my former academic supervisor, "Jesus' life (and therefore his actions) disappears in a comma."[26] (I.e. "he lived, he died.")

Returning to the texts of Wesley's *And Can it Be?* and *The Apostles' Creed*, one can immediately deduce the powerful strain of Christian tradition and thought into which I and millions of Black people have been inducted. In both texts, one notices a huge silence on the life of the historic Jesus. Wesley's hymn (still one of my personal favourites) is, in many respects, indicative of the major thrusts of Wesleyan theology, emphasizing as it does the "Four All's of Methodism" ("All need to be saved"; "All can be saved"; "All can know that they are saved"; and "All can be saved to the uttermost").[27] Wesley does not appear to perceive that Jesus' life might have salvific qualities. Rather, like the earlier creeds, his classic hymn focuses purely on Jesus' death, in isolation and shorn of context; wholly separated from the counter-cultural and life enhancing praxis that made his death inevitable (and redemptive).[28]

Another Way of Conceiving Reconciliation

The emergence of a radical, politically charged polemic for conceiving reconciliation emanated from within the realms of the Civil Rights movement in the US. The theology that emerged from within the Civil Rights movement drew on the long legacy of Black Christian faith in the Americas, dating back to the epoch of slavery. Black theology emerged as the summation of 400 years of oppression and alienation of Black people in the richest and most powerful country in the world. This theology is captured, in part, by the words that open section two of the 1966 *Statement by the National Committee of Negro Churchmen* which read:

> It is of critical importance that the leaders of this nation listen to a voice which says that the principal source of the threat to our nation comes neither from the riots erupting in our big cities, nor from the disagreements among the leaders of the civil rights movement, nor even from mere raising for "black power." These events, we believe, are but the expression of the judgement of God upon our nation for its failure to use its abundant resources to serve the real well-being of people, at home and abroad.[29]

The strength of Black theology has been its ability to "name the sin of racism."[30] The central intent of Black theology has been to challenge the biased self-serving interpretation of the Christian faith that has given voice to and enabled the flourishing of White supremacy. This has been achieved by means of a courageous and unapologetic re-reading of the traditional tenets of "White" Christianity. This latter perspective, by no means popular with all Black people, let alone White ones, has been, for me, the defining quality of Black theology.

This ability to re-read and re-interpret can be seen, for example, in the iconoclastic work of James Cone. In a now legendary passage from *A Black Theology of Liberation* Cone writes:

> In a racist society, God is never color-blind. To say God is color-blind is analogous to saying that God is blind to justice, to right and wrong, to good and evil. Certainly this is not the picture of God revealed in the Old and New Testaments. Yahweh takes sides.[31]

This early section from Cone's second book reads like an incendiary device within the heart of the body politic of White Evangelical Christianity. The work of Black theologians has done much to offer a more radical and challenging perspective on reconciliation. Perhaps the most radical of these theologians is James H. Cone. Cone first argued that White Christianity was able to construct a racist perspective and interpretation of the Christian faith by de-Judaizing Jesus (making him a White Anglo-Saxon male – i.e. one of them) and then relegating his life to a mere prelude before his all atoning death.[32]

Cone seeks to re-interpret both the meaning of Jesus' life and ministry in addition to his understanding of salvation. Cone's Christology (the person of Jesus) and Soteriology (Christ's work of salvation) are shorn of the pious, spiritualized abstractions that has often characterized traditional

White dominated understandings of Christianity. This latter version of the faith is one that makes Jesus a non-confrontational, pathetic and nondescript figure who neither has the will nor the desire to effect any semblance of change in the here and now, save for the fact that his death enables people to be "saved"; but with no accompanying desire for such individuals to change their racist practices or views. Is it any wonder that Black theology did not have any time for this seemingly powerless and pathetic version of Jesus!

By emphasizing the hyper-spiritualized nature of Christ's saving work, White Christianity has been able to replace practice with rhetoric. The doctrinal formulas of Christ's atoning work, often mediated via pre-modern cultural concepts such as "expatiation" and "propitiation,"[33] enables the searing prophetic work of Jesus to be reduced to the point where his followers can assert that they are "naming the name" and are "saved."

In effect, Christian discipleship is reduced to those who are able to say the right words and identify with Jesus' saving work;[34] but with little accompanying need to follow his radical, counter-cultural actions. In short, White Evangelicalism has taught us all to "worship Christ" but not to "follow him." Collective prophetic action has been replaced by private piety.[35]

Is it any wonder, then, that confirmed and unapologetic racists could see no contradiction between loving God and hating their neighbour, especially if that neighbour were Black? When the Christian faith is reduced to John 14:6, there is little need to follow Jesus' actions, for according to many, it is not by following Jesus that we are saved, but only by believing in him. In effect, Christian theology is separated from any notion of counter-cultural praxis.

The theological and philosophical ground on which Black liberation theology has established its connection with the "Jesus of History" (the living, breathing human being who walked the earth and is witnessed in the gospels) has been by means of its identification with the very context in which Jesus was born and nurtured. James Cone writes:

> I begin by asserting once more that *Jesus was a Jew*. It is on the basis of the soteriological meaning of the particularity of his Jewishness that theology must affirm the Christological significance of Jesus' present blackness. He is black because he *was* a Jew. The affirmation of his past Jewishness is related dialectically to the significance of his present blackness.[36]

James Cone remains the most persuasive and eloquent commentator on the basic overarching theological and philosophical grounding between the historicity of Christology and the contemporary experiences and realities of Black people in the post slavery epoch.[37]

So How Does this Usher in an Alternative Formula for Reconciliation?

What is most notable about Black theologians in their approach to reconciliation is that it is grounded in Jesus' life not his death. It is the Jesus of History, the person depicted in the gospels, who challenges us to deal with one another in terms of justice and equity. It is the Jesus who does take sides and who will challenge the unjust to repent and change their ways.

Many Black theologians have asserted that Jesus is Black. This statement should not be taken, necessarily, to mean that Jesus is literally Black. What writers such as James Cone,[38] Jacquelyn Grant[39] and Robert Beckford[40] are stating is that God's preferential option is for the empowerment and affirmation of oppressed Black people. If Black people were enslaved and continue to be oppressed solely on the grounds of the colour of their skin (the mythical "Curse of Ham" – Gen. 9:18–28 – was used to justify the enslavement of Black people), then God in Christ took the form of these exploited people in order to show God's total identification with their plight.

Black theologians continue to argue that in a world where White privilege and advantage is the norm and Blacks continue to die from starvation and economic exploitation, God has sided with these marginalized people through Jesus, who lived his life on earth as a colonized and oppressed Jew, i.e. Jesus' humanity, concrete life, example and his identity (Jewish in the first century and Black now) become the basis for an alternative form of concrete reconciliation.

For Black theologians, this form of reconciliation is one that emerges from the concrete examples of Jesus' liberating praxis as exemplified in his life. So, for example, in Jesus' encounter with Zacchaeus (Luke 19:1–11), we see set forth before us the ethic of reparations, as a means of effecting reconciliation between oppressed and oppressor, and with God's very self. Zacchaeus has to "give back" that which he has wrongly taken in order for him to be reconciled with others.[41]

The pious abstracted logic that chooses to ignore the concrete in favour of the spiritual is challenged. The implications of this ethic for 2007 and the 200th anniversary of the abolition of the slave trade are stark. At the time of writing, not one penny has been given to African peoples in the form of reparations for the monstrous evils of the slave trade, whilst conversely, the White slave owners were paid handsomely to compensate them for their loss of "property."[42]

Similarly, Jesus' praxis as demonstrated in his life demands that his presence be seen in those on the margins (Matt. 25:31–46). By seeing

Christ in the "other," the divine image in the marginalized, despised and oppressed self elevates their humanity beyond the limitations placed upon them by the corrupting power of White hegemony. By concentrating upon Jesus' liberative praxis as the primary scene for effective reconciliation, one is able to detect in this injunction a commitment to see the divine image in the disparaged "other." This is a challenge to move beyond the patrician arrogance of White supremacist ethnocentric conceptions of Black people. Such racist dominated perceptions of people of African descent have given rise to a litany of rape, racist attacks, bodily mutilation and wholesale indiscriminate and disproportionate arrest and detention at the hands of White majority police services and judiciary.[43] Anthony Pinn has demonstrated the extent to which racist notions of Black people led to the extensive paraphernalia associated with the ritualized destruction of the Black body, which found expression in the lynching and murder of countless thousands, by what were often "good Christian White folk."[44]

By concentrating on the liberation Jesus offers to those who are marginalized and oppressed, he throws out a challenge to all who have gained through the exploitation of others.[45] In effect, reconciliation becomes more than just a spiritual idea.

This is not to suggest that spirituality or salvation should be conceived solely in political, systemic or material terms. But if we look at the world as it exists at the present, can we honestly say that the plight of Africa is due to their lack of spirituality or morality? After all, Christianity's future in terms of numerical growth is a Black one.[46] Following the legacy of slavery, Black people don't need more spirituality. One may well argue that the hyper-spiritualized conception of particular aspects of African Christianity, witnessed in the mutilation and death of innocent young children, through fear of demon possession, is testament to the fact that Black can be accused of being *too spiritual* rather than lacking in spirituality.

The growth of Black Christianity all over the world, especially in Africa, is testament to the arid nature of White Western Christian faith and the dynamism and growth of African spirituality. Traditional, spiritualized notions of atonement, based largely, if not exclusively, on Jesus' death will no longer cut it for us. Rather, a Black theological perspective that takes the radical Black Jesus as its norm offers new hope for a more contextualized approach to reconciliation, in which justice, reparations and equity are central to any formulation. This radical Black Jesus is one who sides with the poor and the oppressed, and asks rich exploiters to repent for the Kingdom is close hand and is in our midst. This Jesus becomes the model for an alternative form of reconciliation.

The work of Womanist theologians has been particularly instructive in alerting us to the dynamic, transformative ethic of Jesus' praxis, which is detailed in his life and is not a mere prelude to his all atoning death. Delores Williams, in particular, is adamant in locating in Jesus' life the transformative paradigm that makes reconciliation and partnership a theological and ethical ideal.[47] Williams has argued that reconciliation and salvation that are conceived solely in terms of Jesus' death simply reify and legitimize the *actual* physical suffering and conscription of Black bodies, especially those of Black women.[48]

Jacquelyn Grant has also argued that it is Jesus' life which provides the essential underscoring for a notion of his salvific work in relation to human suffering and estrangement.[49] Whilst not as trenchantly opposed to atonement theories that valorize Jesus' death as Williams, Grant nonetheless argues for repeated attention to be given to the Jesus of History as the paradigm for a liberative praxis that saves.[50] Grant writes:

> More than anyone, Black theologians have captured the essence of the significance of Jesus in the lives of Black people which to an extent includes Black women. They all hold that the Jesus of History is important in understanding who he was and his significance for us today. By and large they have affirmed that this Jesus is the Christ, that is, God incarnate. They have argued that in the light of our experience, Jesus meant freedom.[51]

This form of reconciliation is one that makes justice and equity the central themes for life in the Kingdom, and is a perspective that is not based solely on Jesus' death and individual professions of "being saved."[52]

The legacy of the epoch of slavery still exerts a profound impact upon the collective psyche of all people, both Black and White. From our vantage point of some 200 years since the abolition of slavery in Britain, very little has changed in structural and systemic terms.

For many White people there has been a collective sense of "cheap grace." The price paid by many Black people for the transformation of and reconciliation between Black and White has been immense, and has neither been appreciated nor matched in any reciprocal sense by many White people.[53] There is a significant amount of goodwill between the various communities in Britain, but more work needs to be done to reconcile the privilege of White people with the psychological and societal denial of Blacks.

The resistance to slavery from the churches was very mixed. One needs to differentiate between (often) institutional ambivalence and individual activism. The re-writing of history has seen many churches quick to take credit for individual (often unsupported by their churches) initiative and action.[54] The reconciliation between slave owner and slave, between rich and poor, between Black and White came via the reforming efforts of individuals, and not by means of the institution. Jesus' saving work lies in *both his life and his death* and can become the means by which an alternative form of reconciliation will be affected between all persons. The Kingdom of God is at hand. Repent and believe in the Gospel (Mk 1:15).

[Published previously in *Black Theology: An International Journal* 5, no. 3, 2007, 184–202.]

3 Rethinking Black Biblical Hermeneutics in Black Theology in Britain

This chapter is written from a Black theological perspective. In using this term, what I mean to suggest is that the term "Black" comes to represent God's symbolic and actual solidarity with oppressed people, the majority of whom have been consigned to the marginal spaces of the world solely on the grounds of their very Blackness.[1] I am using a Black theological method as a means of posing a number of political and polemic points about the use and abuse of Holy Scripture and Christian tradition as it collides with contemporary Black experience and human life.

Black theology is committed to challenging the systemic frameworks that assert particular practices and ideas as being normative (normally governed by the powerful), whilst ignoring the claims of those who are marginalized and are powerless; often demonizing the perspectives of the latter as being aberrant or heretical.[2]

Finally, by way of an explanatory overview of this work, I should say that this chapter makes reference to working practices of Black communities, whether African or African Caribbean (in the context of the UK), Caribbean or African American (in terms of the US). It should not be assumed that my reference to these communities or contexts denotes a specific or particular problem for these groups alone. There is a sense that all communities have their "blind-spots" and examples of poor practice, aided and abetted by even poorer theology (more of which in a short while) in terms of their relationship to the Bible. In highlighting this particular issue, I am simply seeking to be honest to my own methodology as a theologian and educator; namely, that I cannot nor do I write for everyone. Instead, I begin from a place that is familiar to me and address my thoughts to the spaces, places and people with whom I share some immediate sense of identity, shared narratives and historic resonances around what it means to be a human being.[3]

Black Christianity in Britain and the Bible

One of the important characteristics of Black Christianity in Britain is the centrality of the Bible. This is not to suggest that the Bible is not central to the formulations of other Christian groups or persons, but it is a generalized truth, however, that every branch of Black Christianity across the world holds scripture to be the supreme rule of faith and the only means by which one can understand God's revelation in Christ. This is most certainly the case with Black Christianity in Britain.

Despite its radical roots in countering racism and Black dehumanization, many Black Churches and the Christians that have emerged from them, whether in the US or in the Caribbean or Britain, have remained wedded to a form of 19th century White evangelicalism. A number of Black scholars have demonstrated the extent to which Christianity as a global phenomenon has drunk deeply from the well of Eurocentric philosophical thought at the expense of African or other overarching forms of epistemology.[4]

Black Christianity has imbibed these overarching Eurocentric, Greek influenced thought forms, often at their expense of their own identity and African forms of epistemology. This adherence to 19th century Biblicism has meant that the blandishments of historical-critical biblical studies have barely penetrated the edifice of Black Christianity across the world. In the case of Black Christianity in Britain, one can still point to a propensity to read biblical texts in "flat" and uncontested ways, often asserting that as the "Word of God" the sacred words of "Holy Scripture" should be read as literal truths.

For the most part, the heart of Black Christianity in Britain, for example, is built upon quasi-literalist readings of Scripture, in which Jesus and salvation is conceived solely in terms of John 14:6. Again, I must make the point that this particular approach to reading the Bible is not unique to Black people. There are many groups who will not only read the Bible in this way, but will also claim it to be normative of historic Christianity as it has been expressed and propagated over 2000 years. As I have asserted, hitherto, I am using Black Christianity in Britain as particular focus for looking at the overarching concerns that are most probably relevant for every ethnic, cultural or geographical grouping in Britain and beyond.[5]

This adherence to scripture is selective like *all approaches to reading the Bible*. I have placed the last few words in italics because I think they are of crucial import in the context of this discussion. All of us are selective, idiosyncratic and contradictory in the way in which we handle the Bible.

In this chapter I want to argue that there are deep religio-cultural factors that underpin the complex and idiosyncratic ways in which Black Christian communities in Britain read and interpret the Bible. My argument in this chapter is twofold. The more minimalist assertion is that using a hermeneutical tool, which I have termed "a Black religio-cultural approach," one can assist faith communities, in this case, African and African Caribbean communities in Britain, to have greater cognizance of the reasons why they interpret the Bible and particular sections of it in certain, distinctive ways.

My more expansive, and dare I say, radical or polemical assertion is this: That in all truth, the Bible does not give human faithful communities authority, for the Bible has no authority other than that which the church, as the main faithful interpretative community, has given it. That in effect, we give the Bible authority by means of the presuppositions we hold, which are then read into the Bible, rather than the other way around. That in effect, we give the Bible authority; whilst many argue that the converse is the case! When what we believe to be true is validated by the Bible then Bible authority as understood in terms of literal truth is preserved and respected. Conversely, when our own presuppositions are at variance with the biblical witness, we then construct alternative reading strategies to reframe what we believe to be true – which result in the Bible being "contextual" "of its time" and only a guide and not a rule book.

Of the two assertions, I am naturally inclined to go with the latter, more radical proposal, but as a Black theological educator, I am willing to settle for the former in the realization that it is not my place to impose my own methodological and hermeneutical considerations upon others. At the very least, however, I do want ordinary Black Christians to reflect more deeply and honestly on the varied and idiosyncratic ways in which they (as do all of us) read and interpret the Bible.

A Black Religio-cultural Framework

For many Black people in Britain their general theism and spirituality enables them to hold a dialectical perspective on reality.[6] The concrete and explicit is not all there is. Talk of Black religious traditions and sensibilities calls to mind the work of such scholars as Albert Raboteau,[7] Robert Hood[8] and in Britain, our own Robert Beckford.[9] Their work is characterized by a pervasive sense of the work of the spirit(s) within Black life. The spirit offers different ways of knowing,[10] and provides an alternative, parallel reality to the concrete nature of the immediate built environment that most commonly confronts us.[11]

I am aware of the tension within Black religious and theological discourse surrounding the relationship between the spirits and the Holy Spirit. The latter is contained within a distinct Christian framework that is often seen as being an anathema to or simply distinct and separate from the former.[12] Recent ethnographic research, in Africa for example, is beginning to tease out some of the complexities of this discourse.[13]

Whilst I accept that for some, more evangelical Christians, the collapsing of Christian and other forms of spiritualities is problematic, I will not be abiding by such orthodox Christian strictures in this work. Drawing on the work of Hood[14] and more recently, Stewart,[15] I will work with the clear intentionality that the spiritualities of Black people extend way beyond the often constricting limitations of Hellenistic influenced orthodox Christianity. But having said that, I need to acknowledge my own positionality, as a Christian Black theologian and religious educator.

I was born into and have been socialized within a Christian Caribbean home of Jamaican migrants to Britain. I have chosen to give you these bare facts by way of an introduction because to understand my approach, commitment to and dare one say, sheer enjoyment of Black-religio cultural production, one needs to understand something of the context into which I was nurtured. My mother, in particular, was (and remains) a committed Christian.

Growing up in a Diasporan Caribbean household in Britain was a fascinating experience. The world that was inhabited by my parents and their children was one that was separated from the wider arena of White working-class life in Bradford, West Yorkshire, UK. My parents, in order to shield themselves and their children from the ongoing shadow of racism that seemed to stalk the lives of Black migrants living in Yorkshire (as many other parts of the country), constructed an elaborate internal universe of ritual, belonging and, best of all, one of familial narratives that was to be our bulwark against the harshness of the outside world.

In this self-enclosed world, living in the back room of our terraced house that also served as a dining room and a kitchen, my parents told of a magical world that was back home in the Caribbean. It was a world punctuated by seemingly extravagant, idiosyncratic characters. This was a world that captured my imagination and that of my three siblings. The storytelling capacity of my parents and their peers was one of juxtaposing the ordinary and the extraordinary in the one narrative structure. African American Womanist scholar Elaine Crawford argues that long before Jurgen Moltmann promulgated the notion of eschatological hope as the foreground for Christian theology[16], one could witness the experiential practices of African women as purveyors of a theology of hope[17]. Similarly, I would submit that prior to the emergence of "Magic Realism"[18] as a category in postcolonial literature, African Caribbean people, such as my parents, were offering a nascent practice of this very same theory. The religio-cultural storytelling and the narratives of my elders were examples of pervasive dialectical spiritualities in which the struggle for truth between often competing realities and notions of self were always clearly in evidence. In this essay, I want to argue that dialectical spiritualities are a facility that are products of experience in which African Caribbean people are enabled to juxtapose alternate realities within their human consciousness. In talking about "dialectical spiritualities" I am referring to this ability to "hold in tension" competing notions of truths, which enable "us" to see deeper shades of reality between that which immediately confronts us and to experience those deeper shades in the ordinary and the expected.

In my socialization amongst the relatively small Black community of Bradford, West Yorkshire, I was aware from the very earliest age that my world was divided into alternate domains. One moment, I might be with my extended family, luxuriating in a quintessentially Jamaican cultural milieu. The next, I might find myself with White friends in the school playground talking in a very earthy and raw Yorkshire dialect and opining on contemporary issues in a manner that would have horrified my God-fearing Jamaican family.

These dialectical spiritualities are ways of responding to the immediacy of one's built environment by seeking to re-cast and re-interpret that context through the lens of one's connection to that which is "other". This facet of Black life is one that, as a corollary, leads to a "Black religio-cultural framework" for reading and interpreting the Bible. In short, in the ability to juxtapose alternative interpretative readings of reality by means of the spirit, Black people in Britain (and possibly elsewhere I am sure) are able to apply their dialectical spiritualities (within a Black religio-cultural framework) to sacred texts in order to construct consonant and dissonant readings when it suits them.

As I have stated earlier, it is not my intention to argue that only Black people do this. I am sure that other cultural and ethnic groups by means of their own learnt behaviours and forms of collective and communitarian experiences have developed strategies for juxtaposing alternative meanings and hermeneutical strategies for interpreting texts. As a contextual theologian, however, I cannot nor do I attempt to write for everyone. Rather, in the first instance, my point of departure is always the Black (British) experience.

An Inductive, Narrative Approach

In the first half of this essay I want to adopt a narrative-driven inductive approach to theological reflection by means of a subjective insider's analysis of my own family. I want to reflect for a few moments on the theo-cultural dimensions of growing up and being socialized in a Diasporan Caribbean household in which the central dimensions of what I am terming dialectical spiritualities were clearly evident. I am using my own remembrances and reflecting on my family as a way of "giving honour" to my parents, particularly my mother and the 34 largely anonymous years she and my father spent in England as racialized fodder for right-wing tabloid newspapers.

I cannot claim that my family are either normative or essentially representative of the wider socio-cultural and economic signifiers of African Caribbean existence in Britain. Rather, they are simply my family. But it is in this familial setting that I witnessed at first hand the symbolic and dialectical features of the subversive spiritualities of Black people.

I have chosen the informality of these narrative encounters within our familial home as the repository for these dialectical spiritualities, as the church that we attended on most Sundays was a very Eurocentric patrician Wesleyan Methodist Mission, in which the phenomenon of cultural dissonance and Black existential concealment were readily apparent.[19] In short, as Black people, we knew that this church was not the place to "let it all hang out." So it is to the familial home that I locate the central features of what I am terming dialectical spiritualities.

I am a Black, African-Caribbean male, born in Britain in 1964. My parents come from Jamaica, in the Caribbean. They arrived in this country, independent of one another, in the late 1950s, were married in 1962 and returned to Jamaica in 1991. At the time of writing, they live in happy retirement on the East Coast of Jamaica. These are the briefest and baldest of facts about my family. Yet beneath the easy utterances lies a whole plethora of emotions and experiences.

My concept of family is an undeniably positive one. The family from which I have emerged has provided the underlying strength and security for my existence thus far. When I state this fact, it is not said in a spirit of short-sighted wishful thinking. Neither is it imbued with tinges of rose-tinted reminiscences. The strength and security of which I speak are a real, vibrant and affirming entity that has been the support for the major part of my life. This family has its faults. There have been strains and inevitable tensions, but its existence has been an affirming and solidifying experience in my life.

To understand my family, you need to know something of the socio-cultural forces that have both fuelled and shaped it.

"Our" Experiences Lay Elsewhere

My family, like many of Caribbean descent, is one that echoes to the formative strains of migration. I am part of that great post Second World War migratory experience. Prior to 1954, and the arrival of my aunt, my mother's elder sister, there existed no immediate links between this country and that of my family. "Our" experiences lay elsewhere. That elsewhere, that sense of "other," is what has shaped and given the context to the individual and corporate experiences of being family. I grew up in a family that always conveyed the idea of "home" as being Jamaica. "Going home" meant returning to the Caribbean. "Back home" was defined as the place where, in some intuitive sense, the family belonged. I did not visit Jamaica until I was 16 years old and on that occasion it definitely did not feel like home. Yet, prior to that time, and in a very strange way over subsequent years, that country still had a sense of being home.

The metaphors that characterized my experience of family were ones of transition and removal. The story is told by my mother of repeated visits to the local church when I was very young, and of me fondly saying "goodbye" to all the other children in the Sunday School at the conclusion of the class. I was giving my farewells, because the following week I would no longer be here, but would be back in Jamaica. My formative years were governed by a powerful sense of the temporal. The talk in the family, all through my early and later years, was of return. My parents never viewed their existence in this country as anything more than a temporary prelude, before a joyous and ecstatic return to life in the Caribbean. That discourse so prevailed upon my impressionable consciousness that I imbibed the stories in a literal fashion and became a central player in that form of powerful narrative.

A Large Blue Trunk

My world of imminent departure was fuelled by the presence of a large trunk in the corner of my parents' bedroom. To a small child, this trunk appeared to hold a store of untold fantasies and seemingly unattainable hopes and dreams. The trunk, as I remember it, was a dark, navy blue container. It looked like a stylized version of a sea chest that often served as an integral plot device in a 1940s Hollywood pirate film. In my feverish imagination, I envisioned Long John Silver thrusting open my parents' bedroom door and bestriding the said trunk, pointing at it with his withered stick, and shouting, "So there be me long lost treasure chest."

My fascination with this trunk lay in the relationship it had with my mother. At periodic moments, my mother would open the trunk and empty the contents across the floor. She would then proceed to inspect each item (usually a shirt, some trousers, or a bed sheet), and then place it back in the trunk. I would watch with fascination as my mother proceeded to arrange and rearrange the contents of the trunk. The opening and closing of the trunk was accompanied by the evocative smell of camphor and moth-balls, placed in the container to preserve the clothes ensconced within.

It is my belief that my mother's constant re-packing of the trunk was an attempt to remind her of the desire to return to the land of her birth. The desire and the hope were enshrined in the contents of the trunk, which contained items she had purchased and stored in order to bring back to Jamaica. The trunk was her commitment to the dreams and promises she had made in a different time and place.

The trunk was both a trunk and symbolically became more than a trunk. Robert Beckford has argued that African Caribbean people in Britain have always been adept at juxtaposing alternative hermeneutical strategies in their reading of events, activities, and even objects.[20] In terms of the latter, one can witness Black people moving interchangeably between an engagement with the signified (the embodied object in and of itself) and the signifier (the symbolic representation and meaning of the object).

The trunk became for my mother a symbolic totem that encapsulated her sense of being the "other" – a Black Jamaican woman in Britain – and her concomitant desires to return "home" to her beloved Jamaica. The trunk was both a practical necessity that would help in the facilitation of her return to Jamaica, but was also a sacramental rite that pointed beyond its embodied reality to a deeper truth of the promise for the future. In effect, the trunk was the nexus between the temporal reality of working-class industrial Bradford and the eschatological promises of "returning home" (figuratively in the theological sense and literally in terms of geographical mobility).

Whilst the trunk occupied a central place in my parents' alternate hermeneutical strategies for engaging with the dialectical struggles of being Black Caribbean migrants in working-class industrial Bradford, there also existed the facility of storytelling as another mode of symbolic self-identity.

Black British life has always been one that has run to a set of narrative pulses that punctuate the ordinary and the mundane with stories of "otherness" and "beyondness."[21] Essentially, Black people have always constructed narratives that confer meaning, within their metaphysical universe in which "there is a point" to why we are here (in Britain) and the expectations that we can and will overcome. In the words of my colleagues, Mukti Barton, "Black people look to the past to understand the present, but since they do not want the humiliating present to continue, vision leads them to a better future."[22]

What I took from this world of storytelling and colourful narratives was the importance of being able to tell a story and hold the attention of an expected audience. The great champion storytellers were my mother and my auntie "Dotty,"[23] my mother's only surviving sister. These two individuals were the special women in my early life, and they were very different. My aunt was strident, ebullient and headstrong, whereas my mother was more quiet, reflective and circumspect; but both of them were united by an amazing ability to tell a good story.[24]

Witnessing the elders in my family and wider community waxing lyrical as they told stories from the dim and distant past and those of a more recent vintage, I learnt one of the central truths of Black cultural life; namely, that the Diasporan Black Caribbean religio-cultural world was one of painting vivid pictures and images in the mind of the listener.[25]

Black religion and its resultant spiritualities inspired the listener through tales of another mythic word. The power of inspired oratory transported the listener to "another space and time." When the elders in my family were regaling their younger charges with dramatic stories of "back home" (in the Caribbean), it often felt like you were there whilst the narrative was unfolding. "Back home" (in my case, the Caribbean island of Jamaica) remained a mythical and tantalizing reality not unlike the notions of home in postcolonial literature,[26] the eschatology of Black Christianity[27] or the powerful notions of homeland for the exilic people of Israel in the Hebrew scriptures.[28]

The power of this narrative was that it held in dialectical tension the realities of the "now" (life in inner-city Bradford, West Yorkshire) and the "not yet" (the anticipated hopes of postcolonial return to the seemingly romantic idyll of the Caribbean) in a manner not unlike the often perilous balancing acts to be found in normative Diasporan Black Christianity. African American religious scholar, Lawrence Jones, contends that the notion of "hope" within Black Christian religious communities possesses two essential dimensions. It is a dialectic, between the here and now, and the promises of eternity – the struggle for truth between the immanence and transcendence of God.[29] Lawrence Jones continues by stating that:

> The Black religious community has not had the luxury of dichotomizing faith and work, or religion and life, or the sacred and the secular. This is surely one beam of light it has to cast. The interface between time and eternity has always defined an area of tension in the Black religious community, the hopes of which have been directed to both.[30]

Given the age stratification in this cultural environment, children were mostly invisible, in that they were rarely seen and certainly not heard. These cultural and community orientated events were most definitely adult oriented affairs. Whilst I was rarely permitted to share any of my stories in these settings I began to appreciate their formational qualities, as I realized I was being inducted into and socialized within a religio-cultural world view that was markedly different from my White peers at the local school I attended.[31]

As the elders congregated in the "front room" and we younger folk were banished to the more mundane climes of the back room, my siblings and I would occasionally peek our heads around the door in order to get a glimpse of the adults at play. Peering through the gap in the slightly opened door I saw my parents and their peers laughing, joking and expressing their exuberant and defiantly hopeful selves in a manner that so rarely found expression in their more public identities in the wider society of Bradford.

People who so often were repressed and diminished by the forces of racism and economic and societal struggle were, in this particular setting, wonderfully expressive and self-conscious entertainers. In effect, the Black elders in my family could hold in tension the struggles and travails of this, the material world and the glories and potential of the spiritual world.[32] This dialectical balance of holding together the immanent and the transcendent has been both the "curse" and the "gift" of being Black in a world where that very Blackness was a pernicious construction of Whiteness and White hegemony. Black people have long learnt the art of being dialectical improvisers![33]

Bible Reading by Means of Participation

Having explored by means of my own family some semblance of what I have termed dialectical spiritualities, I now want to apply this facility to the process of reading and re-reading the Bible. I believe that housing my notion of dialectical spiritualities within a broader framework of Black religio-cultural approaches to reading the Bible one can begin to see how and for what reasons Black people can adopt complex and often contradictory reading strategies for interpreting the Bible.

In this particular method for undertaking Black theology in the British context, I have attempted to create an approach which enables ordinary Black people to become part of a process that allows them to enter into the performance of theological activity[34] and bring their lived experiences into the very heart and dynamic of the biblical text. Entering into the dramatic possibilities of the drama and unlocking the subjectivity of a character is central to this process of re-reading the scriptures in order to create new meaning and praxis from this interpretative method. The substance of this work has been seen in a previous publication.[35]

In the context of this work, the engagement of the participants in the process of reflecting on biblical narratives is part of the process that brings about new forms of knowledge. These forms of knowledge are consonant with the creative energies of dialectical spiritualities, which I would argue is a common feature of oppressed peoples, which various forms of liberation theologies have attempted to harness.[36] In effect, the participants who engage with the biblical text are enabled to possess the narrative and to "put themselves within it" in order to go beyond the text. In doing this, they are operating within a framework of their dialectical spiritualities that can lead to new ways of seeing and engaging with biblical texts.

My ongoing work with ordinary Black people in churches in Britain has been undertaken from within a framework of Practical theology, in which I have used workshops and follow-up plenary as a means of documenting the new learning that has accrued.[37] The engagement within a participative milieu is essential for our reading of a biblical text, for embedded within this method is a commitment to re-thinking and re-assessing the thematic and cultural markers that make us assume certain norms as true. The necessary tension between what is written and what emerges from one's participative involvement within a biblical text is what gives life to one's dialectical spiritualities within the Black British religio-cultural experience.

This chapter seeks to explore an innovative approach to re-contextualizing and re-interpreting texts by means of an interactive and participative method that was first employed in terms of undertaking Black theology in Britain. This approach is one that attempts to harness an experiential and learnt facility of Diasporan African life, namely, dialectical spiritualities in which Black peoples are enabled to interrogate reality and hold in tension differing modes of truth.

I believe that this method for undertaking Bible study, for example, is one that can assist ordinary Black people to "unlock" the scriptures and so find new meaning, relevance and a form of self-actualization from their engagement with sacred texts. In John 10:10 Jesus says that he came to offer full life to all people. In and through an interactive approach to Bible study, ordinary Black people can be empowered to tap into their God-given dialectical spiritualities whose activation through role play and performance can be a catalyst for a dramatic discovery of all the possibilities for full life as promised in Christ.

Doing and Explaining the Exercise

This approach to undertaking Black biblical hermeneutics in which I have attempted to engage with the dialectical spiritualities of Black people in Britain has been by means of a participative exercise. (See the reproduced photograph on the following page. The exercise, like much of my research work, draws on the use of extended metaphor as a means of enabling Black people to "play with reality."[38] When using the term "playing with reality," I am speaking of the ability of Black people to enter into semantic game playing in which the game is both a constructed exercise and is "true to life" at the same time. In much the same way the trunk in my parents' bedroom was both a trunk and more than a trunk, then these exercises are both real and "made up" in equal measure.

The following exercise has been used with a variety of groups over the past two years since it was constructed by me. For the purposes of this book, I have drawn on two encounters to assist me in reflecting on how one re-thinks Black biblical hermeneutics within the context of Black religio-cultural frameworks of Black people in Britain. The two encounters occurred in North London and Birmingham. On each occasion I used the exercise to assist the participants in assessing how and for what reasons they interpret the Bible in particular ways.

In both groups I had around a dozen older Black people, mainly women, with about three or four men, assisting me in the process of interpreting the Bible. I was anxious to assess how their dialectical spiritualities, housed within a Black religio-cultural framework, might enable us to understand how Black people can read the Bible in complex and often contradictory ways.

In this exercise, I have taken the liberty of introducing the group participants to selected members of my family. The reproduced photograph

has been used as a heuristic tool for enabling predominantly Black participants to look at how they "read" texts and interpret their meaning. The exercise commences with me asking the participants to tell me the "truth" of the event in the photograph. The various participants, having looked at the photograph for several minutes, then share their thoughts on the meaning of the picture. Several note the clothes of the people in the picture. Others, however, notice the posture of the people and how they have positioned themselves.[39] The several groups with whom this exercise has been used over the past two years were quickly able to date the scenario in the photograph (the early 1960s) and that the picture took place in Britain.

The photograph in question was taken on the occasion of my parents' wedding – 6 August 1962, in Bradford, West Yorkshire. Interestingly, my parents are not present in this picture. From left to right, the members of my extended family are Alan Reddie (my father's older brother), Elaine Allen (my mother's niece – deceased), Atilia Bryan née Davidson (my mother's older sister – deceased), Enel Dixon (my father's brother-in-law), Elaine Marriot née Hutchinson (my mother's cousin), Mervin Allen (my mother's nephew and brother to Elaine Allen), Myrtle Marriot née Robinson (my mother's cousin and sister to Elaine Marriot) and George Robinson (my mother's cousin-in-law and husband to Myrtle Marriot née Robinson).

When I have asked the groups to tell me what they see in the photograph many have used their existing Black religio-cultural frameworks, born from living as predominantly Black Caribbean people in Britain, to respond to the inquiry. Most will point to the many factors that exist on the surface of the photograph. This event is a happy one because they can see the smiling faces clearly on display. They know that the event is a wedding because of the clothes that the women are wearing. Also, many can tell that this event is from the 1960s for the style of clothing worn by these Caribbean men and women (all are Jamaicans) clearly dates this event to that time period.

And yet juxtaposed alongside the surface reading of this event are the alternate "truths" that emerge when one engages the Black religio-cultural frameworks that are a part of Black life in Britain. The people in the photograph are dressed very neatly and in formal attire. They look respectable and well adorned. Yet, many Black participants have drawn on their familial narratives to explore the sense of alternative truths in the photograph. The people in the photograph, like many Black people at that time living in Britain, would have undertaken largely low ranking, unskilled jobs in factories, mills or public transport.[40] The smart, formal wear masks the largely urban struggle to create a new a life in a hostile and often uncaring world of post-war Britain, following their departure from the Caribbean. Elaine Allen, second from the left and the youngest person in the photograph, had been in England barely a year when this picture was taken. None of the eight people in the picture were in "professional" jobs when this picture was taken.

What has been instructive, as I have asked the group to deconstruct the photograph, are the ways in which different forms of knowledge and truths have emerged as they have engaged with my family picture. For many, there are some "obvious" pointers that can be gleaned from what is simply in the picture. When I asked one group of older Black people as to whether the happy smiling faces in the picture might not mask some more hidden truths around family rivalry and tension, most refuted this suggestion. Whilst many could testify from their own experience that weddings in Caribbean families, having to deal with myriad issues such as class, pigmentocracy, religion/denomination, island rivalries etc., can be explosive occasions, most were prepared to take the picture at face value.

In short, when it came to engaging with the photograph, alternative knowledge or truths could be ignored in favour of a surface reading, particularly if that alternate meaning was perhaps a less palatable or happy one. Many individuals, particularly older Black people in Britain, can point to weddings that have suffered under the tension of many of the issues to which I have drawn attention in a previous piece of work.[41] I am not suggesting that the wedding in the picture was not a happy affair, but it is interesting to note the steadfast attempt of both groups of participants to eschew such possibilities in favour of a surface reading that is eminently more acceptable and pleasurable than any possible alternative reading that exists within the text of the photograph rather than residing on its surface.

Some participants have even admitted that the constructed smile offered to the photographer when he or she exclaimed "Smile" or "Cheese" was but a momentary, fixed truth born of artifice. The hidden or alternate truth not captured on the photograph was the enmity, back-biting and sheer dislike in evidence in often insecure and fledgling communities trying to establish themselves in Britain in the post-war years of the last century. Now this is not to suggest that it was normative for such enmity and dislike to surface at Black weddings in the past or in the contemporary era. The point I am making is that when asked to juxtapose alternative perspectives or truths, the smiling faces on the photograph versus the possible contentious undercurrent in the un-revealed subtext, many opted for the former and not the latter.

Conversely, when asked to comment on the immediate surface reading of the photograph, in terms of the apparent wealth and material success of the characters in the picture, many of these self same participants found alternative and alternate ways of reading the photograph. Whereas the immediate "surface" hermeneutic was appropriate in the previous reading, now these individuals quickly inserted their own familial narratives and background information into the hermeneutical framework in order to add texture and context to their interpretation.

At this point many argued that a "flat" "surface" reading of the photograph was no longer adequate. Now there was a deeper truth to be discerned from the photograph. Although the characters looked prosperous in the photograph, their lives would have been circumscribed by their "race" and class as Caribbean immigrants in 1960s Britain. On this occasion, the participants were quick to remind me of the need to take into account the setting (the context) of the photograph. An immediate or surface reading could be misleading. When asked to comment on the apparent wealth of the Black people in the photograph, as evidenced in their expensive looking attire, all the participants then quickly drew my attention to the deeper, contextual truths contained within the picture. These alternate meanings are readily apparent in any surface reading of the photograph. Suddenly, extraneous information that was ignored in a previous reading was now hugely significant. Personal experience was now inserted into the photographic text in order to put the narrative of the picture into context. Now the participants read the photographic subtext against the surface meaning of the photograph.

Two things should be noted about the process of using this exercise. It should be noted that all the participants took great pleasure in extemporizing around the photograph. What appeared to be a somewhat "flat" two-dimensional photograph dating from 1962 was suddenly infused with a plethora of stories and familial narratives, often dating back some fifty years. Time and space was collapsed as the participants moved interchangeably between the past and the present, articulating their remembrances of people long gone and their recollection of their former selves in an epoch that has shaped Britain and Black people in this country.

I was not born when this photograph was taken. My image of that photograph is dominated by the women standing third from the left, known formally as Mrs. A. Bryan, but loved by one and all as my "Aunty Dotty,"[42] my mother's older sister, who was to all intent and purposes, my second mother in my early, formative years. My Auntie Dotty was an indomitable, "take-no-nonsense" Jamaican woman who was as deeply loved and loyal to her family as she was possessed of a very fiery temper. Engaging with these Black elders enabled me to also access my own familial memories of the people in the photograph all of whom are or were known to me. The inductive and narrative driven approach to assessing the dialectical spiritualities of Black people in Britain, which formed my nascent thinking at the outset of this chapter, was amplified and nuanced by recourse to these Black elders in their engagement with the exercise. Suddenly, my story became our story.

Second, the process also highlighted the alternate ways in which Black people can read texts. Their dialectical spiritualities enabled them to read surface meanings as being undeniably true and in so doing, ignoring alternate meanings drawn from personal experience, when it suited them. In the case of acknowledging painful memories of antagonism and strife, these Black people were simply able to interpret the photograph for its obvious surface meaning when it was convenient to do so. Conversely, when many of them wanted to assert memories and experiences that were infused with defiance and determination, suddenly the additional contextual factors and extraneous information were infused into the narrative of the photograph in order to construct an alternative truth and meaning to the picture.

In effect, when it suited their purposes to interpret the photograph for its obvious surface meaning, they did so. Alternatively, when it did not suit them, they simply constructed an alternate meaning to the picture.

Reflections on the Exercise

Using this particular approach to theological reflection within the framework of Practical theology, one can begin to enable participants to consider what are the factors that influence their perceptions of certain themes in Christian theology? As many liberationist and postcolonial scholars have argued, what happens in front of the page is related to how one constructs meaning within it.[43] In this exercise, I simply invited the participants to read the photograph for its meaning. Given that human beings are embodied creatures living in particular times and spaces, it is usually the case that what we see and how we interpret what is in front of us is influenced by the wider contexts and milieus in which we move, breathe and have our being. In short, our imaginations are influenced by the real world in which we live.

When using this exercise, I have witnessed the ways in which these dialectical spiritualities of Black peoples have influenced how ordinary Black Christians read and interpret biblical texts. When asked to do so, ordinary Black Christians have displayed the ability to conjure dialectical readings of biblical texts in which both conservative and liberative motifs have emerged in their hermeneutics.

Bringing the Bible into Dialogue with our Dialectical Spiritualities

The sense of being able to hold dialectical truths in tension – being able to read literally what is in front of us and also being able to go beyond the surface or immediate meaning – finds echoes in W.E.B. Dubois' landmark work *The Souls of Black Folk*.[44] Elsewhere, I have argued that Dubois' notion of "double consciousness" has proved a very helpful framework for articulating Black theological discourse, in which the Black self has had very limited options in which to navigate the rough vicissitudes of life.[45] In short, Black people can read against the text and with it, depending upon how the text aligns itself with the popular imagination of Black people from within a wider framework of Diasporan African cultures and the often troubled and stunted humanity residing within such socio-religious settings.

In the next part of this chapter, I want to apply the insights of this Black religio-cultural approach to biblical hermeneutics, drawn out from the participative exercise, to two brief passages from the Pauline canon. Both texts are taken from Ephesians in which a contradictory, liberative/anti-liberative dialectic is played out. Namely, that Black Christianity is adept at being liberationist and subversive in one breath and conservative and reactionary in another. I want to highlight the twin texts of Ephesians chapter 5, where wives are asked to be submissive to their husbands and Ephesians chapter 6, where enslaved peoples should obey their masters.

Analysing Ephesians Chapters 5 and 6 in Light of an Imagined Black Religio-cultural Reading

In a previous piece of work I have spoken of the dialectical reading strategies of Black people, when engaging with texts.[46] This tendency can be seen in the ways in which Black Christian communities can read *against* Paul's injunction for enslaved Africans to obey their masters (Ephesians chapter 6) but wives *should be* subject to their husbands (Ephesians chapter 5). These two injunctions come from the same section of writing, but there exists radically different ways of reading the text.

In terms of Ephesians 5, in many African and African Caribbean Christian contexts the truth of this text remains uncontested. Put simply, wives should be subject to and submissive to their husbands. This injunction not only has resonances within African derived socio-cultural settings but also becomes a form of authorial justification for male headship in ecclesial matters. Clearly, if women (in this case, wives) should be subject to their husbands or should "put them first"[47] as it states in the *Contemporary English Bible*, it does not take a great deal of imagination to see how this verse, as a corollary, can become a proof-text for asserting the inviolability of women being in front of and in charge of men.

In *Black Theology in Transatlantic Dialogue*[48] I argue that Black men are happy to read with the literal meaning of the text in terms of this verse because it resonates with the dominant socio-cultural religio-cultural approaches that are prevalent in many African communities. Our religio-cultural norms influence how we read these texts and not the other way around. Recent work by a number of Black women religious scholars in Africa[49] and the US[50] has shown the extent to which Black Christian men are happy to collude with patriarchal structures and teaching, often citing biblical texts as precedent. Mercy Amba Oduyoye offers her usual perceptive and biting critique of African religio-cultural mores as they impact on women when she writes of African Christianity:

> Although the Christian heritage of the biblical, prophetic denunciation of oppression has served Africa well, oppressive strands of the same Bible do reinforce the traditional socio-cultural oppression of women. At this point, prophecy resumes its original characters as a voice crying in the wilderness, ignored by the powerful and the respectable. On the whole, we can say that Christianity has converted the African people to a new religion without converting their culture.[51]

The prevailing attitude that assumes male superiority, often based on age-old historic religio-cultural norms, was not overturned by Christianity. Rather, these religio-cultural norms become reified when they are then conflated with sacred texts. In many circumstances, sacred texts are used as justification for the preservation of human constructions, which are now immersed within allegedly divinely inspired writings that act as metaphysical truth claims for the essential truth of traditional, age-old practices. As I have stated in *Dramatizing Theologies*,

> Claims to Divine knowledge by means of God's revelation through the Holy Spirit can lead to unquantifiable claims for alleged progress and development that by their nature can never be challenged.[52]

In more colloquial terms, the claim that "this is what God says and it is true" becomes an immutable truth that cannot be easily challenged by others. The irrefutable nature of such forms of epistemology becomes all the more corrosive when we consider that it is often the powerful, most usually men, who are the arbiters and interpreters (priests and bishops, who in many traditions can only be men) of what is sanctioned as truth.

Those who are on the margins of such epistemological groundings find themselves snared within an unyielding and tortuous self-referential trap in which they are excluded from participating in the ongoing search for religious truth, whilst being forced to accept the word (and good intentions) of powerful men who are the guardians and arbiters of truth.[53] In effect, women are asked to trust the guardianship of those who by definition of their policing acts demonstrate the clear inability to be trusted.[54]

The contrasts between Black religio-cultural approaches that govern Black Christian communities around issues of gender are in stark contrast to those that exist for "race." Whilst the patriarchal Black religio-cultural approaches that govern male-female relations, which in turn, are validated by recourse to such verses as Ephesians chapter 5, where we read this text literally, are dispelled completely when we come to Ephesians chapter 6. I can safely report that I have not met one Black male who believes that enslaved people *should obey* their masters.

At this point, one can cite almost universal agreement with the notion that as Black people, many of us descendents of enslaved Africans that the author of this text, reputed to be Paul of Tarsus, should not be interpreted literally at this juncture. When one points to the fact, as I demonstrate in my chapter on Womanist theology in *Black Theology in Transatlantic Dialogue*, that there is no compelling evidence to suggest that the Bible has any problem with slavery – in actual fact, there is no prohibition against this institution for non-Jews[55] – Black people still remain unconvinced.

The fact that there is ample evidence to suggest that God, if not actively giving God's blessing to slavery, is at the very least not overly perturbed about it, Black people remain convinced that our God is one of liberation. God is against slavery and has freed us African people from the yoke of forced captivity and oppression.[56] African American biblical scholar, Demetrius Williams, demonstrates how many Black Christian communities have appropriated biblical texts as a means of constructing a liberative hermeneutic that will speak to their existential condition and context.[57] The same author, in *An End to This Strife*[58] demonstrates how a group of older Black Baptist pastors have no problem dealing with the issue of racism and "race" analysis but remain wedded to quasi-literalist readings of Scripture when it comes to gender equality.

I believe the reasons for this obvious disparity can be explained, at least in part, by recourse to Black religio-cultural frameworks and their concomitant methods for interpreting biblical texts. For many Diasporan African Christians the reality that our identities are a critical dialectic between self-affirmation and negative counter-assertion is one that confronts us on a daily basis. For many of "us," the fact that our surnames bespeak of an epoch when we were bought and enslaved commodities,[59] is testament to the psycho-social proximity of the realities of fixed identities.[60]

Robert Beckford's analysis of low-level rage that emerges from the casual incidences of racism in the body politic of Britain is, in part, a manifestation of the ongoing corrosive reality of slavery and the sanctioning of Black oppression by White hegemony in Britain.[61] The reality and nearness of our experience to the remnants of slavery mean that our concomitant Black religio-cultural frameworks are such, that no self-respecting Black person will ever tolerate the justification of slavery, irrespective of the source that is attempting to support such reactionary discourse. Even when the Bible fights shy of wholeheartedly condemning the institution of slavery, such are the religio-cultural frameworks of many Black people that we simply find ingenious ways of reading against the grain of "Holy Scripture."[62] The apparent literal meaning of the text cannot constrain the prevenient spirit within the Black self – our dialectical spiritualities – which speak of an ongoing reality and revelation of God that goes beyond the limited ethic of the Bible.

These two chapters sit alongside one another. Whatever we believe about their authorship, there is little doubt that they emerge from the same source. And yet, in the space of one chapter, we can move from trans-historical literalism as in the case of wives and husbands (Ephesians chapter 5) to relative and contextual readings of the text as it pertains to enslaved Africans and their masters (Ephesians chapter 6).

What are the wider issues of these forms of idiosyncratic and inconsistent reading and interpretative strategies to reading the Bible? What are the implications for biblical hermeneutics to which Black theology should rightly attend?

Black Experience and the Bible

Essentially, there have been three ways in which Black people have read the Bible. These are not mutually exclusive. Indeed, I would describe their inter-relationship to that of a triangle. Each of the three sides of an equilateral triangle is connected at the corners to the other, but none are directly adjacent to one another. I want to highlight the essential characteristics of all three, but would argue that the Liberationist position is both the most honest and the most consistent with how Black people *should* read the Bible mindful of their history of oppression from slavery and sense of exclusion in terms of colonialism, neo-colonialism and globalization. In reproducing the photograph again of my parent's wedding, I now want to make a direct comparison between how these Black elders "read" and interpreted the photograph and how many Black people do something similar in terms of their reading and interpreting of the Bible. I am seeking to use the exercise with the photograph as a metaphor for how people seek to read biblical texts. Whilst there are significant differences between the relative unimportance of my family picture and the overarching authority of the Bible, I would submit that one can observe particular characteristics that demonstrate that Black people read each embodied text in somewhat similar ways.

It might well be argued that the most obvious and straightforward approach to engaging with the photograph (as a metaphor for how we read the Bible) is to concentrate upon what is within the photograph itself. If we transpose this approach, then, to how we read the Bible, I am suggesting that what becomes important is what we literally see before us in the biblical text. This point explains the meaning of the term "reading within the text," i.e. you read for the literate meaning of that which is before you.

By transposing the literal meaning of what confronts us in the photograph with how we then read the Bible it is my belief that this approach most accurately resembles what I would term Evangelical reading strategies of Holy Scripture. I have outlined the basic tenets of such evangelical reading and interpretive strategies below. Of the three approaches, this is the most popular method amongst Black Christians in Britain (and possibly worldwide). It is a straightforward mining of the embodied text for the surface meaning that immediately confronts the interpreter.

The second of the three reading and interpretive strategies for engaging with the Bible are what I would term Liberal approaches. These operate on the basis of looking at the story that exists behind the text – i.e. what is the "back story" that explains how the text came into existence. In terms of the metaphor of the photograph, this can be likened to wanting to know the narrative histories of the people in the photograph, the nature of Jamaican/Caribbean people living in Britain in the post-Second World War era and the larger phenomenon of Caribbean migration to Britain between 1948 and 1965. These additional factors can be used to explain the particular setting of the photograph from 1962 as they represent the larger socio-cultural and political backdrop to this familial scene.

The back story often seeks to problematize or contextualize the seemingly obvious surface meaning of the text, whether that be the photographic text as in this exercise or the biblical text in the broader culture. I have outlined a short-hand descriptor detailing the basic tenets of liberal approaches to reading and interpreting the Bible.

Finally, the Liberationist approach, which of the three is the one that most closely adheres to Black theology, is in many respects the least popular of the three broad typologies I have identified in this study. This approach takes the experience and the insights of the interpreter as the key element in how one reads and interprets any text – whether photographic or perceived as sacred. In terms of the metaphor, this approach would ask people for their own perceptions and perspectives on the photograph. In light of their experiences and social reality, what strikes them as being true when they look at the photograph? This method places greater emphasis upon what resides in front of the photographic text – i.e. what realities and needs does the viewer bring to the embodied text of the photograph, opposed to what lies within it or behind it?

This method, when transposed to the Bible, is one that operates in a liberative fashion, for it seeks to create a relationship between the oppressed humanity of the reader and the perceived truths that reside within the text itself and offers a means by which the experiences of the reader can be acknowledged and transformed. I have outlined a short-hand descriptor detailing the basic tenets of Liberationist approaches to reading and interpreting the Bible.

The different interpretive approaches that I have described above can be likened to the process of viewing and interpreting the photograph of my parent's wedding for meaning, i.e. one can look at the photograph itself, or one can try and discern the story behind its creation or, conversely, concentrate on what is the viewer's prior understanding or concerns as they engage with the photograph.

In the diagram that follows the reproduction of the photograph I have placed the Liberal and Evangelical approaches side by side in order to indicate their parallel nature as the two more normative reading strategies in this three-part typology. The Liberationist approach is placed below, as it is the most marginal of the three. In placing the Liberationist approach below the other two, I also want to suggest that it is the most subversive and transgressive of the three broad typologies. Hence, it is the most radical and "honest" of the three approaches, as it readily acknowledges the subjective bias in all reading and interpretive strategies to engaging with embodied text, whether the photograph or the Bible, as I have demonstrated in the previous section. For the purposes of this work, I am clearly advocating the use of this Liberationist model for re-thinking Black Biblical hermeneutics in Britain.

1. For evangelicals the picture itself is the major arena of importance.

2. For the liberals it is the story behind the picture – what the photographer had intended – how was it created – this is the major arena of importance.

3. For the liberationist it is the perspective of the viewer – what they bring to looking at the picture – this is the major arena of importance.

LIBERAL Approaches to interpreting the Bible	**EVANGELICAL** Approaches to interpreting the Bible
– Places major emphasis behind the text.	– Most popular, perhaps even normative.
– Seeks to interpret the Bible in terms of human reason and human history.	– Places major emphasis on the text. What is happening in the Bible text.
– Shares with the Liberationist the facility to challenge the biblical text and re-interpret it.	– Can handle miracles or supernatural dimensions in the text.
– Shares with the Evangelical the emphasis on the text itself (either behind or within the text).	– Shares with the Liberationist the belief that all things are possible for God. (God breaks into History.)
	– Shares with the Liberal the search for "Grand Narratives" and Universal themes for all people.

LIBERATIONIST
Approaches to Interpreting the Bible

- Places major emphasis in front of the text (i.e. on the reader) and on the experience of the reader and what they bring to the text.

- Asserts the view that there is no one universal reading but that all readings are contextual – i.e. they are influenced by the situation and experience of the reader.

- Shares with the Evangelical an ability to hold in tension the possibility of the Miraculous, if that is consistent with God as the liberator in history.

- Shares with Liberal the facility to re-interpret Christian tradition.

Why Black Experience Matters in Reading the Bible

The Liberationist method for biblical hermeneutics is one, I believe, that is most compatible with Black theology. I am arguing for its use in terms of a critical reading strategy for interpreting the Bible, as it is the main approach that takes Black existential experience seriously, i.e. what happens in front of the text,[63] and the material realities of what it means to be a Black person in a conspicuously Black body matters intensely. The text of our embodied self forms the crucial interpretative data that should inform how we read and interpret biblical texts. Black Liberationist readings of Scripture simply make hermeneutical movement explicit in ways in which Liberal and especially Evangelical approaches do not.

As I have hopefully shown in my use of a Black religio-cultural approach, the human facility of creating meaning via experience and emotion, which leads to multiple ways of construing truth and interpreting the data of human experience, is one that enables people to read their socio-cultural interests into texts, whether embodied or literary. Given that Black religio-cultural approaches arise from existential experience and socio-cultural phenomena, what we often perceive as being biblical authority or teaching is oftentimes nothing more than a form of human projection posited onto the text or a blurred form of reflection of the codified societal norms of the community or group.

For example, in terms of the latter point, I have never met any group of wealthy Christian who literally believe that it is easier for a camel to go through the eye of a needle than it is a for wealthy person to enter the

Kingdom of Heaven (Luke 18:25). Suddenly, this is not a literal text speaking against economic exploitation by the rich and a denunciation of wealth and privilege. Rather, it suddenly acquires a deeper spiritual meaning. Jesus could not be literally castigating or judging the rich, could he?

Is it not interesting that a post-Constantinian church, suddenly flushed with wealth and privilege, should want to find ways of ameliorating the radicality of Jesus' teachings in order to placate the rich people now within her ranks? The changed social location of the church leads to the formation of new forms of hermeneutics around the religio-cultural norms of the compatibility of wealth and the Kingdom of God. The fact that other texts seem to confirm the literal invocation of Jesus' teaching around the rich finding it hard to enter the Kingdom is conveniently ignored. In such passages as "Lazarus and the Rich Man" (Luke 16:19–31), "The Rich Young Man/Ruler" (Luke 18:18–25) and Jesus' encounter with Zacchaeus (Luke 19:1–11), we see evidence of the somewhat unambiguous cautions against wealth, riches and material self-interest.

I am not arguing that rich people will not enter the Kingdom. There is much we can deduce from these texts in terms of how we re-interpret them and whether they should be taken as normative in terms of how Christianity engages with wealthy people and those who are materially rich. What I am arguing for is a greater degree of honesty for the ways in which the material interests that lie in front of the text and the religio-cultural norms that emerge from those with wealth and power have managed to radically alter the "supposedly" clear literal meaning of these passages.

What happens in front of the text, which, as a corollary, is informed by a plethora of personal and societal religio-cultural norms shapes, inevitably, one's interpretation of the Bible. As a Practical Black theologian I am simply asking that as Black people we are more intentional in how we bring Black experience into dialogue with biblical texts. Let us not pretend that it is solely the Bible that influences our notions of social ethics or our religio-cultural codes for determining moral absolutes. Rather, the importation of the myriad religio-cultural norms that exist within all individuals and communities can also assist in shaping our hermeneutical frameworks when engaging with sacred texts.

Whilst my own perspective is to push for a radical expansive polemic that argues that in the name of honesty, Christian religious communities should admit that they give the Bible authority and not vice versa, I am also sufficiently pragmatic to acknowledge that such a proposal will never meet with the approval of most Black Christians. So my more modest proposal is simply one of cognizance. Can we show greater awareness of what governs our hermeneutics? Can we at least own our idiosyncrasies and not blame them on God?

Conclusion

In conclusion, then, it is my belief that particular religio-cultural norms affect how we engage with and interpret the Bible. For Black people in Britain, these norms are shaped by our dialectical spiritualities that enable us to hold divergent truths and perspectives in tension and alternate between them when it suits us. This dialectical facility, which is part of our Black religio-cultural repertoire for interpreting meaning from reality, in turn, affects how we then engage with contemporary issues and ethics in the world. This chapter attempts to highlight the nature of the "problem." Clearly, more work needs to be done in this area in order to assess how and with what strategies Christian adults can be enabled to adopt alternative religio-cultural frameworks, which in turn, will lead to different approaches to reading the Bible.

It is my fervent hope that Black Christian adults will avoid all attempts to justify acts of injustice and exclusion, even if they are writ large in Holy Scripture. Such is the nature of "free will" that as humans, we are not hostages to our past. The future can be remade! Let us have faith in the Spirit of God to banish all examples of bad practice that so often litters our past. We can read and interpret differently! We have done so before as a set of people. Let us continue to do so and to be honest and cognizant of this fact.

4 Jesus as a Black Hero[1]

Why is Jesus Important?

Within any normative understanding of Christianity, the figure of Jesus Christ is seen as central. Jesus, who is believed to be God Incarnated – God who takes the form of human flesh and becomes one of us – remains the basis on which Christianity conceives of itself as offering a unique vision of the world as it is and as it will be. The "prologue" to John's Gospel offers the overarching and supposedly all-encompassing biblical description of who Jesus was and is for Christian believers.[2] Alongside the notion of Jesus being as he was and is, within normative Christianity, is the sense that Jesus continues to live across all time and space; that individual Christian believers and communities, for that matter, can have their own experience of and engagement with the figure called Jesus. Each of us can re-imagine Jesus in the context of our individual lives and the experience of being a human being within history.

My own personal existential quest for imagining Jesus arose in my early teens. It is a story that was once impossible for me to tell, but through repeated telling, often re-enacted for the majority White students (often training for ministry) I teach, I have learnt to control the visceral and emotive power of this narrative.

Why was Jesus so important? In my early teens, whilst attending a prosperous and highly influential Central Methodist Mission in the city of my birth, I had cause to ask one of my Sunday School teachers if the blue-eyed, blond haired Jesus looking so serene and reposed on the far wall of the room was in actual fact the real Jesus?[3] I remember the Sunday School teacher looking quite non-plussed at the question. After what seemed an inordinate pause, she remarked "Well, I yes, I suppose." I replied by asking, "Is it true, miss, that Jesus is the son of God?" She was on surer ground on this one and responded "Yes he is," probably thinking, "I am sure we have been over this already; he should know this without having to ask." I then asked, "So Jesus is the Son of God and we are all part of God's family, miss?" Again she replied in the affirmative, still wracking her brains trying to work out why one of her more studious and observant charges had suddenly developed a major case of amnesia.

In response to her latest brief reply, I then asked, "So miss, if Jesus is God's son and he looks like the man in the picture, and we are all members of God's family, then who am I?"

The pointed question – the so-called "sting in the tail" – suddenly became a deeply political and complex discourse. It was no longer a seemingly amusing and slightly distracting conversation with an apparently absent-minded and forgetful student. The question was pointed as it was fiendishly difficult to answer. I was the only Black child in this Sunday school class. In a White majority church where all the office holders were White, all the preachers were White, where the official vestments were White and the iconography, such as it was in a relatively low Evangelical Methodist church, was also White, my question was indeed a very pointed and fiendishly difficult one.

For who was I? If I were a member of the family, of God's family, then how did they figure with me being so obviously different from the man in the picture and from every other individual in that room? Come to think of it, who was I in relation to the rest of the church?

After an interminable delay, the final reply was, I was a member of the family. That God loved me and that my being different did not matter. The answer was helpful to a point, but only a point. At one level, it was indeed helpful to hear that I was a member of the family, for the truth was, I enjoyed attending church, found it largely fun and had no sense of God not loving me. But it was the second portion of the answer that deeply troubled me. It didn't matter that I was Black! Even as she uttered the words, I could see my Sunday school teacher, a kindly old woman, grimacing slightly at the incongruous nature of her response.

This was Bradford, West Yorkshire, a northern city in England in the 1970s. If there was ever a place where colour mattered, it was here. This was a city that had learnt to turn her back in shame and embarrassment at her long-resident poor White working-class communities let alone the myriad Black and Asian people that had emerged in the city in the years immediately following the end of the Second World War.

The best one can say about the second half of her reply is that it was aspirational. She aspired to believe that colour did not matter. But it did in this church. A church that studiously managed to largely ignore the presence of my parents as potential office holders in the church, despite their near fanatical devotion to Sunday church attendance on a week by week basis. Colour, like social class, mattered intensely.

As many of us can testify, the corrosive effects of White images of normalcy, particularly when wrapped up within Christological images, have exerted a corrosive and dangerously hypnotic vision of White supremacist notions within the minds of Black Christians for centuries.

Josiah Young, the respected African American systematic theologian, recounts the story of accompanying other family members at the burial of his grandmother, and whilst standing observing the body in a traditional

Black funeral home that had been burying Black people for nearly 100 years, spying a picture of a White Jesus on the far wall. Young writes:

> Surely the fact that Jesus remained White after all these years, particularly given the rather intense civil rights struggle that took place in Danville, implied something negative about the Black clergy? Had they read no Black theology, itself a product of the civil rights and Black power movements?[4]

Young is describing a Black majority context, unlike the White majority setting in which I was nurtured, and yet even within the confines of the former, one still witnesses elements of a constricted internalized form of oppression that seeks to elevate one particular image of Jesus over and against others. Namely, a White Jesus predominates. White people may have oppressed Black folk for centuries, yet despite this visceral and emotive context of suffering and struggle that has been our experience for centuries, many Black people still prefer a pictorial image of Jesus that resembles the very people who have subjugated them.

Closer to home, I remember being privy, a few years ago, to an outstanding presentation from a ministerial student at the Queen's Foundation for Ecumenical Theological Education, where I work in the UK. This student had been on placement with two churches in Gloucestershire. One had been at a White majority church from within his own denomination; the other had been at a prominent Black majority Pentecostal church in the principal town/city in the county where he was presently residing.

This White student had studied Black theology at the college with my colleague, Dr Mukti Barton. As part of his placement project, he had devised a piece of participative/empirical theological work that entailed soliciting from the various members of the two churches their preferences for different Christological images. He had approached me for some assistance on the design of the project and for the different ways in which he might approach the congregants of the two churches.

A key resource in the production of this project was the joint (British) Methodist Church and USPG[5] resource entitled *The Christ We Share*.[6] This resource pack is an adult Christian education resource produced with a strong missiological focus, which contains 32 images of Jesus (all on A5-size cards, although 12 of the 32 are also in the form of plastic transparencies for use on an overhead projector), from many different parts of the world, in many different images, poses, identities and ethnicities.

I encouraged the student to adopt the methodology used by Clive Marsh in his attempt to engage with people's visual predilection for particular Christological images as depicted in the many prints contained in the resource pack.[7] This technique for gaining some sense of the nature of the visual Christologies that are operative in people's imaginations required the inquirer to simply place the 32 visual representations of Jesus in front of the various participants and then invite individuals to select the image that most speaks to them. Participants are then asked to account for their choices.

This student had revelled in the Black theology class he had undertaken earlier in his training. Now, at a later juncture in his training, he was offered a chance to put that previous learning into the context of pastoral ministry whilst on placement (field education for some). He was now eager to see to what extent attendees of the White majority and the Black majority churches were willing to engage with the various Black Christologies on show within the eclectic range of visual images of Jesus that were on display in the resource pack.

As the student shared the findings from his study one could sense the acute disappointment that neither group displayed any great enthusiasm for a Black Christ. That the White majority church had failed to do so did not surprise him to any great extent. This was his home church, and from my many conversations with him, the student had shared his own growing consciousness of the importance of Black Christologies in the theological formulation of White people. Speaking of his own learning, having studied the Black Christologies of such scholars as Kelly Brown Douglas,[8] James Cone[9] and Robert Beckford[10] in the Black theology course at Queen's, he remarked, "Anthony, I now know that Black Christologies are not only of importance to Black people...they are crucial for White people as well, perhaps even more so for comfortable and educated White men like me."

What had stunned this most enterprising and committed of White ministerial students was the fact that the members of the Black majority Pentecostal church seemed even more reluctant than their White counterparts to embrace a Black Jesus. I did make the point, highlighted in my previous work, that one could not discount his own Whiteness as being a factor influencing the results. It was not impossible that the Black members had become more diffident in their relationship to Black images of Jesus when confronted by a White student and researcher.[11] Elsewhere, I have argued that researchers cannot take anything Black people say verbatim as being the "whole truth" given our propensity for signifying and the often concealed and codified nature of much that is Black religio-cultural discourse.[12]

What this incident tells us is that there is a complex relationship between Black people and the notion of Jesus being Black like us. This relationship has historic dimensions as witnessed in Josiah Young's observation on the historic Black funeral home in the American south, but it is also not without its contemporary resonances, as witnessed in the story I have just recounted.

Even in Black majority religio-cultural settings the complex nature of our engagement with a Black Jesus is not necessarily dissipated as can be seen in this latter example.

In my White majority setting, I too, found myself in a strange dialectical relationship, with a Black Jesus in absentia. By this I mean, whilst I had never thought openly about Jesus' ethnicity until the particular encounter I had just recounted, I was clear, if only at a subliminal level, that given the choice, whoever Jesus was, he must never look like me. I, like many Black people, was perhaps happier with Jesus looking like anyone except me. As I propose to show in this essay, who Jesus is, is very much connected to what he does, which in turn, is influenced by his appearance.

Who is Jesus, Then?

Given Jesus' central importance to Christianity, it will come as no surprise that more has been written about Jesus than any other subject or category within Christian theology. The study of Jesus (Christology) and his work of salvation (Soteriology) has captured the imagination of writers and thinkers since the earliest times in the history of the faith.

In the centuries following Jesus' historical existence, Christian thinkers began to develop a range of ideas about the implications of this central figure being "God Incarnate."[13] How could Jesus be both fully human and Divine? These deliberations were not only theological but also political. By this I mean it soon became clear that the implications of who Jesus was and what he represented were not only questions for the church and believers of the faith. Rather, Jesus, as the representative of and in the likeness of God, who in turn, is the creator of all that is, has profound political and social and cultural implications for societies and nations.

Is it no wonder, then, that it was the Emperor Constantine, no less, who convened the Council of Nicea in 325 to settle the Christological problem of Jesus' two natures.[14] Jesus' importance, not only to Christian theology and the Church, but to all wider socio-political and cultural structures in the world, lies in the claims made for him by Christian thought.

If Jesus is understood as the "visible image of the invisible God"[15] then who is Jesus, what he represents and, of equal importance, what he looks like, all possess huge political and cultural significance (in addition to theological ones also). For Jesus in this way of thinking becomes the basis for all that we would want to assert as being "of God." That is, Jesus becomes the template for the basis for how we understand what it means to be human. In the words reputed to St. Paul, Christ is the new Adam,[16] the protypical human (the template) on which the new resurrected humanity will be based. Christ's atoning death and resurrection has reconciled us to God (2 Cor. 5:18–20).

From the Universal to the Particular

In the interests of time I am unable to offer a detailed exposition of how the universal symbol that is Jesus became refracted and distilled into a particular image of normalized Whiteness and Eurocentric hegemony. A number of Black scholars have looked at how the person of Jesus came to be possessed and colonized for the purposes of political and cultural control by the dictates of White European elite power. In particular, it is worth noting Jacquelyn Grant,[17] and Kelly Brown Douglas,[18] especially the latter in her more recent book *What's Faith Got To Do With It?*[19] as important works that outline the means by which a White image and vision of Jesus has been used to exploit and demonize Black bodies.[20] African American religious scholar, Anthony Pinn, offers one of the most telling analyses of how White thought control and repressive action was able to use White Eurocentric norms built around a White image of Jesus in order to dismantle and degrade Black bodies.[21]

It is worth noting that around that time of the latter end of the Patristic period (the early Church Fathers), a number of significant developments were already in evidence, which gave rise to the later attack on and the dismemberment of Black minds and Black bodies. As the construction of the overarching doctrinal and creedal building blocks on which much of our Christological understanding of Jesus is based were taking shape, notions of White normativity (White being the assumed norm) and Black being the "other" were already beginning to find their way into the lexicon of Christian thinking. Scholars such as Robert Hood[22] and Gay L. Byron[23] have investigated the way in which notions of Blackness and Whiteness are beginning to get played out in the discourse of Christian thinking, with the latter seen as (at best) preferable and the former (at worst) construed as a state to be feared.

A more sympathetic treatment has recently been offered by Michael Joseph Brown who argues that whilst Blackness was often seen as problematic in early Christianity, there was, nonetheless, a distinct North African perspective on the Christian faith in evidence at this time, which offered a challenging counterpoint to the Greek orientated emphases of the West.[24]

Reclaiming Jesus as a Black Hero

In this section of this essay I outline the ways in which Jesus, for most believers, the central visible figure in Christianity, has been appropriated by people who are marginalized and oppressed as a Black counter-cultural hero. Once again, like the previous section, this assessment cannot hope to do justice to what has become a highly developed and specialized area of research and writing within the theological academy.

For many, the most important person in this development has been the African American Black theologian, James H. Cone. Cone's landmark trilogy of books in the late 1960s and 70s, *Black Theology and Black Power,*[25] *A Black Theology of Liberation*[26] and *God of the Oppressed*[27] remain the dominant texts in outlining the importance of conceiving Christology from the perspective of disenfranchised and oppressed Black peoples.

And yet, not withstanding the importance of James Cone to this ongoing enterprise, it is worth noting the essential contributions of Richard Allen and Edward Blyden in this regard. Allen, the founder of the African Methodist Episcopal Church (AME) in the early part of the 19th century was one of the first Black church leaders to claim that God was a negro.[28] Blyden, on the other hand, argued that Africa's service to the world, and to Christendom in particular, laid siege to any fallacious doctrine enshrining the inferiority of Black people.[29]

"Our" Identification with Jesus: Jesus is Dread – a Black Jesus who is "One of Us"

The concept of Jesus being one of us (a central concept of the Incarnation) remains the key theological theme by which all peoples have sought to identify with him and him with us in our particular contexts. If God became human in Jesus and he became "one of us" and if that same Jesus continues to intercede for us with God, then it would appear to be axiomatic that he (Jesus) continues to be present in the many varied contexts where those who seek to be one with him are found. If then, added to this thought, is the notion that where two or three are gathered, so is Jesus; then it does not seem too outlandish to assert that Jesus' ministry, which is the consistent visible form of God's interaction with humankind, will be found in any place where his followers are in existence.

Black British theologian Robert Beckford has sought to provide a contextualized appropriation of Jesus for predominantly African Caribbean people by identifying Jesus with the Rasta concept of "Dread." Beckford argues that the word "dread" is often taken to mean "an awful calamity" or that which is "terrible and to be avoided,"[30] and often invoked at times of fear and foreboding; it was subsequently inverted and given new meaning by the Rastafarian movement which became a potent religious and cultural group in Jamaica.[31]

"Dread," a term that has often been used within generic Caribbean contexts and Rasta sensibilities in particular, which is often understood as meaning either "catastrophe" (in terms of the former) and "powerful and mighty" (in terms of the latter), is juxtaposed with Jesus, the most holy symbol of God's presence in the universe! In effect, this Christological statement of claiming that "Jesus is Dread" is to identify that Jesus is at once iconoclastic, unacceptable, deeply disturbing of polite social conventions, but also "powerful," "mighty" and "invincible." This Rasta influenced Jesus is one whose mighty and "dreadful" countenance serves to strike fear and foreboding into the heart of the body politic of White polite, corrupt imperial hegemony. A Jesus who is dread is everything an upper middle-class dominated establishment bound English church cannot conceive or countenance. A Jesus who is dread is an oppositional, Caribbean rebel Jesus who denounces all who sits at the heart of hypocritical imperial power and their commonplace rhetoric of assimilation, integration and polite conformity.

Time constraints prevent any serious analysis of the Rasta movement in Britain. This religious and cultural movement became one of the most expressive and significant repositories for Black self-expression, and for social and political dissent.[32]

By identifying Jesus as Dread, Beckford is seeking to relocate the Historical Jesus who was originally alive in Palestine alongside oppressed and marginalized people in that context, with his continued presence in Britain with equally disaffected and overlooked Black people in postcolonial Britain.

A Black Jesus Who Speaks to Us

In a more recent piece of work I have argued that identifying Jesus through the Incarnation with the Black modern day experience is essential if the Christian faith and the ongoing mission and ministry of the Church (which is the "Body of Christ") is to resonate with the reality of Black youth in the twenty-first century.[33] Using a piece from one of my more recent books, *Acting in Solidarity: Reflections in Critical Christianity*[34] as a basic resource, I have recently engaged with a small group of Black young people, reflecting upon the issue of HIV and AIDS. Using one of the pieces in the final section of the book (*Grasping the Chaos*[35]) to address issues pertaining to HIV and AIDS for World Aids Day, I was able to use one of the central characters in the short drama to pose the question of who Jesus is for us in our present setting.

In the sketch *Grasping the Chaos* two characters are in dispute regarding the appropriateness of people suffering with HIV and AIDS being in the church. One of the characters self-identifies as a church attender and believer and is hostile to the idea of "these people" being in the church. The second character does not identify himself or herself as a believer, but is strident in their belief that the church should embrace all who are suffering and in need of love. The latter character says:

> I thought it was Christian… NO, I thought it was a natural human reaction to feel compassion and sympathy, even empathy if you can manage it, for those less fortunate than yourself.[36]

Provocatively, I argued that this second unnamed and unidentified character might be Jesus. How would we read the encounter between the two characters, then, if the one who is challenging the self-righteous and unsympathetic attitude of the alleged believer was Jesus' very own self?

At the heart of this particular sketch and the reflections that follow it is the sense that Jesus is always what he needs to be in order that healing, redemption and salvation are felt and in evidence amongst those who are deemed the "least of these" (Matthew 25:31–46). This dramatic sketch ends on an ambiguous and challenging note, with this second unnamed character possibly identifying himself or herself as being an HIV/AIDS sufferer. How, then, do we read the Christological motif at the heart of this drama, if this unnamed and disturbing character is identified as Jesus' own self? So Jesus is not only a marginal character who disputes the notion of "in" groups and "out" groups within the body of Christ; but this Jesus is also possibly Black (only hinted at in the sketch) and is a person living with HIV/AIDS?

In using this exercise, what I am seeking to argue for is a Jesus who is not constrained by the normative strictures of White Evangelicalism. What I mean by this is the belief that a Black Jesus who is for us, has to be one who is then actually, *truly for us*, and is not a mere imitative model of the White Christ that still seeks to echo the paternalistic and patrician constraints of White power. This Black Jesus I am advocating is not only Black; he is also not bound by conservative religio-cultural mores. This Black Jesus does not imitate the normative thinking of many conservative White evangelicals who are often more concerned with private morality than structural and systemic injustice. Sadly, the many Black conservative church leaders in Britain who have often joined forces with conservative White Christians around issues pertaining to "family values," issues of personal morality or "protecting the Christian faith in Britain" often do so without any serious cognizance of what these factors mean in terms of the economic, material reality of Black people. For many, adherence to the abstractions of doctrine and Church dogma overrule any sense of analysing the underlying causes of systemic poverty and marginalization of Black people in Britain and any resultant praxis that might emerge from such prolonged critical reflection. In essence, Jesus is a spiritual reality in combating hardship and not a practical resource for campaigning for justice and equity for all.

As a participative Black theologian, seeking to combine Black theology with Christian education in order to challenge and conscientize ordinary Black people, I have often witnessed the ways in which African Caribbean Christians have sought to deny their Blackness when faced with the difficult challenge of integrating their material reality with their faith.

For many Black people, the necessity of engaging in a critical re-reading of the Gospels in order to catch sight of a subversive and radical Jesus who is opposed to White normality and hegemony, and is in favour of Black power, is an anathema. This radical Black Jesus I am advocating, like Beckford's "Dread Jesus" cannot be a coloured-coded façade who continues to uphold the limitation on notions of Christian theological election, in terms of who is saved, based on a narrow reading of John 14:6. When I performed the dramatic sketch on HIV/AIDS as described above, I wanted to push this all-Black group to wrestle with their religious and cultural binaries in terms of what constitutes a "follower of Christ." What if a prophetic Black Jesus is revealed in the very presence of the marginalized and the oppressed to such an extent that any sense of those "undesirables" outside of the Church being damned suddenly makes no compelling theological sense?

I want to argue for a Jesus conceived within the tenets of Black theology that is in true and full solidarity with all who are marginalized and oppressed and not only the ones who are deemed to be imbued with the requisite, regulatory moral agency and respectability to be deserving of Jesus' care and concern. My passionate challenge for a prophetic Black Jesus who speaks to us is one that also calls for an incarnated presence of God that denounces all forms of self-interest, including economic self-interest. Itumeleng Mosala has been a key voice in critiquing the ways in which some advocates of a radical Black theology have nonetheless colluded with the materialistic interests of the powerful in and through their uncritical adherence to the "Word of God."[37] In his critique of other Black theologians, Mosala writes:

> The basic question here is: which side of the class struggle in the social history of the biblical communities do we hermeneutically connect with when, like Tutu, we describe our vision in terms of a share in the *royal* priesthood of our Lord (i.e. our ideological landed nobility)?... It is not enough to be existentially committed to the

struggles of the oppressed and the exploited people. One must also effect a theoretical break with the assumptions and perspectives of the dominant discourse of a stratified society.[38]

In citing Mosala, I want to press this need for a Black Jesus even further. I want to argue that just as it is not enough for Jesus just to be Black if all he is going to do is save our immortal souls like the Evangelical White Christ of Faith, then this Black Jesus cannot condone top-down, corporate neo-liberal monopoly capitalism.[39]

In my peripatetic work as a participative Black theologian in Britain I have witnessed some pseudo-radical Black pastors (mainly but not exclusively of the Pentecostal tradition) invoking notions of a Black Jesus. This Jesus belongs to the colourization paradigm I have critiqued in a former piece of work,[40] but he also operates within a normative Evangelical tradition that saves souls and encourages poor Black people to believe that material riches can be found at the end of long rhetorical prayers. A Black Jesus that is Black in pictorial content only, but whose ontological self remains imprisoned within White ethnocentric norms is *almost* as dangerous as the White supremacist Christ of Western Church history.

In preparation for this study, I sat through several services of well-known and seemingly successful Black pastors of thriving Black majority churches, mainly in London.[41] In some of these contexts, the notion of a contextualized Jesus who was with "us," in our present struggles, was often invoked. Whilst the term "Black" was rarely, if ever used, nonetheless, the invocation of the experiential dimensions of Jesus' presence in the liturgical and embodied reality of Black selfhood was such that one could infer that Jesus was being proclaimed as a Black man.[42] This "Black inferred Jesus"[43] was a prototypical ambassador for Black enterprise and commercial success. Just as the pastor would cite his successful church as bearing the marks of Christ's cosmic success over the powers of the "Enemy" thereby winning the victory (for material success amongst other things), so the congregation were encouraged to incorporate Jesus' triumph with their own financial success. This "Black inferred Jesus" is one who comes resplendent in expensive traditional African regalia and is as much at home in the boardroom as he is in the sanctuary. But this "Black inferred Jesus" does not condemn the profit motive or question the shady entrepreneurial practices that leave a few very wealthy, whilst marginalizing the many to survive on the "left overs" from the corporate monopoly capitalistic table. Jesus cannot be just Black if he continues to serve the stratified world, in which a globalized neo-liberal economic system condemns many Black people to poverty.

I have witnessed, on at least three occasions when leading workshops on Black theology, Black participants who have been able to accept Jesus as being Black, but have balked at the notion that he is on the side of the poor and condemns extreme materialism and the selfish values of the rich. A re-imaged Jesus has to be one who is prepared, willing and able to refashion the world order as we know and experience it for the purposes of full life and liberation for all people – especially disenfranchised, poor Black people.[44] This Jesus is one who can do no other.

A Jesus who Refashions the World

The often unspoken presence of Jesus, who resides within the messiness of life and forces those who claim to be his followers to witness to the rightness/righteousness of "his way" in the life experiences and the very selfhood of those on the margins, is also one who forces all people to see the world anew. By seeing the world anew, I am speaking of a way of being, which emerges from an ongoing form of formation and transformation that leads ultimately to seeing oneself and one's wider contexts in a completely new way. I have spoken something of this dynamic in a previous piece of work. In *Dramatizing Theologies*[45] I outlined by means of a dramatic sketch an unnamed "change" agent who transforms the troubled existence of a self-destructive angry combatant who is at the point of implosion.[46]

This very implicit Jesus is one who is known through his saving actions rather than the self-declaimed nature of his Kingly identity. In many respects, the Jesus at work in the sketch *Love is the Answer* echoes the relatively "low" Christology displayed in the lives of many African American women who in their daily lives of servitude, marginalization and oppression find comfort in the saving humanity of an inconspicuous Jesus as opposed to an exalted and high status Christ who is one with God's very self.[47]

The Jesus who refashions the world is one who enables ordinary Black people to see themselves in another light. This entails seeing oneself as God sees us, that is, as unique, interconnected and transformed beings whose ontological and existential vistas are more enhanced and nuanced than the tragic-comic distortions of fixed identity in the present world order.[48]

The language of conversion has proved helpful to many Black scholars in this respect. The term conversion attempts to capture the often elusive psycho-social affects of changed identity and selfhood that accrues from one's sense of being transformed when confronted by the realities of coming into a new relationship with the risen Jesus Christ – the Christ of faith.

It should be acknowledged, of course, that not all Black religious scholars are completely enamoured with the notion of conversion as being an ordinance that has positive connotations for Black self-identity. Scholars like Clarence Hardy have argued, via the writing of James Baldwin (fiction and non-fiction alike), that notions of conversation, so replete and *de rigueur* within a largely Evangelical Christian framework, can lead to the negation of and demonization of the pre-converted self.[49] Given that many of our "pre-converted selves" (the old "us") for Black people, in corporate terms, often entails some engagement with non-European derived religious sensibilities and cosmologies, it could be argued that emphasis upon the new at the expense of the old becomes another means by which the "Black African self" is attacked and disregarded. Anthony Pinn explores the notion of religious conversion as an attempt to re-conceptualize one's world through the rubric of religious faith and observance.[50] For many Black religious scholars, essentially, the power of the rhetoric of conversion for people of African descent can be seen in the facility of this theo-psycho-social phenomenon to become the means of constructing a new self, with enhanced possibilities, within the confines of a so-called sinful and fallen world.

Historically, the new adherence to the Jesus of Faith gave rise to not only a renewed sense of self, which found demonstrable evidence in the changed behaviour and comportment and deportment of the Black body (seen in the aesthetic accoutrements of Black worship),[51] but perhaps of greater import, a new way of seeing the world.

Evidence of this change can be seen in the actions of enslaved Africans in the context of fighting for the abolition of the slave trade in the British Empire.[52] In the lead-up to the abolition of the slave trade in Britain and her dominions in 1807, many White abolitionists fought for the ending of the slave trade but not slavery itself.

There is an old Jamaican proverb, which goes something like this: *Everyday dog has his day, but every puss his 4 o'clock.* The meaning of the proverb is that at periodic moments a lowly dog will have his day, his time in the sun. But cats, which on the whole, are treated with less respect than dogs (in some cases disliked with a passion), even they get, if not a day, then their 4 o'clock; their one hour in the limelight.

As a Black person born of Caribbean parents, I have often thought of this analogy when reflecting on the lead up to and the actual commemoration of the bicentenary of the slave trade in the British Empire. I know that for many, 1807, and the commemoration of the bicentenary of the ending of the slave trade was most certainly not a celebration (one could not imagine "celebrating" the liberation of Auschwitz for example, come 2045). For some others, it barely warrants a mention at all.[53] In terms of the latter, slavery did not end in 1807. The slave trade ended but not slavery.

The White Evangelical Reformers, such as William Wilberforce, were very pragmatic and assiduous in their campaign to end the abomination that was the slave trade. That the trade should end in a timely fashion was indeed a noble cause and one should not be overly unkind or unduly cynical in failing to recognize the assiduous nature of their indefatigable work. But it is interesting that when White paternalism and patrician action gets to work in the service of Black suffering and oppression, there remains the distinct whiff and stain of a form of White moral rectitude that wants to lecture and indeed censure Black people on what is felt to be appropriate for them.

Let me explain the last remark! William Wilberforce, Thomas Clarkson, Granville Sharp et al. could make the fine and moral distinction between the ending of the slave trade and the continuation of the institution of slavery itself in some form, for some years beyond the ending of the former. The argument was one of "patience" and the need for due process, i.e., that there should be the requisite development and progress of Africans in order that they become so schooled in the art of manners that one day they could take their place at the table of humanity and be responsible for their own destiny as free people.

Interestingly, when one hears the words of the Africans themselves they make no such fine distinctions! Rather, they simply wanted full freedom, immediately, without the fine dissembling that wants to instruct the oppressed and the marginalized on what is correct procedure and the requisite moral and societal training to fit one for freedom.

Taking their cue from Holy Scripture, many enslaved Africans simply asserted the often quoted words from John 8:36 "If the Son shall make you free, you shall be free indeed" as the basis for their own freedom. Conversion in the "mighty and saving name of Jesus" meant freedom for many enslaved Africans. Enslaved Africans had no truck with the gradualist agenda of White abolitionists who wanted a piecemeal approach to freedom. For many of the enslaved Africans, taking the central tenets of Evangelical Christian piety directly to heart, conversion and becoming a new creation in Christ (2 Corinthians 5:17) entailed a dramatic change to the very fabric of oneself. In theological terms, this change signalled a new ontological or metaphysical basis for the very nature and reality of being a human being.

This change had both spiritual and material affects. In terms of the latter, slavery was no longer compatible with being a member of the Body of Christ. For Sam Sharpe, the leader of a huge and significant rebellion in Northern Jamaica on Christmas Day 1831, gradual freedom in Christ was an oxymoron. You can be no more partially free than you can be partially a virgin. In terms of the latter, you either are or you are not. For many of the African slaves, identification with Jesus signalled a new form of freedom that was realized in a new vision for themselves and the world in which they lived.

The truth is, for many Caribbean people, descendents of enslaved Africans such as myself, Britain's commemoration of the bicentenary of the abolition of the slave trade act threw up many conflicting thoughts and emotions. 1807 did not bring freedom. In fact, one could argue that 1838 and the ending of the institution of slavery itself did not bring about freedom either. For even when slavery ended, the reality of White supremacy and the notion of White enlightened European superiority in cultural and philosophical terms remained. Just as the former Prime Minister of Britain, Tony Blair and other members of the G8 can see no incongruence between asserting the desire to help Africa whilst wishing to berate her for her own failings (which Europeans themselves helped to create), in a manner reminiscent of "Mother knows best," 1807 marked the beginning of the tired rhetoric of White paternalism. Gradual freedom because we know best![54]

Black people have often looked to Jesus, and within his life, death and resurrection have found glimpses of a realized eschatology that enabled them to view their experience and the reality of that experience in radically new and charged political terms. Sam Sharpe's actions in Jamaica in 1831, or Nat Turner in the same year in Virginia, were examples of the moral vision of Black people being transformed by the visceral encounter with a transforming and transformative Christological event that gave rise to prophetic, sacrificial and sacramental action.[55]

Whilst conversion can be viewed in negative terms, sometimes perceived to be possessed of negative and deleterious effects upon Black peoples' self-concept and existential selfhood, I would contend that seeing Jesus as a Black hero transforms our moral vision, which is also deeply embedded within our historical Black religio-cultural experience.

So Why Do We Need a Black Hero Anyway?

By locating Jesus as a Black hero – i.e. as one of us – Black Christians in general and Black theologians in particular, drawing on the notion of Jesus' particularity (he lived in a particular place with a specific identity), have sought to gain strength from his work of liberation in the lives of those first followers. This form of identification with his historical particularity is in order that they might feel that same power in evidence in their current lives, through his universality (as the one who continues to lives in all places at all times with his people).

The importance of Jesus "being one of us" is crucial. It is in the common humanity of the Christ figure, who reconfigures the meaning of Blackness, Black identity and the nature of what it is to be human that is of huge importance and theological significance to Black people. The realization that Jesus is like us, and we are like him, is essential for the enterprise of Black theology that is attempting to reconstruct the very meaning of our often debased Blackness and African heritage.

The central thrust of this essay was thrown into sharp relief following an incident with two of my colleagues in the Black theology in Britain movement. Prior to a major international conference I had conceived and chaired,[56] myself and two colleagues[57] were invited by another friend and colleague[58] from the national Black Theology Forum (which meets monthly in Birmingham at the Queen's Foundation) to be guests on her weekly gospel radio show.

We were invited, ostensibly, to talk about the forthcoming conference. The conference was to address slavery and the slave trade in light of the bicentenary of the abolition of the parliamentary act in March 1807 that ended the slave trade in the British Empire. Amongst a surfeit of such events in the UK in that year, our event was notable as being the only one that approached the topic from a clear standpoint of Black Liberation theology and the resultant biblical hermeneutics therein. At a later juncture in the show, our host posed the following question to myself and two fellow guests.

"James Cone was once asked, which came first for him,…being Black or being a Christian? How would you answer?" After a short break for the next piece of music, I responded by saying (much as James Cone had) that my primary material reality was as a Black man. So being Black came first. I would readily contend that any understanding of my Blackness is informed, undoubtedly, by my Christian faith and my attempts to be a follower of Jesus. So my Blackness is very much a dialectic between my identity, forged through an ongoing fluid dynamic of Black cultures and my faith, which is informed by and which speaks to that ongoing cultural exchange. My two co-guests replied in a similar manner (but not identically with me, as we are all different, of course).

When our host subsequently took a number of phone calls from the public in response to our utterances, the response so I am told was largely negative. For many Black Christians, the notion that we might want to foreground ethnicity and "race" was not simply problematic, but in one case, abhorrent! I tested out this reaction with a group of Black Christians at a speaking event I undertook a week or so after the radio interview.

From the reactions of the ordinary Black people I met at that event in London, I was saddened to find very much the same reaction to my claims for the inviolate nature of Blackness as a hermeneutic for understanding Christian faith. The claims for an abstract, non-contextualized and colourless faith was replete in the comments of most of the respondents at this workshop event. As I have demonstrated in the opening chapter to this work, such comments are deeply flawed in their theological understanding of the nature and intent of both Jesus' ministry and of the Christian faith.

As contextual theologians such as Bevans[59] and Schreiter[60] have demonstrated, there is no form of Christianity that is not in itself a negotiation between the historic "givens" of doctrine and tradition and the contextuality of human life and their concomitant material cultures, in a given time and space. One can be no more a colourless and ethnically "universal" Christian than one can be a disembodied human being!

And yet for many Black Christians, living within the prevailing negative charge of a holiness culture that not only distrusts "the world," but has also helped to propagate a negation of the materiality of the Black body,[61] the notion that our Blackness has any ethical or theological charge within the construction of one's Christian faith is deeply problematic.

In the context of this work, I want to argue that the necessity of a Black Jesus is essential in order to enable many Black Christians to integrate the inherited material reality of their Blackness with the often expressed intentionality of their Christian faith. The latter does not subsume the former. Rather, I would want to reiterate as I have done in the first chapter that there are dangerous consequences for Black theology, if we are prepared to take the implications of its thinking with the utmost seriousness. It seems to me that if one takes the Black experience as a site for divine revelation with such seriousness then the possibilities for re-thinking the inherited meaning of religious faith, quickly emerge. Just as our thoughts on how one conceives salvation are challenged by the early work of James Cone, so too, are the age-old strictures on how we view sexuality and the Black body, which are reconceptualized by the work of Robert Beckford,[62] or Pinn and Hopkins et al.[63]

In terms of the latter, Beckford uses his reflections on of Black cultures and representational art forms as a means of re-thinking Black Christian thinking on sexuality and Black bodies.[64] In a memorable section in this work, Beckford reflects on Robert Lentz's art work entitled *Lion of Judah*, in which Jesus is depicted as a traditional Masai warrior, complete with a bulge in the lower reaches of his traditional clothes indicating the presence of genitalia.[65]

This re-configuring of Black Christology is intended to incorporate greater levels of holism into Black religious life by rehabilitating the Black body as being worthy of attention and pride and not as something to be overlooked or even disparaged and denigrated.

Jesus as a Black hero – as a hero of colour for all people – is crucial if the ongoing work of redemption and salvation are to be made relevant for the postmodern era where difference and diversity are crucial indices for all world communities.

The final ongoing challenge for Black theology, however, is to remind more conservative Black Christians, particularly those of the second of the three typologies I outlined in the first chapter, that a process of colourization simply will not do. For Jesus to function as a Black hero, he has to operate in a manner that is more than a so-called "coloured" version of the White Christ of faith. In invoking this term, I am not saying that Jesus as the Christ cannot be depicted as a White man. The images of a White Jesus in *The Christ We Share* pack[66] will, I am sure, continue to speak to and resonate with many people. A non-triumphalist White Jesus has legitimacy, particularly for poor and disenfranchised White people. But it is the White Jesus Christ who came to save our immortal souls but who cared nothing for the savage beatings, mutilation, suffering and death of Black bodies, in their millions, to which Black theology is in opposition.

The Black Jesus who is a hero to the mass of Black humanity who represent the marginalized, the forgotten, the dispossessed, the destitute and the dying is one who is not a darker reflection of his paler compatriot. Rather, he is a "hero" precisely because he bears no resemblance to the White imperial power broker who both sanctioned and condoned Black suffering.

A Black Jesus who is a hero to the mass of suffering humanity that is the ordinary, commonplace experiences of many, if not most Black people, is a figure who in his very identification with us, places us right at the centre of God's concern for the whole of creation. This Jesus tells us that we matter. That our Black epidermis matters! That the pursuit of life in all its fullness is a cause worth living for and ultimately dying for! This Black Jesus tells us that full life as conceived in John 10:10 is not about mere existence. Too many of our older forbears largely existed. Too many Black people on the continent of Africa barely live, but largely exist.

This Black Jesus tells us that the material needs of people matter more than fossilized dogmas and religious strictures often controlled and patrolled by those with power. That action matters more than religious observance; for the former gives life and expression to the latter. A prophetic, counter-cultural, "dreadful" Black Jesus is simply a must!

5 A Black Theological Christmas Story

This chapter outlines a Black theological approach to re-reading biblical texts. This interactive process – working alongside ordinary Black Christians – is one that attempts to create an *accessible* and *creative* method for bringing the insights of Black theology into conversation with sacred texts. I have highlighted the terms "accessible" and "creative" in the last sentence, for this chapter represents a slight "change of gear" from some of the previous chapters. I have attempted this methodological and linguistic change in order to acknowledge the other dimension of my scholarly identity and journey.

My early scholarly work was very much located within the area of Christian education and Practical theology. In my initial research work I was attempting to create a more appropriate teaching and learning framework for the Christian education of African Caribbean children, using the frameworks and ideas of Black theology and liberative, transformative education.[1] This work was undertaken between 1995 and 1999 on a research project entitled *The Birmingham Initiative*.[2] This work was concerned with seeking to create an appropriate model of Christian nurture and faith formation for Black African Caribbean children in Birmingham, using the insights of Black theology and transformative pedagogy as educational and theological frameworks for the research.[3] In undertaking this work I was forced to develop a twin-tracked approach to the task of creating Black theological scholarship. Many of the participants with whom I worked expressed the clear desire for a piece of research that did more than create "yet more theory that does not help us in the practical task of ministry." It was this challenge, of seeking to create new scholarly knowledge,[4] whilst developing creative and practical resources for the task of Christian nurture and formation in the light of Black theologies and Black hermeneutics,[5] which absorbed my waking hours.

This approach to Black theological studies was developed further in a later piece of research with Black elders in Britain,[6] where I undertook more participatory work, in which the importance of orality and non-text based approaches to Christian formation was evidently revealed.

In all my previous work, I have attempted to create critical scholarship that is both informed by and engages with the needs of ordinary Black people in local communities in Britain. Attempting to traverse the gap between the academy and the church (the latter remains the most

significant social and communitarian entity in the lives of many Black
people) has been a difficult one. It has led to me being marginalized from
both communities. I am not sufficiently scholarly for one community and
too academic for the other.

Despite the struggles and strains of attempting to hold in dialectical
tension this sense of not belonging to either community, I am nonetheless
obliged to continue in this seemingly foolhardy attempt of trying to straddle
the two sides of my Christian inspired identity. In this chapter, I am seeking
to address the question of how Black people can be enabled to read the
Bible in light of Black theology, within the context of their ongoing ministry
in the local church context.

This chapter arises out of some grassroots engagement with a group of
ordinary Black Christians in Britain. In order to do justice to the needs of
this constituency and also building upon my background as a Christian
educator, I have sought to develop Black theological reflections that emerge
from this encounter with ordinary Black people, whilst also creating a
practical and creative resource that will enhance the process of their
Christian formation.

I am sure there will be many who will find the accessibility of the
language and the lack of technical academic terms a complete anathema.
I make no apologies for this style or mode of engagement.

This chapter is written in critical solidarity with a group of ordinary
Black Christians who desired to see if there was a means by which they
could be enabled to engage with the Bible in a more critical and yet
respectful way. I am not a trained biblical scholar, so I cannot pretend to
offer the critical weight of intellectual and scholarly endeavour of a trained
exegete in my reflections and writing. Yet, I would argue that the lack of
formalized training was not the essential issue in this work. Rather, what
was at stake was how I might be able to work alongside a group of ordinary
Black people in their tentative steps towards incorporating Black theology
into their reading strategies of sacred scripture.

Whilst the desire to be in critical solidarity with a group of ordinary
Black people might be seen as delusional or simply erroneous to some, I
am nevertheless obliged to undertake this work as one who is essentially
a "practiced reflector." The work of many scholars who might describe
themselves as "practiced reflectors" falls within the broader theological
field of "Practical theology." Scholars such as Ballard and Pritchard,[7]
Forrester[8] and Graham[9] have theorized around the development of
Practical theology as a model of reflective activity in which the theologian
interrogates the connections between the theory and practice of Christianity
in a diverse range of contexts and milieus. Practical theology is particularly
adept at utilizing interdisciplinary approaches to theological reflection,
especially those that are drawn from psychology, which has proved a

durable dialogue partner for those engaged in pastoral theology (which is often taken as a synonym for Practical theology).

This chapter, then, is written in an accessible form in order to pay respect and to be in critical solidarity with the needs of ordinary Black people. It was not my intention create a kind of "epistemological deceit" in which the scholar engages with ordinary people, purporting to be "one of them," only to revert to their preferred identity and shed the baggage of accessibility when they return from the field. I am not expecting any of the cohort who assisted in the development of this work to necessarily read this chapter. In all truth, it is highly unlikely that they will ever do so. But should they feel particularly adventurous, I want them to be able to both recognize themselves and to have access to the resultant learning that is contained in this chapter, given that this work arises from their courageous and willing participation.

This chapter is a practical and creative approach to Black theological interpretation or hermeneutics. It represents the developed and practised, group-based approach to knowledge creation. The culmination of this educational and theological process is the creation of a dramatic text – a Black theological re-reading of the Christmas story as depicted in Matthew and Luke's gospels. This following dramatic reading emerged from a number of workshops with a group of Black Christian adults. This approach was influenced by, but is slightly different from, the methodologies first developed in *Acting in Solidarity*[10] and *Dramatizing Theologies*.[11]

Working with a Group of Black Young Adults

In this interactive process to Bible study I asked the group to re-imagine the Christian story and the Incarnation in ways that would be suggestive of Black theology. The group with whom I worked consisted of 10 Black adults, between the ages of 24 and 40. The group was drawn from Birmingham, Nottingham, London and Leeds. All had volunteered to take part in an informal series of workshops[12] that would explore the nature and import of Black theology. Participants were introduced to the work of James H. Cone,[13] Jacquelyn Grant,[14] Delores Williams,[15] Kelly Brown Douglas,[16] Dwight N. Hopkins,[17] Katie Cannon,[18] Linda E. Thomas[19] and Robert Beckford.[20] The initial four sessions, where the participants and I looked at the writings of the aforementioned group of scholars, were not intended to offer individuals an exhaustive account of the development and nature of Black theology. Rather, the intention was to enable the group to re-imagine what Christianity might look like if it were viewed through the lens of Black theological thought as opposed to the rather stultifying, rigid evangelicalism, into which many of them had been introduced as children.

In the previous chapters I have outlined a number of ideas by which a re-imaged Black theology can offer a new hermeneutic and raison d'etre for the overarching framework of Christianity, in which the majority of Diasporan Black people have been socialized and nurtured. In this chapter, I want to highlight a method for enabling a group of Black adults to re-think the Christianity into which they have been nurtured, having first reflected on the nature of Black and Womanist theologies. Following their reflections, I encouraged the group to think through the implications of this learning when applied to one of the central narrative themes in Christianity, namely, the Incarnation.

The reasons for choosing the Incarnation arose from a preliminary conversation in the first session, when I asked all the participants about their attraction to the Christian faith. Without hesitation, all ten members said that "Jesus" was the sole reason for describing themselves as Christians. On further exploration, as I asked the group to work their way through the "Apostles' Creed" (as outlined in Chapter 2), it became clearly evident that all of the group were profoundly Christocentric as opposed to theistic. Jesus loomed large in their religious consciousness in a disproportionate fashion when compared to God or the Holy Spirit. The decision to choose the Incarnation as a central theme for our work together was also influenced by the level of questioning and curiosity exhibited by several members in the group to some aspects of the birth narratives as described in Matthew and Luke's gospels.

I shall say a little more about the process of working with this group at a later juncture in this chapter. In this opening section, I simply want to outline the nature of the following piece and share something of its construction. The following dramatic narrative is a Black political theological re-reading of the story of Jesus' birth. The accompanying text has arisen from my group work with these Black adults and their creative work in thinking through some of the seminal issues in and central tenets of Black and Womanist theologies.[21]

Having been exposed to the basic tenets of Black and Womanist theologies, the group, first working in pairs, and then moving from pairs to two groups of five, then finally the whole group, were invited to reflect upon the traditional story of Jesus' birth as depicted in Matthew and Luke's gospels. Individuals and groups were encouraged think in terms of the parallels between the gospel narratives and the contemporary experiences of Black people in Britain.

Prior to this group work, the various participants had learnt that one of the central purposes of Black theology is to establish, by means of identifying God's liberative work in history, a connection between the biblical narrative and the existential experiences of Black people. That in effect, the liberating acts of God in the past are entirely consonant with the more contemporary struggles and thrust for freedom of Black peoples across the world in the present.[22]

In helping these participants to establish connections between Christian history and tradition and the existential experiences of suffering and oppression of Black people, the task that now confronted the group was to try and find ways of representing and applying this experiential point of departure to an existing biblical narrative.[23] From previous discussion in the group there had emerged a sense that issues of relevance and self-identification were uppermost in their collective concerns. The prevailing question was one of "what has the Bible and Christianity got to do with Black people?" The answers to this question emerged as the group began to explore the ways in which the narrative thrust of God's agency as reflected in biblical texts might be seen as a mirror for the existential crises and struggles of Black people. In short-hand terms, "God's story is our story" and "Our story is God's very own story."[24] Essentially, Black people read biblical texts in light of their own experiences, but then that very self same text then reflects back to them the connections between God's agency or activity and their contemporary experiences – we read the texts and the texts read us!

The developmental process of thinking through questions pertaining to the relationship between Black experiences and the gospel led the group to consider how they might apply the more contemporary insights and experiences of Black people to the biblical text. What might emerge if we, through a process of reflecting on Black theology, could then apply those insights to a biblical narrative? How might the Gospel be perceived if we dared to read it through the eyes of Black experience? Could we construct a Black political reading of, say, the Christmas story using the insights of James Cone, Dwight Hopkins and Jacquelyn Grant?

In order to aid the group in the process of re-reading and re-constructing the text in light of contemporary socio-political and Black cultural concerns, and then applying the insights of Black theology as the means of bringing these issues to the fore, the group was given the following checklist prepared by myself. The list was meant to serve as an indicative reminder of the issues and concerns the group should consider as they went through the process of reading and re-constructing the narratives of Jesus' birth from the accounts of Matthew and Luke. This list was constructed by myself as the facilitator of the group in order to help summarize the teaching and learning that had emerged from the previous sessions on Black theology. The list was intended to affirm their previous learning and to instil in them the confidence to use their own experiences and the concomitant Black theological reflections to re-interpret the traditional narrative of Jesus' birth. This list is detailed below.

Issues to Consider when Re-reading and Re-interpreting the Text

1. When reading the text consider what is happening "in front of the text" in addition to what is happening within the text or behind it. What I mean by this is that you should ask yourself "What am I bringing to this text as I read it in addition to what is already there inside the story or even the historical background to that story? How does the experience I bring affect my reading of the text?"

2. In light of point (1) above, ask yourself what is the social context in which my life is lived? What kind of things are/have happened to me? How do I seek to relate the text to the socio-economic contexts that affect people like me?

3. Remember that your interpretation begins with your concrete experience and not with the Bible or tradition.

4. Remember that you are seeking to find a distinctive and contextual reading of this text for your own liberation and transformation. We need to dispense with the notion of a universal reading for *all people*. Theology (rational talk about God) which underpins the Christian Gospel is *always* contextual, i.e. rich people, men, White people for e.g., will see and experience the Christian faith in different ways than, say, the poor, women or Black people in light of their respective experiences and the contexts in which that faith is understood and expressed.

5. Ultimately, this re-reading and re-interpretation you are attempting is geared towards social and political awareness. In the academic literature this is called "conscientization." This political awareness is the beginning of the transformative process that will lead to reflective action (praxis) and in the end, Liberation! This reading is but the start and not the end in itself!

Having applied the various points in the list as part of a hermeneutical process of re-interpreting the biblical text, the group emerged with a series of ideas concerning the relationship of this narrative to the contemporary experiences of Black people. Uppermost in their thinking was the way in which questions regarding Black deviancy and the corrupting behaviour of Black people in the minds of the predominantly White media can be read into the text. How might we "read" Mary if she were perceived as a Black teenage mother and "benefit scrounger" or "Welfare Queen"? What if the so-called "Wise Men" were simply prurient self-appointed "experts" looking for their next social phenomenon on which to conduct the next piece of research and write that award winning book for academic advancement (tenure)?

Once the group had allowed their imaginations (born of their reflections from personal and collective, contemporary experience) to flourish, there developed a fascinating process of discerning the liberative impulse of God in their ongoing deliberations. The question "what if..." became a constant feature of their conversations.[25]

The resulting discussion gave rise to a series of theological imaginings of the text in light of contemporary Black experience. These reflections, I believe, are the raw materials for a re-imagined conception of the Christian faith in light of Black experience. This biblically-centred hermeneutical approach to Black theology owes much to the pioneering work of James Cone.[26] Reflecting on Cone's use of the Bible as a source and norm for undertaking Black theology, Michael Joseph Brown writes:

> Although Cone, as a follower of Karl Barth, believed in the biblical grounding for his theological perspective, confirmation was not to be found in the writings of mainstream biblical scholarship. In response, Cone wrote his own biblical interpretation of Black theology.[27]

Like Cone and the bulk of those Black theologians who are in the "hermeneutical school," the Bible remains an essential source and norm for undertaking Black theology.[28] My continued use of the Bible as helping to frame the norms of Black theology arises not only from my own personal convictions surrounding the Bible as a hugely significant source for discerning God's nature (in partnership with Black experience, which works with Scripture and is not excluded from it),[29] but it is also a pragmatic one. Gayraud Wilmore describes Black or Afrocentric spirituality as "pragmatic."[30] Wilmore amplifies this point when he states:

> My main point here is that pragmatic spirituality "works" in the sense that Jesus worked. He did not sit round practicing "holiness" and the presence of God. He came down from the Mount of Transfiguration to heal and preach and unveil the Kingdom of God (Luke 9:28–62) with deeds of power.[31]

In using the term pragmatic, I am arguing that so long as Black people believe the Bible is the "Word of God" and that it is the irrefutable basis of their Christian faith, then I, as a Practical Black theologian, am obliged to engage with the Bible and foreground it in my own work. As I have stated on a previous occasion:

> Given that Black folks are not going to let go of the Bible any time soon, how can we become more attuned to the subtle and not so oblique ways in which the Bible has been used as a weapon against us?[32]

Whilst the group of ten Black adults was not chosen according to any recognized scientific method,[33] I have no doubt that many of them remain wedded to a normative Christian gaze in terms of how they connected with the Bible as the "Word of God." My work with this group was not to undermine their devotion or confidence in Holy Scripture. Rather, I wanted them to gain the confidence to re-read scripture in light of Black experience, steering clear of the seemingly arcane arguments about whether the text should be viewed as historical truth or symbolic allegory. Indeed, James Cone punctures the often arcane sterility of these debates when he writes of the Black church (and all Diasporan Black people to my mind):

> In the Black Church, little emphasis is placed on the modern distinction between liberals and fundamentalists as found in White churches. Blacks show little concern about the abstract status of the Bible, whether fallible or infallible. Their concern is with the Scripture as a living reality in the concreteness of their existence.[34]

Following the engagement of the group around the development of this contemporary Black hermeneutic for unlocking this particular biblical narrative, I was charged with the task of attempting to convert their theological insights into an accessible narrative that might be read in the context of a worship service, at a church attended by one of the research participants. Using the method devised from a previous piece of research,[35] I was able to "bring to life" many of the salient points that had emerged from the group work. The following dramatic reading is the completed text that arose from this adult Black theological process of Christian education. The dramatic reading was written in a simple and direct style in order to attract and hold the interest of a Black majority congregation that was comprised of people of varying ages – from those in their eighties down to infants and small children in Sunday School.

Then and Now (A Parallel Christmas Story)
Written and adapted by Anthony Reddie

A dramatic reading of the Christmas story, constructed by Black Christians working in Birmingham, UK.

NO. 1: The story you are about to hear has been called "The Greatest Story Ever Told." That is for you to decide. We hope this story will be an inspiration to all of you who hear it.

NO. 2: This story took place nearly two thousand years ago. It took place in a far away country. A country that had long lay under persecution and oppression from an invading, occupying power. At that time, a census was being taken. All people living under Roman rule were required to travel to the birth place of their ancestors, to register. A young man named Joseph had to travel, like everyone else, to the place of his ancestors.

NO. 3: In our age, there is a basic dislike of government. No one wants to be told where and when to travel. We dislike other people having control over our lives.

NO. 4: Would Joseph have bothered to travel these days? Look at how many people are sent official forms to fill in, or are told that they have to do a certain action by the government, but they choose not to do as they are told. There are so many people, many of whom are Black, who feel they have no stake in society, so they decide not to follow what the government says, as they feel that the government has done nothing for them. Look at how many Black people fail to even register to vote in this country. So when the government form comes, they say, "Nah man, forget it. I ain't moving."

NO. 1: Joseph travelled very slowly. He had a long journey to make. He had to travel from Nazareth, where he lived, to Bethlehem, the town of King David. Joseph travelled very slowly because his fiancée, Mary, was heavily pregnant with her first child. Mary made the long trip upon a donkey. It can't have been very comfortable for her.

NO. 2: As Mary and Joseph finally arrived at Bethlehem, Mary knew that the time for her baby to arrive had come. She needed to find a warm place to rest and prepare herself. Unfortunately, due to the census, there were no places to be rented in the town. All the available rooms had been taken. Joseph was desperate. His wife was about to have a baby and he could find nowhere to place her. In a last-ditch attempt to find a place, Joseph approached yet another Landlord.

NO. 3: Some things don't change. You can imagine trying to find a room at a time when there is some huge festival or event taking place in the city. All the best, medium and even trashy rooms would be taken. In the end, the poor and the powerless are always doomed to receive the last dregs of the barrel. And if you were a Black family trying to find a place? Forget that! Given the way in which our society works, even a stable might be too good for a Black pregnant woman, or should I say "young girl."

NO. 4: In our society, we can easily imagine that a certain group of society would still have to beg a landlord for a small, affordable place to stay for a short while, whilst all those who got there first and who could afford to pay, grabbed all the best places. But still, we've got welfare hostels and cheap Bed and Breakfast rooms for single parent and poor families to stay in. What more do they need?

NO. 1: Joseph explained the situation to the Landlord. He needed somewhere desperately. Sadly, the Landlord had nothing to offer. All of his rooms had already been taken. He had nowhere at all... Well, he did have one place they could stay... But that was only a stable. Surely Joseph would not want his pregnant fiancée to have her baby in a stable?

NO. 2: Joseph and Mary decided that a stable was better than nowhere. So they moved into the stable, along with the oxen and the other animals. Later that night, Mary gave birth to her first child.

NO. 1: When post Second World War Black migrants first came to Britain from the Caribbean in the 1950s, many could only find disgusting, sub-human accommodation to rent. As there was a shortage of housing, many Black families had to share modest, cramped accommodation in order to have a roof over their head. The overcrowding was harsh and dehumanizing.

NO. 2: And yet, in the midst of this hardship that was caused by others – principally, unscrupulous White landlords – it was the Black people who got the blame for "having no standards" and "living like rats" in a sewer. That's probably what they said about Mary and Joseph. They can't find a room, and yet when they have to settle for a stable, they then get attacked for having no standards and living like animals – literally! Typical, huh?

NO. 1. Meanwhile, way up in the hills overlooking the town, a group of shepherds were looking after their sheep.

NO. 2: As the Shepherds were sitting on the hillside, suddenly there was a bright flash of light. The shepherds, not surprisingly, were scared to death... They had never seen anything like this before. The sheep disappeared to all parts of the hill. The shepherds were speechless.

NO. 3: If something like that happened to us in this day and age, we would be speechless. But would we believe the Angel? Would we? In our age when people believe they can explain everything, we have trouble with those things that cannot be easily explained. No one really believes in those way-out wacky things any more. It looks and sounds ridiculous.

NO. 4: Well, Black people and other people of colour in the world might be the only ones still believing in such events. When you have been powerless and have been treated badly for so long, you are more likely to believe in anything that is special or as some might describe it, "supernatural," and which might have the power to change your life and set you free. Of course, if such people believe they saw something very special, we know that the rest of society would never believe them. After all, what do such people know? They're all backward, inferior anyway. What with their poor education and primitive ways! Who could possibly take them seriously?

NO. 1: The bright light was caused by an Angel of God.

NO. 2: The Angel calmed the fears of the shepherds. The Angel told the shepherds that very day, in Bethlehem, a baby had been born. This baby was to be no ordinary baby. This baby was to be the Christ, the Saviour of the World. The Angel informed the shepherds that they should travel to Bethlehem that night, and they would find this special child, wrapped in clothes and lying in a manger, in a stable.

NO. 1: The shepherds did not need to be asked twice. Hearing the news from the Angel, they quickly collected together their belongings and travelled to Bethlehem. When they reached Bethlehem, they found the stable. They entered it and saw the Christ child. The shepherds were overcome with joy and happiness.

NO. 3. In our present age, there are many people who would be seriously upset if they knew that a group of such low-life and social nonentities were the first to see or hear about anything that was supposed to be that special! Imagine if Jesus came back on earth and was seen and witnessed first by the poor – those Black people who feel set apart from society, the down and outs, the gypsies and beggars, the asylum seekers. Imagine that?

NO. 4: The church would be the most upset of all. The important people in the church would feel as if God had insulted them personally. What do those Black people and the poor know? Why them first? It just isn't right. In actual fact, they most probably would not believe it. God wouldn't let these people see anything first. Not without first clearing it with the church hierarchy. The church has been the guardian of God, after all. How could God bypass them like that?

NO. 2: The shepherds, having seen the Christ child, left the stable and began to spread the good news about the birth of the child that was destined to become the Saviour of the world. Mary thought long and hard upon the events of the night. Her son was very special.

NO. 1: Whilst Mary, Joseph and their child remained in the stable, far far away, some wise and scholarly men were consulting their books, maps and charts.

NO. 2: Their research told them that a special child, one born to become a King, was about to enter the world. They had followed a star from the East for many days, and arrived at the Court of King Herod. King Herod knew little of what the Wise men were talking about, but he asked that they keep him informed of the whereabouts of this child, that he too, might pay his respects to the one destined to become King of the Jews.

NO. 3: Wise people usually come in two different categories these days. The first would be journalists. They would have been working on tip offs and other forms of covert information. They would be looking for an angle – looking for a way to hype the story out of all proportion – you can see it now. A headline on the front page of a tabloid: "Slack parents allow baby to be born in stable!" You know that Social Services would be the next visitors to that stable. A child born in A stable? What kind of dysfunctional family set-up is this? My, my, my; these poor Black folk really are to be pitied aren't they?

NO. 4: The second category amongst these wise people would be the intellectuals. Those wishing to do some research and then write a book about it afterwards. You know the type. Travel today, see the event tomorrow, write their book about the phenomenon the day after that – go on a chat show the following day to hype up the whole thing. That family's life wouldn't be worth living. You'd have all the merchandising. "Baby in a manger dolls," cuddly toys and tacky cardboard pop-up books for those who have more money than sense!

NO. 1: Not forgetting the ones who want to get tenure. I bet all those wise men would be White experts. Soon they would know more about the Black family and the deviant "baby-in-a-stable" cultural shocker than most Black folk. In actual fact, these White wise men would be the recognized experts on Black folks.

NO. 3: It's a cultural thing don't you know? That's how Black people like to have their children. I"ve done extensive ethnographic field work and I can attest to the veracity of my discourse! This phenomenon, it's a form of cultural retention from West Africa. I"m writing a scholarly monograph on it for the next international conference on Black religio-cultural practices in the African Diaspora.

NO. 2: So the Wise men travelled on, journeying for many hours in search of this child to whom they wished to pay respect and homage. All through their travels, the Wise men followed a bright shining star from the East that led their way.

NO. 1: Finally, the Wise men, following the star, found the place where the Christ child lay. On entering the stable, the Wise men saw Joseph, Mary and child. The Wise men bowed low and worshipped the Christ child.

NO. 2: The three men gave the baby three expensive and special gifts.

NO. 1: One gave gold.

NO. 2: Another incense.

NO. 1: And the third, myrrh.

NO. 2: Mary accepted the gifts gratefully... She was overwhelmed by it all.

NO. 1: As was Joseph, who could not make any sense of it all.

NO. 3: If the Christ child had been born into a Black family, the whole community and every two-bit Johnny-come-lately looking for a free meal would have been there. Some would bring a present; others would walk with empty hands and fresh air in their pockets. But everyone would be there. There is something symbolic about the birth of a baby. It sort of unites everyone. Brings the community together! Certainly Black communities!

NO. 4: Isn't it ironic? Mary and Joseph were not married. So we know what sort of title one might label their child. If the Christ child had been born today not inside a marriage, to a Black family, the politicians would be having a field day. Especially the Conservative Right! This group would be on the war path; talking about a breakdown in morals – how the family is falling apart – how these unmarried mothers are failing their children – what about the sanctity of the traditional family – should our tax income be spent on such un-deserving folk? I doubt there would be much celebration taking place in the wider society.

NO. 2: Celebration? What, with another pointless bast... [Corrects themselves]... I mean illegitimate Black child to pay for? I don't think so.

NO. 3: No one wants their hard earned taxed income spent on such loose, bad living people like these.

NO. 4: You bet they don't.

NOS. 1 & 2: So Jesus the Saviour of the World has come. Let all the world be glad. Sing songs of praise…

NO. 3 Jesus the Saviour of the world is still here. We often fail to recognize him in amongst the crowded hustle and bustle of our society. When there is so much going on, so many problems and difficulties, we often miss the presence of Jesus who is in our midst.

NO. 4: Most times, when we cannot find Jesus, we are often looking in the wrong place. Jesus is not to be found by only looking inside the beautiful and magnificent churches and cathedrals in this country. Nor inside important offices and decorated palaces. We should look to the stables of our day.

NO. 3: The rubbish tips. Under railway arches as people sleep rough on the streets at all times of the year. In the dole queues. Inside the home of every poor and hopeless family, struggling to survive in this often hostile and selfish society. In the heart of every faithful Black person who continues to fight against the constant enemies that are racism and poverty.

NO. 4: In all these contexts, Jesus is to be found.

NO. 1: By looking at the sight of the despised mass of Black humanity in our world and loving it because that Blackness itself is of God.

NO. 2: Because Christ himself was born into Blackness.

NO. 1: So to look for Jesus.

NO. 3: We just have to know where to look.

NO. 4: And how to look.

NO. 3: And what to look for.

NO. 4: To those who saw Jesus all those years ago, the experience no doubt changed their lives forever.

NO. 3: May we continue in our efforts to find Jesus in our times, and may our lives, like those of so many others, be changed forever.

NOS. 1, 2, 3 & 4: [Together] Jesus the Saviour of the World, is with us. Thanks be to God. Amen.

THE END

Reflections on the Reading – Re-imaging Black Theology

This Black theological interpretation of the Christmas story contains a range of substantive educational and theological themes underpinning the narrative. Central to its construction is the belief in the need for a contextualized Black theological hermeneutic. This particular approach is one that will enable Black people to gain an important sense of affirmation, self-esteem, affective growth and self-actualization in their ongoing Christian development. This Black theological approach to re-reading scripture draws upon educational methodologies found in Black Christian education work such as that of Olivia Pearl Stokes.[36]

This particular approach to Black theology is predicated upon a contextualized, liberative approach to reading the Bible. Olivia Pearl Stokes is of the opinion that any relevant approach to the teaching and learning of the Christian faith must equip Black people to deal with their ongoing struggles for equality, justice, freedom and liberation. In addition to the aforementioned, there is the need for Black people to understand the existential and ontological reality of their Blackness.[37]

By drawing on the themes and ideas provided by my interactions with this group, I was able to construct a popularist dramatic re-reading of the biblical text in order that the contemporary existential concerns of Black people might be affirmed as a legitimate part of God's own story. That in effect, the Divine presence is located within the troubled and dispossessed humanity of demonized Blackness.

James Cone describes Black theology as:

> A theology of and for Black people, an examination of their stories, tales, and sayings. It is an investigation of the mind into the raw materials of our pilgrimage, telling the story of "how we got over."[38]

This Black political re-reading of the Christmas narratives locates Jesus as a part of our Black existential experience. The story of "how we got over" is one of identifying within the biblical text the themes and concerns that speak to the identity, affirmation and "somebodyness" of the Black self.

In developing this approach to re-imaging Black theology[39] I have sought to build upon the insights of my previous work in attempting to marry constructive Black theological work alongside Black Christian pedagogy. This approach is one that is attempting to create a bridge between academic Black theology and the practice of Black Christian faith in Black majority churches in Britain.

Whereas my former work attempted to create a nexus between educational methodology and Black theological thought, this essay offers a more conciliatory and "traditional" method for engaging with biblical texts. In my previous work, *Black Theology in Transatlantic Dialogue*[40] I offer a jazz inspired, improvised approach to biblical hermeneutics and Black theology. Whilst I remain convinced of the efficacy of this improvised approach to moving beyond the sterility of evangelical versus liberal approaches to interpreting texts, I am aware that talk of "playing with text" and re-working existing melodies has proved challenging or frightening to some.

In order to offer an alternative approach to the task of "doing Black theology" I invited a group of Black adults to work alongside me in a process of re-reading biblical texts through the lens of Black theological hermeneutics. This process of re-reading the Bible offers a creative methodology for "ordinary" Black people to bring their contemporary experiences into dialogue with scared texts. This process is one that challenges Black people to honestly place their experiences that arise from "in front of the text" with the sacred narratives of the text itself.

Black Experience and the Bible

I am aware of the critical response that has emerged from some Black Christians when asked to undertake this kind of work. Many will argue that sacred scripture is of a wholly different character and category than the text of Black experience and Black story. Whilst I can appreciate the rationale that gives rise to this form of analysis, I reject it, however, as being one that ultimately seeks to devalue the sanctity and sacred nature of Black experience and Black story. I cannot countenance any form of analysis that will not accord the very highest level of respect for the Black human self. That, in effect, Black humanity (as in the case of all humanity) is the very summit of God's creative potential in the world. The dispensability of Black life at the hands of White hegemony, which finds expression in the form of the casual dismemberment of Black bodies,[41] is too recent an experience for us to surrender the potentialities of our God-created self to the fixity of a written text!

To suggest that Black bodies, and the experiences that arise from their material and spiritual engagement with the cultural milieu in which they are housed, are not sacred texts, opens up the possibilities of Black non-being through oppression. And whilst I accept that privileging the Bible *before* Black experience does not necessarily imply that one is seeking to dismember the Black self, I would argue that the litany of Black humanity is too recent a historical phenomenon to even dare to concede the privileging of biblical texts over and above the living reality of Black existential experience. I have been known to state to students and adult laypeople in the churches, with whom I have worked in workshop settings: "The Bible has nothing to say until we open it and engage with it." The Bible itself is a witness to God's self, but should not be confused with God's being. God is beyond the Bible. The Bible is not God!

The theological concept of the *Imago Dei* confirms the anthropology of Black people and argues against the notion that our bodies are not sacred texts on which the divine author, God, has written (and continues to do so) God's own sacred narrative. Black story, when placed in a dialectical relationship with the Bible, offers opportunities for ordinary Black people to re-read the scriptures in order that a Black political theological hermeneutic can emerge. This approach to re-imaging Black theology allows us to re-interpret the essential meaning of the Christian faith in light of Black experience.

I know that those who hold a more evangelical perspective on the Christian faith would want to suggest that this method for reading the Bible does not take seriously the God-inspired authorship of the biblical text. They will point to the often quoted words of 2 Timothy 3:16 that "All Scripture is God-breathed and is useful for teaching, rebuking, correcting and training in righteousness, so that the man of God may be thoroughly equipped for every good work" as a proof text for arguing in favour of the transcendent, trans-historical meaning of biblical texts.

In this particular theological and biblical schema, the Bible is, for many, beyond criticism and cannot be compared to any other text, literary or human. My belief in the sacredness of the Black self is such that the existential realities of Black experience sit in dialogue alongside the biblical text and are not subservient to it. As I have often said to Black participants in the workshops and classes I teach, when having to defend my theological method: "Black experience has an integrity of its own, which is not subservient to the biblical text. I have no evidence to believe that when the author of any biblical text was writing, they had my reality as a Black person in mind as they were doing so."

As an addendum to my previous remarks, I am at pains to add that *I am not* suggesting that Black experience obliterates or rides "rough-shod" over the biblical text. My argument is that Black Christian radicalism has invariably found ways of linking Black experience to the biblical text in order to affirm the troubled existence of the Black self.[42] In effect, there is an ongoing dialectical relationship between Black experience and the Bible.

In using this approach to Black theology as a means of re-interpreting the Christian faith, thereby creating a liberative agenda for the praxis of Black life, it is my hope that this schema will resource and enable Black people to move beyond passivity to active radicalism.[43] The biblical literalism of many Black Christians in Britain is one that has been challenged by scholars such as Robert Beckford.[44] This form of rigidity in engaging with sacred texts has often had the negative effect of stymieing the liberative praxis of Black Christian expression.

This Black theological Christmas story is both a product and an educational process for re-imaging a biblical text in order to give rise to a Black political theology that can inspire a Christian form of liberation. Black theology challenges the a-historical pietism or abstract spiritualization of conservative interpretations of the Christian faith. A Black theological Christmas story is a material artefact for the historical commitment of Black people to never settle for anything less than their God-given right to be free.

6 Black Churches as Counter-cultural Agencies

This chapter is a Black theological reading of the development, intent and characteristics of Black churches across the African Diaspora. It is based upon a clear theological rationale for the ideological and intentional collective agency of Black people in Black ecclesial spaces. My notion of Black churches is predicated on the notion of the "Black Church" in the African Diaspora. I am writing on the firm premise that there are a number of distinctive cultural and theological markers for Black churches in the African Diaspora.

This chapter is not an exhaustive distillation of the complex literature pertaining to ecclesiology and historical and theological markers that constitute what one might term the "authentic church" in terms of holiness, catholicity, apostolicity. Rather, this work is an attempt to apply the principles of Black theology to the collective agency of God's people meeting together in order to worship God and to undertake the work of God in the world as revealed in the person and work of Jesus the Christ.

This chapter, like all the sections in this book, is written in the form of combative polemic. This chapter, like all the others, is an ideologically driven one. Not all Black churches in the African Diaspora, for example, will either wish to be identified as being Black or perceived as being related to the liberative theological agenda within which this essay is constructed. Despite such sensitivities and blandishments, I remain convinced that the substance of Black Diasporan history gives weight and credence to my liberative contentions for the nature, purpose and intent of Black churches across the past four centuries and into the present day.

What is a Black Church?

Perhaps one of the thorniest problems when trying to talk about the Black Church is the question of definition. What do we mean by the term the "Black Church"? For reasons that will soon become readily apparent, the question is somewhat easier to answer within the US context than it is in Britain or the Caribbean. In the US the notion of the Black Church is an ingrained historical, theological, sociological and experiential reality for many African Americans. The Black Church has an automatic efficacy that finds expression in myriad forms of discourses and academic courses.[1]

The Black Church has been perceived by many scholars as the key social, political, educational and organizational entity in the collective and communitarian experience of Diasporan people of African descent.[2] In Britain, the Black Church is often seen as the key location for the intimations of Black selfhood and collective solidarity.[3] Within the US the Black Church is a normative context out of which the Black religious experience has arisen.[4]

Historic Roots

In this chapter I hope to analyse the development of Black churches in the African Diaspora and sketch out an agenda for the future political and social intent of that development. This development has grown out of the ongoing struggles of Black peoples to affirm their identity and very humanity in the face of seemingly insuperable odds.[5] The "invention" of Blackness, as opposed to being "African," is a construction of the enlightenment.[6] There have long existed deep-seated racialized depictions of people of darker skin within the cultural imagination of Europeans, influenced in no small measure by Greek philosophical thought.[7] Despite the nascent ideas of Blackness as "other" or contrary to theo-cultural norms, dating back from this era, nevertheless, the construction of an overarching doctrine of racial inferiority ascribed to people of Africa descent reached its apotheosis during the epoch of slavery, aided and abetted by specious notions of pseudo-science.[8] In short, somewhere across the "Middle Passage" and the "Black Atlantic," Africans became "negroes."[9]

The use of the term "Black" as a qualifying nomenclature for any particular theological or ecclesiological entity remains a contested and even controversial notion. In using the term "Black" with reference to a particular understanding, development and intent of Church, embodying the Body of Christ, I am drawing upon a particular theological, philosophical and ideological tradition that finds its roots in the epoch of slavery. This particular understanding of the term "Black," having its roots in the slave epoch, adopted an academic conceptualization in the development of Black theology in the 1960s, during the Civil Rights and Black Power era in the United States of America.[10]

In seeking to define a notion of Black church, I am drawing upon a body of literature that has identified African Diasporan Christian religious experience as a struggle for a more affirmed, realized and nuanced humanity that is more than the crude construction of racialized inferiority imposed upon Black people by White Christian hegemony. Anthony Pinn has called this ongoing struggle the "quest for complex subjectivity."[11] Complex subjectivity is the attempt by Black people of the African Diaspora to construct notions of their own humanity on terms that are more amplified and nuanced than the reified strictures of fixed objectification that was a feature of the construction of the "negro."[12]

The roots of Black churches can be found in the radical and subversive re-interpretation of Christianity by enslaved Africans in the so-called New World, during the eighteenth and nineteenth centuries. Black people, having being exposed to the tendentious Christian education of the exploitative planter class in the Americas and the Caribbean, began to "steal away" from beneath the close confines of their slave masters to worship God in their own existential spaces.[13]

The desire of Black people to form their own ecclesial spaces was the process of a long period of history, arising from the "Great Awakening" in the middle of the 18th century.[14] It is beyond the scope of this essay to mount a detailed analysis of the historical development of Black churches in the African Diaspora, but it is worth noting the importance of Black existential experience and context to the historical manifestation of such ecclesial bodies. Black ecclesiological method begins with Black existential experience and not historic mandates born of the often abstract philosophical musings as to the nature of the "Body of Christ." Black churches were born of the existential need to create safe spaces in which the Black self could rehearse the very rubrics of what it meant to be a human being.[15]

The birth of the independent Black Church in the Caribbean can be traced to the arrival in Jamaica in 1783 of approximately 400 White families, who migrated from the United States, preferring to live under British rule than the newly independent 13 colonies. Amongst the White migrants were two former enslaved Africans, George Liele and Moses Baker.[16]

In the United States, Christian ministers and activists such as Richard Allen used Christian teachings and a nascent Black existential theology as their means of responding to the need for Black subjectivity. Richard Allen, a former slave, became the founder of the African American Episcopal Church (AME), which seceded from the American Episcopal Church due to the endemic racism of the latter ecclesial body.[17] Henry McNeal Turner, a descendant of Allen in the AME church, began to construct an explicit African centred conception of the Christian faith, arguing that an alignment with Africa should became a primary goal for Black Americans. This focus upon African ancestry would enable subjugated objects of Euro-American racism to find a suitable terrain for the subversive activism that would ultimately lead to the ongoing path for political, social, cultural and economic liberation and transformation.[18] Pinn acknowledges the link between the African centred strictures of the AME church and the later

Black nationalism of Marcus Garvey and the *Black Star Line* "Back-to-Africa" movement of the early 20th century.[19]

Responding to the ongoing threat of non-being has been one of the central aims of the Black Church that has emerged from the existential experiences of oppressed Black peoples of the African Diaspora. Harold Dean Trulear, writing on the importance of Black Christian religious education within the Black Church in the US, states:

> Rather it [religious education] has carried upon its broad shoulders the heavy responsibility of helping African Americans find answers for the following question: What does it mean to be Black and Christian in a society where many people are hostile to the former while claiming allegiance to the latter?[20]

So the historic roots of Black churches emerge from the Black experience of struggle and marginalization during the era of slavery and was a determined and self-conscious attempt to create liminal spaces where the subjected and assaulted Black self could begin to construct a notion of selfhood that extended beyond the limited strictures of objectified and absurd nothingness of fixed identities.[21]

Black Self-determination in the US Experience

The term Black Church, when used in the US, is a generic one, seeking to denote and describe particular faith communities in which Black leadership, culture, traditions, experience and spirituality represent the norm, and from which White Anglo-Saxon traditions and expressions are largely absent. These churches are termed "generic," because unlike in Britain, they are not confined to any one denominational or theological slant (more of which in a moment).

These churches cut across the whole spectrum of church affiliation and the multiplicity of settings in which Black life is experienced. The development of the Black Church in the United States of America grew out of the racism of the established churches of White, European origin. The worshipping life of these churches displayed discriminatory practices, convincing Black people to leave in order to form their own churches. The denominations most commonly identified with the Black Church are the African Methodist Episcopal Church (AME), the African Methodist Episcopal Zion Church (AMEZ), the Christian Methodist Church (CME), the National Baptist Convention Incorporated, the National Baptist Convention of America and the Progressive Baptist Convention.[22]

Black Churches in Britain

Black churches in Britain are not confined to any one denomination, just like their counterparts in the US. Black churches in Britain can be divided into three broad categories. The first category and by far the most visible is Black-led Pentecostal churches. These churches owe their origins to Black migrants travelling from the Caribbean in the post (Second World) War mass movement of the last century. The first churches were offshoots of predominantly White Pentecostal denominations in the US. These churches were first planted in the early 1950s. The largest and most established of these churches are The New Testament Church of God and The Church of God of Prophecy.[23] The second strand is Black Majority churches in White historic denominations. These churches are demographically determined, as their Black majority membership has grown out of Black migrants moving into inner city, urban contexts, coupled with the White flight of the middle class.[24]

The final strand is that of independent Black Majority Pentecostal churches or Neo-Pentecostal churches. This group is in many respects a dynamic development of those in the first category. These churches tend to be "stand-alone" entities that operate as independent communities of faith outside of any historic national denominational structure. One of the most significant differences between the first and third categories is that whilst the first was almost exclusively Black Caribbean in complexion, those in category three are a mixture of Black Caribbean and Black African, with the latter the more expressive and growing constituent.

Within the literature of Black religious studies particular emphasis is placed on the role of the Black Church as the major (in some respects, the only) institution that has affirmed and conferred dignity upon the inhibited and assaulted personhood of Black people.[25] To put it quite simply, Black folk in the African Diaspora may not have survived up to this point had it not been for their God-inspired genius for creating safe ecclesial spaces in which they could seek refuge from the ravages of racism and White supremacy.

Black Majority Pentecostal Denominational Churches

The origins of these churches in Britain date back to mass post Second World War migration of predominantly Black people from the Caribbean. For many years, it was believed that the formation of these churches emerged from the rejection of Black people from the historic mainline churches, of which these migrants were communicant members.[26] In more recent times, Joe Aldred has put forward a more intentional thesis, arguing missiological perspectives were foremost in the minds of these Caribbean migrants, as many arrived as members of established Pentecostal denominations in the Caribbean.[27] He argued that in effect, these churches were formed not primarily from racism and rejection, but were intentional missiological enterprises in their own right.[28] For many, their arrival in the UK was born of an intense missionary desire to plant and establish their own churches in this new cultural and social context. A detailed history of this largely untold narrative can be found in the work of Black British scholars such as Joe Aldred,[29] Mark Sturge[30] and Doreen McCalla.[31] This new narrative challenges and de-stabilizes the old discourse.

The churches in this category have often been perceived as being the natural equivalents of the Black Church tradition in the US due to their origins and development, which have emerged from within a Black experience. What complicates this particular perspective, however, is the fact that many of these churches, although emerging from within a Black experience, were nevertheless founded by conservative White Americans in the US and then established by means of missionary work in the Caribbean.

Ironically, we now have Black majority Pentecostal churches in Britain who are often seen as the natural equivalents of Black churches in the US due to their Black majority, Black run status. Yet the historical developments of these churches are linked to a form of US White ecclesial exclusivism from which Black people in the US had to separate in order to create a version of Christianity that did not oppress them.

For many years, these churches have been defined using the terms "Black-led." This term (often used by White commentators and not the adherents themselves) has been a highly contested one for many years. Writers such as Arlington Trotman have challenged the use of such terms to name predominantly Black British Pentecostal churches on the grounds that these terms (defining a church on purely ethnic grounds) do not cohere with the self understanding of the churches and the members themselves.[32]

One of the defining characteristics of Black Pentecostal churches is their worship style, which draws upon a range of Black Diasporan (and continental) African traditions, some of which are African American in style. The invocation of the spirit within Black Pentecostal worship, for example, is fused with an expressive, informal liturgy that has been one of the defining hallmarks of Black religiosity. Robert Beckford offers a carefully constructed Black British Pentecostal perspective on this creative dynamic in which participation and movement is an important means by which the liberative impulse of Black life is expressed.[33]

Independent or Neo-Pentecostal Black Churches in Britain

The third typology for Black churches in Britain emerges from within what is the comparatively newer movement of neo-Pentecostalism in Britain. There are a good many similarities between churches in these contexts and those found in category one (see above). Both are based upon an explicit rendering of Black religious cultural expression in terms of music, preaching and liturgy in which the practice of "being church" is reflective of the experiences of the Black people who attend these ecclesial bodies.

In short, attending the worship services of one of these churches is to find oneself located in a cultural setting that is at once removed from the normative, mainstream expression of White Christianity, particularly as it is expressed in most White majority historic churches of European origin. Charismatic worship and a strong emphasis upon the outworking of the Holy Spirit (Pneumatology), coupled with African and Caribbean musicology, characterizes the distinctive contribution to British Christianity of many of these churches.[34]

There are a number of differentiations one can deduce between churches in the first and third categories. In brief, I want to highlight two of them. The first, to which I have already alluded, is namely that these churches, whilst retaining an overwhelmingly Black constituency, tend to have a greater proportion of members who are Africans as opposed to Caribbeans, which was largely the case for those in the first group. Secondly, these churches are much younger in provenance than those in the first. Whilst many of the older Black Majority Pentecostal churches are now approaching or have passed the half century mark in terms of longevity, some of the newer neo-Pentecostal churches are between ten and twenty years old. Amongst the most well-known exponents of these churches (in the third category) include Kingsway International Christian Centre,[35] Glory House[36] and Ruach.[37]

Historically, Black churches of whatever denomination or theological perspective have suffered from two particular flaws. In the first instance, one often witnessed a tendency to spiritualize the central tenets of the Christian Gospel, which has led, as a corollary, to a disengagement from socio-political matters as they affected Black people in Britain.[38] The excellent work of such projects as "The Black Boys Can" of the Church of God of Prophecy or the ecumenical initiative against gun crime and violence, named "Bringing Hope," has tempered this age-old tendency, however.

And finally, a tendency towards factionalism, separation and mutual mistrust has been challenged by the pioneering work of such individuals as Philip Mohabir, Joel Edwards, Ron Nathan and Mark Sturge of the Evangelical Alliance[39] and Joe Aldred from the "Council for Black-Led Churches" and the "Minority Ethnic Christian Affairs" desk at "Churches Together in Britain and Ireland."[40] All of these respective bodies have done much to overturn the suspicions of the past.

The Black churches that can be identified within these first two typologies can trace their roots to the birth of the Pentecostal movement in Azusa Street, Los Angeles in 1906. The manifest outworking of the Holy Spirit gave rise to a new form of church, which in its earliest years attempted to move beyond the racialized division in ecclesial bodies within the Body of Christ that has been a feature of the discourse, hitherto, in this chapter.[41] To my mind, one of the major tragic occurrences in the ongoing development of Black churches from within this Pentecostal typology has been the extent to which they have largely lost the implicit and explicit radicalism of their birth at the dawn of the last century in favour of an abstracted, contextless spiritualized existence. This existence is one that runs counter, not only to the substantive, historical experience of Diasporan Black people, but also to the general liberative and materialist transformative theological thrust of all Black churches in their original incarnation.

White Majority Churches and Black People in Britain

The second of the three broad typologies is that of Black churches in White majority historic churches in Britain. These churches are often identified with such denominations as the Catholic, Church of England (Anglican), Methodist, Baptist and the United Reformed Church.

For many years, it has been assumed that Black members of these White majority churches were not part of a Black church tradition. The Black experience was seen to reside within Black majority Pentecostalism.[42]

The majority of the Black members in White majority historic churches in Britain can trace their roots to Africa and the Caribbean. The majority of these church adherents attend Black majority churches in predominantly inner-city urban contexts.[43] These churches operate, in effect, as Black enclaves within the overall White majority structure and membership of the church as a whole. Among the most significant churches in this category include Walworth Road Methodist Church (in South London) and Holy Trinity Birchfield Church of England (Birmingham).

The development of Black majority churches within these White majority historic bodies has emerged due to demographic changes in inner-city areas within the larger cities and towns in Britain, and not through a self-conscious separation along the lines of "race," as has been the case in the US. Research recent by Peter Brierley has shown that the majority of Black Christians in Britain belong to White majority historic churches (by a factor of almost 2:1 when compared to Black Pentecostalism in Britain).[44]

The place and role of Black churches in predominantly White majority historic denominations remains a deeply contentious issue. David Isiorho, a Black Anglican priest in Britain, has written about the dominant images of "Whiteness" and "Englishness" (the latter often taken as a synonym for the former) in the Church of England, which fails to acknowledge the plural and multi-ethnic nature of the Church.[45]

Writing about the seemingly inextricable link between the overarching construct of "Englishness" and "Whiteness" and that of the Church of England, Isiorho argues that these twin seminal building blocks in the established churches' self-understanding combine so as to exclude Black people.[46] This combination of Whiteness being associated with Englishness (and the established church being the "Church of England") means that it becomes structurally and symbolically difficult for Black people to feel a representative part of this White dominated edifice.

Defining Characteristics of Black Churches – Adherence to the Bible

One of the important characteristics of Black churches is the centrality of the Bible. This is not to suggest that the Bible is not central to other formulations of the Christian Church, but it is a generalized truth, however, that every branch of the Black Church across the world holds scripture to be the supreme rule of faith and central to their understanding of God's revelation in Christ.

Despite its radical roots in countering racism and Black dehumanization, many Black churches, whether in the US, the Caribbean or Britain have remained wedded to a form of 19th century Biblicism. A number of Black scholars have demonstrated the extent to which Christianity as a global phenomenon has drunk deeply from the well of Eurocentric philosophical thought at the expense of African or other overarching forms of epistemology.[47]

Black churches worldwide largely adhere to a form of pre-modern White European Evangelicalism that is a product of a post Reformation Biblicism. Black people on both sides of the Atlantic may have learnt how to utilize a "hermeneutic of suspicion" in terms of White supremacist overlays on the Gospel, in terms of the existential experiences arising

from slavery, but have been reluctant, however, to challenge the
Evangelical basis of faith as they have received it from the period of the
"Great Awakening", in the early to middle part of the 18th century.

For the most part, the heart of Black churches are built upon quasi-
literalist readings of Scripture, in which Jesus and salvation are conceived
solely in terms of adherence to Jesus Christ as the only means of salvation.
One of the important defining qualities of Black churches is the
Christocentric nature of their doctrine and worship. Within parts of Black
Pentecostalism in Britain, for example, there remains a powerful "oneness
tradition" which does not recognize the alleged, speculative Trinitarian
formulation of the historic church.[48]

In terms of Christology, Black churches on both sides of the Atlantic
have adhered to an orthodox Johannine Christology. Through a-historical
and de-contextualized readings of John 14:6, Jesus becomes the only
means by which people might be saved. The extent to which the Black
Church has traditionally been loath to engage in interfaith dialogue has
been, to a great extent, influenced by the strictures of this normative,
classical Christianity, in which the benefits of salvation are confined to
those who acknowledge Christ's atoning work on the cross.

Within the literature of Black theology a number of writers have located
within the suffering of Jesus a sense of divine solidarity with their own
historical and contemporary experiences of unjustified and unmerited
suffering. Scholars such as Douglas,[49] Cone[50] and Terrell,[51] to name but
a few, have all explored the theological significance for Black people of
Jesus' suffering on the cross. Writing with reference to this theme, Terrell
states:

> Yet the tendency among Black people has been to identify wholly with the suffering
> of Jesus because the story made available to them – Jesus' story – tells of his
> profound affinity with their plight. Like the martyrs, they are committed to him
> because his story is their story. Jesus' death by crucifixion is a prototype of African
> Americans' death by *circumscription*.[52]

This radical identification with the undeserved suffering of an innocent
individual has exerted a powerful hold on the imagination of many Black
people and other marginalized and oppressed groups in the world.[53] The
Christocentrism of Black churches in affirming Jesus (as opposed to God)
as the central point of departure in its ecclesial method has led to an over
reliance on notions of orthodoxy in their doctrinal and missiological
practices. Placing less emphasis upon the Trinity – the "Jesus-ology" of
Black churches – has seen many of them fall prey to the unwitting trap of
emphasizing a single-trajectory notion of faith (in Jesus only), which loses
the inter-penetrative reflections of perichoresis that has been one of the
hallmarks of Christian Trinitarian theology.[54]

In claiming a "High Christology" of Jesus in light of the seeming exclusivism of John 14:6, Black ecclesiological development in the 20th and 21st centuries has become trapped in the cul-de-sac of doctrinal adherence and dogmatic certitude. One of the problems of this adherence to neo-orthodoxy is that it runs contrary to the historic development of Black churches, in that the majority of Black ecclesial settings in the Black tradition came into existence not to replicate the arcane sterility and anti-modernist resistance of many forms of White Evangelicalism,[55] but rather, as an oppositional response to the corruptions of White Christian hegemony and its tendencies towards spiritualized abstraction in the face of Black oppression.

The roots of the Black Church lie in a radical appropriation of the Gospel in order that those who are the "least of these" (Matthew 25:31–46) might live, and have that life in all its fullness (John 10:10). That work was a praxis orientated one and was not mindful of either doctrinal purity or biblical literalism.[56]

Helping Black Churches to Conceptualize their Missiological Task – an Experiential Experiment!

One of challenges for many Black churches, particularly in Britain (but I guess all over the African Diaspora), is the need to discern their missiological task for the present age. What are we to do and to what end? Whilst this chapter has highlighted a more generalized perspective, drawn from African Diasporan history over the past four centuries, there is, I believe, a need for each individual Black Christian faith community to discover its own specific reason for being.

The following exercise was developed a number of years ago, and was re-enacted more recently with two Black churches[57] as a means of attempting to assist them in re-framing their sense of mission for their worshipping communities. The four typologies that are identified in the exercise function as diagnostic tools to assist Black people in Black churches to reflect on their role and positionality (and commitment to committed faithful action) in the Christian settings to which they belong. The four typologies were generated from a number of informal conversations with Black people, both within and external to the church.[58] The two questions I asked in these very informal interviews were (1) What should the church be doing? and (2) How would you describe your relationship to the church at this time? The responses were either tape recorded or the underlying sentiments of the comments written down in note form and amplified at a later point.

What emerged from these two questions were a variety of responses, which when juxtaposed with the scholarly literature on Black churches, assisted me in creating the following participative exercise for use with these Black participants. The exercise seeks to reflect back to the groups the substantive content of their thoughts and concerns about the Black Church and their individual role within it. The exercise also serves as a diagnostic tool that attempts to assist these participants in acknowledging the different ways in which Black churches seek to operate in their missiological task of proclaiming the good of Jesus, in word, deed and sign in Britain. The crucial question for many in the group was "And what am I to do?"

The work of the many scholars highlighted at an earlier juncture in this chapter assisted me in delineating four typologies that are used in the exercise.[59] These scholarly texts have enabled me to make a historic assessment as to the many different ways in which some Black people have sought to engage with the Church. The reflections that emerged from these texts were then juxtaposed with the comments of contemporary Black people, in this participative work, in order to give rise to the typologies that are identified in this chapter.

The typologies are not meant to serve as normative evaluations on the place and positionality of Black people in churches. Neither are they definitive in any sense. Rather, they are simply created as diagnostic tools that will assist me in my own theological reflections when juxtaposed with a group of ordinary Black people. My engagement with these groups was to enable them to conceptualize their relationships with Black churches of which they are a part, and to assess these positions for what they connote, in discerning the missiological task for such bodies and themselves.

The exercise is detailed below. My reflections on the exercise follow the description of this experiential learning activity.

Get on the Bus – an Experiential Consciousness Raising Exercise

* You will need four volunteers to assist you in the following exercise. The four volunteers should be asked to come to the front. Ask them to stand in a row, one in front of the other.

* Inform the whole group (including the four at the front) that they are all members of a particular church. The church can be from any denomination

or tradition of their choosing, i.e. Church of God of Prophecy, New Testament, Methodist, Anglican, URC, Baptist, Assemblies of God, etc.

* Inform the group that this church from this point onwards will be compared to a bus or a large coach. The bus/coach is about to start its great historic journey. The bus has a mission to travel towards the "Promised Land," the place of destiny. The bus decides to start on the long journey. It is the duty and the destiny of the bus to travel towards the ultimate place where God is leading it.

The four people at the front represent four different types of people who have a particular relationship with the bus.

PERSON ONE: (Invite the first of the volunteers to come to the front.) This is the person who decides that they do not want to be on the bus. They too want to get to the end of the journey, the Promised Land, but they have decided that they will not travel on this particular bus. They may not like the route the bus is taking, or the speed at which the bus is moving. In fact, there may be lots of reasons why this person will refuse to travel on the bus. Instead, they will make their own way. This person is committed to getting to the Promised Land but not on the bus. This person may have the best of intentions for the bus and may well have been members of that bus at an earlier point in their lives. But for now, and for this time, they prefer to make their own independent way towards the destination point in the journey.

PERSON TWO: (Invite the second volunteer.) This person has agreed to get on the bus, but they have decided to sit at the back of the bus. They are interested in being a part of the bus and travelling with others on the journey towards the Promised Land. This person likes to sit at the back because they do not want to be a part of the crowd or the main group on the bus. They enjoy being "difficult," being "subversive" or enjoy making harsh or honest comments about the bus, where it is going and who is guiding it on its journey. These are the "back row" people. The people who are not afraid to voice their opinions, make their presence felt, but as they are the mavericks, they prefer to stay on the edge, or in this case, at the back of the bus.

PERSON THREE: (Invite the third volunteer.) This person represents the ones who make up the central body of the bus. They sit in the seats from near the front, going back towards the rear of the bus. The majority of members in the bus are located in these seats. They are willing to be on the bus, but unlike their compatriots at the back, they are not mavericks. These people like the "quiet life." They want to be anonymous, so they sit quietly on the bus and simply take in the ride and watch the view.

These people have no desire to be involved in the navigation or the direction of the bus. They are happy to let others decide that for them.

PERSON FOUR: (Invite the fourth volunteer.) This person represents those who sit right at the front of the bus. They can see what the bus driver is doing. The can look out of the front window and see the road ahead of them, and get a clear idea of where the bus will be going next. These people are the ones who will want to know where the bus is going, at what speed the driver is going, and why he/she is taking that particular direction. These people have decided quite deliberately to sit at the front to watch the driver and to inquire about the progress of the bus.

Ask people in the main congregation or audience to decide upon which of the four groups they would naturally wish to join. Or, alternatively, is there another typology or category that more accurately describes their relationship to the bus? Where will the group participants locate themselves? Are they happy at the front of the bus, taking decisions, commenting on navigation and direction? Or are they happy sitting in the main body of the bus with no real comment or opinion to make? Some may want to be the dissidents sitting at the back. Some may even prefer not to be on the bus at all. Invite the people to stand behind one of the original four people who represent each of the four groups.

Initial Reflections

Person One

Right at the outset it was the bus that was compared to the church. In this metaphor, the bus is on its journey. The four different sets of people represent the many categories of people in the church. The model is relevant for all people, but is especially true for Black people in the church. There are some Black people for whom the bus is too restrictive. They find it claustrophobic on the bus. They do not like the bus, the direction, the speed or the people who are making the decisions or even driving the bus. The confines of the bus and the rules for being a part of it are too regimented for those whose spirit is too effusive, iconoclastic and prophetic to be contained within this vehicle and the set journey it is taking in order to reach the Promised Land.

Point to note: **Black churches must always appreciate the alternative forms and ways of "being church" that are represented by the dissidents who sit outside of, but perhaps are travelling alongside the established bus, using their own means of transport. Historically,** this is represented by those breakaway movements that represent alternative forms of church that are in critical solidarity with those on the established journey.

Person Two

Then there are the people who are sat at the back of the bus. These people make up the critical element on the bus. These are the mavericks. They will not conform. They remain on the bus, but only just. They make their own entertainment, say what they please and keep themselves apart from the others at the back of the bus. These people are in a definite minority. Every church needs a good number of these people. They take the bus journey with the utmost seriousness, but will not be dictated to or censured on how they should express their sense of belonging on the bus. Many young people would prefer to sit at this point on the bus. In effect, they want to be a part of the journey, and are concerned about the direction and the speed, but do not wish to sit near the front and become involved in the "official" politics of decision making on how the bus should proceed.

Point to note: **This group represents the critical edge of any Black church. Black people in this typology are in "critical solidarity" with the church, but feel more comfortable on the edge of any ecclesial setting. Reflecting on the work of Victor Anderson[60] and his critique of African American religio-culture mores and the pervasiveness of essentialism in these communities, these individuals struggle to sit in the main body of the life of the community of faith. The irony of Black people sitting at the back of the bus as a self-styled position of critical engagement with the institution will not be lost on many African Americans, given the emotional and visceral energy of the Montgomery "Bus Boycott" and Rosa Parks' stance as a prelude to the Civil Rights era. Many in this typology, in light of the exercise, understood their positions as ones of internal critique; but were also aware of the irony of choosing to sit metaphorically in places and spaces from which many Black people had once fought to be freed. I guess the difference for a more modern generation is their sense of "choice" in making that positional statement.**

Person Three

The next group are those who sit in the middle. Most Black people will find themselves at this particular place on the bus. They will feel comfortable being in the middle, being anonymous. They are happy just to go along for the ride. For many Black people, coming to church on a

Sunday, sitting in worship and then going home is about as much as they want to do. These people make up the central body of the church. Others in this position will play a full part in the life of the church, attending Bible studies, prayer meetings, fellowship groups, in addition to attending church; but they will not necessarily aspire for leadership roles or expect to be at the vanguard of helping to direct the direction in which the church should move.

Point to note: **This group, whilst they can be critiqued for their passivity, can also be seen as the solid base of many faith communities who, at their best, are able to provide a platform that enables others on the bus to adopt more radical positions and forms of praxis. At their worst, those in this typology can limit and constrain the activism and progressive actions of Black people towards the rear of the bus and those outside it. James Fowler,[61] the chief exponent of "faith development theory,"[62] and others[63] have noted the extent to which many adult believers in a number of churches never progress beyond the mid-range on the six-stage developmental schema for faith development. Those at "stage three" (synthetic-conventional") are often characterized by notions of conformity and an adherence to the established norms and values of the faith community of which they are a part.**

Person Four

Then there are the ones who want to know what is going on, and want input in all decision-making processes. These people sit at the front in order to see what is going on. These people will sit on church councils, Parochial Church Councils (PCCS), elders and deacons meetings, etc. and will hold office in the church. Many historic churches have traditionally not encouraged many Black people to be in this area, as it has often been perceived as the natural position for White middle-class leadership! In many Pentecostal churches in Britain, the question remains as to what extent they themselves are in the front seats of the bus, or is it their White "overseers" in the US? Too often, Black people have been encouraged to sit in the middle, simply watching others decide on the direction and the speed the bus is taking.

Point to note: **This group are right at the front of the bus and have a major role to play in determining the direction the bus takes, at what speed it travels and the route along which it should progress. As I have written in a previous piece of work, often, even in supposedly "counter-cultural" Black churches, a specious form of "classism" is at work in which those who possess greater formal education and social** status are the ones who are permitted to sit near the front and exercise authority over others.[64] Whilst there are, undoubtedly, good practical and procedural reasons for this mode of action, I wonder to what extent can it be said to articulate the practical theological and ecclesiological commitment to Jesus' injunction that the "first being last and the last being first" (Matthew 20:16). The counter-cultural Black Church of the 18th and 19th centuries, with its capacity for empowering and conferring status on the lost, least and the lonely, is one that has been stripped away by the vicious status bound creature that is the shiny, visible and corporate capitalism of the late 20th and early 21st century goliath of the "Mega Church" phenomenon. To what extent have "post modern" Black churches now become obsessed with respectability, status and social class? These obsessions then deny opportunities for those with lower levels of social status in the wider society to find any sense of belonging and an expression of representative status within the decision making structure of the church and its exercising of authority and power.

What about the Driver?

In my reflections with the two church groups that engaged in this exercise it was important to note that Black people should be seen at every position on the bus (and therefore the church). It vitally important that the crucial position, that of the driver, is also Black, when the opportunity arises. If the majority, if not all, the people on the bus are Black, it would seem only natural in those situations that the driver, the one who actually has ultimate responsibility for driving, should be Black also. The bus needs to reflect the experiences, expression and aspirations of all the Black people on the bus. The speed, the direction, the route and the driver, etc. should reflect and be decided by those people who constitute the membership of this bus.

Final point to note: For the church to gain an authentic sense of how the journey should be undertaken (as a metaphor discerning its missiological task) it is imperative that a Black theology inspired vision of leadership is in operation. This form of leadership eschews the status bound and exclusive exercising of power that has been modelled by White hegemony in Christian history and to which too many Black pastors have both aspired to and imbibed, often in an uncritical fashion. As Jagessar and I have stated: *"We have noted that the old dictum of 'needing Black people in office' can become a false panacea given the ways in which ecclesial and secular examples often simply* demonstrate that Black men and women who assume power and influence can be as authoritarian, non-collegial and myopic in their thinking and actions as the White people who preceded them... Black theology does not doubt the need for Black people to be involved in all forms of political processes, seeking to influence from the top, and engaging in the arenas of power, but we would remind all such persons that authentic change has always come from the bottom-up and not the top-down. Black theology must continue to align itself with the needs of ordinary rank and file Black people and not the blandishments of the powerful."[65]

Post-Exercise Reflections

This exercise operates as part of a process I have termed "performative action." Performative action operates within a mythical space in which religious participants are invited to imagine themselves sitting on a bus. The aforementioned exercise, which is entitled *Get on the Bus*,[66] invites participants to decide where they are going to sit on a mythical bus journey. The bus journey represents the collective journey of the Christian Church towards the "Promised Land" of racial justice. This is a mythical place/ space, which Martin Luther King once described as the "Beloved Community."[67]

The journey towards the beloved community is one in which the process is as important as the destination that is reached. By this I mean that the challenge to engage with one another, across our tangled and complicated lines of class, ethnic and theological differences, is one that is essential if the arrival at the destination is to make any kind of sense.

What has been challenging for the participants of the two church groups with whom I engaged in this exercise was the question of how one discerned where the corporate bus should be going, in addition to the more micro or individual question of where they would place themselves on the bus (if at all). The missiological task of any church is always a tripartite one.

In the first instance, one has to attempt to discover in which direction and to what destination is the spirit of God leading a particular group of people. The temptation, to my mind an erroneous one, is to attempt to answer that question in some form of ecclesiological and experiential vacuum. By this I mean that where a church might find itself being led by God cannot be ascertained outside of the context of the lives, experiences and narratives (individual and corporate) of the people that constitute that communitarian setting.

My post-exercise reflective work with the two groups was very much influenced by the work of Thomas Groome. Groome has developed a notion of shared, critical Christian reflection, which gives rise to committed praxis in the name of the gospel, and constructs an overarching concept for a radical approach to Practical theology.[68] In this seminal work, he outlines an approach he calls "shared Praxis," which he describes as being

> A participative and dialogical pedagogy in which people reflect critically on their own historical agency in time and place and on their socio-cultural reality, have access together to Christian story/vision and personally appropriate it in community with the creative intent of renewed praxis in Christian faith towards God's reign for all creation.[69]

Groome details an approach that attempts to link the individual to a process of critical reflection and dialogue. This reflection and dialogue arises through a shared process where individuals are encouraged to enter into dramatic exercises that attempt to address major issues and concerns in the lives of that group of people – in this case, their own positionality in the larger missiological identity of an ecclesial body. This dramatic exercise is, in turn, combined with the sacred stories (or narratives),[70] in order that the Christian story/vision, namely the gospel of Christ, can be realized.

This process culminates in the final phase of this approach, which is a search for the truth that enables participants to make the Christian story their own.[71] Groome argues that participants should be empowered to appropriate the story/vision in order that they can own it, and then remake it, so that they can be set free. Groome's approach is heavily influenced by Liberation theology and seeks to speak to the experiences of those who have been marginalized and oppressed.

In order to discover the missiological task into which they are invited by the prevenient spirit of God, it is imperative that Black churches are able to discern some sense of where their congregants and adherents might be in the positional make-up of their faith community. For example, a church cannot propose to undertake radical counter-cultural work, such as an active engagement in local politics for example, if that ecclesial body has a preponderance of those sat in the middle, but no one sat at the front or at the rear of the bus.

Those in the front can provide the intellectual and professional sustenance and know-how that will enable the church to access the often labyrinthine processes for engaging in political action. Those at the rear, however, can provide a sense of critical comment that will offer the necessary "checks and balances" less those at the front let their enthusiasm lead the church into the politically choppy waters of compromise and expediency.

Similarly, if the bus is comprised of too many sat at the front, one may find their sense of importance and respectability a bar to engaging with external radicals who are outside of the bus, but maybe travelling in solidarity in their own vehicles alongside the bus. I have witnessed too many Black congregations who only wish to ally themselves with external people "who are just like us." Some do not even wish to go that far and cannot countenance accessing support from anyone outside of their gathered community of supposedly like-minded souls (often any internal dissention is suppressed in such settings).

I have used this exercise to challenge a group of people from two Black churches to reflect on how they perceive their own individual positionality within the collective setting of a mythical bus journey. Individuals are then asked to reflect on that position in light of those adopted by their peers. What is the overall shape and balance of the collective whole, given the various praxiological positions adopted by the different members of the ecclesial body?[72]

In the exercise, the different participants are challenged to determine their individual agency and positionality in this process. Where will they sit on the bus? Is it important that they sit near the front and direct the driver and, as a corollary, assist in influencing the route the bus should take? Traditionally, in Britain, this has been the role paternalistic White people have played in their efforts to engage with Black people. This can be seen in the historic churches in Britain and the role White leadership has played in individual congregations and these denominations as a whole. Conversely, within Black-led Pentecostal churches, the role of White people has been in the overarching shaping of doctrine and ecclesiology, which, while at a distance in many respects (most of the main "head" leadership is in the US), still has the net effect of shaping or even controlling the direction and the route the bus takes on its journey.

Alternatively, are the Black people going to opt out of the bus journey, on the basis that they will refuse to engage with White paternalist constructs? Conversely, will they seek alternative ways of engaging that do not require them to collude? This may be the challenge of creating completely alternative and diverse forms of faithful communities, ones that may not even adhere to any notional view of what it is to be Christian.

One witnessed examples of these kinds of movements in the 1970s in Britain, under the aegis of Rastafari.[73] Similarly, in a more contemporary epoch, Black British Womanist theologian Lorraine Dixon is undertaking work as a DJ priest in Birmingham (in the Church of England) under her performance name of DJ Ayo, and is seeking to develop faithful communities of resistance amongst members of the dance community in the city.[74] These nascent forms of faithful communities[75] are part of a wider development of "emerging" or "Fresh Expressions[76] of church in Britain.

The challenge for many Black people struggling with particular ecclesial models of faith community is one of whether you "hang in there" trying to reform it, or simply bid church a hasty retreat? This challenge, as is sometimes stated in Jamaican speak, is to "stay and burn and not cut and run," and is one that poses hard questions for many Black theologians and religious scholars such as myself.

The development of the Black Church in the US, for example, as a repository and incubator for the creation and development of Black theology, came into being due to the decision of African Americans to leave the racialized ecclesial body of White America.[77] In seeking to answer the vexed question of what should the church be doing (characterized in the exercise with the metaphor of where the bus is heading and which route it is taking), many Black people have sought recourse in alternative ecclesial models.

In short, some have simply left and moved away to "do their own thing"! In more recent times, I have acted as a form of theological consultant and reflector to an emerging, informal faithful grassroots community in Leeds. This group is comprised of a dozen Black young professionals, all in their mid 30s, who have left the Pentecostal churches of their birth. The decision of these young adults to leave their respective churches has been a difficult one. Two members of the group (both males, it is important to note!) have taken the decision to undertake theological education in order to fit themselves for ministry as leaders of this nascent group.

The individuals in this group are self-consciously seeking to create an alternative, looser and less confined notion of church, one that still echoes to the distant call of Black cultures and African Diasporan experience, but is not determined by rigid doctrinal rules or top-down impositions of power and hierarchy. All members of the group would, to my mind, be defined by the first typology in the exercise. None of the members of the fledgling community are hostile to their former traditions and some still return to them periodically. But essentially, the decision to create something new has emerged from a form of prevenient spirit that has inspired them to seek an alternative space in which to discover a new way of being authentic, faithful Christian communities.

The group are using their professional skills and expertise to create alternative health-care, educational and counselling services for poor Black people in their part of West Yorkshire. I have been invited to accompany them on their faith journey as a consultant Black theologian (at no charge, I hasten to add) in order that this new community might seek to embody the central tenets of Black theology in their liberative praxis.

The dangers for this type of group are all too evident. What happens when the brave new dream begins to fade? Will some leave this fledgling community for other ecclesial spaces, forever seeking the next "magical space beyond the rainbow"? History shows that people can develop a propensity for schism. Also, of equal import, perhaps, are the challenges this form of attitude and behaviour pose for the self-emptying and sacrificial themes that are replete within Christianity? As I have stated elsewhere, the desire for personal fulfilment can soon lead to self-absorption and the sense that Christianity and the church exists solely for the individual to fulfil the self-congratulatory desire of inherently selfish people.[78] The "selfish faith" that Robert Beckford identifies is one that is consumed with thoughts of personal blessing and self-aggrandisement and has no conception of the necessity to fight injustice or to be committed to pray and work for social change.[79]

I am inclined to believe that the excellent praxis of this newly developing group in West Yorkshire – evidenced in their determination to serve the wider community in addition to engaging with the political process in their local electoral ward – is testament to their desire to be a form of church that is more than "feeling good and have one's needs met" (often to the detriment of a lack of care and concern for others).

I am not suggesting that only those in this first typology can be described as being church in the spirit and according to the tenets of Black theology. As I have stated at an earlier juncture in this chapter, Black people can legitimately adopt a variety of positions and roles in terms of their participation in the bus journey. What is important is that individuals, however they might describe their present role and position (as I state previously, these typologies are not normative or definitive), are enabled to reflect theologically on why they are located at a particular point. But, perhaps of greater import, through the use of this experiential exercise, is the question related to the direction and to what end do they think God is calling the bus on its continuing journey towards the "Beloved Community"? How and in what ways are they prepared to be a part of that journey?

Ongoing Challenges for the Future

The historic development of Black churches over the past four centuries has not been without its troubles. Gayraud Wilmore has asserted that the radicalism of the early Black church movement in the US was ceded to the strictures of conventional, normative pseudo White social mores and theological and ecclesial respectability.[80]

Within the British context there are issues pertaining to the ongoing struggles for familial cohesion and a sense of the loss of cultural and historical memory. Contemporary postcolonial Britain is a context where lives are governed by the all-pervasive influence of a form of societal postmodernism. The old assumptions surrounding family life and collective identities are fast disappearing. In this particular epoch the realities of social and geographical mobility are constantly challenging the traditional notions of collective and communitarian cohesion. These social and cultural factors have been the bedrock on which Black churches have gained their traditional strength, and from which the majority of their adherents have been drawn.

The challenge facing Black churches in their historic task of offering safe ecclesial spaces for affecting the liberative impulse for Black existential freedom can be seen in my own formative experiences. I was born into a Black Caribbean Christian family, and although my family attended a White majority church for a good deal of my formative years, the values of Black Caribbean Christian traditions, learnt from the Black church of my mother's childhood in Jamaica, were nevertheless highly visible in my Christian nurture and socialization.

Prayer remained an important component in my Christian nurture and formation. I can still remember being taught the traditional prayer of "Gentle Jesus" by my mother. An informal survey amongst a group of forty-something Black Christians a few months ago revealed that this prayer seems to represent some form of signifier in connoting aspects of an African Caribbean religio-cultural heritage. Learning this prayer was an important moment in my own sense of identity in religio-cultural terms. I still retain the distinct memories of being taught this prayer on my mother's knee at a very young age.[81]

Black people have found in God, who is defined in psychological terms as the "Ultimate Reality,"[82] through the facility of prayer a constant and accessible mediator for their troubles and hardships.[83] In this particular understanding of prayer, God is identified in immanent terms. God, through the life, death and resurrection of Jesus, and by and through the power of the Holy Spirit, is manifested in God's own creation, as mediating alongside humankind.

Reference to the importance of a literal, immanentist approach to prayer has been highlighted in a previous publication.[84] My mother, in particular, inculcated the importance of praying to God at all times. Accompanying this approach to prayer was the literal, almost eager expectation that God would answer one's petition. There was never any doubt within my mother's conceptualization of God that this God was not in the business of assisting and supporting the presence of God's own people. The faithful would be upheld and no forces of evil, such as racism, would overpower them. In this respect, the words of Romans 8:37–39 ring true. The author of this text writes:

> In everything we have won more than a victory because of Christ who loves us. I am sure that nothing can separate us from God's love – not life or death, not angels or spirits, not the present or the future, and not powers above or powers below. Nothing in all creation can separate us from God's love for us in Christ Jesus our Lord![85]

One of the central challenges facing Black churches as we continue into the 21st century is the ability to meet the existential concerns of Black people, whether in Kingston, Jamaica, New York or London. The challenge that faces Black churches is the need to harness the historic resources that have informed and governed her existence to date, juxtaposed with the possibility of discerning new ways of being and doing.

In order to address the challenge of postmodernism, the Black Church, inspired by an improvisatory approach to Black theology, will gain the confidence to move beyond the strictures of a stultifying form of conformity into which so many of us have been herded. In a previous work I have questioned the conformist strains of many Black churches, influenced by a strict "holiness" code, which in turn, are governed by the twin concerns of "shame" and "racism."[86] Scholars such as Kelly Brown Douglas,[87] Robert Beckford,[88] Jacquelyn Grant[89] and myself,[90] have all explored, in our many differing ways, the challenges faced by the Black Church to move beyond the seemingly endemic forms of conservative thinking and practice that has limited the scope of its prophetic agency.

The challenge that faces Black churches is one of attempting to connect with the postmodern realities that presently face Black people and to construct new ways of engaging in the historic mission of challenging injustice and proclaiming the good news of individual and corporate transformation.

In this respect, Black churches need to re-learn the strident and polemical forms of radical Christian praxis that galvanized Diasporan African peoples in previous epochs. This newly imagined paradigm of the Black Church is one that will continue to work within the historic tradition that has sustained countless generations of Black people of the African Diaspora, and the younger generations born and socialized in this country.

The challenge is to model examples of good praxis that inspire prayerful dedication and discipleship, which can provide new paradigms by which Black children and young people can begin to gain some semblance of the factors, both immanent and transcendent, that have enabled people of African descent to survive the many travails of the past. Janice Hale says something to this effect when reflecting upon the importance of re-telling stories of experience, by word and example. She writes:

These stories transmit the message to Black children that there is a great deal of quicksand and the many land mines on the road to becoming a Black achiever... They also transmit the message that it is possible to overcome these obstacles.[91]

Black churches of the 21st century must develop a model of Christian mission that inspires and transforms. This cannot be the kind of theological moribund framework that seeks to offer a simplistic and spiritualized placebo for the contemporary and more historic ills that have plagued Black people for the past half millennia. This cannot be the type of Christian practice that seeks refuge in certain forms of abstractions that describe a personal piety, which retreats from the world rather than seeking to transform it.

The kind of Black ecclesiological Christian praxis of which I speak is the facility that connects with the very heart of God. It is a form of praxis that demands reflective action, the kind of action that is an integral component of faith, whose practical demonstrable consequences are described in James 2:14–26. The demand for praxis (action and reflection) finds expression in the salient words of Paulo Freire who opined that "Action without reflection is mere activism, and reflection without action is pure verbalism."[92]

Black churches need to return to these historic roots in order to be reminded of the factors and facets that once made them amazing centres for rescue, resistance and renewal. This is not to suggest that there are no Black churches presently doing this type of missiological work in the world. That would be an erroneous proposition on my part. I think it is true to say that there are insufficient churches, of this ilk, for me to rest secure in my bed at night.

At a recent visit to a friend's house, I was somewhat surprised and not a little perturbed at her almost Pavlovian relationship to the "God Channel" on cable television. I sat dismayed, watching this once radical, critical and challenging Black Christian peering in a seemingly hypnotic state at the television screen entranced at the plethora of expensive suits and lacquered hair on show as the "men and women" of God strutted their stuff and sold their wares. What price now for a Black church that is proclaiming the radical "upside-down" Kingdom where the first are last and the last are first? In arguing for Black churches as counter-cultural agencies, I am pressing for an articulation of the gathering of God's people who are committed to structural and societal change and not simply instant personal gratification and blessing.

The title of this book is "Working against the grain." Many Black and Womanist theologians are witnessing the seemingly remorseless rise of neo-conservative Black churches (many that do not even want to be identified as being Black) in Britain and in other places in the world. We are spectators at the soufflé-like tendencies of such churches, in which one witnesses a surfeit of rhetorical bombast and vacuous, sententious moralizing. These soufflé-like Black churches are long on rhetorical utterance, often through the loquacious sermonizing of conservative Black pastors, but beneath the puffed thin crust of supposed relevance lies a hollow space of empty thinking and non-existent theology. As a Black theologian I remain committed to a version of church that is against the apparent natural flow of things. I am seeking to work against the grain.

I am particularly exercised by the "Prosperity Gospel wannabees" in Britain, who may be able to attract impressive numbers to their places of worship, but once the people are within their "temples of Glory" they are subjected to simplistic anachronistic teachings of the Christian faith that are neither contextually drawn or theologically credible.

In terms of the latter, too many of these "high profile" pastors of Black churches in Britain (principally London) almost make it a badge of honour or some perverse form of virtue to be uneducated and without any substantive theological training.

This chapter argues for a form of Black church that is not constrained by the need to be respectable or acceptable. Neither is it concerned with the need to present its pastors with extravagant and obscenely expensive gifts or trying to make a theological virtue out of poor financial governance. The counter-cultural Black church needs to return to the pioneering spirit of such heroes in the faith as Sam Sharpe. Sharpe's total identification with the liberative message of freedom that is the Gospel of Jesus Christ forced him to put himself at the service of his Saviour in order to work for the social transformation of all people. He was not afraid to challenge injustice as a sacramental and kenotic act of self-giving.

His costly discipleship was an act of theological hubris, which shamed the powers and principalities of oppressive control in Jamaica. It was this form of radical, counter-cultural action that gave life to the Black Church in the African Diaspora. The truth is, as we observe the dangerous tentacles of the new world order, as it chokes the life out of the poor and the marginalized in our present age: we know that nothing less than this sort of Black liberative praxis, emanating from the heart of the Black Church, will do!

7 A Black Theological Approach to Violence against Black People: Countering the Fear and Reality of Being "Othered"

One of my earliest memories is of standing in a playground of my primary school, aged five, as the only Black child being taunted by a larger group of White pupils. I remember clearly standing in the playground as a sea of White faces pointed little jabbing fingers in my direction followed by a well-known expletive "N***r."

Up to that point in my life, I did not know that I was Black. As the eldest child of Black Caribbean migrants, I had been cocooned within the comparative safety of my extended family and the normativity of that sub-contextual world. Nothing in my previous four years had prepared me for the reality of being in an apparent and conspicuous minority of one. I remember looking around in vain for a familiar and friendly face with which I could identify, but none seemed to exist. I huddled into the corner of the playground, near the far wall, as the White jabbing fingers came closer and ever closer, mouthing in unison the racial epithet "N****r." In an interesting case of "psychological remembering" or flashback, I remember my first viewing of Michael Jackson's epoch-making musical video, *Thriller* and witnessing the climactic scene where the frightened and embattled heroine is holed up in a bedroom as an army of fiendish zombies make their way ever so remorselessly towards her bed to devour her, and thinking, "Now this takes me back!"

OK, so memory is a fickle business and my experience in the playground was not outlandish as the events depicted in Michael Jackson's video; but nonetheless, the visceral shock of that moment has never left me. The intense fear of that moment was suddenly dissipated as a booming voice was heard from behind the mass of White bodies, "Leave him alone!" Suddenly, the White bodies halted. The fingers stopped jabbing in my direction. The name calling ceased. In through the mass of now silent agitators came a tall Black figure. Looking back at that incident, I am not sure what was more shocking: that a group of White kids were going to beat the hell out of me or the sight of another Black person who suddenly descended from nowhere.

The Black figure was the toughest kid in the school, as I was to later find out. In the popular parlance of the time, he was the "Cock of the school." This phrase, invoking the imagery of the farmyard, meant that he was the head rooster – he "ruled the roost" amongst the student population.[1]

This Black salvific figure not only saved me from a likely beating, he also graciously identified with me. Whilst the social protocol of the school yard meant that he, in the top class of the school, could not associate with me in any direct sense (I guess it would have ruined his street-cred to be seen hanging around with a "wet-behind-the-ears newcomer), he nevertheless let it be known that anyone who messed with the new "coloured kid" would have to deal with him.

As I reflect back on that incident two things immediately come to mind. First, was my sense of "otherness" in that context. I was new to that context. There was no warm welcome or sense of much vaunted English fair play upon my arrival in the school. Conversely, my Black skin immediately marked me out as different and that difference was perceived as a threat. At the other end of the spectrum was the other Black body in the school. I suspected that he may have faced the same reception squad when he had started the school some time earlier. But now, at this moment in time, he was the toughest kid in the school. Whether he was liked or merely respected in a manner one learns to respect the mafia, for example, has been a point of much speculation over the years.

What is without doubt is that he being the toughest kid placed him in a completely different category from myself, even though the two of us had parents who had come from the Caribbean to Britain in the previous ten years. My erstwhile protector was the "bad Black boy" who should not be trifled with or displeased. As I will demonstrate at a later point in this essay, such typologies have not changed significantly in the last thirty or so years in the UK.

This was Bradford, in the North of England, and the year was 1969. I was the eldest child of Caribbean migrants who arrived in Britain in the winter of 1957. They came as strangers to the Britain that was then the remnant of the British Empire. They found themselves to be different and found that experience a painful and dispiriting one.[2]

Admittedly, 1969 seems like a whole lifetime away. A distant country to which I never want to return! As I reflect upon my life as a Black British person in his early 40s, in the early part of the 21st century, I believe that things are so much better for Black people now in Britain. Postcolonial Britain in the early part of this new century is very different from 1969. It is argued that the lessons of multi-culturalism have supposedly made us all a more tolerant nation. Britain, as a nation, is now able to deal with strangers and outsiders differently than it did all those years ago. In this chapter, I want to challenge and problematize this notion. I am not arguing that Britain has not changed. Neither am I arguing that, in a great many ways, the life experiences and opportunities for Black people have not improved either. The very fact that I am writing this book, perched in my third-floor office of a genteel middle-class institution that is a theological college in Birmingham, is testament to the extent to which things have changed in the fifty years since my parents came to this country. What I want to argue in this essay, however, is that whilst the surface level indices of social, cultural and economic opportunities for Black people have improved, what has remained largely unchanged is the unreconstructed, substantive underpinning notion of what it means to belong and be acceptable in Britain. That in effect, Black people are still the "other" in this context. We are not authentically of this place in the fashion that is readily accepted by White subjects in this nation.

The Ongoing Legacy of Being the "Other" – Assessing Christianity in Britain

To belong to British society and that of the church, for a Black person, necessitates at some intuitive level, a denial of one's self. To be Black is to have one's experiences, history and ongoing reality ignored, disparaged and ridiculed. It is to be rendered an insignificant presence, amongst the many who are deemed one's betters and superiors.[3] Reflecting upon a Caribbean aphorism, which states that "Who feels it knows it" – to be Black and "other" in 21st century Britain is to find that what I know or have felt is of no consequence to the nation or world as a whole.

What I know and have felt is dismissed as untrue and without any social, political, cultural or theological consequence. The collective entity that is Britain will often invoke the rhetoric of its Judeo-Christian heritage as a basis of defining itself as a Christian nation. This socio-historical and religious heritage does not come to us in a value-free, non-ideological baggage. As Robert Hood has shown, within the development of Christian thought and tradition, the post-Constantinian imperial church of Christendom, flushed with power and hubris has drunk deeply from the well of Western epistemological thought, but has shown scant regard for the contribution of African cultures and traditions in the shaping of Christian doctrine.[4] For the most part, European inspired norms, values and political expediency have helped to shape the direction of Christian thinking, which as a corollary, have influenced the development of predominantly English identity. These developments have largely ignored or even disparaged the presence of Africa as a major contribution to the ongoing development of the collective whole.[5]

The awful truth a so-called Christian country like Britain has to face is the extent to which its own Judaic Christian traditions have been and continue to be a source for violence and hatred against the other – the foreigner – those who are "not one of us."[6] The violence that exists within Judaic-Christian practices (sacrifice, atonement, crucifixion and the cross) have all contributed to the development of a set of thinking and ideas, which ultimately make violence seem like an acceptable and redemptive idea.[7]

Attempts to reify Christian culture and learning have led, almost axiomatically, to the exclusion, marginalization and oppression of others.[8] When Christianity has insisted on parading human constructions as metaphysical, essentialized truth, this has often led to the reification of the aesthetics and conventions of the powerful, whilst marginalizing and oppressing those outside the traditional hegemonies that govern many societies.[9]

This tendency is exemplified and has had deadly consequences for Black people when we assess the seemingly rigid determination of mainstream Christian thought to cling onto patriarchal, Judaeo cultic beliefs and doctrines such as our often violent, blood-thirsty doctrines of Atonement. The corollary of this for Christian learning and ethics has been the reification of suffering, mutilation and servitude for Black women and those groups whose existential experiences would seem to suggest such eventualities as being their normative lot in life.[10]

There has been much emphasis upon poor, marginalized and oppressed Black people identifying with Jesus' suffering and death.[11] For Black people, there is the necessity for us to live with and accept our suffering and oppression in a stoical fashion, à la the Jesus "who never said a mumbling word."[12] Within Black theological thought a number of writers have located within the suffering of Jesus (whose struggle and ultimate death, it is believed, is foreseen by the writer of this text) a sense of divine solidarity with their own historical and contemporary experiences of unjustified and unmerited suffering. Scholars such as Douglas,[13] Cone[14] and Terrell,[15] to name but a few, have all explored the theological significance for Black people of Jesus' suffering on the cross, believed by many Black Christians (and others of course) to be foretold in Isaiah 53.

The Relationship between Religion and Violence

The relationship between religion and violence has gained a greater potency since the events of September 11, 2001 in New York and July 7, 2005 in London. Historically, religion was often seen as something that offered security and certainty. Religion, Christianity in particular, for the purposes of this study, was something that provided the overarching macro-theory for the collective identities and sense of purpose of many societies that experienced their generative formation within the epoch of Christendom.[16] The notion of something that provided security and certainty, particularly within Christianity, could be deduced, perhaps most clearly, within the concept of salvation and the assurance of everlasting life.

Since the rise of the social sciences in the 20th century, a religion that offered security and certainty took on a different meaning, now becoming linked with notions of improved consciousness and social and individual identity.[17] One of the implications of this change was the removal of religion from most aspects of corporate life in the West.[18] Religion has become linked with individual awareness and now has become privatized truth. A consequence of the latter is that individuals can utter outlandish claims and subsequently gain some form of immunity by claiming a particular exemption by way of their affiliation to some religious code.

The work of Rudolf Otto in the area of phenomenology shows how the study of religious experience highlights the way in which the human experience of God has often been one that has been described in terms of "terror" or "dread."[19] Being confronted with the holy is to often experience a sense of the "awesome." Some of the theories for the relationship between terror in religion come from the world of "religious experience" where it is often believed that the extreme emotions generated by an encounter with the Divine can lead to extremes of behaviour, often leading to religiously inspired (and often dangerous) action.[20]

James Cone, the "founding father" of Black Liberation theology, once remarked in an address given at the Queen's Foundation in Birmingham in 1997 that the most dangerous people in the world are those who claim to have an untrammelled line of communication to God and know exactly what God wants and what can be construed as God's will. In effect, these are the frightening people who later claim, "God told me to do it" when they are arrested for some extreme atrocity. One only has to recount the events at Waco in Texas and in Georgetown, Guyana to see the grisly truth of this contention.

The great Christian missionary movements from the 16th through to the early 20th centuries were marked by the use of violence.[21] One can see the relationship between biblical and theological traditions and violence by looking at how particular classic theories of the atonement have given sustenance to the notion of violence and the shedding of blood as being redemptive and indeed necessary.[22]

The work of René Girard has shown how violent images that are inherent within Christianity can lead to communal and societal violence. The scapegoat is vilified and then worshipped.[23] Girard's work has been helpful in assisting me to locate a framework in which the scapegoating tendencies of the British state can be located. In times of social unrest and public tumult, Black people become the scapegoats for the collective, systemic ills that have plagued Britain, problems that existed long before non-White people were ever visible in significant numbers in this country.

My experiences of being taunted in that playground was simply the symptomatic playing out of the intrinsic dis-ease that was prevalent in that poor, largely uneducated White working-class environment of inner-city Bradford. I became the sublimated "other," whose presence and conspicuous difference offered a cathartic and therapeutic outlet for the latent aggression, malevolence and vitriol that existed in this marginalized and deprived urban context. The anger, shame and frustration felt by many Black people in Britain is a direct response to the "othering" of their Black selves within postcolonial Britain.

Kelly Brown Douglas' more recent work is a stunning dissection of the impulse towards violence that lies deep within the "belly of the beast" that is top-down, Imperial White Christianity.[24] Douglas offers a historical and theological analysis of the trajectory from the platonized epistemological foundations of Christianity to the construction of White privilege and Eurocentric norms that demonize the Black body whilst creating an unhelpful and heretical dichotomy for the preservation of the Black soul. Douglas tackles the seeming paradoxes (indeed makes a very helpful distinction between paradox and dualism)[25] that run through Christianity like the manufacturer's seam in a stick of rock/candy. Christianity follows the "Prince of Peace" and yet has developed a particular predilection and penchant for violence against the "other."[26]

An interesting aside to the Christian predilection for violence can be seen in the actions of Messrs Blair and Bush, two self-confessed Christian leaders, whose actions, they claim, in propagating the "War on Terror" were influenced by their Christian faith. Clearly, for them, the biblical injunction to "Love one's enemy and do good to them" (Luke 6:27) or even love and bless them (Matt. 5:44) are not to be taken *too* seriously. It seems that one can construe a strange notion of blessing and loving, which involves military aggression and myriad bombs being heaped on one's enemies! As self-confessed Christians with a personal faith, the teachings of Jesus are perhaps to be understood in more spiritual or abstract senses than as material and embodied forms of ethics that will govern contemporary actions.[27] I would argue that whilst the Jesus of Faith that is depicted in the New Testament is the one who saves them, it is the belligerent, bellicose and strident God of the Old Testament who provides their ethics for engaging with the other. In effect, Jesus' primary function is to provide a form of rhetorical focus for the basis of Christian faith, whilst the substantive context of the ethical rubrics of religious practice belongs to the combative teachings of an "eye for an eye" from the Hebrew Scriptures. Loving one's enemy is not a characteristic that is necessary replete throughout the entirety of the Old Testament or Hebrew Bible canon!

In the actions of traditional Christian teaching, notions of reconciliation and redemption are based upon the relinquishing of power from within the Divine self and yet many believers in "the way" have found it convenient to monopolize power and use it shamelessly in their own plans for self-aggrandisement and hegemony.[28]

Most tellingly of all, perhaps, this faith that has enslaved and played a significant part in assisting in destroying the Black self remains the religious code of choice for millions of Black folk the world over. This faith remains a force for self-affirmation and survival. The latter reflections find expression in Douglas' words which state "I am a Christian because my grandmothers were, and it was their Christianity that helped them to survive the harsh realities of what it meant for them to be poor Black women in America."[29]

Black Christianity and Black theology must engage with the extent to which it has both colluded and become involved in supremacist notions of theological normativity. This facet of imperial Christianity can be found in the demonizing and othering of people of differing religious faith, often in a manner not dissimilar to our own marginalization and oppression at the hands of White Christianity.[30] It is interesting to note the extent to which Black Christianity in Britain has often eschewed any notion of inter-faith dialogue with people of other faith on the basis that we are "saved solely by the blood of Jesus." Aside from the problematic nature of this form of theological construction, the myopic tendencies in this type of analysis lies in the way in which it fails to interrogate the logic or lack of it, in its own position. In the first ever reader in Black theology in Britain,[31] Jagessar and I argue for the need for this discipline and form of context praxis to become a "serious voice in inter-faith conversations"[32] in this country.

I would argue that the normativity of racialized forms of "othering" within Britain has always existed within the context of a Judeo-Christian framework. The 1662 "Act of Uniformity," following the Restoration of King Charles II to the monarchy, states in its preamble the notion that uniformity is a pre-requisite to unity. The stark effects of this Anglican-centred conflation between crown, church and state were the marginalization and indeed oppression of non-conformist and "Free Church" Christianity in Britain, and the supremacy of the Church of England. In effect, Britain became a one-church-state oligarchy.

Seventeenth-century Britain had already learnt how to persecute White people who were different long before Black people entered the nation in significant numbers. The relationship between Christianity and Whiteness has been explored in exemplary fashion by David Isiorho.[33] Isiorho argues that the Church of England, with its links in the landed aristocracy and White middle-class privilege serves as a crude barometer for a symbolic notion of Whiteness and English normalcy within the psyche of the nation.[34]

It is interesting to note the extent to which the British National Party is now using religion and the construction of Whiteness and Christianity as a means of arguing against the continued presence of Black and Asian people in Britain on the grounds that we are threatening the "Christian heritage of the nation," i.e. Christianity equals Whiteness.[35]

The challenge facing Black Christianity in Britain is to make sense of the post Reformation Evangelical heritage – the tradition (the one to which I am trying to work against the grain) into which "many of us" have been inducted. This tradition is one that makes us the losers, in terms of racialized othering, whilst offering us the tantalizing prospect of belonging, by adhering to the same Jesus that White power has used to pathologize us and other people of colour as the "enemy within." In effect, even the losers can become the winners if we are willing to join the exploiter's club! In this respect, the usage of the Exodus narrative in the Hebrew Scriptures, by Black and other Liberation theologians, is telling. As Randall Bailey reminds us, what is it about dehumanized and oppressed peoples that make them want to so identify with the winners that they sublimate their own concrete, contextual experiences at the expense of other marginalized peoples with whom they so clearly have so much more in common?[36]

The use of violence that is replete within the Exodus narrative, which is exorcised with frightening regularity upon those that are othered, has been explored with great eloquence and honesty by a number of postcolonial scholars. Naim Ateek[37] and Robert Warrior[38] remind us that the Exodus narrative functions as a liberation paradigm if one ignores the subjectivity and positionality of the indigenous people whose identity with the land is obliterated by invading forces – people who clothe themselves in the "Word of God." Warrior, commenting on the Exodus narrative, writes:

> The obvious characters in the story for Native Americans to identify with are the Canaanites, the people who already lived in the promised land. As a member of the Osage Nation of American Indians who stands in solidarity with other tribal people around the world, I read the Exodus stories with Canaanite eyes. And, it is the Canaanite side of the story that has been overlooked by those seeking to articulate theologies of liberation. Especially ignored are those parts of the story that describe Yahweh's command to mercilessly annihilate the indigenous population.[39]

Warrior's claim to identify with the marginalized and oppressed others across the globe has been adopted with great alacrity by my colleague in

Birmingham, R.S. Sugirtharajah. In such landmark texts as *The Bible and the Third World*[40] Sugirtharajah demonstrates the many ways in which colonial exegetes ruthlessly exploited the images of violence within biblical texts as justification for their subjugation of native peoples.[41]

Similarly, within *Postcolonial Criticism and Biblical Interpretation*[42] the author demonstrates the extent to which Liberation theologies' methodological and thematic decision to work within the hermeneutical frameworks provided by the "Word of God" leads them to undertake often uncomfortable "deals with the text" in order to preserve its overarching status as the primary source against which human experience is interpreted.[43] This means that when the Bible advocates unremitting violence against those who are othered, many Black Liberation theologians (myself included if truth be told) have to find some means of "reading against the text" (thereby still making it normative) as opposed to de-centring it as being the major problem itself. Sugirtharajah cites Latin American Liberation theologians who state that "the Bible itself is not the problem, but the way it has been interpreted."[44] The author makes a sharp critique of Liberationist approaches to the Bible when he states:

> There is a danger in liberation hermeneutics making the Bible the ultimate adjudicator in matters related to morals and theological disputes. Postcolonialism is much more guarded in its approach to the Bible's serviceability. It sees the Bible as both safe and unsafe, and as a familiar and a distant text.[45]

Sugirtharajah's comments are directed at the much larger enterprise of contextual hermeneutics than the more narrow concern of this essay on the use of violence within Christian theology and Christian practices. Whilst I would still want to identify myself with the hermeneutical school in Black theology,[46] nevertheless, I want to question the use of the Bible. I am particularly concerned at the ways in which a form of normative hermeneutical posture to the Bible in Black theology seems potentially guilty of explaining away or even sanctifying violence within the biblical text.

In advancing this critique, I am aware that I am very much attacking my own methodological point of departure, within this very same Christian hermeneutical frame (one that relies on the Bible as a major source of its modus operandi) that provides the basis for the Black theological "angle of attack." My response (which is given in the first chapter and is largely determined in terms of practical pragmatism) must, nevertheless, be constantly on its guard against a form of neo-conservatism that has plagued Black theology since its academic inception in the late 1960s. This, to my mind, is the danger of becoming too enamoured with the normative frameworks of Christian thought that the radical and necessary work of seeking out alternative thematic and methodological constructs that can liberate Black people are abandoned at the seductive altar of White acceptability. My colleague, Michael Jagessar, and I have argued previously against the false doctrine of Black acceptability within the White Eurocentrically dominated academy and Church practice.[47] Jagessar and I write:

> Black theology must never seek to sit at the top table or luxuriate in the corridors of power. Black theology adopts the position of the prophet and not that of the priest... Black theology continues to argue for a bottom-up model of structural change and societal and world transformation that eschews any sense of placating the status quo.[48]

I use these words as much to remind myself of the need to constantly pose critical questions of the Bible, particularly around the ways in which normative readings of it have enabled the flourishing of violence to be unleashed on Black bodies at the behest of an allegedly benign God of love. In the context of this essay, I am looking at how violence has been unleashed on Black bodies from within a Christian purview. The violence we have faced and experienced has emerged from the long historical process of Black people being othered. I want to reflect for a few moments on the internal, psycho-social effects of this process of being othered, which as a corollary, leads to the now, all too familiar, attacks on Black people within the British context.

The Effects of Being Constantly Othered

One of the concomitant effects of this constant "othering" of Black people, in which violence is the physical and psychic end point of an escalating continuum of societal negation, is the debilitating and de-stabilizing existence of psychological rage. In *God of the Rahid*,[49] Robert Beckford tackles one of the most pressing issues affecting Black people in Britain – namely that of rage. This text commences with an analysis of postcolonial Britain, particularly in the aftermath of the Brixton nail bomb in April 1999. Beckford argues that Britain is the country in which racialized oppression permeates the very fabric of the nation.[50]

In 21st century postcolonial Britain, Black people are trying to come to terms with and exist within a context that both validates and legitimizes the institutional and casual incidences of racism against people of colour.[51] It is within this climate that Black people are struggling with a phenomenon Beckford terms as "low level rage." He defines the latter as "related to internalized rage in that it is experienced in mind and body. It is manifested in anger, depression and anxiety."[52] The high incidence of mental ill health (particularly schizophrenia) amongst African Caribbean communities in

Britain adds substance to Beckford's contentions. Having initially analysed the many contexts in which Black rage is to be located, the author outlines his own personal collision with the pernicious and debilitating nature of Black rage.

The Theological Legitimization of Violence against the "Other"

The importance of Jesus in Christian theology in connection to this theory displays this point in very obvious terms. As I have argued in an earlier chapter,[53] one can trace a trajectory for the glorifying of violence in terms of the concentration on Jesus' death as opposed to his life. The centrality of Jesus' death can be juxtaposed with the almost complete removal of his life as depicted in the narratives of the gospels. The latter can be seen as clear evidence of a form of liberative praxis in which followers of "The Way" are invited to follow. Yet the almost complete concentration of Jesus' death leads almost inevitably to Christian theology finding convenient ways to ignore the claims of those who were different from them, whether on grounds of ethnicity or nationality.[54]

Once Jesus' life is removed from its socio-political context he can be commandeered to become the mouthpiece for a form of epistemological conscription in which his symbolic silence becomes the justification for the oppression of others[55] (especially Black bodies). If Jesus' life and his Jewish identity were to be emphasized, then White Euro-American Christianity would need to engage directly with the "otherness" of Jesus. This, then, would immediately call into question their notions of cultural and political hegemony through the conscription of Jesus as one of them.[56] In effect, by concentrating solely on his sacrificial and all-atoning death, White Euro-American Christianity has been able to turn the "Christ of Faith" into one of them.

By eradicating his otherness (through downplaying the historical Jesus who is depicted in the gospels)[57] and concentrating upon his more abstract saving acts on the cross, White hegemony has been able to ignore the materiality of Jesus' life. Once Jesus' materiality is downplayed (and in some cases ignored altogether), he can then be construed as "one of us" whose presence then sanctions the otherness and oppression of those who are deemed not "one of us" – i.e. Black folk. This pernicious Christological construction is predicated on the notion that Jesus is White and is in opposition to the bestial and fallen nature of Blackness.

Contemporary Resonances

There are many educational implications for dealing with the relationship between Christianity and violence. There is a need for a form of Christian education as a means of preventing Christian inspired violence towards Black "others." In Christian theology, the cross is central to how Christian educators deal with violence. How do we deal with the cross and the violence associated with that act? Too much Christian education that takes place in churches lacks the necessary theological resources to help believers make sense of the seeming justification of violence that lies at the very heart of the Christian faith.

There is a challenge to those who might be described as educators to commit themselves to directing their work towards enabling their learners to walk the paths of peace, not by ignoring the realities of terror and violence, but by dealing with it in our work. This is the challenge of enabling those who profess to follow Christ to become critical thinkers who are able to handle the ongoing threat of religiously sanctioned violence in our increasingly complex world.

The ways in which a violently executed White Jesus is placed alongside the oppression of Black and Asian people in Britain is much too complex to detail at this point.[58] What one can say at this juncture, however, is that being non-White in Britain, and having to deal with the reality of one's demonized Blackness, is to be in a context where one is always perceived as a threat. The truth is we are often told that we do not belong. We are the "enemy within" and are policed and detained on the basis that our presence is not conducive to the country as a whole. It is interesting looking at the assumptions governing Black and Asian bodies in Britain in terms of so-called "race relations," as they are predicated on the notion that too many of us means trouble! Good "race relations" in Britain is about limiting our numbers because at some intrinsic, intuitive level, we somehow do not belong. Hence, the apparent impunity with which disproportionate numbers of Black people are stopped by immigration officials and then refused entry into the country.

This form of policing and monitoring is sufficiently bad to lead to significant numbers of Black young people believing that they have no legitimate place in this country.[59] Many consequently choose to vacate the mainstream for their own subversive forms of subcultures and constructed identities.[60]

The irony of our residency in this country is that it has never been a benign or non-contested existence. The socio-politicized nature of Black bodies residing in Britain is neither a new nor is it a surprising phenomenon.[61]

Once you start from the premise that some people really do belong and deserve to do so and others do not, then it becomes almost axiomatic that particular practices and customs will develop, which in turn lead to the penalizing and detrimental treatment meted out to Black people. The racist frameworks of "them" and "us" create the template in which stereotyping, discrimination and struggle become commonplace, leading to the blunt instrument of Black detention and incarceration in disproportionate numbers in our prisons. The punishment of Black people fits into a long, established pattern, deep within White religious discourse, that Black people and other people of colour deserve to be ill-treated, because deep down they are not of the same substance as "normal White people."[62]

The death of the Black teenager, Anthony Walker, in the Huyton area of Liverpool on July 29, 2005 has once more reminded us of the ongoing and pernicious threat of racism and racial violence that continues to stalk British society. It is interesting to note the extent to which the largely White-run media made much of Walker's grief-stricken mother's Christian ethic of love and forgiveness for the murderers of her son. I do not want to comment on the merits or otherwise of Anthony Walker's mother's decision to forgive the murderers of her son. I am not in her position nor do I know anything of her own faith journey or relationship with God to interpret her actions. What is interesting to note, however, is the ease with which the media and the British public felt able to engage with her declarations of forgiveness as opposed to a more trenchant call for justice.[63]

Walker's death was not a new phenomenon. Prior to Anthony Walker's violent murder at the hands of a group of White assailants, there was the death of Stephen Lawrence, another Black teenager of blameless character. Stephen was brutally murdered on April 18, 1993, in the south-east London borough of Eltham.

In both cases, what one witnesses within the body politic of Britain is what I have termed in a later essay as "contractual forgiveness."[64] In using this phrase I am arguing there is an existing theological framework that is expressed in an oppositional form of dualism, which divides the world and people into those who are righteous and "of God" and those who are of "the world" and are not. This framework is one that then creates dichotomies between those are deemed deserving and those who are not; those who are "saved" and those who are not.

In the case of Black bodies, because we are seen as the "other" and are inherently bad (or at the very least, of lesser worth than White people), sympathy, and therefore justice, as a response to racialized violence can only become operative when the recipient of such violence is seen to be blameless. It is no coincidence that in the case of Stephen Lawrence, when the police first arrived on the scene of his murder, their first instinct was to assume that he was guilty of something, even though he lay on the ground fatally injured.[65]

The next line of inquiry was predicated on the notion that he was a member of a gang and that this incident, which subsequently led to his death, was a product of gang-related violence. It was only when all the traditionally racialized lines of inquiry had been exhausted and no apportion of blame could be levelled at this Black youth of "dubious character and virtue" that the British press then threw their weight and influence behind the campaign to find his killers. The support of the British press emerged once all the hitherto, non-contested frameworks that posit the notion of Black people as the "other" had been exhausted and not before. In effect, the reluctance of the police force or the press to support, unequivocally, the thrust for Black justice was not appreciably different from the "othering" of myself in the playground from my early childhood.

Seeking to Embody the Theory into Practice: Some Preliminary Thoughts from a Real Encounter

This line of specious hermeneutical reconfiguring of the Black presence within the body politic of Britain, by White authority, was one I remember trying to articulate at a high profile event in 2007. As a leading Black theologian in Britain I was invited to be a speaker at a conference on slavery and its legacies in Britain during the year of abolition. There were three speakers at this conference in Oxford; all of us were of African or Caribbean descent. I was the final speaker on the programme. Unlike the two speakers that preceded me, I decided against speaking from a carefully prepared script. Rather, I decided that I would use one of my many experiential exercises[66] with which to challenge the critical consciousness of the predominantly White audience. It is interesting to note that the presentations of the previous two speakers went unchallenged and without any major dissent. Both speakers located their work in the historic past rather than in contemporary Britain. When I used my experiential exercise[67] in order to show that the underlying theological frameworks that assisted in the enslaving of African peoples are now very much evidence in contemporary Britain in terms of how they are expressed in wholesale violence against Black people, with comparatively little success in apprehending the largely White assailants, the room almost descended into uproar.

So long as our conversation could be remitted to the past, then the conversation could proceed in a polite and tidy fashion. When I challenged the ways in which contemporary Black bodies are conscribed to marginal spaces within a normative framework for articulating what is distinctively and characteristically British, suddenly the seeming veneer of polite English conventions dissipated. When the largely White participants were forced to reflect upon the relationship between past and present epochs, suddenly, I, as a Black theologian in Britain, was "othered" as the "bad guy" who was being unfair and unreasonable.

So deep is the thread connecting past with present that most White people in Britain are singularly unaware of the nature in which Black bodies are circumscribed in this country. Once one moves beyond the stereotypical frame of being "grateful," "forgiving" (like the mother of Anthony Walker) and "jolly," then one suddenly becomes the "bad guy" and is wholly unacceptable.

Using the Exercise

In preparation for the writing of this essay, and in a manner consistent with my vocation as a participative Black theologian in Britain, I sought out a group of Black and White people[68] with whom I could undertake some experiential theological work. The nature of the exercise was to gain an approximate perspective on how Black and White people view the acceptability or otherwise of Black people. What had prompted this undertaking was the visceral encounter in Oxford that I have described previously. I was intrigued as to what had given rise to such an explosive moment?

As a participative Black theologian, I have long sought to undertake my constructive theological work alongside and with ordinary people. In doing so, I want my reflections and resulting work to be shaped by the lived experiences, perspectives, insights, limitations and strengths of ordinary people of faith, especially those of African descent. In this particular undertaking, I wanted to gain some sense of how a small group of ordinary Christians perceive Black people. My interest was sparked, not only by the liveliness of the encounter at the conference, but the manner in which the largely White audience had turned on me and not my two Black colleagues who had preceded me to the tribune.

The exercise consisted of me asking the group to imagine a long line that ran along the floor across the length of the church hall in which we met. I asked the group to imagine a series of numbers dividing the line across its entire length. The group were asked to consider two types of Black person in the world. At the near end of the line, closest to them, was a Black person standing at no. 1. This person was someone who was perfectly acceptable to White authority and ordinary Black people. Then at no. 30, at the opposite end of the line, across the other side of the room, I asked the group to think about who might be antithesis of person no. 1.

The group reflected for several minutes, in pairs, and then in the whole group, as to the characteristics that would describe person no. 1. Words or phrases like "passive," "jolly," "always smiling," "never a threat," "conservative in dress and manners," and "embarrassing" were quickly recorded on the flip-chart. I asked the group to "give a name" to the person who might be identified as no. 1. Without much hesitation, the group mentioned the familiar figure of Frank Bruno.[69] When asked why they had chosen Bruno, a number of people in the group said that he fitted all the compliant and non-threatening stereotypes expected of Black people in terms of their acceptability within conventional British socio-political mores.

The group were then asked to consider the characteristics of person no. 30. Words and phrases like "war monger," "highly dangerous," "hates White people," "un-Christian" were shared and recorded on the flip-chart.

In deconstructing their meaning and intent in using these words and phrases, the group were very clear that person no. 30 was in clear opposition to person no. 1. I was struck quite forcibly by the term "un-Christian" when attributed to no. 30. Why would this person be at no. 30 and why would they be identified as un-Christian? After some reflection, the group stated that, whilst they had no proof that Frank Bruno (the person identified with no. 1) was indeed a Christian, their sense of the compliant and controlling nature of establishment Christianity[70] in Britain and the way in which it attempts to control Black bodies informed them that Bruno could well be a Christian. What was interesting to note from their reflections was the perception that Christianity demanded nothing less of Black people (especially the men) than total subservience and an accompanying lack of dignity.

When asked to give a name to the person at no. 30, some said Bin Laden, others Louis Farrakhan. At this point, the significance of the term "un-Christian" became clear. Once again, when asked to elaborate, the group believed that the Islamic identity of both men was somehow the key to their being at no. 30. That in effect, to be Islamic and male was an essential signifier for the unacceptability of "Black"[71] males in a so-called Christian country like Britain. It may be this perceived controlling mechanism on the autonomy of Black bodies in Britain that has persuaded many Black young males to see, ironically, greater levels of freedom within the seemingly "restrictive" religious frameworks of Islam (either the "Nation of Islam" or conventional Islam).

Is it this imperial form of Christianity, with its emphasis upon a supine and passionless Jesus who emasculates Black malehood, a cause for many Black men to depart the Christian faith and the church for other religious traditions? What was interesting to note is that whilst some Black famous women figured at various points across the range from 1–30, the exemplars that defined the continuum at either end were both male.

The final, and for me, the most interesting question, was "How far from no. 1 would you have to go before you began to identify a Black person whom you would consider a threat to the White establishment? What number?" After some discussion, six of the ten said no. 7 (of the six, five were Black – i.e. all the Black respondents in the group), and the other four (all of whom were White) said no. 4.

In the final set of reflections, the various participants all agreed that it did not take much deviation from the passive and supine figure at no. 1 to become unacceptable to White authority. The differences between the Black respondents and the White ones was very instructive, but not conclusive.[72] What I mean by this phrase is that the intention of the exercise was not to prove any particular hypothesis in empirical terms. Rather, this exercise was a simple diagnostic tool. Being on the receiving end of a litany of challenges from a largely White audience at the conference at Oxford had been a strange and enlightening experience. What was also of interest at that event was witnessing the merest hint of embarrassment from the small numbers of Black people present. In response to this experience, I wanted to create a heuristic device that would assist me, in some way, to understand what occurred in that room in Oxford, several months earlier.

The idea for this exercise, incidentally, arose from my reflections on an outcome from a previous piece of participative theological work looking at Black popular, cultural production and Black theology.[73] Some of the reflected "fruits" of that previous encounter posited the idea in my head that using this particular form of heuristic device might be a helpful approach towards teasing out from a group their perception of Black bodies in the popular imagination.

The fact that the Black people in the group did not place the possibility of Black acceptability significantly higher than their White counterparts was instructive. The sense that some of the Black people at the Oxford conference were slightly embarrassed by my seemingly strident attack on "all White people" was perhaps given some credence by Black people's perceptions of Black acceptability in the exercise. Had I gone beyond the bounds of acceptability in my experiential game-playing in Oxford that day? In a different time and place, would my "uppity" Black body have been castrated, dismembered and even lynched for having the temerity to stray beyond the narrowly conceived demarcations for Black people in White controlled spaces?

The noted African American theologian, Anthony Pinn, has explored the internal and external theological constraints and controlling devices that have exerted a measure of coercive power over the Black body.[74] Pinn illustrates the limited room for manoeuvre for Black people within the Christian-inspired New World of North America. I wonder if it is fanciful of me to speculate as to the constrictions on my Black body in that space in Oxford, daring to challenge polite, Christian sensibilities in the citadel of White power and normative superiority? Whilst I was not five years old any more and I was not under threat from physical violence, the underlying sense that I did not belong or at the very least, did not know my place, still remained. The group with whom I had worked on this experiential exercise were quite adamant in their belief that no Black person could stray beyond no. 7 on a scale of 30 and still remain acceptable to White authority. Can any Black theologian in Britain, then, expect to be acceptable in such a case?

The Challenge for the Church and Christianity

This chapter seeks to analyse the means by which Black people are constantly seen as the *other* within the fabric of British life. I believe it is the central task of the Christian faith, through a prophetic Black theological approach to education, to raise the critical consciousness of Black and White people in Britain, in order to overcome the threat of violence that emerges from racism.[75] It is my belief that a radical and prophetic practical model of Black theology, by means of Christian education, can contribute to challenging the ongoing scourge of racism in Britain and so offer a new paradigm by which Black and White might work together in solidarity to affect a working model of inter-ethnic discourse.

As a participative Black theologian, one of my primary interests is looking at the Bible and the Christian traditions that accompany it. This is allied, in turn, to historical and contemporary experience, in order that these sources should inform our present-day practice. How are we to relate to one another, our environment and to issues of justice and equity?

Looking within Scripture we are given examples of the importance of welcoming and affirming the stranger. In the Hebrew Scriptures, in the book of "Ruth" we read of the experience of Ruth who is a foreigner in Judah. Personal and domestic difficulties lead Naomi, and Ruth (who is from the country of Moab), to travel to Bethlehem in order to start anew.

Prototypical economic migrants perhaps? In chapter 2, Ruth a foreigner is offered sustenance by Boaz a wealthy land owner.

In the New Testament, Jesus in one of his teachings that has been interpreted as a comment on the final judgement, remarks upon the seemingly harsh treatment that will befall those who failed to show due care and concern for those described as the "least of these" (Matt. 25:40).

Clearly, within Jewish and Christian traditions there is something significant about the stranger – about those who are different. In the Gospel passage I have just mentioned, Jesus even suggests that Christ will be found in those who are amongst the "least," including the stranger. In making recourse to the stranger, I am not suggesting that Black people are strangers in Britain in terms of our presence in the body politic of the nation. There is clear evidence to suggest that Black people have lived in Britain for over a thousand years.[76]

Rather, what I am asserting is the sense that our otherness – our not being White – marks us out as strangers according to the construct of the White romantic rural idyll of Englishness, from which Black people are so conspicuously excluded.[77] It remains the case that Black people know far more about White people than the converse, particularly within a so-called multi-cultural, postcolonial context that is Britain. The truth is Black people and their concomitant cultures are largely strangers to many White British people.[78]

In amongst the vitriol and vituperative comments that are often levelled at those who are deemed undesirable to the body politic of postcolonial Britain, we should remember the salutary warning of Jesus in his response to those upon whom judgement is being made. In response to their entreaties Jesus states "Truly, I say to you, as you did it not to one of the least of these, you did it not to me" (Matt. 25:31–46).

There is much rhetoric pertaining to those who are different and are often deemed to be strangers – those who are identified as "not one of us." I still remember being different in that playground. The difference and apparent strangeness of Stephen Lawrence led to his death in South London.

As Britain continues the slow, painstaking journey towards being an equitable nation that affirms and even celebrates difference, we have much to learn from and critique in our Judeo-Christian heritage. The greater challenge is not only to learn from that heritage, but to move towards a more radical position of also being able to confront it, and perhaps move beyond its strictures when necessary.

In this chapter, I have sought to show that particular theological readings of Christian tradition have given comfort to racialized othering and violence against Black bodies in Britain. As I have demonstrated in Chapter 1, colour blind abstractions do not help us in the ongoing task of dealing with and handling difference. We need to find ways of moving beyond abstract, non-material forms of hermeneutics that have dominated Christian tradition for far too long, particularly post Reformation Protestant Evangelicalism – the very fount from which the majority of Diasporan Black Christianity has been drawn.

The challenge of engaging with difference is one that confronts all communities of faith or otherwise, where notions of homogeneity are often writ large in the very modus operandi of that collective and corporate sense of self.[79] As Parekh has shown, it can be all too easy for communities to define themselves in homogeneous ways in order to "police their border" so that the other is excluded.[80] It can be all too easy for those who are deemed as strangers to find themselves on the receiving end of violence as the price for being different.

A radical Black theology will challenge the often silent corrosive nature of Whiteness and will insist on a healthy constructive use of Christian tradition to venerate and uphold the stranger and those who are different from ourselves. Welcoming the stranger can be a means of grace. They offer us renewed opportunities to show hospitality and care. They enlarge our capacities to be human. In their very presence we may even see the benevolent presence of the Divine.

8 A Biblical and Theological Case for Reparations

This chapter consists of some preliminary thoughts and reflections on the biblical and theological case for reparations in the wake of the terrible legacy of the Atlantic slave trade, in which Britain was a notable contributor and chief custodian of economic benefit and profit. This chapter will argue for a distinctively Judeo-Christian framework and rationale for the economic restitution to people of African descent for the horrors and the unbridled profit of the slave trade.

At the outset of this piece, I think it is worth stating a few important caveats regarding this chapter. First, I am not a biblical scholar. I am not attempting this work as a specialist in exegetical work on ancient sacred texts. Rather, I am approaching this task as a Practical Black theologian. I am attempting this work, looking at particularly at biblical texts, in order to engage with the hinterland of predominantly White evangelicalism in Britain. White evangelists in Britain, through their engagement with William Wilberforce and the "Clapham Sect,"[1] often wish to claim some kind of moral justification for themselves, by appealing to their supposedly righteous forebears. In their theological method, the Bible is the essential and inviolate resource for assessing the veracity of any discourse that purports to be about and from God. It is in this context that I have sought to undertake my Black biblical theological work.

This chapter is also a "first thoughts" on the subject, in that I am not pretending that this work is in any sense a detailed exploration on the full scholarly intent of the necessary detailed theorizing on the rationale for "reparations."

In the context of this work where I construct a biblical and theological case for reparations, I understand the last term as that outlined by the prominent dictionary definition as "The act of making amends, offering to pay the penalty, or giving satisfaction for a wrong or injury."[2] There is a secondary meaning to this term, which often denotes the payment of money for damages – i.e. compensation for past wrongs.

In this chapter, I am speaking primarily to the first usage of the term, but in order to activate the former, I feel it is necessary that the latter is also borne in mind as a materially constructive means of giving substance and actuality to the first definition.

This chapter is not an in-depth exploration of the semantic meaning of the term "reparations" and its outworking as a concept in contemporary and historical socio-economic and political discourse. I am not suggesting that such questions are of little importance. On the contrary, it is precisely due to its grave importance that as a trained Practical theologian, I am choosing to leave this particular area within this debate to those who possess much greater experience and skills than any I may possess.

This work does not seek to deconstruct our notion of reparations and how it might be applied to the question of the grisly epoch of the enslavement of African people over a 400-year period and the legacies that exist therein. Rather, I want to look at what can be construed as the underlying theological issues for informing this discussion. From my experience of undertaking a number of teaching, preaching and speaking engagements during the bicentenary year of the commemoration of the abolition of the slave trade in Britain[3] I have recognized the need to "puncture" the rhetorical verbiage of White conservative Christians in their attempts to negate the validity of asserting the importance of reparations as a means of engaging with the reality of Britain's slave owning past.[4]

One aspect of my work as a Practical (participative) Black theologian is to undertake "Racism Awareness"[5] sessions with predominantly White students training for ordained ministry within the theological education system in Britain. On such occasions, I am often struck by the ways in which many White Christians will seek refuge in the Bible and Christian tradition. Adherence to the Bible (sometimes nothing more than a "tactical move" to outwit the Black theological educator) is used as a means of negating the social-scientific forms of epistemology often used by left-of-centre religious scholars in the task of countering racism and White supremacy. This form of Christian obfuscation becomes all the more risible when one witnesses, hitherto, very liberal White Christians suddenly seeking recourse in the Bible as a means of countering the need to treat the "other," i.e. their neighbour as themselves, with any degree of respect or mutuality.

For many White evangelicals, the Bible is their non-negotiable point of departure in discerning truth and the agency of God in all matters. Consequently, when engaging with them on issues of racial justice, one hears the plaintive cry of "Well, show me the evidence in scripture for this." Over the years, my approach to undertaking Black theology, often by recourse to the methods and intent found within Christian education, has become more biblically-centric, as I have sought to challenge my adversaries using the tools and resources that they themselves view as being essential. So this chapter is a biblically-centred approach to mounting a theological polemic for the case for reparations to be paid towards those of African descent for the horrors of the transatlantic slave trade.

I should also acknowledge that there is no one "unanswerable" case for reparations, with regard to the slave trade. This chapter draws on numerous strands of theological thought in the Bible and the resultant Christian traditions. I am making **a** case for reparations drawing on biblical and theological material. As I am not a political economist or strategist and neither am I a specialist in biblical studies or a Christian ethicist, the case I am arguing for in this chapter is from that of a Christian educator in Black theology. The thematic frame that informs this work is that provided by "postcolonial theory." The resultant technique that arises from this methodological framework is one which, in turn, gives rise to particular models for reading the Bible.

In the context of this work, I am reading the Bible, not as a trained specialist, but as a Black Liberationist Christian seeking to engage with this sacred text in order to find resources that will do justice to the suffering and oppression of my ancestors and the continued marginalization of Black people in the present epoch. My engagement with the Bible is one of trying to apply the biblical text, using a postcolonial, reader-response hermeneutic, as a means of establishing a link between the ancient world, first-century Judea, the epoch of slavery and our present "New World Order."

This work is influenced by my own particular position/social location. I am a Black male, who has been trained and operates as a Black Liberation theologian and Christian educator and whose work is informed by Liberationist and postcolonial perspectives on the Bible.

Finally, by way of my introductory remarks, this piece, like much of the chapters in this book, is written in the form of a polemic. In this chapter, as in the book as a whole, I am making no pretence to engage in the somewhat dubious practice of so-called "scholarly neutrality" and "objectivity." Neither am I overly concerned about how this makes White Christians feel. I am not writing this chapter to placate polite, White English convention, but to give voice to the anguish and pain of people of African descent. In terms of the latter, many of us have to constantly negotiate with the machinations of White officialdom and their marked reluctance to even apologize[6] for the evils of the slave trade, let alone engage with the justice issues pertaining to reparations.

Reconciliation is Still the Key Theme

To understand the call for reparations from within a Christian purview, one has to recognize the essential importance of the theme of reconciliation, which runs through Christian thinking like the maker's name through a stick of rock. There is no avoiding the centrality of reconciliation within Christianity. Cognizance of this fact is crucial, for it enables us to locate this debate, particularly within the context of reconciliation; a call for restoration and forgiveness and not one of exacting revenge. In writing this chapter, I am not arguing for "revenge" or "pay back," in terms of punitive damages for Black people. Rather, I am arguing that if we are to take the central biblical and theological concepts within Christianity seriously – i.e. to actually practice the very form of Christianity imposed upon Black people by corrupt White power – then we need to engage in issues of justice, which form the basis for reconciliation.

As is now commonly accepted, Paul's writings form the earliest documented texts in the New Testament canon, and these are replete with references to God's reconciling work in Christ on the cross. One can point to such texts as Rom. 5:10, 1st Cor. 5:14–21, 2nd Cor. 5:18–20 and Col. 1:18–23. This theme, however, needs to be read in terms of Jewish thought: that Paul, although a Roman citizen, remained Jewish in terms of ethnicity and culture. So in order to make sense of the notion of reconciliation one also has to understand the Jewish antecedents that inform Paul's writing, and allow these ideas to inform our arguments around the notion of reconciliation and reparations.

Two Main Hermeneutical Keys for Establishing a Basis for Reparations

Jewish Traditions on "Restorative Justice"

From my reading of the Hebrew Scriptures, it appears to me that in Jewish thought atonement and salvation are collective and corporate concepts, not solely individual ones (as often conceived in post Reformation Protestant theology). Essentially, being in right-standing with God necessitated that one should be in right relationships with others. In fact, one could argue that it appears to be the case that one cannot be in a right relationship with God unless you were doing right by the other.

The above can be seen in Leviticus 6:1–6. These verses clearly state the notion of restorative justice for that which was wrongly taken and used, which is described as a "sin against God" (v. 1). One can also see this concept or formula evident within Deuteronomy 15:12–18. The key for me is verse 12 which states "if any of you buy Israelites as slaves, you must set free after six years. And don't just tell them they are free to leave – give them sheep and goats and a supply of grain and wine."[7] Essentially, you are to compensate the slave for the length of time they have been in captivity and how much you have benefited from their use/service/labour.

As is the case when engaging with the Bible, it is important to hold a cautionary and critical perspective on so-called Scripture and the normative political undercurrents that inform the cultural production of biblical texts.[8] It is important to note that only Israelites who are purchased as slaves are to be compensated for the length of time in which they were under the obligations of slavery. What of Gentiles? There is insufficient time in this chapter to investigate such issues (plus I am not the right person to explicate this point further), but it is a semantic point that must not be lost! The Deuteronomic code does not include Gentiles. What are the implications of this issue for the question of restorative justice or reparations? I am sure that, for some, particularly those on the evangelical right, compensation if it should be paid, must be directed at those who would claim to be within the "Covenant"; namely anyone who can self-identify as a Christian and is "saved" through faith in Jesus Christ. But as my colleague at Queen's, Michael Jagessar, and I argue, we resist and indeed reject out of hand such narrowly conceived notions of justice and God's righteousness being the preserve of those who are "saved" in Jesus Christ. Rather, our conception of God's justice is for all people and not only those who feel themselves as part of the "elect."[9]

Nevertheless, despite the inherent weaknesses within this biblical strain for justice for those wronged, one can see evidence of this continued stream of thought in the New Testament, particularly in the Synoptic Gospels. In the Gospels, Jesus' two great commandments indicate the continued balancing of this Jewish tradition, namely, loving God, and your neighbour as yourself (Matt. 22:37–39). You cannot love God without loving and showing justice to other people. This link was weakened, if not lost in Reformation theology. It was the reformers of the 16th century, who in their anxiety to downplay or even remove "Works" from the formula of salvation diminished the interpersonal dimension in soteriology. This was one that spoke of mutuality, relationship and full regard with and for the other, as a means by which being saved might be conceived.[10]

A Postcolonial Framework

The second hermeneutical key to unlocking the scriptures in order to discern a theological pattern for reparations for those who have been enslaved can be found in the focusing lens of postcolonial theory. The postcolonial framework emerges when the reader recognizes that the context in which much of the New Testament canon was composed was one that echoed to the restrictive strains of colonialism. Judea, in which Jesus' ministry was largely located, was an occupied colony of the Roman Empire. Scholars such as William R. Hertzog II[11] and Mark Lewis Taylor[12] have shown the extent to which wealth in this province was always connected with economic exploitation. So when Jesus challenges the rich, he is doing so in light of the socio-economic exploitation of that first-century context.

In light of postcolonial hermeneutics, one can see that Jesus' teachings around wealth and its relationship to discipleship and living the "Jesus way" has political and economic implications. Scholars such as Musa W. Dube[13] and Catherine Keller, Michael Nausner and Mayra Rivera[14] have shown the similarities between first-century Palestine, the slave epoch of the 16th, 17th and 18th centuries and our present globalized, postcolonial context. Each context is based upon imperialistic/colonial expansion, capital accumulation, forced labour and exploitation of the poor by the rich.

Luke's Gospel is believed by some scholars to be written by a non-Jewish source, mainly as a rebuke and a challenge to rich gentile followers of Jesus.[15] Chapters 16–19, for example, are all challenging teachings against the rich, who, in the context of occupied Judea are symptomatic of economic exploitation.[16] In all of the examples from these chapters, the rich are asked to give up their wealth in order to live the "Jesus Way." This "Way" is one that speaks against the exploitation that was endemic within Jewish theocracy. The prophetic challenge in the religious ethics of "The Way" can be seen in the now legendary chasing out of "the money changers from the Temple," which serves as a classic example of this genre of thinking. It is not that people did not barter or exchange goods in the temple, for that was how people were able to purchase the necessary objects for sacrificial worship. Rather, Jesus' anger is directed at the economic exploitation of the system. This "Jesus Way" is one that not only challenges the Jewish theocracy of the Pharisees and Sadducees, it is also against the Roman occupation.[17]

The aforementioned postcolonial framework can also be seen in "Lazarus and the Rich Man" (Luke 16:19–31) and "The Rich Young Man/Ruler" (Luke 18:18–25). In Jesus' encounter with Zacchaeus (Luke 19:1–11), we see set forth before us the ethic of reparations, as a means of effecting reconciliation between oppressed and oppressor, and with God's very self. Zacchaeus is expected to "give back" that which he has wrongly taken in order for him to be reconciled with others. I will make greater reference to Zacchaeus' ethic of reparations at a later juncture in this chapter, for it provides us with a compelling account of the need to effect restitution in response to one's own sense of forgiveness at benefiting from the economic exploitation of others.

One can argue that the culmination of Jesus' teaching is perhaps found in Luke 21:1–6 when Jesus condemns the exploitation of the poor (this is evidenced by the narrative often termed "the widow's mite") and in so doing, challenges the whole system of temple worship. In issuing this prophetic denunciation, Jesus is attacking the very seat of economic power in colonially run Judea, and announcing as he does so, the ultimate destruction of the temple and the ushering in of the Kingdom of God. In this latter example, the widow is not meant to serve as an example of personal piety (i.e. she gives all that she has), but rather as a denunciation of a corrupt system that makes a vulnerable person like a widow feel compelled to give all she has. Why should a rich socio-religious institution like the temple demand everything from a poor widow? You might imagine that a rich temple should be giving her money and not the other way around.

It is interesting the extent to which many of us have been taught to spiritualize our readings of the Bible. When I was taught the so-called meaning of this text in Sunday school, it was always impressed upon us that the point of the passage was to help us to see that we should give all that we had to God. This form of reading encourages the poor to leave their social reality and material interests at the door of the church, whilst an often biased, middle-classed base institution that has favoured the rich and the economically comfortable seeks to exploit the theological naivety of the poor. Let me ask the question again – why should a poor widow give up all she has to a rich institution like the temple?

The point of the postcolonial hermeneutic, above, is, I believe, that it challenges the wholesale spiritualization of Jesus' message. This largely evangelical pious form of abstraction that chooses to ignore the concrete in favour of the spiritual is challenged. Jesus challenged those first believers to practise a form of restitution or, one might even say, reparations, in light of existing Jewish thought (which Jesus does not overthrow) in which salvation and restorative justice went hand in hand.

Working on the assumption that wealth was accumulated by means of exploitation, Jesus' ethic expects Zacchaeus to give back that which he has taken from others, in order to be reconciled to God, through faith in Jesus. Interestingly, Zaccahaeus does not need to be told to pay back that which he has wrongly taken. It would appear that his understanding of the "Jesus Way" demands restorative justice as the self-sacrificial price to be paid for entry into this new way of living. *Salvation is by means of faith and (restorative) action.* Zacchaeus can do it, but the rich young man in Luke 18:18–25 cannot!

I think the example of Zacchaeus is a classic example for us to consider as we look at the whole question of reparations in light of Black Atlantic chattel slavery. Jesus meets Zaccaheus in the immediacy of his context and offers to come to his house to break bread and partake of a meal. That is, Jesus offers forgiveness by way of accepting his hospitality in the form of a meal, which some have seen as Eucharistic. Jesus' presence "at table," in fellowship with Zaccheus, can be seen as a sign of God's outpouring of love and grace on the sinner. But this act is not done in isolation. The "Eucharistic" meal[18] is accompanied by Zacchaeus giving back the monies to all the people he has wronged and cheated.

Spiritualized Theology and Concrete Obfuscation

I know that many contemporary White Christians in Britain will argue that they cannot seek forgiveness for wrongs they themselves did not personally inflict. Therefore, to ask for forgiveness in the context of slavery, they will argue, is inaccurate or incorrect. I think this is a specious argument for two reasons. First, White British people may not have participated in the slave trade but they and countless generations have benefited from it. Britain did not become rich in isolation from her colonial history. I am always bemused by those who will insist that (a) teaching and learning about the British Empire be made central to the National Curriculum (in schools), but (b) will make no link between that history and the contemporary call for reparations.

If slavery is long etched in the midst of time in British history – therefore, being too far removed in the past to be retrieved for the purposes of engaging in reflections around state-sanctioned wrong-doing – then why also insist that our present children learn that history in schools?

Even more scandalous, for some, if the passage of time calls into question the relevance of such past events to our present epoch, then what are we to make of the cross? After all, might not present generations of people say, quite legitimately, "why should they be held to account for the sins of humanity against God, when such sin was committed by our forebears, with whom we have no connection?" If one should not apologize, and therefore as a corollary, not pay reparations because the crime was committed by one's ancestors and not the present generation, then explain why countless future generations should be held to account for the sins of one man (symbolically) way back in the midst of time? If the guilt of our ancestors does not have implications for us in the present, then the traditional understanding of the cross as atonement for the sins of humanity no longer carries any theological weight!

As I have argued in a previous essay,[19] corporate White Christianity is wonderfully adept at spiritualizing all the central tenets of Christianity, thereby shoring them of any contextual or material power. The trans-historical nature of Christianity can be appealed to as we can be content that it is evoked in generic, universalizing and spiritualizing ways, which enable the material basis and self-interest of the powerful to remain untouched and untroubled. When Black theologians or African-centred activists[20] argue that the past does pose major political, economic and moral implications for us in the present, we are suddenly told that present generations cannot be held responsible for the actions of others in the past.

I know that many have argued with me on this point, saying that it is facetious, and even blasphemous, to compare human slavery with the divine sacrifice of the cross. The two are not the same, many will argue. One is trans-historical and is not to be compared with the other. When I have asked what makes it different, the answer has usually been "Well, the cross is about the sin of all human beings." This sin is one of cosmic disobedience to God. So we are bound, across all space and time, by the actions of our ancestors? This connection is maintained, no doubt, by the spiritual basis involved in the inherent sinfulness of humanity!

The response of some White Christians (and some Black ones also, I should hasten to add) simply reinforces the critique I levelled a few moments ago, about the spiritualizing of Christianity. This process of spiritualization has the marked effect of making us all guilty, thereby absolving those who benefited from the former crimes of slavery from having to make any particular response to the sins of the past. Once such issues are spiritualized, there is no problem at all in asserting that all of us are guilty. Consequently, the price to be paid for our collective guilt is undertaken by a universal and generic salvific figure. This salvific figure is one who then allows all who benefited from the exploitation of others to keep whatever material advantage they have accrued *whilst still remaining* within the "Body of Christ" – in stark contrast to Zaccheaus' experience, it should be added!

The truth is Britain gained a distinct and marked economic advantage from slavery, which has benefited millions of White British people over the past 400 years. The necessary capital that funded the Industrial Revolution, on which British economic prosperity was based, came via the stupendous profits accrued from slavery.[21] If White British people wish to avoid the stain of the past then let them repudiate the wealth and economic advantage that came from colonialism and the forced, un-free labour that built the British Empire.[22]

The knock-on effects of slavery are stark and confront us in many realms of contemporary life in Britain. I believe that the British government should make an unambiguous apology for its involvement in, and profit from, the slave trade. The nation should offer an extensive package of reparations to Black community groups and African nations in response to 2007. As Robert Beckford reminds us:

> We have to remember that the greatest export from slavery that's still with us is racism. So if we want to counter racism, we need to deal with how it was established and its legacy.[23]

As Beckford so rightly opines, racism was the damnable offspring of slavery, which has far outlived the parent. Racism remains one of the most toxic and noxious phenomena in our present world order. The "dash for Africa" culminating in the Conference of Berlin in 1885, which "carved up" Africa for the major European powers, was one that was built upon a manifest racism that viewed Africa as a *tabula rasa* ripe for White conquest. The notion that Africa should be ruled by White Europeans was part of a specious doctrine of "White Supremacy" that asserted the ranked inferiority of Africans.[24]

The sad indictment of the failure to connect the past with the present can be seen in the G8 Gleneagles summit in July 2005,[25] when the leading industrial powers met to discuss the problems of Africa, at which the African presence arrived as a (seeming) after-thought. In effect, despite the problems that face Africa being ones that impact with greatest severity on Africans themselves, it was still legitimate for the meeting to commence without people from that continent being present.[26]

Prior to that meeting, leading spokespersons such as the then British Prime Minister Tony Blair spoke of Africa being "a scar" on the conscience of the developed world,[27] which led, in turn, to the creation of the "Africa Commission" in March 2004.[28] At that conference, Blair felt sufficiently emboldened by his "good intentions" in seeking to help Africa, to offer a number of sharp attacks on the poor governance of African leaders. Blair also attacked the endemic corruption in many African states as being major causes for Africa's contemporary plight. And yet, in this mountainous acreage of platitudinous verbiage, there was little talk of Europe's systematic and wholesale under-development of Africa, as outlined by the great Walter Rodney.[29] As Richard Reddie reminds us, the White slave owners received compensation for their loss of "chattel" when the prohibition against slavery became law in 1838 (a sum of 20 million pounds was paid to slave owners; equivalent to 40 per cent of the national budget at the time[30]). Over a century later, America offered approximately five billion dollars in reconstruction aid to Europe in order that the continent could recover from the structural damage caused by World War Two.[31] The "Marshall Plan" was instituted to assist Europe in recovering from the horrors of war and to assist in the reconstitution of the economic and trading relationship between America and Europe, and for the flourishing of liberal democracy and capitalistic free trade. In the words of Richard Reddie, "There was no Marshall Plan for Africa following centuries of blight from the savage evils of slavery."[32]

The slave owners were compensated for the supposed "wrongs" of their loss of chattel, upon the ending of slavery in 1838 in the British Empire. America, who bore no direct responsibility for the wrongs of war in Europe, nevertheless saw sufficient self-interest in offering huge sums of aid to Europe. It should be noted that this aid was not punitive, in that it did not involve sums of money being "clawed back" under the dictates of so-called "free trade" and structural adjustment programmes.[33] Yet, Africa in comparison did not receive one penny in compensation for her travails. The descendents of enslaved Africans have, similarly, not received a penny in compensation. Perhaps as scandalous as the lack of monetary recognition is the failure of Blair to readily acknowledge the role slavery and the European under-development of that continent exerted on Africa and the peoples connected with that continent.

Dealing with the Legacies of Slavery

The legacies of slavery for the children of the African Diaspora and for Africa itself are myriad. In calling for reparations, I am arguing for a specific fund to assist Black communities in Britain. The monies should be used to help establish capacity building within Black communities that are a part of the African Diaspora and the continent. For example, why is the educational attainment of Black children low, in comparison to their White middle-class counterparts? Why are Black communities amongst the poorest in the nation? Why are there disproportionate numbers of Black males languishing in our prisons in Britain?

I have witnessed, at first hand, the desire of many White Christians to want to engage in wholesale acts of collective memory loss and "cheap grace" when having to deal with the terrible legacy of slavery and the complicity of the Church in England and her dealings with Black people. The notion of "cheap grace" owes much to the inspirational writings of Dietrich Bonhoeffer,[34] who, incidentally, is one of the few privileged White theologians for whom the great James Cone[35] has any time or regard.[36] The notion of costly sacrifice that runs through the heart of Christianity and which is reflective of the cross is one that has largely escaped most White Christians in the West, in terms of their dealings with Black people. The costly actions of Christ, which we are asked to imitate, has not been much in evidence when White European Christianity has wanted forgiveness and reconciliation without repair, restitution, or recompense.

Taking on the mantle of Bonhoeffer, my mother has been known to remark that "Talk is cheap" and words can be cheaper. Saying sorry is commendable, but it is just a start, not the end in itself (even though at the time of writing, the British state has not managed it yet). In one of my previous books[37] I talk about a notion I term "a theology of good intentions." This is where the perpetrators of all kinds of humiliating and offensive acts feel that closure can be gained by simply invoking the words "sorry." There is rarely any analysis on why particular events or phenomena might have taken place in the first instance. Neither is there much reflection on the implications of their actions or the legacies that might exist because of them.[38] Rather, the magic word "sorry" is issued with no cognizance of what that might mean in concrete systemic terms. "Sorry" is meant to suffice in isolation from any concomitant actions or reflection.

Such is the moral force of the word "sorry," any hesitation, equivocation or reluctance on the part of the recipient to automatically accept the apology then brings with it the sobriquet of "not being Christian." I have argued elsewhere that the blandishments of a "theology of good intentions" can only be overturned when White people are prepared to question their unearned privilege, accrued from their Whiteness.[39] This involves them seeking to be in creative and dramatic dialogue with Black people, in order to unlearn the pernicious and toxic dangers of White supremacy.[40]

In the discourse surrounding issues pertaining to slavery and its legacy, the onus is always upon Black people to undertake the greater journey in order to affect reconciliation. Failure to engage with or to forgive the horrors of the past, without the accompanying presence of anything remotely like justice and restitution, is to be branded as "un-Christian." In the end, the victim ends up being the "bad guy" and not the abuser or oppressor. The recipient of the abuse or oppression is castigated because they did not acquiesce to the dictates of the latter – who, let us not forget, was the one who created the issue in the first place. Saying sorry is but the start of an extremely long process. Those who try to use this word as a way of circumventing this process are indulging in "cheap grace."

There can be no forgiveness without penitence, admission of guilt and wrong-doing, which is followed by forgiveness and restitution. The first thing that individuals, organizations – indeed, the British state – need to do is to unambiguously acknowledge their wrong-doing. This form of acknowledgement must be more than the disingenuous excuse-making variety one often hears in Britain. I am rather tired, if truth be told, of having to engage with such platitudinous nonsense as the comments one hears, such as "we didn't know better," "You need to understand the context of the time" or "It was legal at the time." I would rather the British state and her major representatives simply acknowledge guilt and begin to make repair.

One never hears of any such obfuscation and other forms of expediency-ridden responses to the Jewish holocaust, for example. I have yet to hear any mainstream White Christian seek to excuse themselves from the collective sins caused by anti-Semitism – which as a corollary, led to the horrors of the Jewish holocaust in Germany. As a descendent of enslaved Africans, I want the British state to acknowledge the sins of the past and to make restitution for the gains they made from the horrors of that past.

The need to make amends cannot be addressed solely from a structural or systemic perspective (although this is paramount to my mind), but needs to be accompanied also by a more micro framework. This latter framework is one that asks White people to reflect on the unearned privileges, accrued from their Whiteness, and to seek to use that positively for the flourishing of racial justice. Speaking from a very personal perspective for a moment (some would ask when have I done anything other!), I am often stunned into mock laughter at the number of occasions I have met allegedly radical White Christians who can argue for (racial) justice in the abstract, and yet have no means of engaging with Black people in the flesh.

I remember being present at a very prestigious Christian festival and meeting a well-known, radical White Christian whose books and writings have inspired many, and yet seeing his patent dis-ease at engaging with me and my Black male colleague. It remains the case that Black people are far more adept at engaging with White people than is the reverse. Throughout many centuries, Black people have developed a plethora of strategies for learning to engage with the socially constructed normalcy of Whiteness, especially that of White power.[41]

The formula for making repair – for reparations is one that requires many White people to learn how to engage with Black people – is also a call for White people to engage with their Whiteness. A formula for reparations needs to include White Christians meeting with the descendents of enslaved Africans and listening to their anger, pain and hurt – and I mean listen without trying to editorialize our comments or re-interpret them for us.[42] The perpetrators of rape, for example, are not in a place to tell the rape victim how they should feel or how they should behave. I am aware of the dramatic nature of this analogy, and it may even strike some as being a highly contentious and controversial image to use at this juncture. But I make no apologies for using such extreme images. How else can we describe the desecration of a whole continent and millions of people being torn from their heritages, identities and cultures?

Reparation is a very difficult subject, and I am not advocating any simplistic notion of money being given to individual Black people; but there is a sense that forgiveness without cost is simply cheap grace. I am rather tired of people saying "how long ago" these events were for which Britain is being asked to apologize and make amends. The basic ethic of justice demands nothing less than an honest account of the ways in which

Britain was enriched by the slave trade, thereby, making her name as a great trading nation.[43]

In the more micro dealings of the criminal justice system in Britain, one never hears of a defence in law, which states, "Well your honour, I know the item in question was stolen or used illegally, but look at how long ago that happened, and besides, it was my ancestors who did it. So let's forgot about the whole thing and simply move on." The beneficiary of wrong is always required to make amends.

The notion that slavery was technically legal is also a specious argument. This line of argument, if taken seriously, would be an "oppressors' charter" if accepted at face value. Arguing from within a Christian purview, corrupt and immoral agencies, such as the apartheid regime in South Africa prior to 1994, argued for the justification of their practices by pointing to the law. Many cited literalist readings of Romans 13:1–7 as justification for the oppression of Black Africans in that nation. If the powerful are able to fashion law, based on their self-interest, and then justify their actions from within that self-referential framework, a specious form of legal defence can always be invoked. In effect, the powerful frame the law for their self-interest and then appeal to that same law for their justification. If the weak and the powerless are unable to break this self-referential hermeneutical circle of privilege, then they are morally and legally unable to fight for their freedom. Such a scenario, if taken literally, would have negated the struggle outside and inside South Africa for the overturning of apartheid, for example.[44] What, then, of such states as Burma, at the time of writing? It is simply a nonsense to state that such actions were legal, when it was the rule of oppressive power that constituted the legality of slavery. The British state and the capitalistic greedy merchant's class ignored the rhetoric of "natural law" or the Judeo-Christian framework of hospitality and justice for the poor, when seeking to justify their actions.[45]

Incidentally, the very fact that British life and manners in the late 18th century were not governed by the Judeo-Christian framework to love the neighbour as oneself poses major questions for those of a more conservative evangelical mindset (especially if they are Black). I have no doubt that there are some evangelical Christians (both White and Black), who are committed to reclaiming the glories of Britain's mission history. I believe that such individuals need to re-interrogate British history more carefully. Can one seriously argue that Britain, as the major "missionary powerhouse" in history, should return to that past, and take her place once more at the epicentre of Christendom?[46]

The question I want to pose to such protestations is: Can the propagation of the gospel be seen as any kind of recompense or amelioration for the tragic occurrences that emerged from such missionary activities? As a descendent of enslaved Africans, I will not countenance any form of theological construction that seeks to offer up Black bodies as the counter-weight to the propagation of the gospel on the Divine scales of providence. Black life is too sacred to countenance any form of theological escapology that seeks to safeguard the Gospel or the church, at all costs, from any historical critique of its role in the enslavement and dismembering of Black bodies in the past. The material reality of Black bodies in history matters more than the dictates of theological abstractions, particularly when such protestations, as evinced in Matthew 28:19–20, gave licence to wholesale murder and plunder – all in the name of the Gospel!

Life in post-bicentenary Britain – post 2007 – must be a time in which this nation no longer puts its collective head in the sand. Rather, let this era be one of healing and reconciliation as Christ commands us, but not one built on a failure to acknowledge the benefits and advantages accrued for Britain from the broken bodies and desecrated spirits of enslaved Africans!

9 What is the Point of This? A Practical Black Theology Exploration of Suffering and Theodicy

In the previous chapter I outlined a tentative proposal for reparations based upon a postcolonial-inspired Black theological reading of the Bible and Christian tradition. As I stated in that chapter, I am not a political economist, so the fiscal and procedural mechanisms for affecting this form of restorative justice is not within the orbit of my competence.

In this chapter, I want to move from more theoretical considerations to those that arise from the need for the praxis of Black people, particularly in terms of how we engage theologically with the legacy of slavery, which shapes the macro and micro dimensions of life in the African Diaspora.

The impetus to write this chapter arose from my engagements, in 2007, across the length and breadth of Britain, as we marked the bicentenary of the abolition of the slave trade. What struck me, repeatedly, as I preached, led workshops, taught seminar classes, wrote new material and edited other work,[1] was the marked reluctance of many Black people to engage with the subject from a theological perspective.

As I have outlined in the prologue to this work and in the first chapter that follows, there continues to exist within many Black Christians in Britain an unhelpful dichotomy between the rhetoric of their Christian faith and the material realities of their Blackness. Far too many Black Christians in Britain, to my mind, seem unable to integrate these two arenas of human experience. For many, their Blackness is to be sublimated beneath their Christian identity, as if the latter can ever exist in a cultural or ethnic vacuum. In short, we are all some sort of Christian. The fact that White Christians rarely term themselves thus should not be seen as something Black folk should necessarily seek to emulate. Rather, it should be viewed as an un-deconstructed escapism and a denial of self. The invisibility of Whiteness, and the dangers that lie therein, seems to me to be reason enough for the assertion of Blackness as a means of both affirming self and holding up a mirror to the Whiteness that never wants to "speak its name."[2]

The reluctance on the part of many of my Black brothers and sisters in the Christian faith in Britain to juxtapose their material realities alongside the rhetoric of faith finds particular expression (or the lack of it) within the discourse pertaining to slavery. The immutability of Christianity, particularly when interpreted through an inerrant Bible and propagated by fundamentalist theologies, has led some Black Christians to entertain forms of theological rhetoric that have profound consequences for the psycho-social well-being of Black people in Britain. Let me explain this remark.

On the many occasions I have engaged with ordinary Black people, seeking to address the issue of slavery and its legacy in Britain (and across the world), I have noticed an all too frequent form of obfuscation when asked to address this topic in theological terms. In terms of history, many Black people are cognizant of the need to challenge the White patrician mythology of Wilberforce and the seemingly endless verbiage of hagiography that has emerged in the bicentennial year in Britain.[3] Increasing numbers of Black people have gained a greater appreciation of the pioneering work of Black abolitionists such as Equiano, Sancho, Cugoano and Gronniosaw.[4] Some have even taken the political high road, inspired no doubt, by Eric Williams' groundbreaking treatment on slavery and economics,[5] to argue for the necessity of reparations for African peoples in Britain.[6]

Yet, when the question is addressed from a theological perspective – such as, "What do we think God was doing when African peoples were being butchered and maimed in their millions?" the trail goes silent. Suddenly, intense insouciance is met with sobering silence.

Two incidents from 2007 have brought this issue sharply into focus. The first one concerned a major "Commemoration Service" to mark the bicentenary of the abolition in Britain. A major city was seeking to identify a "Black Pentecostal preacher" who would be entrusted with delivering the "Word" during their major act of Christian worship marking the passing of the parliamentary act in 1807. A number of names were proffered and one significant person was approached. He was a Black conservative evangelical preacher.

When approached and asked if he would preach, he responded, affirmatively. Further conversations with this individual, however, brought to light a most disturbing theological interpretation of the epoch of slavery – and was one which he was prepared to share with the congregation on the occasion of the service: namely, that slavery had been an unexpected blessing for Black people, as through the evils of the slave trade we had found Jesus, become Christians and many of us were now "saved."

The silence that followed this rather brutal admission was perhaps more eloquent than the "unfortunate nonsense" of this highly respected Black church leader. Further conversations led to a withdrawal of the invitation and another preacher was found.

In the second incident, which took place at a major conference seeking to mark the abolition, another high-profile and visible Black evangelical

Christian was asked for his theological interpretation on the evils of the slave trade and its relationship to Black people. This individual opined that, as difficult as it might be to accept, perhaps there was a sense in which this epoch could be understood in terms of God's "providence": namely, that such evils were all part of some grand cosmic plan of God, in which the senseless deaths of millions of Africans were somehow caught up in the Divine action of God. No doubt, at some point in the future, God would deign to enlighten us as to the ultimate purpose of allowing this event to happen in the first place.

The reaction of the audience to this second example of theological myopia was no less striking than the first. What was galling for sections of the audience on this second occasion was the sense that this speaker was a much more respected and highly sophisticated individual in theological terms than the first. And yet, such high intelligence could yield nothing more sensible than a more polished version of the vacuous rhetoric of the first, abortive speaker.

In both cases, the material reality of Black suffering was not used to re-configure and rearticulate one's understanding of the nature of God and the meaning of the Christian faith. Rather, Black experience was sublimated beneath the faith and not given equal importance alongside it. On hearing the first story and witnessing the second, both occasions caused me to ponder ruefully, "What kind of faith makes people want to negate the historical reality of themselves in favour of religious myth and rhetoric?" Now, it is important to add, these are only two speakers of a great many in Britain, and I am sure there are many other preachers and commentators who might not have said anything quite so deleterious in their pronouncements. Whilst I accept these are but two examples, they nonetheless represent the views of two prominent Black church leaders in Britain. In colloquial Jamaican speak, these are not "dibby dibby" people![7]

The second speaker, in seeking to place the realities of Black suffering within a theological framework of "providence," invoked the "Joseph Paradigm." The "Joseph Paradigm" takes its name from the narrative of Joseph, the favoured son of Jacob, who is sold into slavery in Egypt and later prospers, as depicted in Genesis 37–50. In the narrative, what appears as a deleterious event in Joseph's life turns out to be a propitious chapter, as at a later point in the story he has the power to save his brothers from complete economic ruin. The providential act of an omnipotent and omniscient God is one that enables a concrete reversal of events to occur within the life experiences of a family following a seemingly vengeful and sinful act at the outset of the narrative.

In this case, the ends clearly justify the means. If the biblical narrative is correct (which of course, for an inerrant holy text, it must be) and is to be taken literally (the same logic of faith applies once again), then the theological meaning of enslavement, exile and finally redemption are axiomatic. If God is all powerful and all knowing and is the "Lord of History" then that same God somehow could accommodate the evils inflicted on Black people as a means of enabling something "good" or "better" to emerge at a later point.

The horror for me (and I guess for many others, but I cannot speak for them) is that this theological account is prepared to countenance God as a Divine sadist in order to preserve the sanctity of our inherited theological systems. So, God is all powerful and all knowing, and the normative-literalist readings of the Bible are to be believed as "literally" true and an example of how God acts in history. The preservation of these biblical and theological axioms leads to the absurdity of conservative White people then opining "Well, if it's all providential, then how can we be blamed for slavery? We were only doing what God had planned and willed already in history!" The fact that conservative White Christians might be pleased with such theology does not take too much imagination to fathom, but the realization that Black people, as a corollary, have accepted this notion is an altogether different matter!

As I have tried to demonstrate in previous chapters, it is only by submitting theological axioms to the acid test of our material experiences in history can the truth of any religious tradition, particularly as they are explicated in the sacred texts, be better understood and known.

If either of these Black evangelical church leaders were prepared to interrogate the Christian tradition and the Bible through the focusing lens of Black experience, particularly that which emerges from the historical reality of the slave epoch, I do not see how one could remark that slavery was providential. As I will demonstrate shortly, the work of such scholars as William Jones and Anthony Pinn have pushed me further than I am naturally comfortable, in acknowledging the theological fault lines in terms of what we construe as God's agency and any notion of Divine providence.

One of the problems with these forms of theological reflection is the absence of any critical engagement with notions of lament, sorrow or anger – which are replete within Hebrew sacred texts. Any cursory glance at the Psalms will alert us to the sense in which writers sharing their reflections whilst struggling with the raw emotions of anger, confusion and doubt, give vent to these feelings through the searing poetic writing, which expresses their sense of lament. In Psalm 10, for example, we see the writer bemoaning God for God's silence as they are besieged by their enemies. The writer cries out "Why, O Lord, do you stand far off? Why do you hide yourself in times of trouble?" (10:1).[8] I have no doubt that many of my enslaved African forbears uttered such cries of anguish in the midst of their despair.

Black and Womanist theologians, such as James Cone and Cheryl Kirk-Duggan, have explored the varied ways in Black (African-American) spirituality sought to give voice to their existential condition and seek answers to profound questions of suffering and theodicy through their varied musical traditions, perhaps best exemplified in the spirituals. Cone, commenting on the role of the spirituals as a means of giving voice and agency to the reality of Black suffering, states:

> The Spirituals are historical songs which speak about the rupture of black lives; they tell us about a people in the land of bondage, and what they did to hold themselves together and to fight back. We are told that the people of Israel could not sing the Lord's song in a strange land. But for blacks, their *being* depended upon a song. Through song they built new structures for existence in an alien land. The spirituals enabled blacks to retain a measure of African identity while living in the midst of American slavery, providing both the substance and the rhythm to cope with human servitude.[9]

In a later work, Womanist theologian Cheryl Kirk-Duggan, in a penetrating and exhaustive study, outlines the functional strength of the spirituals as a means of encompassing the depth of sorrow and lament of Black people.[10] More recently, Womanist religious educator, Yolanda Smith, assesses the pedagogical potential of the spirituals for shaping the faith formation and cultural consciousness of Black people in the modern or postmodern epoch.[11] Smith, commenting on the historic function and contemporary potential of the spirituals to foster critical, honest reflections on the nature of Black struggle, says:

> Spirituals were also important educational tools that taught worshippers about the Bible, God, Jesus, sin, Satan, and communal ethics as well as personal and collective empowerment… The Spirituals also provided a means of expressing the hope and despair that arose out of the living conditions under the brutal system of chattel slavery.[12]

What emerges clearly from these authors is that the eschatological hope that resides deep within the lyrical content of the spirituals is one that is dialectical in its engagement with the existential context and condition in which the Black self resides. Namely, that the spirituals speak to the often prevalent sense of despair, confusion and hope "against" hope of Black suffering during the tumult and existential misery of Black bodies during the epoch of slavery.

This struggle for meaning is located in the context and conditions in which the Black self exists, in which one's daring to hope is fused in dialectical tension with the realities of one's existence that seem to point to the futility of that hope. This existential, dialectical tension sits right at the heart of the Diasporan African slavery and post-chattel slavery existence. As I have pointed out in a previous piece of work, in regard to

Job's quest to seek a measure of understanding of the catalogue of suffering that befalls him, there can be no easy "quick fix" theological formulas for the colossal reality of Black suffering, in both historic and contemporary terms.[13]

The sense of hope that emerges from the spirituals is not a declamatory and exuberant spirituality. It does not celebrate in the midst of evil nor does it give God thanks for the providence of acquired insight and revelation as a consequence of that evil. The tone is down-beat, reflective, circumspect and yet still hopeful.

My sense of the reaction to these two significant Black Pentecostal leaders was that their theological and spiritual armoury contained little or even no resources that drew upon the notion of lament and critical hopefulness as the most honest response to the presence of evil in the life experiences of Black people.[14] It is interesting to note that for the first of the two individuals, the theological approach to the bicentenary services was one of "celebration" and "thanksgiving."

The sense of "celebration" and "thanksgiving" arose from his belief that the epoch of slavery had been providential. The providence of God had enabled Black people to find salvation in Christ through the whip and the lash of the slave master. The fact that countless millions had died meaningless and pitiful deaths in order that this so-called act of "providence" could be achieved did not seem to merit any undue consideration from this Black church leader.

In response to the unacceptable convictions of this church leader, I remember remarking to a colleague, Can you imagine Jewish people, come 2045 and the centenary of the "liberation" of Auschwitz choosing to "celebrate" and "give thanks" for that event?

The inability to move beyond a prevailing sense of "manufactured joy" in the face of colossal evil represents one of the major theological challenges for more conservative Black Christian people in Britain. It is the challenge to face the horrors and brutalities of the slave epoch and its continued legacies and to ask sharp pertinent questions, such as "And where was God in all this?" One can neither hide from beast nor seek to offer up bland theological platitudes in the face of this ravenous leviathan.

Testing out my Theories

The previous discussion on how some Black people have struggled to engage with the latent theological issues connected with the enslavement of African people was one that challenged me to think creatively about how I would seek to address this issue as a participative Black theologian in Britain. In the course of the "bicentenary year"[15] in Britain, I have been struck by the marked absence of any substantive, critical theological work seeking to address this phenomenon.[16]

In order to attempt to address this issue as a participative Black theologian, I once again sought recourse to an experiential exercise in which I could engage ordinary Black people in embodied action and critical Black theological reflections. In order to engage with ordinary Black people of predominantly Christian faith, I decided to use the following exercise. The exercise is entitled "What do you want from God?" This exercise was undertaken with a number of groups over a seven- month period in 2007. In a variety of settings, I used the following exercise to tease out the underlying or latent theologies of ordinary Black people towards the issue of God's presence and activity, in terms of suffering and evil arising from the Atlantic slave trade.[17] In using this exercise, it was my hope to connect with some previous research work and juxtapose that with my present concern around the issue of slavery.

This exercise is one of my favourite analogies for explaining the importance of Black theology and its response to the idea that God sides with oppressed Black peoples.[18] When I have used the exercise in the past, I have explained to the group that they will be reflecting on the following "mythical tale" concerning an encounter between God and two people, involved in a struggle on a pavement.

God sees the two people struggling with one another. One of the people fighting is a strong White man who has his foot on the neck of a Black woman, who is pinned to the floor. Both characters recognize God is walking on the other side of the road, on the opposite pavement and they both call out to God. The White man with his foot on the Black woman's neck asks God for the strength to continue doing "God's will" and work by subduing this Black savage. The Black woman, conversely, asks for God to intervene and to save her from possible death. God replies by saying that neutrality and objectivity is all important and, as such, God cannot intervene or take sides.

Having explained the scenario, I then split the group into two halves. Side one, becomes the powerful White man. The other side becomes the woman. When recounting this tale I usually ask the group, "which person is most content with this response from God?" The answer, of course, is "the person who is most advantaged by the status quo" – the one who is being oppressed would have good reason to doubt the goodness of God in such circumstances.[19]

On previous occasion when I have used this exercise, it has been mainly as an experiential means to assist predominantly White ministerial students (or seminarians) to get to grips, in the most basic of terms, with the essential point of departure for understanding Black theology. In the context of using the exercise to address issues of theodicy, in light of slavery, I was hoping for a more prolonged and in-depth level of engagement.

For the purposes of this group exercise, participants in the two groups were required to stay in role for a full two hours. Whereas in past situations, I had asked one half of the main group to become the powerful White man, on recent occasions, I divided the main group into a number of subgroups (depending on the overall size of the body of people with whom I was working) and invited all of them to become the poor, weaker Black woman fighting for her life.

In this particular scenario, God does not walk by (for that would presume that God exists – a critique I had taken from a previous piece of work[20]); rather, participants are simply asked to reflect on what they would want God to do in this situation, assuming that God exists.

Leaving the participants in their groups for two hours, I asked them to consider what were the different options that might emerge as they considered the presence of God (or not) in their situation? What would the Black woman struggling for her very life want from God in this situation?

For the first forty minutes or so, I let the group discuss this existential question in the belief that God might appear at any minute (as "she" has done in a previous piece of work[21]) to save them from their struggle. After forty minutes or so, I approached each group and informed them that in the likely event that God might not literally appear, how would they then seek to rationalize their existential situation? If God did not appear, could one then deduce that God did not care? Alternatively, could one construe God's non-appearance as conclusive evidence of the nonexistence of God?

Armed with this additional (and disturbing for some) piece of information the various groups continued to formulate their theological responses to the crisis situation in which they found themselves. A number of them began to develop ideas of this crisis being one in which God, as allpowerful, loving and acting as sovereign, would reveal God's self to the participants in the "fullness of time." That the passage of history would give rise to the sense of "God's will" is becoming increasingly clear to those who were suffering in the present. I would conclude that approximately one in six, or around fifteen percent,[22] would have argued that God's agency (if at all) was best expressed in this way.

From the various comments and reflections of the groups, I was able to construct four broad typologies for the theological reflections of around 120 ordinary Black people across several months, the during bicentenary years, in 2007 in Britain.

Like the experiential and participative models of Black theology that have been generated from other forms of engagement with ordinary Black people,[23] I am at pains to stress that these typologies are neither definitive nor normative. In many respects, they are very much tentative heuristics, created for the purpose of discerning and interpreting the responses of the many Black participants with whom I have engaged. In this work, I have used the exchanges between the various members to create a four-pronged typology for Black accounts of theodicy, as expressed and reflected on by the various participants.

In my first attempt to synthesize the feelings and expressions of God's presence (or lack of it, as we shall see), I worked notionally with eight and then six typologies. After further reflection and thought, I realized that a number of the different perspectives crossed each other, resulting in a number of very fine demarcations and differentiation, which upon further analysis proved far too convoluted. Upon further analysis, I realized that there were actually four broader categories, in which other finer distinctions could be made by the researcher.

The four basic positions are indicative and not conclusive of the experiential models of theodicy of ordinary Black people. There is a final substantive point I should add about the responses of the group participants and their resulting theodicy. It is, namely, that during the final plenary sessions when I had shared my summative work with the various groups, a number of individuals spoke honestly about their own faith formation and resultant theologizing. A number asserted that in their daily faith operations, their concomitant implicit or latent theologies were not necessarily anchored in any one position alone. I have accepted such declarations as being true, in the knowledge that my positionality in terms of the four-part typology is one that can encompass elements of no. 2 (in moments of despair and anger) and large doses of nos. 3 and 4. It is has always been my belief that people in general, and perhaps the mercurial abilities of Black people in particular, exhibit greater levels of flexibility and mutability to confuse, defy and frustrate any attempt of the researcher to categorize and tabulate Black religiosity and spirituality.

Four-part Typology to Understanding God's Role in the Evils of Slavery

1. It is God's will and can be redemptive

This view states that God may have even made the evil or injustice happen or, at the very least, allowed it to happen. As God is an all-powerful and ever-present force in Creation, nothing can happen without God's agreement. Historic slavery and the modern forms of this institution, whilst *not necessarily* of God's making, can be understood as being within the orbit of God's will. The important thing to realize, however, is that slavery, like other forms of evil and oppression, can be redemptive. Basically, transformative change can emerge from such events in history. Something "good" can come out of such suffering.

This position was the most controversial of the four and is, to my mind, the one least acceptable to the substantive hinterland of Black theology. As I have stated previously, around one in six people chose this position. For the most part, individuals representing this position tended to be older persons and from the Pentecostal tradition.

2. Brings God into question and can never be redemptive

This view states that if God is an all-powerful and ever-present force in Creation, then by definition the presence of evils, such as slavery (historic and contemporary) calls God's existence and alleged "goodness" into question. Is God to blame? Does God care? Is God completely absent? Does God even exist? Whatever one might say of God, this position asserts that the suffering that is a part of such evils as slavery is never redemptive or transformative. It is simply evil and has nothing but bad consequences for those caught up in it.

William R. Jones' classic text, *Is God a White Racist?*,[24] was a withering critique on the presumptions of Black Christian theism, in terms of the non-foundational underpinning of Christian Black theology. Jones posed a number of challenging questions surrounding the basic presupposition of Black Christian faith that lies at the heart of Black theology, particularly in light of Black suffering. Starting from the basic premise of Christian theism – that God is all powerful – then what are we to make of evil and suffering of people, particularly innocent Black suffering?

If God is all powerful, then why cannot God intervene and banish suffering and the oppression of Black people? Maybe God chooses to do nothing? In doing nothing, God, then, appears to sanction Black suffering. Given that Black people suffer disproportionately more than White people, God, therefore, can be seen to be on the side of White people. Ergo, God is a White racist. If this is the case, then perhaps this God should be opposed and denounced?

The alternative view is that God is not all powerful. Due to the need to preserve human agency and free will, God will not impose God's will on us. In this scenario, it is the duty and responsibility of human beings to solve their own problems as God cannot and perhaps will not intervene. In which case, why worship God at all, if God can be seen to be impotent? A third view might hold that God is to be best understood from within the framework of "humanocentric theism."[25] This theological frame accomplishes its particular understanding of Black suffering by "removing God's overruling sovereignty from human history."[26] Responsibility for the genesis, the perpetuation and the ultimate eradication of evil and suffering, especially that which emerges in the form of slavery and racism, are ultimately the responsibilities of human beings and are not God's!

This form of explanation for the evil and suffering of Black people during the epoch of slavery, essentially, "takes God out of the equation" and leaves the moral responsibility for effecting change down to human beings. This view seems to gesture towards that of no. 4 (as we will see in a short while), but whereas for no. 4, one will still argue that God is love and is on the side of those struggling for systemic change, no. 2 negates such notions. Jones emphasizes the point when he writes:

> The consequence of humanocentric theism is to remove God from anyone's side. History becomes open-ended and multi-valued, capable of supporting either oppression or liberation, racism or brotherhood.[27]

In effect, no. 2 asserts that all people, Black or White, are charged with the responsibility of effecting systemic change and that there is no "get-out clause" in which God will ultimately intervene to put right that which humankind is singularly unable to accomplish. The starkness of this position, when juxtaposed with the theological certainties of the traditional Christian theism, was one that concentrated the minds of many in the various workshops I facilitated. For many, no. 2 was simply too stark an alternative, in terms of their engagement with the monstrous evils of the slave trade. The notion that we are in this by ourselves and there is no external Ultimate reality, on which humanity in general and Black people in particular could depend for the final victory was one that was too bare and devoid of hope for many.

3. We cannot know where and what God is doing, but we know that God is love

This view states that trying to "know" the reason for something happening is almost impossible. The one irrefutable "fact" we do have is that God is love, and that love as displayed by Jesus on the cross suggests that God is with us in our suffering. So God was and continues to be with those who are enslaved.

In this context of the various groups, a number of people, approximately half, argued for this position. Many of them asserted that God was a god of love and hope, and these twin dimensions in God's nature were facets that encouraged those struggling with the reality of "social death"[28] to believe that death itself would not be the end. This sense of hope that was encapsulated in the thinking of the participants who held onto this view was one that finds echoes in the work of African-American Womanist theologian Elaine Crawford.[29] Crawford argues that ordinary Black women, much like the mythical character in the exercise, have always declared a defiant "hope against hope" ethic in their daily operations. Crawford argues that many Black women were able to hold in dialectical tension the struggles of holding together family, life and the church; in much the same way as that found in the *seemingly* more erudite work of such luminaries as Jurgen Moltmann.[30] Moltmann and his development of a "theology of hope," which is grounded in an "end before the beginning" teleological framework that places the notion of the eschatological at the foreground of systematic theology,[31] is one that echoes the experiential struggles of ordinary Black women. The theology of hope,[32] as outlined by Moltmann, is given historical and contextual agency by the embodied life stories and experiences of Black women.

The sense that the hope of those who are suffering is informed by their association with and identification with God's suffering, as exemplified in the experiences of Jesus on the cross, is one that has been explored by a number of Black and Womanist theologians. Within Black theological thought a number of writers have located within the suffering of Jesus a sense of divine solidarity with their own historical and contemporary experiences of unjustified and unmerited suffering. Scholars such as Douglas,[33] Cone[34] and Terrell,[35] to name but a few, have all explored the theological significance for Black people of Jesus' suffering on the cross. Writing with reference to this theme, Terrell states:

> Yet the tendency among Black people has been to identify wholly with the suffering of Jesus because the story made available to them – Jesus' story – tells of his profound affinity with their plight. Like the martyrs, they are committed to him because his story is their story. Jesus' death by crucifixion is a prototype of African Americans' death by *circumscription*.[36]

This radical identification with the undeserved suffering of an innocent individual has exerted a powerful hold on the imagination of many Black people and other marginalized and oppressed groups in the world.[37]

For many in this, perhaps the largest of the four groups, Jesus' death, coupled with the "promise" of resurrection hope is one that offers a theological grounding for a form of passive and active resistance to the evils of oppression facing the Black women in the mythical exercise. For some, passive radicalism seeks recourse in the spiritual resistance, in which the sheer life force to praise God and to "keep on keeping on" counters the sheer absurdity and mockery of the existential plight in which the oppressed are housed. Black British Pentecostal scholars, Valentina Alexander[38] and Robert Beckford,[39] have explored this facet of Black spirituality in their respective scholarly work. Active radicalism can be seen in the participants' desire to use the promises of God's presence (in Christ) as the basis for seeking a response with violence (if necessary) to the imposition of the foot upon the extended Black neck of the woman in the exercise. Beckford argues that radical Black action motivated by Black Christian faith has been one of the hallmarks of a tenacious Black spirituality that has drawn on an experiential and immanent Jesus for its strength to tackle and oppose White hegemony.[40]

Beckford identifies Jamaican hero, Sam Sharpe, to be an integral part of this active-radical tradition. "For Sharpe, freedom in Christ (Colossians 3.11) was a vindication for rebellion against the English planters."[41]

Whilst there are inevitable dangers in a kind of religious quietism at play in those who seek to wrap themselves in a comforting blanket of God's love and suffering presence alongside them, nonetheless, such protestations gave rise to greater resources of radicalism and resistance than those found in group one.

4. Looking to God is to look in the wrong place, as countering evil is our (human) responsibility

This view states that as human beings have free will, it is both unrealistic and unhelpful to be looking to God for answers to questions such as the evils of slavery. Rather, taking our human freedom seriously, we should spend our energies and efforts trying to counter evil in all its forms, such as modern-day forms of slavery. The existence of such evils as slavery tells us more about the human capacity towards horrid acts of selfishness than it does about the nature of God.

This perspective falls short of Jones' open-ended view of history, in that those who adhered to this perspective would still want to argue for a notion of "eschatological hope" in which God will decisively enter into human history and ensure the completion of God's purposes for righteousness and justice.

Those who advocated this typology would argue that human beings are charged with the responsibility for campaigning and fighting for justice within history. This active campaigning for justice is accomplished, as a forward-orientated journey through the continuum of human experience, in the confident belief that the "God of History" will meet them at the "other end of History." This view might be challenged by those in no. 2 as the "so-called radicals who want to have their cake and eat it," i.e. such proponents want to preserve human free will and autonomy, but still want the comfort of an interventionist and activist God who will enter history to complete the task that human beings cannot accomplish through their own efforts.

The lack of any historical data by which one can attribute any notion of a God who is actively working in partnership with humankind to banish evil and suffering has to be acknowledged. The notion that God is "with us" in the struggle to overturn evil and suffering is based on the presupposition of Christian faith, which when examined in the light of historical experiences, can be shown to be speculative at best and delusional at worst. For those who adhered to typology no. 4, such exhortations of faith cannot be sustained in empirical terms. The challenges of those in no. 2 to the inherent weaknesses of those who hold to no. 4

can only be countered by the latter by appealing to notions of faith. To quote my mother, "if you want proof that something is going to happen and you also want the exact time and date at which this event is going to happen, then you don't need faith, do you?"

Reflecting on my own position vis-à-vis the four positions, I have to confess that on a good day I can remain sanguine that God who "is all in all," will work out God's own purposes, working in partnership with Black people throughout history. That in effect, God's active involvement in history, in partnership with human agency, will give rise to peace, justice and God's righteousness! This ongoing movement throughout history is one that will, ultimately, in the fullness of time, prevail over and against all the forces of evil. I hold to this view, as result of my own ongoing struggle with faith, and the recognition that this corporate faith is always elusive and slightly ahead of us. We cannot, therefore, depend upon it for empirical proof.

Conversely, in my more negative moments – for example, watching television during the remaking of the latest Band Aid single, or listening to the various broadcasts about the 20th anniversary of the Bhopal disaster in India – I am forced to ask the question "Maybe God does hate Black people and other people of darker skin?" "Why do so many people have to live miserable lives that are an insult to the word 'life' itself, when a seemingly all-powerful God could do something about it?" But maybe God can't? In which case, why are many of us still bothering? Are we not just kidding ourselves?

In the final analysis, from my reading of Scripture and my own faltering perceptions of who is God, perhaps I have convinced myself (maybe because the alternative does not bear thinking about) that a God of truth and justice will prevail in the end. Maybe my belief in a God of righteousness who acts within history on the side of the oppressed is nothing more than a theological "comfort blanket" to keep me warm against the ravages of historical reality. So long as we can wrap ourselves in the "faith blanket" and continue to utter our prayerful mantras then we might convince ourselves that the icy cold of oppression that surrounds us will one day disappear.

My belief in the continued goodness of God is not fool-proof or inviolate. Such are my modest powers as a systematic and constructive theologian, when compared to the likes of such eminent scholars as William Jones and Anthony Pinn, that I would not be much of a match for their philosophical and mental gymnastics in any intellectual "Black theology slam"!

Rather, in this chapter, in answer to the pointed question, "What is the point of this?," I have, as a participative Black theologian, sought to engage ordinary Black people in reflecting critically and honestly about this important challenge. To ask the question, "Where was, and is God, in all this?" is to stand naked, in metaphorical terms, in front of an abyss, with all the attendant vulnerability that is expressed at such a moment. To stand before that abyss, with all one's assumptions stripped away, when we are made vulnerable, lacking our hand-picked garments in which we chose to hide our nakedness, is indeed a frightening existential moment. This existential moment of encounter is one in which our mordant fears arise as we consider the potentially frightening realization that our faithful assumptions may have dissipated forever. One may not be able to return to the place from which we had come!

For the many participants who took part in the various group exercises and workshops I conducted across the many Black communities in Britain, in 2007, their engagement in this work was a frightening and vulnerable moment. For some, refuge was to be found in no. 1: the sense that all the events of history, including Black suffering in the epoch of slavery, could be best understood as falling within God's sovereign nature as the "Lord of History."

This notion is deeply problematic one, and is a notion from which I recoil. But the truth is, in my habitual life as a Black theologian living and working in Britain, who is sponsored by a major historic church,[42] the bulk of my worshipping and liturgical existence echoes to the theological certainties of no. 1. For many of us who declined to sit within the framework of no. 1, there remained the ongoing challenge of seeking to reconcile our more private fears with the often stated positions of our churches, which hold to the view that God is omnipotent, omniscient and omnipresent and is indeed the "Lord of History" – the alpha and omega.

How these notions are to be squared with the historic reality of slavery and the ongoing existence of Black suffering is a subject on which most, if not all, of "our" churches have remained, conveniently and not surprisingly, silent.

This chapter has not sought to seek a conclusive answer to the question "What is the point of this?" Rather, in my own participative way, I have sought to draw on the experiences and thinking of ordinary Black people to create a framework that can enable them to reflect critically, from a Black theological perspective.

It was interesting to note that for a small minority of participants, none of whom had undertaken any significant work in Black theodicy, the work of William Jones became an important resource for their faith formation. For these individuals, the notion that God is not sovereign of history is one that opens up abundantly more creative possibilities for a critical understanding of the reasons for Black suffering in slavery than any potential problems it may create. In short, the pluses outweigh the minuses.

I remember well the sheer sense of relief felt by some of the participants when they realized that their supposedly "heretical" reflections on God's lack of agency in accounting for Black suffering and evil found accord and was substantiated in the works of Jones and Pinn. Many felt a sense of justification when they became cognizant that in Jones' "humanocentric theism" there existed a term and a concept that gave voice to their, hitherto, submerged theological reflections. This, in itself, was an important outcome of this work.

This particular project, following my more individual work looking at a biblical theological basis for reparations in light of the slave trade in Britain, was undertaken to give agency to ordinary Black people in terms of how they can make sense of this tumultuous breach in Black peoples' history. The participative exercise, and the approximate four positions that emerged from our prolonged discussions, provided me with invaluable opportunities to assist ordinary Black people in constructing their own nascent Black theology that responds to the reality of Black struggle with evil and suffering.

It is my hope that this work of attempting to confront our past in light of the presuppositions of faith will continue, and that the reflections of ordinary Black people will help supplement the incisive work of our Black systematic and constructive theologians and ethicists. In the final analysis, seeking answers to one of the most foundational of all existential questions, namely: "what is the point of this" requires the skill, ingenuity, passion and dedication of us all; and even then, we may never assail to the summit of this philosophical mountain and be in a position to say that we have "cracked it." But we must continue to try and never settle for nonsensical responses that fail to do justice to the dignity of Black bodies and our suffering presence in western history.

10 Peace and Justice through Black Christian Education

The development of appropriate Christian education curriculum materials for Black people owes much to the pioneering work of Olivia Pearl Stokes, in the late 1960s and early 70s. Stokes argued for the need for Christian education within the Black church in the United States of America to be informed by the discipline of Black theology.[1]

When Olivia Pearl Stokes argued for the need for Black theology to be the first point of departure for Black Christian education, she was making recourse to a basic conviction of Black existential experience: namely, that central to the development of a Christian religious experience is the ontological reality of Blackness: the condition of being Black in the world.

The rationale and import for Black Christian education has arisen, in part, due to the encounter between White Europeans and Black Africans some five hundred years ago. The emergence and development of the Atlantic slave trade unleashed a terrible legacy of oppression and exploitation upon the African self. Upwards of ten million African people were transported from continental Africa to the "New World" for profit. The major historic denominations of the West were involved directly and indirectly in this pernicious and violent assault upon African people.[2] Prior to the development of this movement in capitalistic greed and economic expediency[3] there had been in existence a philosophical belief in the inherent superiority of European peoples over and against those of African descent. Africa as a continent was peopled by savages who were barely human!

One of the chief pernicious legacies of the epoch of slavery was the rationalization of the economic machinery of captivity. This was achieved through a rigid ideology that asserted the inferior status and sub-human nature of the African slave.[4] This form of insidious indoctrination was so pernicious that to quote the notable reggae singer Bob Marley, it was a form of "mental slavery."[5]

The effects of such tendentious instruction are still being felt – the continuing tendency of Black people to internalize their feelings of inferiority, coupled with an accompanying lack of self-esteem. The internalization of this demonized instruction has led to Black people directing the fire of their repressed and negated selves onto their own psyche and that of their peers with whom they share a common ancestry and ethnic identity. Franz Fannon describes the aggression shown by colonized and repressed people towards their peers and members of their own clan or ethnic grouping. Conversely, argues Fannon, greater insults can be levelled at these people by the oppressor with comparatively little response from the individuals concerned.[6]

Erikson, writing from a clinical, Freudian perspective, posits a notion of the self-negated identity and repressed personhood in a manner that finds echoes with the assertions of Fannon. He, like Fannon and many others, recognizes the psychological damage that has been unleashed upon, and which continues to plague, the ego identities of people of African descent. Erikson writes:

> Therapeutic as well as reformist efforts verify the sad truth that in any system based upon suppression, exclusion and exploitation, the suppressed, excluded and exploited unconsciously accept the evil image they were made to represent by those who are dominant.[7]

Jocelyn Maxime, in an address given to young Black Methodists at the 1990 Connexional conference for Black young people, details the central importance of racial identity in the formation of the personal identity of Black people.[8] Individuals unable to construct a positive racial identity will invariably harbour within their cognitive framework negative self-images of their race and concomitant cultures.

There are a number of substantive issues relating to notions of identity that affect children of the African Diaspora. For example, there are questions related to the sense of dislocation felt by many African-Caribbean children in Britain. This sense of dislocation is manifested in both psychological and physical terms. The forbears of these children were plucked from the ancestral cradle of Africa and transplanted to the Caribbean and the Americas. In light of the rupture and breach in African Diasporan history, the past five centuries have been a perpetual and substantive struggle for self-definition – a search for a sense of identity that has not been dictated and imposed by White hegemony.

The search for a positive self-identity and the difficulties evinced by Black youth in their identity crises must be placed within a wider context – a context that is informed by the socio-cultural and historic frameworks that have governed Black and White relations for five centuries. Winston James, writing on Caribbean slave societies, explains at length the disastrous effects that emerged from the widespread miscegenation of White slave masters with their Black slaves.[9]

The direct consequence of these sexual liaisons was the construction of an all-pervasive "multi-layered pigmentocracy."[10] In these contexts the place of the individual in the social hierarchy was dictated by their shade of skin. Higman writes of eight such gradations of skin pigmentation existing in the British colonies, ranging from "Negro"[11] through to "Octoroon."[12]

Remarkably, in the Spanish Americas there existed no less than 128 such gradations."[13] Commenting further on this phenomenon James has stated:

> Those who approximated most closely to the European type (in terms of hair texture, skin colour, facial characteristics, etc.) were accorded high status (which almost invariably corresponded with their location within the class structure of society), and those who were deemed to have been without, or with few such characteristics, were likewise relegated to the bottom of the social hierarchy.[14]

There is a continuing tendency of Black people to internalize the negative self-images of Blackness. This continuing self-negation remains one of the primary difficulties for Black people in general, and Black youth in particular, to construct helpful identities with which to underpin their notions of selfhood. Walter Rodney has commented on the incongruity of Black people continuing to elevate White aesthetics that connote a sense of beauty whilst denigrating characteristics that are synonymous with their own identity.[15] Rodney goes on to state that: "But we continue to...express our support of the assumption that White Europeans have the monopoly of beauty, and that Black is the incarnation of ugliness."[16]

The privations of Black people in macro terms over the previous five centuries, it can be argued, have become distilled and relocated within the micro experiences of Black youth living in post-war Britain. The sense of displacement, disaffection and marginality that exemplifies life for many Black young people living in Britain today is in many ways typified by Caryl Phillips in his book *The European Tribe*.[17]

In an early passage in the book, Phillips recalls a painful experience from his childhood. In a classroom discussion focusing upon identity of pupils derived from the surnames of all class members, his surname of Phillips becomes the butt of classroom humour. The humour that envelops the class arises from the patently obvious fact that Phillips is not perceived as being Welsh as his surname would seem to imply. The other White pupils are able to derive some sense of identity from their surnames. One boy is called Greenberg and is Jewish, whilst another boy is called McKenzie and is Scottish by descent. Phillips, meanwhile, finds himself rootless and is exposed to the merciless taunts of his peers. Phillips writes: "The truth was I had no idea where I was from as I had been told that I was born in the Caribbean but came from England. I could not participate in the joke, which made my identity a source of humour."[18]

Consistent with and directly related to the search for a positive self-identity has been the sense of detachment and exclusion that has been keenly experienced by Black young people living in Britain. In crude notional terms, Black young people although the greater majority are born in Britain[19] are largely denied positive affirmations governing their presence within British society because they do not look British.

The grim residues of some five centuries of low self-esteem, internalization of racism and the negation of the self manifests itself in the lives of people of African descent in a number of alarming ways. Cornel West speaks of the nihilistic threat at the heart of the Black experience in America. African-American youth have lost hope. They have consequently become a threat to themselves and to the body politic of corporate America.[20] African-American youth are over-represented in the criminal justice system, under-represented in higher and further education; at threat due to intra-cultural and communal violence and have become a grim statistical indictment upon a racist system.[21]

The situation in Britain regarding the education and socialization of African-Caribbean males does not make for pleasant reading. Tony Sewell has highlighted the many difficulties experienced by state schools in engaging with and educating African-Caribbean males in an effective and successful manner.[22]

Without wishing to delve into the worst forms of pathological reductionism, it is the case that a significant proportion of Black people in general, and Black youth in particular, are a threat to themselves and the wider societies as of whole to which they notionally belong. What are the possible solutions to this malaise and where are they to be found? One significant location where assistance might be found is within the discipline of Black Christian education.

Black Christian education has attempted to engage with the existential questions of African people's struggles and tumult in a racially oppressive world. A variety of Black Christian educators and theologians have sought to utilize Black Christian education as a means of affirming and empowering people of African descent within the African Diaspora.

Michael Ross argues that effective Christian education must be formational, helping young Black people, particularly young boys, to make the transition into responsible adulthood. This pedagogy and curriculum should enable Black boys to gain a sense of the historical legacy and the more recent developments in Black masculinity. This educational process will assist such individuals to locate appropriate identities that are informed by the ongoing legacy of faith of which they are a part.[23]

Writing from a more generic position, Grant Shockley outlines an approach to the Christian education of Black youth that looks at the historical development of Black Christianity and faith in the United States of America. Shockley argues that the Civil Rights Movement in the United States of America radicalized Black youth, but the churches' response, and the developments in Christian education curricula, did not follow suit. Appropriate and credible programmes for the Christian education of Black youth did not emerge until the late 1960s.[24]

In the same book, Jacquelyn Grant offers a theological framework for the Christian education of Black youth. Grant's discourse, framed within her perspective as a Womanist theologian, asserts that Christian education for Black youth must possess an ideological intent. This approach is one that understands the nature of power and racism within the world and how these realities have affected Black people historically.[25] Grant believes that Christian education must assert the personhood of Black youth in the here and now. This form of Christian education utilizes a praxis methodology, which is informed by experience and context, and underscored by Black theology. Ultimately, it should teach Black youth to be proud of being Black and resist the spurious universalism that asserts that all people are the same under the guise of White hegemony and ethnocentric norms.[26]

Romney Moseley argues for a process of Christian education that is not only intergenerational, but is also inter-cultural. Commencing from an African-centred perspective, Moseley argues for a pedagogy that enables Black youth to make connections between themselves and people of other cultures and situations who are struggling with oppressive structures not dissimilar to their own.[27] Moseley contends that Christian education and youth ministry must engage with the existential struggles for self-identity indicated by Black youth. These forms of Christian youth work must possess as a principled aim the goal of self-actualization for young African American people.[28]

Evelyn Parker uses Womanist frameworks as a basis for identifying characteristics, qualities and themes for the liberation of African-American youth.[29] Parker writes of her approach: "I used Womanist religious–moral value theory to test the, life stories of African-American adolescents to determine the presence of elements germane to a Black liberation struggle."[30] Parker interviewed 20 African-American adolescents, looking at their life stories and experiences for paradigms that indicate the liberative impulse within contemporary African-American life.[31]

An early advocate to assert the importance of the ideological intent of Christian education with reference to Black children was Helen Archibald, who stated that Christian education for such children must "Combat the poison they know lives about them."[32] Archibald continues by stating that "Religion is that which interposes itself between the bent back about to be broken and the whole crushing weight of the world's evil and injustice."[33]

The amelioration of contextual woes as detailed by Archibald is continued by Andrew White, who states that Christian education under the auspices of the Black Church must be a practical exercise in liberation.[34] White believes that Christian education should introduce Black youth to the often disguised and suppressed militancy of Jesus, upon whom Christian teaching must be predicated. He states that:

> Jesus was militant and a revolutionist who understood justice to have a specific and practical meaning. The young Blacks will identify with him if they are informed about his program for peace, justice, brotherhood and equality, in practical observable actions.[35]

In a more recent epoch, Nelson Copeland has written of the need for Christian education to be conscious of and informed by the contextual realities of Black youth culture. Copeland makes the case for a Christian education that is linked inextricably to the ongoing experiences of Black youth and equips young people to develop the necessary tools for their own liberation.[36] The importance of encouraging and enabling Black young people to begin to locate appropriate stratagems and solutions to their own problems is a theme to which Copeland returns at a later juncture in his writing. He argues that Black young people should be empowered to gain a reflective criticality that refuses to accept superficial solutions, whilst continuing to pose hard questions.[37]

Copeland asserts that many Black young people no longer possess the capacity to be critically reflective because they have lost the inherent self-belief that is often a pre-requisite of that particular facet of human consciousness.[38] This theme is echoed in the work of Na'im Akbar. Commenting upon this psychological deficiency amongst Black people, Akbar refers to a term he calls "plantation ghost." Akbar claims that those struggling from this malaise are individuals who have been dehumanized and psychologically shorn of any shred of belief in their own abilities and self-worth. In effect these people have become brainwashed.[39]

Copeland contends that Christian education must have, as one of its core aims, the restoration of autonomy, dignity and belief amongst Black youth. He writes "The ability to dream is the highest gift given to the intellectual."[40]

Whilst Black Christian education has been associated, in almost symbiotic terms, with the promotion and affirmation of the African self, its efficacy has a much wider resonance than the utility and applicability to African people. The maxim of "No justice, no peace" is one that has echoed through the many contexts where oppression and injustice have been evident. One need only think of South Africa during the apartheid era to realize the essential truth of this aphorism.

In a world of globalization, White hegemony and structural inequality, Black Christian education possesses the critical ideological force to counter the worst excesses of racism and economic exploitation. Black Christian education at its best is a radically prophetic enterprise that challenges the status quo.

The importance of education as a prophetic tool for liberation is a perspective that owes much to Paulo Freire. Freire argued that for oppressed people to be free, they must first recognize the condition in which they find themselves. One of the primary ways in which the oppressor controls the actions of the oppressed is by restricting the thinking of the oppressed. The latter view the world and perceive their reality in terms that are determined solely by the oppressor. This constricted world-view prevents the oppressed from claiming their freedom.[41] Freire asserts that the oppressed need to recognize the situation in which they find themselves before liberation can become a reality.[42] This process of coming to an informed knowledge of one's existential condition, and the accompanying process of developing the necessary tools for liberation, has been termed by Freire as "conscientization."[43] Freire concisely expresses both the dialectical dilemma and challenge that confronts the oppressed in their quest for liberation, when he writes:

> The central problem is this: How can the oppressed, or divided, unauthentic beings, participate in developing the pedagogy of liberation? Only as they discover themselves to be "hosts" of the oppressor can they contribute to the midwifery of their liberation pedagogy.[44]

Freire's work has proved an important influence on a number of Black Christian educators. Grant Shockley, one of the most important Black Christian educators, has argued that one needs to go beyond Paulo Freire in developing a liberative model of Christian education for Black people.[45] Shockley outlines a five-stage implementation programme for a liberative model of Christian education for Black people.[46] Continuing to outline this theological apologetic for a programme of Christian education that arises out of the Black experience, Shockley states that:

> The center of education for liberation occurs when persons are able to utilize their capacities of self-transcendence to evaluate reality, and as subjects, of naming the world instead of being named by it.[47]

This point is important, as it inspired me to see the necessity of self-definition as being an essential core component of any practical curriculum that might be conceived within the development of my own work. Whilst there are a number of occasions in which this expressed intent is manifested within the Christian education curriculum I created,[48] its most explicit rendering can be found in the section on Advent week one, in the material for the oldest group.[49]

In this material I wanted to find a means of bringing issues of self-definition from the abstract into the concrete. My attempt to accomplish this task came by means of an exercise that portrays in a graphic sense how oppressed and marginalized people have their reality defined for them, and they are subsequently named and their essential meaning as human beings is determined by those with power. The exercise involves Black young people becoming objects.[50]

The theological intent of Shockley's conception for Christian education is rooted within the paradigm of Black theology.[51] This particular understanding of Christian education is one that asserts God's predisposition for the poor and the marginalized of the world.[52] This thinking led me to utilize Black theology as a means of highlighting the liberative impulse of the Gospel.[53]

Shockley argues that appropriate Christian education for people of African descent should be anchored to the existential realities of the Black experience. Shockley's work draws upon the wider discourse of Liberation theology, particularly the work of Schipani.[54] Schipani, who in turn, is influenced by Gutierrez,[55] seeks to fuse the ideological tenets of Liberation theology with the intentional engagement of the teaching and learning process. Schipani incorporates the pedagogical and methodological processes inherent within Liberation theology, with the Bible.[56]

Schipani argues that Liberation theology provides the ideological dynamism that confers relevancy and ownership to the process of religious education for oppressed and marginalized peoples of the world.[57] Schipani reminds us that the Kingdom of God is in essence a subversion of the traditional values that govern a world dominated by global capitalism and White hegemony. He states that "The divine Commonwealth is an upside down kingdom that calls for personal conversion and a comprehensive restructuring of the world."[58]

This radical restructuring of the world challenges the existing norms of White hegemony. As Black Christian education has emerged, in many respects, as the offspring of Black theology, it has been born through a process of political ferment, marginalization and oppression. Its birth was as a direct consequence of racism and subjugation. Delores H. Carpenter argues that the Christian education of Black people in America has been a struggle against the historic forces of oppression. This Christian education struggle is linked to the fight for relevance and affirmation, and the parlous nature of this enterprise within an overall context of poverty and marginalization.[59]

Let us return, finally, to the seminal work of Olivia Pearl Stokes. Stokes advocates that the development of Black Christian education, especially in light of the burgeoning social and political upheavals of the 1960s, was driven by the exigency of relevancy and liberation.[60] Stokes amplifies this point when she states "Thus education in the Black Church, with insights from Black theology, must become a part of that indispensable structure for survival and transformation that ameliorates these societal ills Christian faith is committed to remedy."[61]

The remedy of societal and global ills such as racism, exclusivism, sexism, classism, world poverty and economic exploitation are tasks that a liberative approach to education can attempt to counter and challenge. This approach to education is one that is not born out of economic advantage, material gain, vested interests or political and economic power. Rather, it is an approach that in its very weakness, the weakness of marginalization and denigration, has drawn directly upon the life and teachings of Jesus and the liberative, transformative power of the Gospel, in order to grant freedom to both the oppressed and the oppressor. When Jesus reverses the social norms in the "sermon on the Mount" (Mt. 5:1–12), the new principles he advocates are ones that cannot be obtained by the powerful. It is the poor, the marginalized and the oppressed, who in the process of their transformation and liberation possess the power to gain the insights and the vision to look beyond the immediate and the temporal, to transform the existing norms and so challenge the status quo. Black Christian education possesses the power to transform the lives, experiences and thinking of people of African descent. It can assist them to discover their authentic selfhood. This discovery will, I believe, create an opportunity for a greater sense of peace between rich and poor, Black and White, male and female. A new peace that is predicated on justice, equality and equity. For authentic peace is more than just the absence of conflict. It is the realization of the principles inherent within the Kingdom of God.

(This essay was first published in *Black Theology in Britain: A Journal of Contextual Praxis* 6, 2001, 73–85.)

11 HIV/AIDS and Black Communities in Britain: Reflections from a Practical Black British Liberation Theologian

In this essay, I will be addressing the social mores and theological frameworks that have influenced the reaction of Black, African Caribbean peoples in Britain to the growing incidences of HIV/AIDS within their communities. I am writing this piece as a Practical Black Liberation theologian, whose principal area of expertise is in Liberative models of Christian education and formation that are cognizant of Black cultures and histories. I am not, I hasten to add, a specialist nor have I undertaken specialist work in HIV/AIDS. In this essay, I want to offer a brief snapshot of how and for what reasons many African Caribbean Christian communities have been unwilling to either confront or offer any meaningful support and pastoral care to those suffering from HIV/AIDS from within their ranks.

This work will be approached by means of some participatory fieldwork I undertook some years ago[1] and to which I returned in order to write this essay. This initial work has been supplemented by a more recent return to one of the groups with whom I worked a number of years ago in order to continue the quest of teasing out their theological reflections on the whole nature of suffering and illness in respect to the scourge of HIV AIDS.

The experience of poor, marginalized and oppressed peoples within Christian history and the church has largely been one of struggle, opposition and invisibility. Black people have often been perceived as problems rather than opportunities. We have been controlled, denigrated and treated with suspicion. Only in recent history has our presence within White majority churches been celebrated.[2]

One of the most significant impacts on African Caribbean communities that arise from their ongoing struggles against the seemingly insuperable edifice of racism in Britain has been the creation of neo-conservative patterns of socialization and their concomitant cultural norms.

A number of scholars have written extensively about Black family life, and the social and cultural factors that affect Black families and their structure.[3] One of the hidden factors of Black life and the cultures that reflect these experiences are the sometimes negative aspects that exist within Black communities that are often overlooked or even excused.

One such hidden issue is the sense or rivalry, competition and conformity that exist within many Black communities. Often times, Black communities can exert strong patterns of socialization and conformity due to the external factors that have historically oppressed and limited them.[4] There are many Black people who have been accused of not "really being Black" or not being "Black enough."[5] In effect, these are the Back people who have been perceived as "letting the side down" in terms of their actions and behaviour. Writers such as Victor Anderson have challenged the way in which other Black scholars have perpetuated aspects of this internal conformity by refusing to acknowledge the inherent diversity within Black cultural life in the African Diaspora.[6]

There is the sense that within oppressed and marginalized groups, where racism and poverty are amongst the main factors that define the nature of community, the struggle to maintain a coherent and collectivist stance against a hostile and uncaring world often leads to particular forms of neo-conservative stance regarding such matters as sexual ethics and their resultant social mores. In such contexts, to be perceived as being different offers a dangerous challenge to the whole community and their notions of what is permissible or acceptable. To be different is to potentially bring shame upon the whole community. The notion of shame remains a very strong regulatory factor in defining the limits of behaviour, identity and actions within many Diasporan African communities.[7]

I have offered a brief microcosm of aspects of the historic underscoring of African Caribbean life and experience in Britain in order to provide a basis from which I can investigate the attitudes and theological thinking of a group of Black Caribbean Christians. I am in no way suggesting that the reactions of this group are emblematic of every community of African Caribbean Christians in Britain. Clearly, one would need to undertake a very different mode of theological inquiry in order to gain that sort of data to make such generic and overarching findings for any group of people.[8]

Rather, in this work, by looking in more detail at one particular group of African Caribbean Christians in Britain, I want to suggest that there are themes and patterns of thought that provide the underscoring of a host of societal and attitudinal responses to the phenomenon of HIV/AIDS.

Working with the Group

The group with whom I worked, initially, in the late 1990s and subsequently, for this study is located around the south west area of

Birmingham. Birmingham is the second largest city in England. It is a vibrant multi-ethnic city whose population numbers approximately 1.3 million. The group of African Caribbean Christians with whom I worked were drawn from largely Black majority Methodist, Pentecostal, Anglican and Reformed Churches in the area. Of the group of twelve, seven had originally travelled to the UK from the Caribbean island of Jamaica, whilst of the other five three traced their roots to the island of St. Kitts and two were from another Caribbean island called Montserrat. I met with the group on three occasions, each meeting lasting approximately two hours.

The first meeting was largely taken up with a recap of the previous meeting some seven years ago. Seven of the twelve were veterans from the previous meeting. The five newer members of the group had been chosen by myself from a more recent piece of work I had undertaken.[9] Subsequent meetings explored the role of God and God's agency in dealing with suffering and disease in the lives of believers and those who would not describe themselves as Christians.

Biblical Reflections

In order to assist the group in focusing upon how they might reflect upon the issue of suffering and illness with particular reference to HIV/AIDS, I asked the group to engage with Luke 8:40–48. This narrative is Luke's account of Jesus' encounter with a woman haemorrhaging.

I split the group of twelve into four groups of three and invited them to reflect on the passage by adopting the persona of a particular character in the narrative. One group became Jesus, the second the woman with the "issue of blood," the third the disciples and the fourth the crowd. I invited the group to imagine that they were present as this narrative unfolds and to record their feelings (in character) as the action takes place around them.

Having set the exercise up, the remainder of the session was spent exploring the text in character. After the exercise, the groups were de-briefed in order that they could come out of role and would not take any negative or difficult feelings home with them. Finally, immediate feelings, thoughts and overall reflections were recorded on a flip-chart for further analysis in the third and final meeting.

A number of important themes emerged from the different groups as they immersed themselves in character within the framework of the biblical narrative. The main theme that emerged was what I term "contractual compassion." In using this term I am referring to the ways in which the group asserted that God's grace and healing for any individual suffering from HIV/AIDS was a direct correlation to how that individual might have contracted the virus in the first instance, and whether they were repentant of their sins.

When the group was asked if it mattered how the sufferer had contracted the virus, nine out of the twelve said yes. For most in the group it did matter. If the sufferer were gay or a lesbian or an intravenous drug user, for example, then this knowledge has a major impact upon their resulting response. Whilst no one in the group displayed a particular hardened response of "they brought it upon themselves," there was, nonetheless, a sense that contracting the HIV virus was the naturally corollary of such forms of sinful behaviour. "If you defy God's law then there are consequences" argued one member of the group.

What is interesting to note is that the reactions of most members of the group was influenced to a great extent by the societal and historico-cultural factors impacting on African Caribbean communities to which reference was made at the beginning of this essay. For most members of the group (all of whom were over 50)[10] the struggles against racism, marginalization and societal indifference were such that the means by which many Black Christian communities seek to challenge such systemic ills was through a retreating into themselves, buttressed against such forces by neo-conservative religio-cultural mores and their accompanying theological norms.

Robert Beckford has addressed particular aspects of Black Christianity in Britain and its restrictive self-serving brand of faith that seeks to engage only those who adhere to the religio-cultural norms of the faith community and might describe themselves as being saved.[11] In an earlier work, Beckford analyses the praxis of particular Pentecostal churches in London whose mission theology is unable to bridge the gap between the structural socio-political concerns that exert a disproportionate hold over those on the margins of the church and society and those who are "saved" within the faith community.[12] People suffering with HIV/AIDS are clearly located as those who through inappropriate behaviour and actions are not saved – for sanctification and holiness would have precluded these forms of actions in the first instance.

When I asked the group to correlate their reflections with the praxis of Jesus and his engagement with the woman in the text, the group were convinced, at least initially, that the woman was an "innocent sufferer." Essentially, her plight was not of her making and so Jesus' response of healing her was one that was entirely in keeping with the righteousness of God.

When the group was challenged by myself to reflect on what might be construed as "deserving and undeserving suffering," i.e. could any one of us really deserve God's love and grace, all the members clearly recognized the fault lines in their initial responses. Many recognized that their initial responses were ones coloured by the often restrictive and inhibited cultural norms that they had unconsciously imbibed, which themselves are products of an overarching framework of racism and oppression that has dominated the lives of most Black people living in Britain since the mass post-war migration movements of the mid part of the last century.[13]

When the group was invited to re-think their initial reactions, it was heartening to see the extent to which uncritical generalized assertions were replaced with a desire to try and understand and respond better.

The group were offered some reflections and thoughts by a number of North American theologians and educators, in particular the work of Gary Gunderson. Gunderson uses the insights of an interfaith health programme in Atlanta to illustrate how congregations can share ideas and experiences in order to support and be in solidarity with those who are broken and suffering.[14] I have found Gunderson's notion of the church as sanctuary, or a "safe space," to be particularly apposite in the context of this essay.[15] The notion of the church as safe or hospitable space is one that is utilized in the ecumenical report on children in the church, entitled *Unfinished Business*.[16]

Charles Foster has done much to raise our awareness of the need for congregations to create educational models to assist in the task of trying to construct communities that can handle diversity and conflict in a creative fashion.[17] In a collaborative piece of work with Theodore Brelsford, Foster has undertaken case study research, highlighting the differing (and successful) approaches of a number of churches to engaging with issues of difference, and how plural communities of faith learn how to celebrate their diversity.[18] The challenge that confronted this group was one of how to demonstrate hospitality and inclusivity. How can churches become safe, hospitable spaces where those who are vulnerable and broken can find a welcoming home? In respect to this central defining issue, Foster writes:

> The movement from messages of hostility to hospitality is required for congregations seeking to embrace the strangers they find in their communities. The difference is seen in comparing the posture of the Prodigal Son's father – standing out on the road expectantly waiting – to the posture of the sulking brother, refusing to participate in the banquet.[19]

The challenge for all of us is to learn to live out the generosity of spirit that is displayed by the father to his son in this famous passage. As this narrative hopefully demonstrates, this generosity is ultimately a gift of grace for it often runs contrary to what we would normally want or choose to do. The members of the group saw this form of praxis as a possibility for themselves as they reflected further on the Lukan passage and their existential engagement with the text and its correlation with contemporary experience.

A Black Theological Re-reading of Luke 8:40–48

I was conscious that the group remained wedded to notions of "contractual compassion." Whilst they acknowledged the all-embracing and inclusive reality of God's grace in the lives of "all sinners," I was struck, nevertheless, by the fact that there remained a sense in which the existence of this abundant grace was one that tolerated particular groups of people rather than celebrating their life and any concomitant experience. In order to push the group to reflect further on this issue I invited them, in the final section of the third meeting, to see how a Black theology reading of this Lukan text might open up new vistas for a renewed and more expansive form of praxis as it pertains to those suffering from HIV/AIDS in Black communities in Britain.

One of the great challenges facing all our Christian faith communities is trying to find relevance from the task of reading the Bible. The Bible remains central to the faith of virtually all Black Christians.[20] How can those of us who are charged with leading Bible studies become so energized and inspired that we find new ways of opening up the scriptures for the adults and children we may lead?[21] In this, the final section of this essay, I want to offer a Black theology reading of Luke chapter 8 and demonstrate how a politicized reading of this text can challenge African Caribbean Christian communities to re-think their praxis as it relates to those suffering with HIV/AIDS.

One of the first things to note about Jesus' engagement with the crowd and the woman in the Lukan text is that he is fully engaged in the context in which he is situated. First, Jesus is close to the action. He is within the crowd, not distant from it. Jesus' actions involve being emotionally and physically involved with the context in which he finds himself.[22] This very intentionality of Jesus acts as a counterbalance to the non-contextual and often abstracted theologies of predominantly prosperity-led practitioners of Black Christianity as seen in the likes of Creflo Dollar[23] in the US and Matthew Ashimolowo in the UK.[24] Jesus engages with the context in which he is located in a real and embodied way and does not retreat into spiritual banalities as a means of avoiding being labelled "political."[25]

Jesus' public engagement eschews any sense of the closed binary of "them and us" that seems to characterize aspects of the worse forms of self-congratulatory, over-regulated models of holiness inspired conceptions of Black Church practice and Black Christianity, as a whole, across the African Diaspora.[26]

A Black theological reading of this text is an ideological form of hermeneutical practice that challenges the casual ethnocentric and ecclesiological certainties that belittle, oppress and marginalize some people over and against others.[27] Such a Black theology re-reading challenges the notions that some people are created more in God's image than others. It challenges those who feel that some people belong more than others. It challenges those who think that some people are a part of the "us" and others who are different are a part of the "them."[28]

For those who think that some belong, and deserve to be noticed, i.e. the Jairuses of this world, but others can and should be ignored because they are unclean or seemingly not worthy, i.e. the woman who was suffering from a blood disease, this text can and should be an immense challenge. In terms of the woman, I read her plight in hermeneutical terms as a Black gay, lesbian, bi-sexual, trans-gendered person or intravenous drug user who is seen as "beyond the pale" due to her social condition. Her plight of being on the edge or beyond the pale is one that is recognized by many sufferers with HIV/AIDS in a number of Black communities in Britain. Jesus' actions bring her from the margins into the centre of the action and the narrative. She is affirmed and healed. No questions are asked as to whether she is deserving, or in what contexts she contracted her illness.

A Black theology inspired reading of this text, in which Jesus is seen as an iconoclastic disturber of the status quo, challenges us to re-think what we mean by the bounded nature of our theologies that still work on the binaries of "in" and "out." A Black theology reading suddenly challenges us to reassess who is upset by the "Good news" of Christ? Is it those who think they are on the inside, in which their cultural taboos are tolerated and affirmed, or those on the so-called outside who suddenly find themselves acceptable and welcomed? For all these people in the former category, a Black theology re-reading of this text is bad news, because it is a disturber and a denouncer of all that they hold to be true.[29]

A Black theology reading of this text can open up new ways of seeing established and well-worn patterns and practices. It can challenge, hitherto, conservative African Caribbean Christian communities to reassess their praxis as it impacts and engages with those struggling with HIV/AIDS in Britain. It can move beyond "contractual compassion" and "mere tolerance" to radical affirmation and hospitality, where the first truly become last and the last and the least are made first within the communal practices and ways of being the "Body of Christ."

(First published in *Concilium* no.3 [July 2007], eds Regina Ammicht-Quinn and Halle Hacker [London: SCM Press, 2007].)

12 Making the Difference

This chapter sketches some nascent thoughts around how a re-imagined Black theology for the twenty-first century, approached through the lens of Practical participative Black theology, might begin to be "cashed out" in the messy and grossly unequal world in which we presently live. This chapter draws on five case studies,[1] using them to pose critical questions around how a Black theology of practice can remain committed to challenging the vested interests of those at the centre from a position of apparent weakness, working on the margins. This chapter, like the rest of the book, seeks to demonstrate how a subversive and polemical Black theology can re-interpret traditional, Judeo-Christian themes and concerns in order to become a resource for personal and systemic change during this century. I have termed this chapter "Making the difference" because at the very heart of this exploration of Black theology, it is essentially about just that – how do we make the difference?

This chapter is something of a personal credo. A decade or so has elapsed since I made the fateful change in careers or vocations. In the early 1990s, I was working for the Asbury Circuit of the Birmingham District of the British Methodist Church. I was employed as a Youth and Community worker in the Handsworth area, North Birmingham, working with Black children, young people and their families. My work was multifarious and involved working with people of all ages, either inside the church or external to it. The central task in this role was that of working alongside Black communities helping them to re-contextualize and re-interpret the nature and task of the Christian faith in light of the particular contexts in which they were living. It was this experience of trying to connect the Christian faith to the reality of the lives led by urban, Black Christians, many of whom lived at the bottom of the socio-economic ladder, that first persuaded me to seek out opportunities for further study at the Queen's Foundation and the University of Birmingham.

When I did finally begin my doctorate in the mid 1990s, my central concern was to see whether my studies could give rise to not only new knowledge, but of equal import, new ways of embodying Christian praxis in light of the "Word of God." In effect, it was my hope to combine Practical theology with Black theology. As that work has continued over the course of the last decade, I have not lost my passion for trying to make that connection. How can Black theology connect with the realities of ordinary Black people?

In this chapter, working through these five case studies with a group of Black people, I have tried to pose practical questions and challenges, in order to assess the means by which there might emerge forms of praxis that are governed by the frameworks provided by Black theology.

This chapter, as the closing piece in this book, is written in order to re-affirm the need for a radical, challenging polemic that continues to push for systemic and systematic change, which is juxtaposed alongside issues of personal formation and Christian discipleship. I know that for many, such talk will seem anachronistic. There are some Black religious scholars in Britain who want to assert that we have moved beyond notions of liberation.[2]

Such notions are either predicated on one of two bases. First, that Black people have asserted their rights in such a confident and non-apologetic manner that the old notions of Black oppression (therefore requiring liberation) can be displaced by the more emollient and persuasive rhetoric of "Respect." Alternatively, the other thesis argues that the dynamic and transformative power of the Holy Spirit gives rise to a pneumatologically inspired identity that asserts the defiant and emancipated selfhood of Black people beyond the claims of suffering and oppression. Both approaches are ones that eschew the need for liberation.

It is my belief that whilst there is a modicum of truth in both perspectives, they both ultimately, fail, due to their inability to engage with the materiality of Christian praxis as the basis for authentic living. Elsewhere, I have argued for a Black theological approach to pneumatology and Pentecost, in which the dynamic work of the spirit both recognizes materiality and structural change, whilst also recognizing that there is always more to life than just matter.[3] As I have tried to emphasize in the first chapter, central to the workings of Black theology is the utilization of Marxist forms of analysis, which seek to unmask the material basis of oppression in a world with which Christianity has often found it easy to collude – often by seeking recourse in abstract spirituality.

Throughout this text, I have repeatedly called attention to the need to engage in material and practical forms of analysis in order to move beyond the strictures of the status quo and the vested self-interests of the powerful. Whether in terms of notions of reconciliation[4] or arguing in favour of reparations,[5] I have pressed for contextual and systemic forms of theological analysis that have eschewed the tendencies within Christianity to sacrifice embodied practice for spiritualized rhetoric.

In both of the perspectives I have outlined, in brief, there is the sense that their efficacy is best expressed in the abstract rather than the embodied. For "Respect" to work, it pre-supposes that there is already a measure of equality between Black and White in order for the former to assert their rights to be respected. This framework also assumes that as long as Black people assert their God-given humanity and demand to be respected, then the material and structural elements of oppression will somehow dissipate. But as a host of Liberation theologians have long argued, oppression is not solely an internalized subjective affair.[6] Clearly, within the frameworks in which oppression and marginalization operate, there remains a corrosive effect on the Black self from hundred of years of systematic and systemic psychological attack. Grant Shockley was perhaps one of the main proponents of the need for Christian religious education to attend to the internalized oppression arising from many Black people's labour.[7] As I have demonstrated, in terms of visual Christologies, the fact that many Black people still prefer the representation of Jesus that prioritizes Whiteness over Blackness, attests to the continued levels of internalized oppression that resides within many Black communities.[8]

Yet, not withstanding the corrosive and pernicious affects of psychological damage unleashed on Black people by White tendentious teachings of Black inferiority and non-being,[9] Anthony Pinn has shown that the machinery of White hegemony, particularly during the epoch of slavery, was geared primarily to the destruction of the Black body.[10] The worst excesses of globalization in our present epoch finds its worst effects on the structural poverty of darker skinned peoples of the world.[11] Whilst one should not discount the spiritual and psychological impoverishment that is impacting on Black communities and peoples across the world, in all truth, 30,000 people die in Africa everyday because they do not have enough to eat, which is not due to the insufficiency of their mental attitudes or spiritual acuity.

The fact is oppression is best conceived in material, structural and objective terms. The material poverty of many Black communities in Britain, the failure of the state to adequately educate Black boys or the disproportionate numbers of Black males in the criminal justice system in Britain all challenge the notion that the language or the concepts of liberation are anachronistic. It remains the case that the lives of the majority of Black people are blighted by the structural injustices of poverty, ill health, racism, blighted environments, mis-education and societal alienation. These contextual and largely material ills require concrete action that is underpinned by protesting and radical Black theological analysis that is prepared, in the word of James Cone, "to name the sin of White supremacy."[12]

The weaknesses of the two aforementioned approaches I have highlighted are their twin failures that can be summarized thus: (a) Conceiving of oppression in purely internalized and subjective terms rather than as structural and objective and (b) a continued failure to seriously interrogate the inherited meaning of Christian faith in light of Black material existential (and not just ontological) existence. If one imagines that oppression is a phenomenon that is located purely in the mind of the marginalized person who is objectified (oppression may begin in the mind but it does end there), then it seems axiomatic that changing one's mindset will therefore change one's materiality. The weakness of the "Respect" thesis can be summed up in a Caribbean aphorism I have heard my mother say, which states "If wishes were horses, then beggars would ride!" If all it took for the poor and the marginalized to change their mindset and imagine an alternative reality, then even beggars could have horses if they possessed a sufficiently powerful imagination to conceive of this hoped-for eventuality. In the other thesis that argues for going beyond the rhetoric of Liberation, the pneumatologically framed notion of Black subjectivity, as conceived from within the realms of conversion and Christian identity, fails for it can only construct Black subjective agency from within a normative Evangelical perspective. In effect, Black radical expression is subject to the normative constraints of largely post Reformation European Biblicism, opposed to the exigencies of the Black experience. Essentially, in this latter thesis, Black theology is reduced to the notion that Jesus is Black, but he is operates from within a frame of meaning that is consistent with Evangelicalism as largely conceived by White thinkers. So the only thing Black about Jesus is his façade and not in terms of any existential or ontological intent!

The *modus operandi* – Working with a Group of Black People

As a Practical Black theologian with a passion for engaging with ordinary Black people, this work of trying to think through the practices of Black theology with a view to "making a difference" has been undertaken via a number of workshops. Subsequent meetings explored the role of Black Christian praxis in terms of working in partnership with God and God's agency in order to make a difference in local communities.

My challenge in this work has been to try and map out a trajectory for Black theology that seeks to create greater synergy between the church and the academy, between Black theology in its systematic or ethical form and the more inductive processes of pedagogy and formation to be found within liberative models of Black Christian education.

In a previous chapter I returned to a previous piece of work outlining an approach to peace and justice by means of Black Christian education for Liberation. This liberative approach to Christian education is not a separate discipline in itself, to my mind. Although a good deal of my work can be described as being "Christian education," I have never viewed my scholarly activities and practical ministry as a separate discipline from Black theology. Rather, I have always viewed it as a subset of the larger, overarching practice and discipline of Black theology. Black Christian education for Liberation (BCL), as I have conceived it, is the "practical wing" of Black theology, one which seeks to root its radical intent in the contextual messiness of ordinary people's lives and the practice of Christian ministry.

As a participative Black theologian, I am constantly engaging with ordinary Black people in local churches and in other networks in order to bring the insights of Black theology into dialogue with their experiences – in addition to seeking to create new theological knowledge from such encounters. This dialectical process of teaching and learning and dialogical theological exploration and reflection has been the ongoing substantive model of my scholarly work since its inception.

In this final chapter, I have continued that work, seeking to develop a range of reflections from the context of a number of workshops. Like most of the previous chapters (where Black theological insights have emerged from workshops and group work), this final section of the book is drawn from a number of encounters with ordinary Black people in Britain.

Where is Black Theology to be Rooted?

Ever since I first became enamoured with this exciting notion termed "Black theology," I have struggled with the question of how one makes this Godly enterprise "Practical"? In what ways can Black theology become more than wondrous esoteric rhetoric? For many Black theologians, for good or ill, the church has been identified as a context in which the practice of Black theology can be rooted.[13]

Prior to undertaking these series of workshops with the various groups, I felt it was necessary to outline some of the basic markers that would shape our various encounters. As all the members of the different groups had some connection with the church, one of my immediate concerns was that we should be clear about our own expectations and experiences of the church itself, prior to any further collaborative work we might undertake.

One of the important issues that emerged in many of the early meetings was the question of gender. In all the participative work I have undertaken for the writing of this book, the majority of volunteers for the workshops have been Black women. In terms of the various participative encounters I have undertaken over the past two years, only 30 per cent of the participants, on the whole, have been Black men, although this figure has been considerably higher, depending upon the nature of the workshop itself and the tasks undertaken in the group work. At the outset of this tranche of workshops, the lack of Black men volunteering to take part in the group work was palpable. The few Black men present (20 per cent of the overall number taking part in this set of exercises/workshops/group work) felt very conspicuous. The greater number of Black women looked on, some in marked irritation, others in amusement.

I remain unsure as to the extent to which this ratio of females to males represents the macro picture of gender (im)balance in church attendance in Black majority churches in Britain.[14] The Black church in Britain continues, for the large part, to be a female centred context in numerical terms at least.[15] What is it about the church, which makes a seemingly compelling space for Black women and a setting of trepidation and suspicion for Black men?[16]

In order to make sense of the ongoing disparity between Black women and Black men in the series of participative encounters I have undertaken that constitute the heart of this book, I felt it necessary to undertake some preliminary reflections. As a reflective and reflexive participative Black theologian, my initial starting point, as is *always the case*, in my work, was myself. Who am I? Who is the constructive self that seeks to be in critical solidarity as a participative theologian with the many others with whom I work?

Deconstructing Myself as my Point of Departure

I first became aware of my Black body at five years old, as I have stated in a previous chapter.[17] Being the eldest of Caribbean migrants to Britain, I was the first in my family to enter the British school system. Suddenly, in a seemingly never ending sea of conspicuous Whiteness, I became very much aware of my own Blackness.

Whilst I have been constantly aware of my Blackness from an early age, the same cannot be said of my gender. The author of this text is a Black single heterosexual Christian male in his early forties. He is from working-class roots in West Yorkshire, but has lived in the West Midlands for over twenty years, and presently earns his living as a Black religious scholar in the predominantly White middle-class arena of theological education.

I offer these brief biographical notes by way of a contextual introduction to this section of the work. As I do so, as I am conscious of the ways in which many religious commentators and theologians are apt to ignore their own points of departure and cultural and social location when beginning to write and speak about issues as they see them in the world. It seems patently obvious to me that all people are shaped, in part, by the formative social and cultural frameworks and concerns that exert some influence upon how they see the world. Basically, we all see and experience the world from within a particular skin, and that skin is acted upon and acts upon the world.

As self-conscious animals we are aware (to a greater and lesser extent) of our own place and subjectivity in history, and in our daily human operations we are enabled to act upon the world, as moral agents who are able to take and make decisions for ourselves. And yet, alongside that basic sense of agency or activity is the realization that whilst we might be autonomous beings with some semblance of power, none of us lives in a vacuum. We are also acted upon and are constrained and influenced by the societal and legal norms that are replete in the wider contexts of which we are a part.

Constraints of time prevent any detailed or even cursory glance at the wealth of literature pertaining to how human beings construe meaning from the most fundamental questions governing their existence; namely who am I and how do I relate to the world and the world relates to me?

Whilst I am not going to attempt to unwrap or deconstruct these most basic and foundational of all human questions regarding existence, I have stated them, nonetheless, in the most rudimentary of terms in order to frame the following discussion regarding Black male Christian identity. I am addressing this brief discussion to Black male Christian identity as they are the ones under-represented, numerically, within the church. Black women, seemingly, have no major structural, philosophical or experiential difficulty in attending or taking part in church. For the most part, Black men do. So what is it about Black male identity that makes the church a less than appetising proposition for many Black men?

Black and Christian or Christian and Black?

There is, within Christianity, those from a particular conservative, evangelical perspective who often assert a colour-blind doctrine and theology[18] that does not see colour, "race" or difference in terms of human identity. For such individuals and groups, Christian identity falls completely outside of any tribal, cultural, sociological and political framework.

For many, the proof text for this form of transcendent notion of Christian religious faith is found in Galatians 3:28, where it states "In Christ there is no longer Jew or Greek, there is no longer slave or free, there is no longer male of female; for all are one in Christ Jesus." I have offered an alternative hermeneutic of this text in a recent piece of work.[19] I argue that it is not difference that is exploded by this supposedly Pauline text, but rather, notions of "in" and "out" groups within the newly emerging religious tradition based[20] upon the life, death and resurrection of Jesus who is now understood as the Christ.[21]

As a participative Black, born into a Jamaican family and raised in West Yorkshire, I refute any notion of Christian identity and faith that exists outside of any cultural and social location. In the most prosaic of terms, the skin in which we live (not only determined by epidermis but also by class, ethnicity, nationality, geography, sexuality, age and so on) does not suddenly disappear or cease to become of any symbolic or religious consequence once we adopt the nomenclature of "Christian" with which to name ourselves. As I have stated on numerous occasions when leading workshops with ordinary Black people in Britain: no matter what I may feel about the depth of holiness that imbues my life, I have no evidence and remain to be convinced that any White person, when spying me walking along the street, sees my incipient Christina faith writ large as opposed to the materiality of my Blackness.

I am a Black Caribbean British male Christian. This work is written out of the many influences and confluences of that hybrid sense of identities and subjectivities that dominate my life. I am a multi-layered individual who is also a member of a religious code, namely Christianity, which seeks to provide an overarching theory (a macro-narrative) for construing meaning from my life and that of the whole world, across all space and time.[22]

As I reflect upon my own positionality as a prelude to engaging with a group of largely Black women, I am forced to consider what it means to be a Black Christian male. Is there a causal link between the absence of Black men in church and the developmental psychological and theological building blocks that support the traditional notions of what it means to be a Christian? Why did so few Black men accept the invitation to attend these later series of workshops on Black theology and practical discipleship?

It strikes me that there is a need to address this important phenomena that is a salient truth within Black Christianity in Britain, indeed across the broader contours of the African Diaspora; namely, that Black Christian faith is a largely female orientated affair. If one were to go to any Black majority or Black led church[23] on a Sunday one would see a plethora of Black women and a relative scarcity of Black men. Whilst Black men often "head up" the church, it is Black women who, often selflessly, run it.

My reflections at this point are not predicated on the notion that the absence of Black men is pathological for Black churches or contrary to

Divine sanction in terms of male headship – views often propagated by conservative Black religious leadership.[24] I am not seeking to attack Black churches for being too feminine or to plead that the church *necessarily* needs more Black men. Undoubtedly, the community of faith that is the church should reflect the broader contours of human life and the inter-dependence and mutuality that is often perceived as being a Divine image for the ideals of human communitarian living.[25] There is a difference between wanting more Black men in church and believing that authentic church cannot happen without men. I am arguing for the former and not the latter!

One of the subtexts, therefore, in the various workshops to which repeated attention will be given, in a short while, is that we may have to investigate the whole arena of Christian religious faith development and ask whether there is need for an alternative theological framework and developmental schema? It may be the case that our present constructs may be inimical to Black Christian male identity and discipleship.

Hearing from the Men

In order to get some sense as to why Black men had neither responded positively to my invitation to take part in the workshops, or of greater import, why so few did not attend church in any significant sense, I invited a group of Black men to a pre-workshop consultation. I wanted to pose a number of questions to the Black men that had agreed to take part in the various workshops. I felt that exposing them to a series of "pre-workshop" questions would be helpful in preparing them for the cross gendered work that was to follow. I felt that such exchanges might create an additional level of consciousness around their gendered identities as Black men, which would be of some assistance in the subsequent workshops, possibly making them more sensitized to issues of power relations and un-earned privilege. The relatively small percentage of Black men wishing to explore the meaning of Christian faith in light of Black existence and personal experience was in itself a telling statistic. Having invited some two hundred Black men to meet with me, only ten volunteered, in the final analysis.[26]

My interactions with these ten Black men were telling. I asked each one of them to complete the exercise that is detailed in *Dramatizing Theologies*[27] as a prelude to our meeting. The exercise invites individuals to re-interpret their own formative narrative by means of a chart on which they place crosses to denote the significance of particular events in their past. Participants are invited to consider how and in what ways (if at all), their lives have been shaped by the dual nomenclatures of "Black" and "male" and to assess how these dual influences are further textured by the additional label of "Christian."

The completed forms were then reflected on via the Matthean text of the "Parable of the Talents"[28] in order to place their thoughts within a Christian theological purview. What emerged from this day-long activity is no more than a snapshot of some necessary additional, substantive practical/pastoral theological work on the issues pertaining to Black Christian male discipleship in Britain. What was interesting from our encounter was the sense that these men's experiences were at variance with the strictures laid down in Christian theology and the literature pertaining to Christian discipleship.

The traditional literature stresses that Christian maturity is in essence a reversal of the normal humanist perspectives on actualization, i.e. people achieve their highest form of personhood through a *denial of self* and an ongoing process of imitating Christ. Pauline theology stresses the necessity of losing oneself in Christ (see 2 Cor. 10:5 and Gal. 2:20).

Within the related areas of practical/pastoral theology, the literature pertaining to faith development theory (whether Fowler,[29] Nipkow[30] or Westerhoff[31]) stresses the importance of faith/spiritual growth. This literature stresses that people should seek to surrender the self to the "Ultimate Reality" (often termed as God or the Divine Self) in order to take on the character and identity of Christ's very own self.[32]

The problem with these prevailing theories when applied to Black men, as evidenced by our many conversations, is that they run counter to Black male nurture and socialization. Black masculinity is often predicated on notions of self-sufficiency, self-containment and invulnerability. These are precisely the traits which seem to militate against mature Christian faith and discipleship!

Reflecting upon the many accounts from these Black men, issues of autonomy and control were central to their self-definition. It is my belief that we need a new developmental theory for what constitutes authentic Christian identity and discipleship. I suspect that we need a radical re-think as to how we socialize and nurture Black boys, particularly during their formative years, before they grow into men.

As a corollary, we need to re-think what it means to be a Black man, in postcolonial Britain. Given the continued importance of Black churches in particular, and Black Christianity in general, to the nature, definition and intent of Black communities and their identities in Britain, many of these men were posing critical questions of Christian faith development and Black male identity in this country.

In short, many posed the following simple question: "Are Black men in Britain so socialized that many of us have become (at best) suspicious of the Christian faith or (at worst) even allergic to the whole phenomenon of Christianity?" Is this the time for the construction of a new Black British Christian male based upon a different notion of what it means to have Christian faith?

In the course of several hours together, these ten men and myself were unable to construct any workable paradigms that assist in addressing this issue in any direct fashion. In many respects, this conversation was but a first point of departure in addressing the issue. Time constraints prevented any further work at this juncture, as this issue had arisen, not as a specialized issue in its own right, but rather from the low numbers of men volunteering for the workshops in the first instance. The direct question at hand was not one of why Black men are largely absent from Christian contexts. Instead, our concerns as Black men arose from the need to address the question of how Black theology can become rooted in the ethical practices of Christian discipleship, especially within the context of the life of the church? The issues pertaining to the questions posed by the absence of Black men is one that is in need of further, in-depth qualitative work.

Undertaking the Workshops

In my construction of the workshops, I was interested in finding ways of enabling ordinary Black people to reflect critically on their faith and to identify contexts and situations to which Black theological Christian praxis could be directed in order to attempt to "make a difference." It was my intention, by means of my usual participative approach to doing Black theology, to locate a framework that would enable Black people to both identify problems and reflect theologically on what might be the "good news" for such troubled situations.

In working with these ecumenical groups, it was my hope that in a collaborative fashion, we might be able to identify challenging questions and possible points of action to which their local (Black majority) churches could respond. In order for this participative and collaborative work to emerge, I returned to a past educative exercise to assist me in shaping the critical consciousness of the group.

Over the course of a number of months, I informed a number of people of the next project on which I was working and asked if they were interested in assisting me in its development. To my delight, a number of people answered in the affirmative.

So over a period of several months I managed to gather around me fifty Black people to assist me in undertaking some participative Black theological work by means of an experiential learning exercise. The fifty people were drawn from approximately a dozen churches spread across the West Midlands, with five persons (related to some of the first people I had invited) travelling from London to attend our meetings. The group met in five sub-groups over five successive weekends. We met in a local church in the North of Birmingham, to which I had access, and for which there was no charge. Participants brought their own lunch and the group celebrated their time together through a sharing of food and fellowship whilst we discussed and reflected on what Black Christian faith should be saying to the socio-political problems and issues facing Black people in Britain in the 21st century.

At the outset, I promised all the groups with whom I worked complete anonymity in order that I might gain more honest and critical reflections from our various interactions. The following "Black theological vignettes" emerged from a series of five workshops in which ordinary Black people were invited to identify contextual issues drawn from the media and then asked how, and in what ways, does Black theology seek to pose critical reflections and subsequent contextual action on these issues.

The procedure for undertaking this work was as follows:

- Scene setting – Anthony Reddie introduces the day and asks the participants to identify themselves. (20 mins.)
- Ice-breaker exercise – led by Anthony Reddie. Participants are asked to divide into pairs and spend five minutes listening to their partner describe themselves. When both individuals in their pairs have undertaken this task, the whole group re-assembles and each individual has to introduce their partner to the whole group and relate to them what that person told them; and visa versa. The exercise is completed when all persons have been introduced to the whole group. (40 mins.)
- Participants are invited to describe the role faith plays in their life in no more than one side of A4 paper. What are the central elements of their faith and how are they represented and expressed? (30 mins.)
- Participants are invited to reflect on their accounts and those of their peers. What role does Christian faith play in their lives? How are they attempting to make a difference? (1 hour.)
- Break for refreshments.
- Anthony Reddie shares his understanding of Black theology with the group in order to show how it both affirms and critiques their religious experiences and any resultant practice. In what ways does Black theology confront us with the righteousness of God, as revealed in Jesus Christ? (1 hour.)
- Lunch

- Participants are encouraged to look at a stack of newspapers, magazines, and other published media in order to discern what are some of the substantive issues as reported in the media which Black theology, as expressed in the lives and practices of ordinary people (collectively, as the church), should address. (40 mins.)
- Participants were asked to choose one substantive topic/concern/ theme on which to reflect, in light of Black theology, with a view to creating plans for further action.

Creating a Framework for Participative Black Theological Reflections

As in a previous work the scholarship of Thomas Groome proved invaluable.[33] I have long sought to utilize the critical thinking of Thomas Groome in my participative Black theological work. Thomas Groome has been a major proponent of an interactive, participative approach to Practical theology. Groome argues that activity and joint participation are central to the teaching and learning process of Christian education.[34] Groome, in a later work, develops further his notion of critical reflection, which gives rise to committed Christian praxis action in the name of the gospel. Groome constructs an overarching concept for a radical, liberationist approach to Practical theology.[35] In this seminal work, he outlines an approach he calls "shared Praxis," which he describes as being

> A participative and dialogical pedagogy in which people reflect critically on their own historical agency in time and place and on their socio-cultural reality, have access together to Christian story/vision and personally appropriate it in community with the creative intent of renewed praxis in Christian faith towards God's reign for all creation.[36]

Groome details an approach that attempts to link the individual to a process of critical reflection and dialogue. This reflection and dialogue arises through a shared process where individuals are encouraged to enter into dramatic exercises that attempt to address major issues and concerns in the lives of the group. This dramatic exercise is, in turn, combined with the sacred stories (or narratives)[37] in order that the Christian story/vision, namely the gospel of Christ, can be better realized.

This process culminates in the final phase of this approach, which is a search for the truth that enables participants to make the Christian story their own.[38] Groome argues that participants should be empowered to appropriate the story/vision in order that they can own it, and then remake it, so that they can be set free. Groome's approach is heavily influenced by Liberation theology and seeks to speak to the experiences of those who have been marginalized and oppressed. The final act in this liberative cycle is one that calls for shared praxis, as the means of realizing and "making good" the inherent promises of freedom from within the Gospel of Jesus Christ.[39]

Having re-discovered Groome's work, I wanted to see if there was a way in which I could use his methodology within these workshop settings. My purpose in doing so was to raise a number of important theological and educational points concerning the role of Black theology in addressing contemporary problems facing Black people in Britain. In short, can this approach engage with and challenge ordinary Black people?

As a working heuristic, I began by synthesizing Groome's ideas with some practical educational and theological material I had first created a number of years ago. This exercise attempts to raise the critical consciousness of ordinary Black people by enabling them to inhabit a biblical narrative and explore the intersections between themselves, the Bible and the contemporary context.

The exercise I used was entitled *Are You in the Story?* This exercise was taken from the introductory material in my second book, entitled, *Growing into Hope* (vol. 2).[40] This exercise was intended to help Black people of faith to interrogate their present reality by means of climbing inside a sacred text and using that actualizing process to reflect back on their context, in order to see what is the "good news" for their particular setting and environment. The process of climbing inside a text was meant to serve as an opportunity to relate their individual stories within a broader set of sacred narratives that are perceived and believed by many Black people to be God's story.

The exercise asks individuals to imagine a scene from the Bible. I decided to choose the account of the "Feeding of the 5,000" in John 6:1–15. My reasons for doing so were more pragmatic than theological. I chose this text for the wide range of characters on show within it and the fact that people can adopt a number of positions within the narrative. All participants are asked to imagine the scene in the narrative in as much detail as possible. What does Jesus look like? What are the disciples like? What is the boy wearing? How do they see the crowd? Where are they located within the crowd?

Having imagined the scene in great detail, individuals are then asked to reflect upon where they are in the story. If individuals see themselves as one of the disciples at the centre of the story, then they are encouraged to walk to one particular side of the room. Conversely, if they are mere bystanders, standing near the back of the crowd, then they are encouraged to walk to another side of the room. Finally, I ask some if they are even in the scene at all? Are they watching the action as if they are in a living room, far removed from the whole event, viewing everything on television?

The crucial learning that resulted from this exercise was the sense that many marginalized and oppressed Black people tend to see themselves as distant spectators in God's story, not as central players.[41] What was interesting about this revelation from the group was the sense that their distance from the centre of story was one that spoke of their positionality vis-à-vis corporate Christianity. That, in effect, within the corporate, global brand that is Christianity, many of these Black people felt somewhat on the margins. And yet this sense of distance and marginality was juxtaposed with the firm belief that Jesus was close at hand, who was in many respects described as their "best friend."[42]

The dichotomy between a close at hand Jesus and a sense of distance and marginality in terms of corporate Christianity should not surprise us. In terms of the postcolonial nature of Christianity in Britain, Black people have often had to hold in tension the sense that Jesus is not understand as being bound up with the power structures and the exclusive and sometimes repressive power of the corporate church.[43]

The fact that many members of the group felt estranged from the corporate identity of the "established" hierarchical bound Christianity is not surprising. The corporate edifice that is Christianity is uniquely bound up with power, patronage and prestige; and its corporate Whiteness often militates against an active identification for many Black people in Britain.[44]

This exercise was created in order to bring to life a central idea of Groome's; namely, the notion of inculturation: the expression of the gospel through a specific culture (located in a specific period of time). This process includes the appropriate re-setting of the sacred narrative, bringing the story to life and localizing the story/vision.[45] On this subject Groome writes:

> Christian faith is expressed in peoples' lives through symbols and modes native to their culture. It is a source of transformation for the cultural context – each cultural expression of it renews and enriches the universal Christian community.[46]

In using this exercise, I was able to challenge this group to think about the images, symbols and cultural contexts in which the Christian faith was both expressed and imagined. I impressed upon them the need for people to be empowered to imagine themselves and their accompanying cultures at the centre of the gospel narrative, in ways which counteracted the often marginalized and humiliating status imposed upon them in the wider society.

By using this exercise, I was able to assist the group in posing the question "where am I in this narrative?" followed by the supplementary concern of "and what troubles are we bringing to Jesus?" These questions are of significant import, for they challenge Black people of faith, in experiential terms, to note their proximity to Jesus (what kind of Jesus to whom they related was also noted) and to ask honestly, what, if anything, their faith had to do with the contexts and concerns that informed their lives.

The question was posed in this fashion as, for the majority of group, their faith, like a good deal of Black theology, possessed a very strong Christocentric focus. Jesus was both the means and the focus of their devotion and religious practice.[47]

In using this exercise, I asked the groups to bring their "generative themes" into dialogue with the Bible through imagining themselves in conversation with Jesus and others in small base community meetings/ groups. The purpose of such a small base community setting was in order that they might reflect on the substantive issues for them as people and what forms of actions should follow.

The development of this methodological point of departure, whilst owing a great deal to the work of Groome, is influenced also by Hope and Timmel and their groundbreaking participative community development work in Southern Africa.[48] In the second volume of their quartet of books, the authors explore the role of group work in the process of raising critical consciousness towards the holistic paradigm of individual, group and societal transformation. Group work is identified as a shared activity, not unlike that conceived by Groome, but their emphasis is on practical application as opposed to intellectual theorizing.

In utilizing their methods, I was anxious to create opportunities for shared learning, and for theological insights to emerge from our collaborative conversations across the five separate meetings, involving some fifty persons. Hope and Timmel seek to embody and make operative the searing insights of Paulo Freire and his vision of conscientization of grassroots peoples for the purposes of transformation and radical faith-based praxis.

Central to the task of collaborative group work is the importance of dialogue. Freire says:

> Dialogue also requires an intense faith in human beings; in their power to make and remake, to create and recreate; faith that is the vocation to be fully human is the birthright of all people, and not the privilege of an elite. Founded on love, humility and faith, dialogue becomes a horizontal relationship of mutual trust... Nor can dialogue exist without hope. Hope is rooted in our human incompleteness, from which we move out in constant search, a search which can be carried out only in communion with other people... Finally, true dialogue cannot exist unless it involves critical thinking, thinking which sees reality as process, in transformation, thinking which does not separate itself from action but constantly involves itself in the real struggle without fear of the risks involved.[49]

This process of group work was one in which ordinary Black people were encouraged to reflect theologically, juxtaposing their own faith experiences with Black theology, through the interactive and imaginative re-reading of a biblical text. It was intended to enable them to identify themes and ideas for individual and corporate, critical transformation. This methodological point of departure was informed by Hope and Timmel who argue that

> Group methods are meant to help structure our work time together so that we can learn better ways of uniting our efforts towards the transformation of this world. Group skills can be used to help people become sensitive to how others see them and more realistic about how one sees oneself. For some people, this has become an end in itself, ignoring the need for justice in the wider society. But self-knowledge needs to be seen in relation to the community and our role in it. Methods are not neutral, just as content is not neutral. If we believe that the participation of people is essential in the transformation of society, then our methods must be consistent with the aim: that is participatory education. If we also believe that people need to be involved in transformative action which breaks the structures of domination, then methods must lead to the unveiling of the values and structures which dominate them.[50]

Bible Reading by Means of Participation (John 6:1–15)

So, in this participative approach to undertaking Black theology, using the facility of group work, I encouraged a number of ordinary Black Christians to imaginatively enter into a biblical text. This process was one that encouraged them to dialogue with one another, imaginary others, and Jesus around a topic of concern that the group themselves had identified.

By approaching this biblical text in this fashion, the group was enabled to imagine themselves within the text and to ask critical questions of it in terms of their socio-political, cultural and economic concerns. This particular method was one that assisted these Black people in opening up the Bible to the scrutiny of their fears and concerns. This form of approach can minimize the incidents of cultural dissonance that are often a feature of Diasporan African religious consciousness, particularly in terms of its engagement with sacred texts.[51]

What I mean by this statement is that, for many Black people in Britain, the Bible represents an inviolate world that remains beyond the contaminating stain of context and contemporary experience. Prior to this exercise, several members of the different groups claimed that the Bible had no direct relationship to the Blackness of the people who might be reading it. That in effect, the Bible (and therefore God)[52] has no direct interest in the material realities that affect Black bodies.

In this particular method for undertaking Black theology in the British context, I have attempted to create an approach which enables ordinary Black people to become part of a process that enables them to enter into an active engagement with the biblical text using their performative abilities[53] to bring the text to life.

In the interests of space, I shall offer a fuller set of reflections from only one of the groups (group one), showing how their imaginative reading gave rise to some critical reflections on the meaning of the text and its consequences for socio-political action. In response to their re-structuring of John 6:1–15, I detailed their reflections, seeking to put into narrative form the substance of their inspired conversations. I have written up their disparate reflections into a narrative form that can be read and used in a more practical fashion. Their initial comments were very much episodic in nature, and therefore hard to follow and utilize in their original form.

Prior to offering up the extended narrative of this re-reading of John 6, first let me say something about the "generative themes" which the five different groups developed from their critical analysis of material culled from printed media in Britain. Group one, after much discussion, settled on the theme of the "environment." This theme emerged from the many stories reflecting on the issue of "climate change" and the consequences for the "global south" of the continuing change in climatic conditions on the earth.

For the second group, the issues that arose as their primary concern were capitalism, money and greed. This focus emerged from the many articles and stories concerning the effects of profit maximization on the poor. Why are corporate shareholders seemingly more important than single mothers who are already earning a pittance in particular industries in Britain?

The third group of people were concerned with entertainment and the media. What should be the stance of the church in relation to particular genres of music that seem to glorify in objectifying people? Why are they so much more popular than other, more redemptive pieces of work?

Group four focused on the question of belonging and commitment. What does it mean for the church and other voluntary agencies when many people are over-burdened with countless demands on their time and the old sense of devotion and responsibility to serve others seems to have evaporated?

Finally, group five discussed the issue of time and lifestyles. In what ways are Black Christians expected to be stewards of their time and how is that time spent? Is what we do with our time a theological issue?

I have chosen to concentrate on the reflections from group one as I found their comments very evocative. This, in turn, inspired me to write in a very poetic (or at least I hope so) and challenging way in order find words that did justice to the substance of their conversations.

As the group entered into the text, they imagined what would happen if the issue of "climate change" that arose from their own experiences and analysis of the media was then juxtaposed with this biblical text? How would environmental concerns affect their reading of this text? Utilizing a reader-response[54] approach as outlined in a previous chapter in this book on biblical hermeneutics,[55] I encouraged the group to imagine their way into the text and see how it might read when it is confronted with their concerns.

Clearly, there are always dangers associated with this approach, for one can imagine the all too easy tendency to stretch one's interpretations of the text in order to justify the presuppositions of the reader. The group were very much aware of this temptation. The regulatory factor in the imaginative, re-imaging of this biblical text was provided by the framework provided by Black theology – in particular, a Christocentric focus on justice and liberative praxis.

In short, the group was not re-imaging this text in order to assert an ethnocentric conception of the Christian faith that de-humanizes or limits the creative potential or agency of any other group. At the start of this particular meeting (of group one), two members of the group of ten posed the honest question as to whether this group exercise was about attacking White people? There was some concern that time should not be spent objectifying and traducing others. When the group was enabled and encouraged to relate personal experiences of faith from within the frameworks provided by Black theology, it became clear that the central focus of the day was that of justice and not stereotypical attacks on others. The group utilized James Perkinson[56] and Robert Beckford's[57] respective work on Whiteness as a helpful means of assisting them to differentiate between two central norms in what is often termed "Critical White Studies"; namely, the need to differentiate between challenging White hegemony and the un-earned privileges associated with the socio-cultural construct that is Whiteness, and that of White people. The former is essentially an examination of the specious nature of the untrammelled authority and power of invisible Whiteness that is the conflation of power and the structured template of Euro-American normativity.[58] In terms of the latter, I must admit that I hold to the view that all White people possess un-earned privileges simply from the symbolic power attributed to Whiteness in a world of Eurocentric normativity. But as Beckford reminds us, the individual agency lies within the orbit of every human being, including many radical White people, is one that enables them to act in ways that are consistent with the thrust of justice and equity for all persons. That in short, not all White people have to act in ways that are consonant with the worst excesses of White privilege and hegemony.

In re-reading and re-imaging the biblical text, the group, whilst engaging in their collective hermeneutical work, were careful to ensure that their reflections were in line with the inclusive and justice-orientated liberative praxis of Jesus. In effect, one's utilization of a reader-response approach does not permit one to "do or say what you like" with the text. This was clearly the case with the group in their collective, imaginative re-reading.

Before I offer you the re-written narrative I created in response to the group's extensive hermeneutical discourse, it is worth saying something of the final outcome of the process. Both Hope and Timmel[59] and Freire[60] are clear that the end point of any faithful group-enacted process in critical consciousness raising is not more satisfying and clever forms of thought, but rather, in practical reflective action or praxis. The end for all five groups was the question of what to do next? How would their Black theological reflections lead to further action?

Upon the completion of the exercise (and prior to my writing up the final story of their shared narrative work), the group was asked to construct their action plans for the next three, six and twelve months. The action plans of this group, the first of the five, were summed up in the following three questions.

Questions:
1. In what ways have we failed to acknowledge God's sovereignty over creation?
2. The African American a capella group Sweet Honey in the Rock have a song called "If the Earth could run away." Here, they imagine that the earth is taking flight from the violence that is committed on her by humans. What do you think God is saying to us about our stewardship of the earth and the people that populate it?
3. In what ways can we, as Christians, contribute to developing a more respectful and sustainable attitude to our environment?

In response to question one, participants in the group committed themselves to remain in touch with one another. They were committed, through regular correspondence and meetings, to monitor their own individual and familial behaviour. How can Black people be encouraged to examine their lifestyles and subject them to critical questions of sustainability?

This first pledge was very much at an individual and familial level. Contrastingly, question two called for more strategic action in terms of lobbying members of parliament and possibly joining campaigning groups. As one will see from their re-imagined narrative, for there to be environmental justice, the rich must be forced to share the realities of the poor and experience the effects of environmental racism as it impacts on of the poor – who for the most part, are people of colour. Many in the group committed themselves to joining campaigning groups like Christian Aid, Friends of the Earth and Greenpeace, in the words of one member, "to Blacken them up." It was agreed amongst members of the group that this re-imagined narrative of John 6 had enabled them to re-conceptualize their task as Black Christians in the ongoing task of Christian discipleship to make a difference. That difference was to be made operative at a number of levels.

Whilst some emphasized the "personal action" of question one, and others, the more macro, structural and systemic work of lobbying and campaigning in question two; still others concentrated on the collective response of their churches as outlined in question three. Various members of the group argued that their respective churches could do more in terms of sustainability. Did their churches buy energy-saving light bulbs? Did they have thermostats that could reduce heat waste by regulating temperature? Could their congregation challenge the corporate denomination as a whole to consider its purchasing power in order to persuade companies to amend or change their trading policies?

The group recognized that no one action would automatically serve as an adequate expression of Black theological praxis arising from their re-imagined theological reflections from this particular biblical text. Yet, it was also recognized that one had to start somewhere, and that the content of the actions plans resulting from this one-day event was considerably more than anyone in the group had imagined, prior to their collaborative work.

The final point I would like to make before I offer you the scripted narrative of the creative imaginative hermeneutical work of group one is that the resulting text you are about to read has been checked with the group for its veracity. I was anxious that my creative writing should not transgress the reflections and ethical comments of the group.

This work, like the other participative material in this text and in my former research, is not offered as a piece of scientific, empirical investigation. I am not seeking to make any conclusive proof of objective, reliable and replicable scientific discovery in this work. As I reflect on the writing of this chapter in light of the events that gave rise to it, I am forced to conclude that, with the benefit of hindsight, I would do all manner of things differently if I had the opportunity to do so! I am not a scientist, but a participative educator and theologian. My working methods are often idiosyncratic but not careless or sloppy! I aim to do the best and most rigorous work I can, but in the final analysis, my overarching priority is my concern for people and the belief that all people matter and that God cares for all people. My scripted reflections on John 6:1–15 are not final in any sense. They are simply the outworking of an exciting group exercise with ten ordinary Black people who were encouraged to let their imaginations run free, fired up by the passionate challenge of Black theology.

This re-imagined new reading was achieved in dialogue with a biblical text in which the group themselves became the central agents of change. My pleasure and honour was being the invited guest as this fantastic story unfurled. The continued honour was that of the writer, charged with the frightening and pleasurable task of putting their workshop themes and ideas into story form. It was a truly inspiring moment for us all!

Reflections from Group One: Re-imagining John 6:1–15

When group one were asked to look at the text (John 6:1–15) in light of their own faith, Black theology and an analysis of the media, the issue that ignited their passions was that of the environment. The group reflected what would have happened if they had been a part of the crowd at which climactic conditions had radically altered the very basis on which this type of event had taken place. What would have happened, they surmised, if torrential rain accompanied the meeting? The poor would usually be the ones who would have been at the mercy of the elements. The richer folk would have tents and caravans at this major festival event, at which the main speaker was Jesus.

The group imagined the setting of the narrative as one in which people from a wide geographical area had attended the event. The weather forecast was one of "un-seasonal weather." The organizers have invested too much in the event to cancel it at the last moment. In fact, the local police force and other authorities, concerned for public order and the propensity of an excited and disappointed crowd to riot, may have insisted that the event go ahead as planned.

Sadly, the poor and those unable to make alternative arrangements, such as hiring tents or other forms of covering, or purchasing waterproof clothes, were unable to protect themselves from the falling torrents of rainwater. As Jesus stands amidst the torrents of water, what does he do? For the participants in this group, a Jesus of integrity, who is in solidarity with the poor, leaves the dry confine of the stage where he is safely ensconced from the rain, and joins the poorer folk towards the sides, who are cowering from the deluge falling from the heavens. The poor who are getting wet consist mainly of darker skinned people. Many of them have travelled thousands of miles to be in this country. They were poor in the lands of their birth, and now they are here today, in this country, getting wet and they are still poor.

The richer folk, who are all White, are secreted on the surrounding hills in their expensive tents, trailers and assortment of mobile vehicles; they are sheltering from the rain and are not happy. In moving away from the stage, Jesus has to walk away from the microphone in order not to be electrocuted in the downpour. This means he can no longer be heard by those in the distance.

As Jesus stands amongst the poor, being soaked from head to foot, he shares their concern for the environment. As food is shared amongst the people, he cannot help but notice the incessant rain that is not a common occurrence at this time of the year. He is reminded by the poor that the rich folk on the hill, safely sheltered from the rain in their expensive apparel, are the ones whose greed-filled activities have changed the climate. Yet they are the ones who are dry! It is the poor who are getting wet. One older Black woman shouts out "It's always the poor who end up being the innocent victims of the greed of the rich." Jesus smiles and says, "Ain't that the truth!"

Jesus puts his fingers to his mouth and says 'Ssshh.... Watch what happens now." With this, he crouches down on his haunches and begins to speak in a very low voice amongst the poor. The rich folk on the hill are not best pleased. When Jesus left the stage to go amongst the crowd, they could no longer hear him. A number of them muttered irritatingly that this 'Simply isn't on...We didn't pay all this money hiring tents and motor homes in order to sit here, not being able to hear anything." But at least they could see him. But not now! Now Jesus has crouched down low and he cannot be seen. This makes some of the rich folk very angry. "What is he playing at?" some of them cry. "That man has simply got his priorities wrong" cry many others. A very rich elderly White gentleman resplendent in matching pea-green corduroy trousers, woollen sweater and waterproof footwear exclaims, "Well he can forget my vote now, after this absolute fiasco."

Undeterred and seemingly unconcerned, Jesus continues to hand out food as he walks amongst the poor. The field is getting very muddy and waterlogged due to the rain. Although the rain is continuing to fall, a remarkable thing begins to happen amongst the poor. Some of them begin to sing. "Always look on the bright side of life!" Others begin to join in. "Always look on the bright side of life." The whistling isn't too hot, but nobody really cares. Many of the children begin to dance in the ever widening puddles that are emerging all across the sodden field. Jesus begins to laugh when he is splashed by two young teenagers. He splashes them back and shouts "Got ya... Like I didn't see you comin'!" They run off into the crowd, looking to find some other victims of their pranks. Jesus laughs again. He is wet through.

Despite the rain and the miserable conditions, a carnival atmosphere begins to break out. Many of the poor are simply happy to have Jesus amongst them and are relieved that he understands what they are going through. Jesus also notices the rain and how the increasingly un-seasonal weather is affecting them all. But still, it is only the poor who are getting wet. Meanwhile, up on the hill, the rich are being driven to distraction by their increasing anger. If Jesus does not mind getting wet, then why isn't he walking up the hill to speak with them?

After a short period, a number of the richer people decide that they have had enough of this blatant insult. They came to this event with good intentions and now Jesus is insulting them by "frolicking" amongst the poor and displaying not one ounce of the kind of dignity you would expect to see from someone who has leadership aspirations. "I'm definitely not voting for him," cries one man as he turns on the engine of his large camper van and then finds that it is stuck in the mud.

A number of the rich begin to drive away. Some of them motion to the poorer people down the hill, demanding that they leave their unruly behaviour and come and assist them to move their vehicles, which are stuck in the mud. Many of the rich are calling out to those they recognize as their employees. To their astonishment, the poorer folk at the bottom of the hill are having too much fun basking in the rain and the mud listening to Jesus and enjoying each other's company to come and help their so-called social betters. There will be hell to pay when they go back to work on the following Tuesday. But for now, on this wet Bank Holiday weekend, the mainly Black poor folk are enjoying their moment in the rain. The chant goes out again, "Always look on the bright side of life!" The ironic refrain echoes across the dark skies, overlooking this massed throng of drenched humanity. Poor clothes, which barely looked appealing in the baking sun that had preceded this bank holiday weekend, now look even less appealing when weighed down with dirty water. But no one cares.

After some of the rich folk have managed to get their cars and vans working and others have packed away their tents and vacated the muddy field, some of the more curious amongst the rich decide that they will venture down the hill to hear Jesus. Having come this far, some feel it would be a waste – a missed opportunity even – not to hear what he has to say.

So, some of them, taking off their expensive and ill-suited shoes, begin to tip-toe down the hill towards the riotous action that is opening out before them. Jesus is still walking in a crouched position, his Black matted locks looking somewhat bedraggled in the rain. His dark skin is glimmering underneath his modest work clothes, which are now looking anything but impressive. Can this really be the person who is the supposed spokesperson for the liberal intelligentsia and is the media darling of the glitterati? Looking like this? Acting in this undignified way? Surely not!

Jesus crouches even lower than before so he can speak to the small children and those whose disabilities and infirmities mean they are unable to move very far from where they are sitting on the muddy ground. He tells them that things will change. "We can't go on as we are," he says. The people nod and shout back in agreement. "Damn straight" cries out one man. "Talk, mek dem hear" cries another older woman.

By this time, the richer folk are coming down the hill. They, too, are now getting wet. The rain is becoming something of a leveller, in that it is soaking everyone. The rich folk, who are getting wet as they walk down the hill, choose to do so! The poor never had any choice in the first place. They simply got wet!

Soon, the rich have arrived at the edge of the muddy party. A woman, in what one can imagine was a rather expensive dress which is now drenched in mud, stands looking at the scene in a very nervous manner. Her pale White skin is at variance with the preponderance of darker skinned people all looking at her intently from their muddy perches on the waterlogged earth. Her husband, a rather rotund man, looking very flustered having had more exercise than is his want, slipping and sliding down the hill, is stood cowering behind her. They look on at the mainly poorer Black folk sat around in the mud. They party has stopped. The crowd are looking at the rich couple and the numbers of others slowly making their way down the hill in the distance.

An elderly Black woman takes out a paper plate from a plastic bag and places some snapper fish and two fried dumplins onto it. She hands it to the woman and says, "Com' darlin' yu look lik yu cud do with a good feed. Mi sarry yu 'ave no place fi sit." The woman accepts the plate of food and begins to pick at the fish. Meanwhile, a younger Black man hands a glass of sorrel to the husband. "Watch it," he says, "Mikey overdid the rum when he was making it this morning."

Mikey is not impressed. "I didn't hear you complaining when you were wapsing it down a short while ago." The couple join the party.

Jesus looks on at the mainly White people making their way down the hill through the ripples of mud and debris in the over-ploughed field. "Today we party," he says. "We all party. There is enough to go around, as we all get wet together. But tomorrow, when the party is finished and we all have to go back to where we came from and what we were doing, the difficult task of living really begins. There is plenty of work to be done. Things cannot go on like this. Something's gotta give. We are all in this together."

Notes

Prologue

1. I accept as an intellectual proposition that there are other ways of conceiving Black theology in methodological terms. Indeed, the Philosophical or Human Sciences schools of Black theology would not identify Liberation as the dominant generative theme in terms of how one conceives Black theology, and some would eschew its dependence on Christian-inspired themes and its constant recourse to the Bible and the norms of Liberation as understood from within a Judeo-Christian framework. See Frederick L. Ware, *Methodologies of Black Theology* (Cleveland, OH: Pilgrim Press, 2002) for further details on the various methodological points of departure in the different schools of Black theology. In aligning myself with the most dominant of the three approaches outlined by Ware, namely, the "hermeneutical school," I would want to assert that this model is most representative of the bulk of scholars who would identify themselves with the cause of Black theology. In making this claim, I in no way wish to diminish the importance and value of other approaches or perspectives to Black theology. Even if one does not anchor one's methodological approach on an ongoing dialogue with the Christian tradition or use Liberation as the dominant generative theme, I am still convinced that the broader notions of emancipation and full life remain the overarching goal for all forms of *genuine* Black theology, as conceived within the tripartite typologies outlined by Ware. It is also worth noting the comparative schemas developed by many Caribbean theologians such as Kortright Davis, *Emancipation Still Comin'* (Maryknoll, NY: Orbis Books, 1990); Noel Erskine, *Decolonizing Theology* (Maryknoll, NY: Orbis Books, 1983); Lewin Williams, *Caribbean Theology* (Frankfurt: Peter Lang, 1994). South African perspectives include Allan Boesak, *Farewell to Innocence: A Socio-ethical Study on Black Theology and Black Power* (Maryknoll, NY: Orbis Books, 1977); Itumeleng J. Mosala, *Biblical Hermeneutics and Black Theology in South Africa* (Grand Rapids: Eerdmans, 1989); Itumeleng J. Mosala and Buti Tlhagale, eds, *The Unquestionable Right to be Free: Black Theology From South Africa* (Maryknoll, NY: Orbis Books, 1986).

2. See Anthony G. Reddie, *Nobodies to Somebodies: A Practical Theology for Education and Liberation* (Peterborough: Epworth Press, 2003).

3. See Anthony G. Reddie, *Dramatizing Theologies: A Participative Approach to Black God-Talk* (London: Equinox, 2006).

4. See Anthony Reddie, *Growing into Hope: Christian Education in Multi-ethnic Churches. Vol. 1: Believing and Expecting* (Peterborough: Methodist Publishing House, 1998) and *Growing into Hope: Christian Education in Multi-ethnic Churches. Vol. 2: Liberation and Change* (Peterborough: Methodist Publishing House, 1998).

5. See Reddie, *Dramatizing Theologies*, 129–61.

6. See Anthony Reddie, *Acting in Solidarity: Reflections in Critical Christianity* (London: Darton, Longman and Todd, 2005), xi–xv. See also Anthony G. Reddie, *Black*

Theology in Transatlantic Dialogue (New York and Basingstoke: Palgrave Macmillan, 2006), 8–13.

7. Anthony G. Reddie, "Editorial," *Black Theology: An International Journal* 4, no. 2 (2006): 135–37.

8. One of the most influential people in my intellectual development has been the African American educator James A. Banks, whose long and distinguished career has been devoted to looking at how education as an ideological enterprise can shape the consciousness of (particularly) adult learners, around issues of "race" and culture. See James A. Banks, *Race, Culture and Education: The Selected Works* (London and New York: Routledge, 2006).

9. John Ruskin (1819–1900) was an essayist, social critic and a Christian socialist whose wide interests spanned art criticism, the arts and crafts movement in Britain and education. One of his chief legacies was the foundation of Ruskin College, in Oxford. Ruskin is an independent educational college (not part of Oxford University) that specializes in providing opportunities for adults with little or no previous formal education. Ruskin has been an important resource for the political left in Britain, improving the educational attainment of Trade Union activists and Labour Party politicians such as Dennis Skinner and John Prescott. See John Ruskin, *Letters Addressed to a College Friend during the Years 1840–1845* (London: George Allen, 1894). See also Programme for Research and Actions on the Development of the Labour Market, *Developing Support Structure for Workers' Cooperatives / by Trade Union Research Unit, Ruskin College* (Luxembourg: Office for Official Publications of the European Communities, 1986).

10. See Kenneth Cracknell, *Our Doctrines: Methodist Theology as Classical Christianity* (Calver: Cliff College Publishing, 1998), 68–74.

11. See Margaret Jones, "Growing in Grace and Holiness," in *Unmasking Methodist Theology*, eds Clive Marsh, Brian Beck, Angela Shier-Jones and Helen Wareing (New York and London: Continuum, 2004), 155–65.

12. See Reddie, *Black Theology in Transatlantic Dialogue*, 8–13.

13. I was briefly a member of the Socialist Workers Party (SWP) at University and was much influenced by the left-wing sentiments of Revd Dr Stuart Burgess, the Methodist Chaplain at the University of Birmingham in the 1980s. Whilst it would be unfair, and inaccurate, to describe the Methodist Society (Meth. Soc.) at the time as being "left wing," it did seem to me that there existed a distinct left-of-centre bias amongst the students at the time, many of whom were trying to link their Christian faith to social activism. Many of us were also members of the "Student Christian Movement" (SCM) and committed to Christian Aid and issues of Fair Trade.

14. A major service marking the slave trade was held in London at the City Hall, on August 23, 2007, which is often seen as "Emancipation Day" amongst African and Caribbean people of the Commonwealth. Many postcolonial activists consider the August 23 date to be preferable to the March 25 date (on which the National Commemoration service was held) as the former marked the "full" (of a fashion) emancipation of enslaved Africans in the Caribbean, in 1838, as opposed to March 25, 1807, when only the slave trade itself was abolished, which still left enslaved Africans in their existing condition. At the Commemoration service at the City Hall on August 23, the (then) Lord Mayor Ken Livingstone apologised unreservedly for the slave trade and

the continuing effects that slavery continues to exert on the life experiences of many Black people in Britain and across the world.

15. See Reddie, *Dramatizing Theologies*, 14–22.

16. See Donald M. Chinula, *Building King's Beloved Community: Foundations for Pastoral Care and Counselling with the Oppressed* (Cleveland, OH: United Church Press, 1997).

17. See Gayraud S. Wilmore, *Pragmatic Spirituality: The Christian Faith through an Afrocentric Lens* (New York: New York University Press, 2003).

18. Wilmore, *Pragmatic Spirituality*, 4–5.

19. See Allan A. Boesak and Charles Villa-Vicencio, *When Prayer Makes News: Churches and Apartheid – A Call to Prayer* (Philadelphia: Westminister Press, 1986).

20. Boesak and Villa-Vicencio, *When Prayer Makes News*, 1.

21. See Robert Beckford, *Dread and Pentecostal: A Political Theology for the Black Church in Britain* (London: SPCK, 2000).

22. Beckford, *Dread and Pentecostal*, 173–74.

Chapter 1

1. See Mike Phillips and Trevor Phillips, *Windrush: The Irresistible Rise of Multi-racial Britain* (London: HarperCollins, 1999).

2. See Emmanuel Y. Lartey, *In Living Colour: An Intercultural Approach to Pastoral Care and Counselling* (London: Cassell, 1997), 9–18.

3. See "Introduction," in Anthony G. Reddie, *Black Theology in Transatlantic Dialogue: Inside Looking Out, Outside Looking* (New York: Palgrave Macmillan, 2006).

4. See Robert Beckford, *Dread and Pentecostal* (London: SPCK, 2000).

5. Like the editor of this text, the collective and corporate nature of Methodist theological method has shaped my own particular approach to the doing of theology. See Angela Shier-Jones, *A Work in Progress: Methodists Doing Theology* (Peterborough: Epworth Press, 2005). See also Anthony G. Reddie, *Dramatizing Theologies: A Participative Approach to Black God-Talk* (London: Equinox, 2006).

6. See Joe Aldred, *Respect: Understanding Caribbean British Christianity* (Peterborough: Epworth Press, 2005).

7. See Kate O. Coleman, "Exploring Metissage: A Theological Anthropology of Black Christian Women's Subjectivities in Postcolonial Britain" (unpublished PhD thesis, University of Birmingham, 2006). See also the website of "Ligali" – who describe themselves thus: "Ligali (*pronounced lee-ga-lee*) is the African British Equality Authority. We are a Pan African Human Rights Organisation that challenge the misrepresentation of African people and culture in the British media. Our remit is to actively campaign for cultural, economic, political and social justice on behalf of the African community." They prefer the term "African British." See http://www.ligali.org/ for more information.

8. See Reddie, *Black Theology in Transatlantic Dialogue*, 92–102.

9. See Anthony Reddie, *Growing into Hope: Christian Education in Multi-ethnic Churches. Vol. 1: Believing and Expecting* (Peterborough: Methodist Publishing House, 1998) and *Growing into Hope: Christian Education in Multi-ethnic Churches. Vol. 2: Liberation and Change* (Peterborough: Methodist Publishing House, 1998). See also

Anthony G. Reddie, *Nobodies to Somebodies: A Practical Theology for Education and Liberation* (Peterborough: Epworth Press, 2003).

10. See Michael N. Jagessar and Anthony G. Reddie, eds, *Postcolonial Black British Theology* (Peterborough: Epworth Press, 2007), xiii–xiv.

11. Jagessar and Reddie, *Postcolonial Black British Theology*.

12. Reddie, *Black Theology in Transatlantic Dialogue*, 160–64.

13. See Michael N. Jagessar and Anthony G. Reddie, eds, *Black Theology in Britain: A Reader* (London: Equinox, 2007).

14. See chapter 6 "Black Churches as Counter-cultural Agencies."

15. Jil Brown was a promising Black British Womanist theologian who died tragically of a brain haemorrhage in October 1999, aged 31. A book, which contained many of her unpublished work, was edited in her honour. See Anthony G. Reddie, ed., *Legacy: In Memory of Jillian Brown* (Peterborough: Methodist Publishing House, 2000).

16. Anthony G. Reddie, "The Christian Education of African Caribbean Children in Birmingham: Creating a New Paradigm Through Developing Better Praxis" (unpublished PhD thesis, University of Birmingham, 2000).

17. I accept that being "Black" or trying to understand the conceptual realities of what constitutes "Blackness" are not simple propositions and indeed have given rise to myriad reflections and scholarly discussion. In this work, I am not seeking to operate within a reductive vein regarding the conceptual understanding of "Black"; rather, I simply want to propose a tactical heuristic as a means of undertaking this conversation and providing Black British people with an initial point of departure. For further thoughts on the term "Black," see Algernon Austin, *Achieving Blackness: Race, Black Nationalism and Afrocentrism in the Twentieth Century* (New York and London: New York University Press, 2006).

18. I am forced to admit that this is a major generalization, but the recent statistical figures on religious observance in Britain clearly demonstrate the overwhelmingly Christian complexion of Black British communities since 1948. The growing percentage of Black people in historic mainline churches alongside the growth of neo-Pentecostalism is testament to the realization that "Black Christianity" in Britain is a phenomenon of major import. This text is an attempt to speak to the developments of the phenomenon and to demonstrate how Black theology can be of service in providing the much needed critical insights of this growth.

19. This work, like all my scholarly research, is undertaken from a subjective-insider's perspective, using personal narrative, experience, dialogue and accessible reportage as methods for undertaking Black theological discourse.

20. See Jagessar and Reddie, *Postcolonial Black British Theology*, xxi–xxii.

21. See Peter Brierley, ed., *The UK Christian Handbook: Religious Trends*, 2002/2003 (London: Christian Research, 2003). See also Joe Aldred's report entitled "Stronger Together, Weaker Apart" at http://www.churches-together.net/Publisher/File.aspx?id=12445

22. Aldred, *Respect*.

23. Mark Sturge, *Look What The Lord Has Done!* (London: Scripture Union, 2005).

24. See Robert E. Hood, *Must God Remain Greek? Afro-Cultures and God-Talk* (Minneapolis: Fortress Press, 1991).

25. What Frederick Ware terms the "hermeneutical school." See Frederick L. Ware, *Methodologies of Black Theology* (Cleveland, OH: Pilgrim Press, 2002), 28–65.

26. Jagessar and Reddie, *Postcolonial Black British Theology*, xvii.

27. See Anthony B. Pinn, *Varieties of African American Religious Experience* (Minneapolis: Fortress Press, 1998).

28. See Ware, *Methodologies of Black Theology*, 28–65.

29. See Ware, *Methodologies of Black Theology*, for an assessment of the different methodological and thematic approaches to Black theology that do not draw exclusively on Hebrew and Christian Scriptures and the traditions that emerge from the former.

30. See chapter 1 of Jagessar and Reddie, *Black Theology in Britain*.

31. See Anthony B. Pinn and Dwight N. Hopkins, eds, *Loving the Body: Black Religious Studies and the Erotic* (New York: Palgrave, 2005); Kelly Brown Douglas, *What's Faith Got To Do With It?* (Maryknoll, NY: Orbis Books, 2005).

32. See Dwight N. Hopkins, *Being Human* (Minneapolis: Fortress Press, 2005), 118–59.

33. African American Black theologian, Dwight Hopkins offers a very helpful and nuanced perspective on "being human" and the myriad ways in which this common phenomenon is impacted on and responds to the complex factors of "race," ethnicity, cultures and religion, across the many contours of the globe. See Hopkins, *Being Human*.

34. The work of rehabilitating the Black body has been undertaken to excellent effect by Pinn and Hopkins, *Loving the Body*.

35. See Emmanuel Lartey, "After Stephen Lawrence: Characteristics and Agenda for Black Theology," *Black Theology: A Journal of Contextual Praxis* 3 (1999): 79–91.

36. See "The Pentecost Narrative from a Black Theological Perspective" in chapter 4 of Reddie, *Black Theology in Transatlantic Dialogue*.

37. See Emmanuel Lartey, "Editorial," *Black Theology: A Journal of Contextual Praxis* 1 (1998): 7–9. See also Lartey, "After Stephen Lawrence," 79–91.

38. See Sturge, *Look What The Lord Has Done!*

39. See Aldred, *Respect*.

40. The term "Womanist" was coined by African American woman writer Alice Walker as a way of defining the subjectivity of Black women in the US. See Alice Walker, *The Color Purple* (London: Women's Press, 1983) and *In Search of our Mothers' Gardens: Womanist Prose* (London: Women's Press, 1984).

41. Womanist theology is the theological articulation of God as understood through the lens of the experiences of Black (predominantly African American) women. It seeks to address the tripartite jeopardy of being Black, female and poor in the wealthiest nation in the world. Significant Womanist theological texts include Delores Williams, *Sisters in the Wilderness: The Challenge of Womanist God-Talk* (Maryknoll, NY: Orbis Books, 1993). See also Kelly Brown Douglas, *The Black Christ* (Maryknoll, NY: Orbis Books, 1994); Emile Townes, *Womanist Justice, Womanist Hope* (Atlanta, GA: Scholars Press, 1993); Renita J. Weems, *Just a Sister Away: A Womanist Vision of Women's Relationships in the Bible* (Philadelphia: Innisfree Press, 1988); Katie G. Cannon, *Black Womanist Ethics* (Atlanta, GA: Scholars Press, 1988).

42. See Walter Raushenbusch, *Christianity and the Social Crisis* (New York: Association Press, 1912).

43. See Ludwig Feuerbach, *The Essence of Christianity* (New York: Harper and Row, 1957).

44. See Paulo Freire, *Pedagogy of the Oppressed* (New York: Herder and Herder, 1993).

45. See Gustavo Gutteriez, *A Theology of Liberation* (Maryknoll, NY: Orbis Books, 1973).

46. See Joel Edwards, ed., *Let's Praise Him Again* (Eastbourne: Kingsway Publications, 1992).

47. See Reddie, *Nobodies to Somebodies*, 67–73.

48. See Robert Beckford, *Jesus is Dread* (London: Darton, Longman and Todd, 1998).

49. Reddie, *Dramatizing Theologies*.

50. See Sturge, *Look What The Lord Has Done!*, 113–34.

51. A traditional Jamaican aphorism which when translated has an approximate meaning of "when things reach their heated conclusion."

52. See Pinn and Hopkins, *Loving the Body*.

53. See James H. Cone, *A Black Theology of Liberation* (Maryknoll, NY: Orbis Books, 1986).

54. See Williams *Sisters in the Wilderness*.

55. See Beckford, *Dread and Pentecostal*.

56. James H. Cone, *God of the Oppressed* (SanFrancisco: Harper, 1975), 183–94.

57. Williams, *Sisters in the Wilderness* (Maryknoll, NY: Orbis Books, 1993), 161–77.

58. See Joe Aldred, "Paradigms for a Black Theology," *Black Theology: A Journal of Contextual Praxis* 2 (April 1999): 9–32.

59. See chapter 5 of Reddie, *Black Theology in Transatlantic Dialogue*.

60. Verbatim comment made by the Revd Dr Inderjit Bhogal, the former Director of the Urban Theology Unit, in Sheffield.

61. Beckford, *Dread and Pentecostal*, 67–130. See also Anne H. Pinn and Anthony B. Pinn, *Black Church History* (Minneapolis: Fortress Press, 2002).

62. See Valentina Alexander, "Onesimus's Letter to Philemon," *Black Theology: A Journal of Contextual Praxis* 4 (2000): 61–65.

63. Alexander, "Onesimus's Letter to Philemon," 61–62.

64. See Robert Beckford, *Jesus Dub* (London: Routledge, 2006).

65. Robert Beckford, *God and the Gangs* (London: Darton, Longman and Todd, 2004), 18–28.

66. Reddie, *Nobodies to Somebodies*, 132–40.

67. Ibid., 132–40.

68. Ibid., 132–40.

69. Ibid., 139–40.

70. See Robert Beckford, *God of the Rahtid* (London: Darton, Longman and Todd, 2001), 1–30.

71. Kenneth Leech, *Race: Changing Society and the Church* (London: SPCK, 2005), 102–11.

72. See William R. Hertzog II, *Jesus, Justice and the Reign of God: A Ministry of Liberation* (Louisville, KY: Westminster John Knox Press, 2000).

73. See Reddie, *Growing into Hope: Vol. 2*, 40–62.

74. See Lewis V. Baldwin, *Toward the Beloved Community* (Cleveland, OH: Pilgrim Press, 1995).

75. I actually prefer the term "participative," as will be deduced from several of the chapters that follow.

76. Gayraud S. Wilmore, *Pragmatic Spirituality: The Christian Faith through an Africentric Lens* (New York and London: New York University Press, 2004).

77. See Joseph Washington, *Black Religion* (Boston: Beacon Books, 1964).

78. See Donald M. Chinula, *Building King's Beloved Community* (Cleveland, OH: United Church Press, 1997).

79. See Pinn, *Varieties of African American Religious Experience*.

80. Pinn, *Varieties of African American Religious Experience*, 1–10.

81. See Douglas, *What's Faith Got To Do With It?*, 3–65.

82. See Chapter 7 on Violence against the other.

83. I am indebted to Randall Bailey, Professor of Hebrew Bible at the Interdenominational Theological Center, Atlanta, Georgia, for this insight. In a public lecture given at the University of Birmingham (March 2005), Bailey poses the question as to whether the endemic violence against women and the "other" in the Hebrew canon can be attributed to the violent propensities of a jealous God of wrath who permeates the pages of this section of the Bible? When is jealousy ever a positive emotion that leads to enlightened and thoughtful behaviour and actions, asked Bailey?

84. My own religious and theological position can be deduced from my last sole authored text, where I argue against the compatibility of Evangelicalism and Black theology. See Reddie, *Black Theology in Transatlantic Dialogue*, 35–38.

85. Reddie, *Black Theology in Transatlantic Dialogue*, 68–70.

86. See Dianne M. Stewart, *Three Eyes for the Journey: African Dimensions of the Jamaican Religious Experience* (New York: Oxford University Press, 2005) for an excellent study on the nature of the religious experience of Jamaican/Caribbean peoples, which extends beyond the mere efficacy of Christianity.

87. See Cone, *A Black Theology of Liberation*, 6.

88. See Reddie, *Dramatizing Theologies*, 10–25.

Chapter 2

1. See Anthony G. Reddie, *Acting in Solidarity: Reflections in Critical Christianity* (London: Darton, Longman and Todd, 2005), 72–74.

2. Margaret Jones, "Growing in Grace and Holiness," in Clive Marsh et al., eds, *Unmasking Methodist Theology* (London and New York: Continuum, 2004), 155–65.

3. Reddie, *Acting in Solidarity*, 59–67.

4. I am at pains to add that as all memory is selective, it should not be doubted that this reminiscence carries within it a healthy dose of historical revisionism. My recollections are filtered through a consciousness that is informed by my current practice and reflections as a Black British Liberation theologian.

5. See Clarence E. Hardy III, *James Baldwin's God: Sex, Hope, and Crisis in Black Holiness Culture* (Knoxville, TN: University of Tennessee Press, 2003).

6. See Dwight N. Hopkins, *Down, Up and Over: Slave Religion and Black Theology* (Minneapolis: Fortress Press, 2000), 13–50.

7. See Tissa Balasuriya, *The Eucharist and Human Liberation* (London: SCM Press, 1979). See also Inderjit S. Bhogal, *A Table For All* (Sheffield: Penistone Publications, 2000), 11–34.

8. See John W. De Gruchy, *Reconciliation: Restoring Justice* (London: SCM Press, 2002), 44–76.

9. See Anthony B. Pinn and Dwight N. Hopkins, eds, *Loving the Body: Black Religious Studies and the Erotic* (New York: Palgrave/Macmillan, 2005) for a challenging and insightful analysis of Christianity and Black Church traditions that have demonized the Black body, even within supposedly liberative agendas such as Black theology and Womanist theology.

10. See Anthony B. Pinn, *Terror and Triumph: The Nature of Black Religion* (Minneapolis: Fortress Press, 2003), 27–80.

11. I am indebted to Randall Bailey, Professor of Hebrew Bible at the Interdenominational Theological Center, for this insight.

12. See Demetrius K. Williams, *An End to This Strife: The Politics of Gender in African American Churches* (Minneapolis: Fortress Press, 2004).

13. See Philip F. Esler, *Galatians* (London: Routledge, 1998).

14. See Balasuriya, *The Eucharist and Human Liberation*.

15. Bhogal, *A Table For All*, 11–34.

16. See Tissa Balasuriya, "Liberation of the Affluent," *Black Theology: An International Journal* 1, no.1 (November 2002): 83–113.

17. See James H. Cone, *God of the Oppressed* (New York: Seabury Press, 1975).

18. See James H. Cone and Gayraud S. Wilmore, *Black Theology: A Documentary History. Vol. 1 1966–1979* (Maryknoll, NY: Orbis Books, 1992).

19. See Hopkins, *Down, Up and Over* and Dwight N. Hopkins and George Cummings, eds, *Cut Loose Your Stammering Tongue: Black Theology and Slave Narratives* (Maryknoll, NY: Orbis Books, 1991).

20. W.E.B. Dubois, *The Souls of Black Folk* (New York: Bantam Books, 1989), 3.

21. See Robert E. Hood, *Begrimed and Black: Christian Traditions on Blacks and Blackness* (Minneapolis: Fortress Press, 1994). See also Gay L. Byron, *Symbolic Blackness and Ethnic Difference in Early Christian Literature* (New York: Routledge, 2002).

22. Byron, *Symbolic Blackness and Ethnic Difference*.

23. See Balasuriya "Liberation of the Affluent," 83–113.

24. In challenging White Evangelicalism, I am not juxtaposing this with White liberalism. My attack on White Evangelicalism is due to its proximity to and relationship with Black bodies and Black religious experience. I have failed to mention White Liberal theology in this study because, for the most part, it has been irrelevant to Black religious sensibilities. The non-realist interpretations of Christianity that are evident within aspects of White Liberalism has never found favour with the bulk of Black Christian religious experience, which for the most part, coheres with (without being synonymous in any substantive way – see Robert Beckford *Dread and Pentecostal* [London: SPCK, 2000] and Cone, *God of the Oppressed*) White Evangelicalism.

25. It is my contention that the creeds, particularly the Nicene Creed, tells us more about the capitulation of the Christian Church to the top-down patrician elements of Roman Imperial rule than they do about a Galilean Jew in a politically charged context that resisted colonial occupation. Is it any wonder, then, that the Creeds fail to mention the Jesus of History and his liberating praxis, when a good deal of his actions and teachings critique the very top-down imperial support of the powerful and wealthy at the expense of the poor and the marginalized that is evidenced in the very formation of the Council at Nicea and later at Constantinople? See Mark Lewis Taylor's *The Executed*

God: The Way of the Cross in Lockdown America (Minneapolis: Fortress Press, 2001), 70–98 and 127–54.

26. Comment made by Professor John M. Hull in an address to the annual Conference of the British Methodist Church, Southport, 1999.

27. See Kenneth Cracknell, *Our Doctrines: Methodist Theology as Classical Christianity* (Calver, Hope Valley: Cliff College Publishing, 1998).

28. See Taylor, *The Executed God*, 70–98. See also William R. Hertzog II, *Jesus, Justice and the Reign of God: A Ministry of Liberation* (Louisville, KY: Westminster John Knox Press, 2000).

29. "Black Power: Statement by The National Committee of Negro Churchmen, July 31, 1966." Wilmore and Cone, *Black Theology: A Documentary History, 1966–1979*, 24.

30. James H. Cone, "Theology's Great Sin: Silence in the Face of White Supremacy," *Black Theology: An International Journal* 2, no. 2 (July 2004), 139–52.

31. James H. Cone, *A Black Theology of Liberation* (Maryknoll, NY: Orbis Books, 1990), 6.

32. See Cone, *A Black Theology of Liberation*. See also Cone, *God of the Oppressed*.

33. JoAnne Marie Terrell, *Power in the Blood?: The Cross in the African American Experience* (Maryknoll, NY: Orbis Books, 1998), 17–34.

34. See "Christian Jargon" in Reddie, *Acting in Solidarity*, 59–67.

35. Of course it should be noted that *not all* White Evangelicals can be accused of the theological myopia I have just described. One can point to the indefatigable work of such individuals as William Wilberforce, Thomas Clarkson, John Newton and The Clapham Set in South London as notable exceptions to the argument I am proposing. Having acknowledged the dangers of over-generalization, however, it worth noting that these examples (as fine as they are) do not invalidate the contention that this theological myopia was and, to a great extent, remains the norm for White Evangelicalism. One only has to note the actions of the President George W. Bush (a self-avowed White Evangelical) whose personal professions of "being saved" are not affected unduly by any attempt to match the liberating praxis of Jesus with his personal piety. It should also be noted that the likes of Wilberforce, Clarkson or Wesley, whilst abhorring the slave trade, did not believe in equality between Whites and Blacks. Their thinking was still infused by a White Eurocentric supremacist framework that believed that White people were inherently superior to Blacks. Their work was one of moral rectification not societal restructuring or equity between the "races."

36. Cone, *God of the Oppressed*, 134; original italics.

37. See Mokgethi Motlhabi, "The Problem of Ethical Method in Black Theology," *Black Theology: An International Journal*, 2, no.1 (January 2004): 57–72. Motlhabi assesses the ethical method of five Black theologians, including James Cone. He is of the opinion that Cone's work represents the most consistent ethical method for articulating a sustainable praxis for Black theology.

38. See Cone, *God of the Oppressed*.

39. See Jacquelyn Grant, *White Women's Christ and Black Women's Jesus* (Atlanta: Scholar's Press, 1989).

40. See Beckford, *Dread and Pentecostal*.

41. When presenting this paper to the monthly "Black Theology Forum" (which I chair) that meets at the Queen's Foundation for Ecumenical Theological Education (in

Birmingham, UK), I was asked by a number of respondents about the question of "forgiveness." I have to confess that such thoughts did not enter my mind when writing this paper. My reluctance to engage with the issue is due to the propensity for White hegemony to "impose" upon Black people the necessity of forgiving, without entering into any significant attempt to engage in "restorative justice" (perhaps reparations is a more politically charged term) as a prelude to and as an outcome of forgiveness. In effect, forgiveness becomes yet more empty rhetoric. My colleague at Queen's, Dr Mukti Barton, reminded me that in the Jewish tradition forgiveness is seen to belong within the divine purposes of God (and is something left to God to effect) and is not something into which the victims themselves enter. One can see something of this tradition in evidence in Jesus' words on the cross. Jesus asks the Father to forgive those who have crucified him. Jesus himself does not forgive (Lk. 23:34). The work of Black Pastoral theologians, such as Edward P. Wimberly, have demonstrated the importance of forgiveness as a means of the oppressed to gain psychic healing from the internalized bitterness and corrosive nature of hatred and enmity. (See Edward P. Wimberly, *Relational Refugees: Alienation and Reincorporation in African American Churches and Communities* [Nashville, TN: Abingdon Press, 2000].) But I am quite clear that forgiveness is something that comes from God – it is incumbent upon those who have or are being oppressed, to forgive, as a basis for their own healing. This is somewhat different from being morally obliged to do so, as a form of imposition, by those who have or are exploiting you.

42. See Eric Williams, *Capitalism and Slavery* (London: Andre Deutsch, 1964). See also Walter Rodney, *How Europe Underdeveloped Africa* (London: Bogle-L'Ouverture Publications, 1972).

43. See Anthony G. Reddie, "Pentecost: Dreams and Visions (A Black Theological Reading)," in *Discovering Christ: Ascension and Pentecost*, ed. Maureen Edwards (Birmingham: International Bible Reading Association, 2001), 27–42.

44. Pinn, *Terror and Triumph*, 27–80.

45. See Luke chapters 16–18 for Jesus' many injunctions against riches and people who are rich.

46. See Lamin Sanneh and Joel A. Carpenter, eds, *The Changing Face of Christianity: Africa, the West, and the World* (Oxford: Oxford University Press, 2005).

47. See Delores Williams, *Sisters in the Wilderness* (Maryknoll, NY: Orbis Books, 1993).

48. Williams, *Sisters in the Wilderness*, 161–67.

49. See Grant, *White Women's Christ and Black Women's Jesus*.

50. Grant, *White Women's Christ and Black Women's Jesus*, 195–230.

51. Grant, *White Women's Christ and Black Women's Jesus*, 215.

52. See Kelly Brown Douglas, *The Black Christ* (Maryknoll, NY: Orbis Books, 1994), 110–12.

53. See Michael Battle and Tony Campolo, *The Church Enslaved: A Spirituality of Racial Reconciliation* (Minneapolis: Fortress Press, 2005).

54. See Reddie, *Acting in Solidarity*, 38–45.

Chapter 3

1. See James H. Cone, *A Black Theology of Liberation* (Maryknoll, NY: Orbis Books, 1986).

2. See Kwok Pui-Lan's excellent text in this regard. Kwok Pui-Lan, *Postcolonial Imagination and Feminist Theology* (Louisville, KY: Westminster John Knox, 2005).

3. See Dwight Hopkins for an imaginative and incisive exploration of the shared and complex nature of what it means to be a human being. See Dwight N. Hopkins, *Being Human: Race, Culture and Religion* (Minneapolis: Fortress Press, 2005).

4. See Robert E. Hood, *Must God Remain Greek?: Afro-Cultures and God-Talk* (Minneapolis: Fortress Press, 1990). See also Gay L. Byron, *Symbolic Blackness and Ethnic Difference in Early Christian Literature* (New York: Routledge, 2002).

5. See Kenneth Cracknell, *Our Doctrines: Methodist Theology as Classical Christianity* (Calver: Cliff College Publishing, 1998).

6. See Anthony G. Reddie, *Faith, Stories and the Experience of Black Elders* (London: Jessica Kingsley, 2001), where I argue that Black Caribbean Christian faith is generally possessed of a dialectical quality that sees God in the ordinary and the mundane and in the work of the spirits that are beyond the conventional boundaries of the human senses.

7. See Albert J. Raboteau, *Slave Religion* (New York: Oxford University Press, 1978).

8. See Hood, *Must God Remain Greek?*

9. See Robert Beckford, *Dread and Pentecostal* (London: SPCK, 2000).

10. Cheryl Bridges Johns, *Pentecostal Formation: A Pedagogy among the Oppressed* (Sheffield: Sheffield Academic Press, 1998), 62–137.

11. Beckford, *Dread and Pentecostal*, 168–82.

12. Peter J. Paris, *The Spiritualities of African Peoples: The Search for a Common Moral Discourse* (Minneapolis: Fortress Press, 1995), 27–57.

13. Brigid M. Sackey, "Spiritual Deliverance as a Form of Health Delivery: A Case Study of the Solid Rock Chapel International," *Black Theology in Britain: A Journal of Contextual Praxis* 4, no. 2 (May 2002): 150–71.

14. See Hood, *Must God Remain Greek?*

15. See Dianne M. Stewart, *Three Eyes for the Journey: African Dimensions of the Jamaican Religious Experience* (New York: Oxford University Press, 2005).

16. Jurgen Moltmann, *Theology of Hope: On the Ground and the Implications of a Christian Eschatology* (London: SCM Press, 1967).

17. See A. Elaine Brown Crawford, *Hope in the Holler: A Womanist Theology* (Louisville, KY: Westminster John Knox, 2002).

18. See Stephen M. Hart and Wen-chin Ouyang, *A Companion to Magical Realism* (Woodbridge: Tamesis, 2005).

19. See Anthony G. Reddie, *Nobodies to Somebodies: A Practical Theology for Education and Liberation* (Peterborough: Epworth Press, 2003), 11–13.

20. See Robert Beckford, *God of the Rahtid* (London: Darton, Longman and Todd, 2001), 10–24. See also Robert Beckford, *Jesus Dub: Theology, Music and Social Change* (London: Routledge, 2006).

21. This narrative thread can be seen some of Robert Beckford works. See Beckford, *Jesus Dub*, 28–62. See also Mukti Barton, *Rejection, Resistance and Resurrection: Speaking Out on Racism in the Church* (London: Darton, Longman and Todd, 2005).

22. Barton, *Rejection, Resistance and Resurrection*, 30.

23. It is not uncommon for many Caribbean people to be given "pet names," which become the popular means of identification of the person, often-times, in preference to their given "Christian" names.

24. See Anthony G. Reddie, "An Unbroken Thread of Experience," in *Family And All That Stuff*, ed. Joan King (Birmingham: National Christian Education Council [NCEC], 1998), 153–60.

25. See Carol Tomlin, *Black Language and Style in Sacred and Secular Contexts* (New York: Caribbean Diaspora Press, 1999), 103–24.

26. See Richard Werbner, ed., *Memory and the Postcolony* (London: Zed Books, 1998).

27. See Lewis V. Baldwin, *Towards the Beloved Community: Martin Luther King Jr. and South Africa* (Cleveland, OH: The Pilgrim Press, 1995) for excellent analysis of Martin Luther King's Christian eschatological vision, juxtaposed alongside the Black anti-apartheid struggle in South Africa.

28. See Richard Coggins, *The Book of Exodus – The Epworth Commentaries* (Peterborough: Epworth Press, 2000), 3–8.

29. Lawrence N. Jones, "Hope for Mankind: Insights from Black Religious History in the United States," *Journal of Religious Thought* 34, no, 2 (Fall – Winter 1978): 59.

30. Jones, *Hope for Mankind*, 59.

31. See Caryl Philips, *The European Tribe* (London: Faber and Faber, 1987), 2.

32. See Reddie, *Faith, Stories and the Experience of Black Elders*.

33. See James W. Perkinson, *White Theology* (New York: Palgrave, 2004), 51–114.

34. Some of my initial thinking has been inspired by Jose Irizarry and his notion of theology as "performative action." Irizarry argues for a dramatic process of doing theology in which participants and the educator enter into a process of performance in which there is an inherent dialectic and from which new truths can be discerned. See Jose R. Irizarry, "The Religious Educator as Cultural Spec–Actor: Researching Self in Intercultural Pedagogy," *Religious Education* 98, no.3 (Summer 2003): 365–81.

35. This work is explicated in greater detail in Anthony G. Reddie, *Dramatizing Theologies: A Participative Approach to Black God-Talk* (London: Equinox Publishing, 2006).

36. Robert Beckford, *God and the Gangs* (London: Darton, Longman and Todd, 2004), 96–114.

37. The development of a plenary arising out of the dramatic engagement first emerged in a previous piece of work. See section entitled "The Process" (in the introduction) in Anthony G. Reddie, *Acting in Solidarity: Reflections in Critical Christianity* (London: Darton, Longman and Todd, 2005).

38. See my use of the "Barn Dance exercise" in *Dramatizing Theologies*, 112–18.

39. I am aware of the impressive work undertaken by Black cultural theorists in Britain on the cultural tropes and meaning of Black iconography. I am not unmindful of this work but I have largely ignored it for the purpose of this exercise as my intention in using this picture is not to explore socio–cultural, symbolic meanings of Black post-Second World War iconography in Britain; rather, my intention is to use this picture purely as a heuristic for teasing out the different approaches of Black British people to reading biblical texts. For a useful examination of Black pictorial iconography see Paul Gilroy, *Black Britain: A Photographic History* (London: Saqi Books, 2007).

40. There is a huge literature detailing this period in Black British history. Two texts of many are Mike Phillips and Trevor Phillips, *Windrush: The Irresistible Rise of Multi-racial Britain* (London: Harper Collins, 1999). See also Kwesi Owusu, *Black British Culture and Society: A Text Reader* (London: Routledge, 2000).

41. In the dramatic sketch, "It could have happened like this," I explore the sense of rivalry and endemic tensions in some African Caribbean communities in Britain where internal conflicts around handling difference and external pressures in terms of racism from White society are the overarching frameworks that have exerted profound pressures on how "we" often engage with one another. See Reddie, *Acting in Solidarity*, 45–53.

42. This was a "pet" name, the provenance of which no one is able to deduce, including my auntie herself. When I asked her personally for the derivation of this name, she said simply that she had been called this name for as long as she could remember.

43. See Miguel A. De La Torre, "Scripture," in idem, ed., *Handbook of U.S. Theologies of Liberation* (St. Louis: Chalice Press, 2004), 85–86. See also R.S. Sugirtharajah, *Voices from the Margin* (London: SPCK; Maryknoll, NY: Orbis Books, 1996).

44. See W.E.B. Dubois, *The Souls of Black Folk* (New York: Bantam Press, 1989).

45. See Reddie, *Dramatizing Theologies*, 97–98.

46. See Reddie, *Dramatizing Theologies*, 113–27.

47. Ephesians, 5:21 in *The Contemporary English Bible* (Nashville: Thomas Nelson Publishers, 1995), 1414.

48. Anthony G. Reddie, *Black Theology in Transatlantic Dialogue* (New York: Palgrave Macmillan, 2006), 85–87 and 111–12.

49. See Isabel Apawo Phiri and Sarjojini Nadar, eds, *African Women, Religion, and Health: Chapters in Honor of Mercy Amba Ewudziwa Oduyoye* (Maryknoll, NY: Orbis Books, 2006).

50. Cheryl Townsend Gilkes, *If It Wasn't for the Women* (Maryknoll, NY: Orbis Books, 2001).

51. Mercy Amba Oduyoye, *Beads and Strands: Reflections of an African Woman on Christianity in Africa* (Maryknoll, NY: Orbis Books, 2004), 92–93.

52. Reddie, *Dramatizing Theologies*, 188.

53. Reddie, *Nobodies to Somebodies*, 132–40.

54. Reddie, *Dramatizing Theologies*, 64–71.

55. Reddie, *Black Theology in Transatlantic Dialogue*, 111–12.

56. See James H. Cone, *God of the Oppressed* (San Francisco: Harper San Francisco, 1975).

57. Demetrius K. Williams, "The Bible and Models of Liberation in the African American Experience," in *Yet With a Steady Beat: Contemporary U.S. Afrocentric biblical Interpretation*, ed. Randall C. Bailey (Atlanta: Society of biblical Literature, 2003), 33–59.

58. Demetrius K. Williams, *An End to This Strife: The Politics of Gender in African American Churches* (Minneapolis: Fortress Press, 2004), 9–10.

59. Robert Beckford, *God of the Rahtid* (London: Darton, Longman and Todd, 2001), 66–97.

60. See Anthony B. Pinn, *Terror and Triumph: The Nature of Black Religion* (Minneapolis: Fortress Press, 2003), 52–80.

61. Beckford *God of the Rahtid*, 31–65.

62. Reddie, *Black Theology in Transatlantic Dialogue*, 85–87.

63. Or the picture if we want to use the metaphor as a means of talking about the biblical text.

Chapter 4

1. It is important to note that the author is a contextual Black British Liberation theologian. As such, his point of departure is his own context and identities as a Black British Christian of Caribbean descent. In identifying Jesus as a Black hero, I am not asserting that this identity should supersede all others or become a normative form of hegemony in a manner similar to how White conceptions of Jesus have been used. Rather, in identifying Jesus as Black, I am simply seeking to be accurate and honest about my own points of departure. Jesus is who he needs to be. In this case, and for the purposes of this essay, Jesus needs to be Black.

2. See John 1:1–14.

3. A very edited fragment of this story was first shared in a previous book. See Anthony G. Reddie, *Nobodies to Somebodies: A Practical Theology for Education and Liberation* (Peterborough: Epworth Press, 2003), 11–12.

4. Josiah Young, "Envisioning the Son of Man," *Black Theology: An International Journal* 2, no. 1 (January 2004): 11–17 (12).

5. USPG stands for The United Society for the Propagation of the Gospel, which is a successor to the historic SPG, which was a leading player in the evangelization, initiation and socialization of enslaved Africans into the Christian faith in North America and the Caribbean.

6. See *The Christ We Share* (London: The Methodist Church & USPG, 2000).

7. See Clive Marsh, "Black Christs in White Christian Perspective: Some Critical Reflections," *Black Theology: An International Journal* 2, no. 1 (January 2004): 45–56.

8. See Kelly Brown Douglas, *The Black Christ* (Maryknoll, NY: Orbis Books, 1994).

9. See James Cone, *A Black Theology of Liberation* (Maryknoll, NY: Orbis Books, 1990).

10. See Robert Beckford, *Jesus is Dread* (London: Darton, Longman and Todd, 1998).

11. Reddie, *Nobodies to Somebodies*, 97–99, 105–6.

12. Anthony G. Reddie, *Dramatizing Theologies: A Participative Approach to Black God-Talk* (London: Equinox, 2006), 117–27.

13. See Alistair McGrath, *Christian Theology: An Introduction* (Oxford: Blackwell, 1999), 5–26.

14. See McGrath, *Christian Theology*, 5–26.

15. See 1 Colossians 1: 15.

16. 1 Corinthians 15:22.

17. See Jacquelyn Grant, *White Women's Christ and Black Women's Jesus* (Atlanta: Scholar's Press, 1989).

18. See Douglas, *The Black Christ*.

19. See Kelly Brown Douglas, *What's Faith Got To Do With It?: Black Bodies/Christian Souls* (Maryknoll, NY: Orbis Books, 2005).

20. Anthony B. Pinn, *Terror and Triumph: The Nature of Black Religion* (Minneapolis: Fortress Press, 2003).

21. Pinn, *Terror and Triumph*, 27–80.

22. See Robert E. Hood, *Begrimed and Black: Christian Traditions on Blacks and Blackness* (Minneapolis: Fortress Press, 1994).

23. See Gay L. Byron, *Symbolic Blackness and Ethnic Difference in Early Christian Literature* (New York and London: Routledge, 2002).

24. See Michael Joseph Brown, *The Lord's Prayer Through North African Eyes: A Window into Early Christianity* (New York: T & T Clark, 2004).

25. See James H. Cone, *Black Theology and Black Power* (New York: Harper SanFrancisco, 1989).

26. See Cone, *A Black Theology of Liberation*.

27. See James H. Cone, *God of the Oppressed* (New York: Harper SanFrancisco, 1986).

28. See Anne H. Pinn and Anthony B. Pinn, *Black Church History* (Minneapolis: Fortress Press, 2002), 31–43.

29. Edward Blyden, "Africa's Service to the World" (Discourse delivered before the American Colonization Society, May 1880). In Cain Hope Felder, ed., *The Original African Heritage Study Bible* (Nashville, TN: The James C. Winston Publishing Company, 1993), 109–21.

30. Beckford, *Jesus is Dread*, 25–41.

31. See Horace Campbell, *Rasta and Resistance: From Marcus Garvey to Walter Rodney* (London: Hansib, 1985).

32. See William David Spencer, *Dread Jesus* (London: SPCK, 1999).

33. See Reddie, *Dramatizing Theologies*.

34. Anthony G. Reddie, *Acting in Solidarity: Reflections in Critical Christianity* (London: Darton, Longman and Todd, 2005).

35. Reddie, *Acting in Solidarity*, 127–35.

36. Reddie, *Acting in Solidarity*, 131.

37. See Itumeleng J. Mosala, *Biblical Hermeneutics and Black Theology in South Africa* (Grand Rapids, MI: Eerdmans, 1991).

38. Mosala, *Biblical Hermeneutics and Black Theology in South Africa*, 39; original italics.

39. I am indebted to Dwight N. Hopkins, Professor of Theology at Chicago Divinity School, University of Chicago for this insight. See Dwight N. Hopkins, *Head and Heart: Black Theology, Past, Present and Future* (New York: Palgrave Macmillan, 2002), 127–52.

40. See Reddie, *Nobodies to Somebodies*, 68–70.

41. I have chosen not to name these churches nor the pastors who oversee them. My presence in the service was that of a participant. No attempt was made to interview any persons in the pews or the leadership of these churches. I attended six such churches, visiting each one twice. I did not make any contemporaneous notes in worship. Rather, I simply entered into the worship along with all the other participants. Notes and reflections were written on my return to my research base. As the research was not intended to be either conclusive or definitive, nor am I seeking to make any substantive

sociological analysis of these worship encounters, save for my attempt to assess how Jesus is presented and conceived in such settings, I think my improvisatory heuristic method is sufficient for the purpose in which it was used.

42. I acknowledge the problematic basis of this analysis. Trying to impute implicit meaning into the discourse of others without attempting to interview or converse with them in order to test out one's hypothesis is always fraught with danger. I acknowledge this fault line in this analysis and accept that my reflections are largely self-generated, impressionistic, and are my tentative hypotheses at the time of writing. This line of reflection is in need of further work at a later juncture.

43. I am terming this model of Christology as a "Black Inferred Jesus" as his Blackness is not stated, but the experiential dimensions of the "son of God" who is one with us, within a largely Black (if not exclusively so) religio-cultural setting, seems to echo many of the trappings and nuances of a Black Christ for Black people. See Kelly Brown Douglas' *The Black Christ*.

44. A helpful text that has assisted me in unpacking some of these thoughts is Leonardo Boff, *Global Civilization: Challenges to Society and to Christianity* (London: Equinox, 2005).

45. See Anthony G. Reddie, *Dramatizing Theologies: A Participative Approach to Black God-Talk* (London: Equinox, 2006).

46. Reddie, *Dramatizing Theologies*, 91–99.

47. Grant, *White Women's Christ and Black Women's Jesus*, 63–83.

48. See Pinn, *Terror and Triumph*, 157–79.

49. Clarence E. Hardy III, *James Baldwin's God: Sex, Hope, and Crisis in Black Holiness Culture* (Knoxville, TN: University of Tennessee Press, 2003), 17–36.

50. Pinn, *Terror and Triumph*, 157–79.

51. Reddie, *Dramatizing Theologies*, 40–42.

52. For a brief discussion on the differences between the ending of the slave trade in the British Empire (March 1807) and the end of slavery per se (August 1838) see "Editorial" in *Black Theology: An International Journal* 5, no. 2 (July 2007).

53. Organizations such as Ligali have largely sought to refute any sense of commemoration or substantive remembrance of 25 March 2007 – i.e. the bicentenary of the abolition of the transatlantic slave trade – on the grounds that the parliamentary act of 1807 did not end the institution of slavery. If slavery did not end then what is the point of any commemoration or remembrance? "Ligali is a non profit voluntary organization. Through investigation and monitoring, we aim to challenge, identify and recommend workable solutions to current social issues that refuse to recognize the equal and inalienable rights of African people in the UK. Our main objectives are to turn talk into action and apathy into productivity. Ligali began its growth in early 2000 with the aim of challenging the negative representations of the African British community across all forms of media." For further details see http://www.ligali.org/ (accessed December 10, 2007).

54. This issue is explored in one of my recent books – see Reddie, *Dramatizing Theologies*, 10–25.

55. See Anthony Reddie, *Growing into Hope: Christian Education in Multi-ethnic Churches. Vol. 2: Liberation and Change* (Peterborough: Methodist Publishing House, 1998), 58–62.

56. The International Conference in question was entitled *Freedom is for Freeing* and was held at the Queen's Foundation for Ecumenical Theological Education, July 13–15, 2007. The event looked at the slave trade and its legacies from the perspective of Black theology. International guests included Revd Professor Randall C. Bailey, Professor of Hebrew Bible at the Interdenominational Centre, Atlanta, Georgia and Professor Elizabeth Amoah of the University of Ghana, Revd Dr Delroy Reid Salmon, who although resident in the US, is a visiting fellow at Regent's Park College, Oxford, UK, and Revd Dr Marjorie Lewis, lecturer at the United Theological College, Kingston, Jamaica.

57. These were Revd Dr Michael N. Jagessar, a colleague at Queen's and the Reviews Editor of *Black Theology: An International Journal* and Revd Lorraine Dixon, a Church of England Priest and a Missioner in the Bordesley Deanery of the Birmingham Diocese.

58. Dulcie Dixon is an experienced gospel DJ and radio host, whose show "The Dulcie Dixon Show" airs on Radio Leicester, every Sunday afternoon.

59. See Stephen R. Bevans, *Models of Contextual Theology* (Maryknoll, NY: Orbis Books, 2002).

60. See Robert J. Schreiter, *Constructing Local Theologies* (Maryknoll, NY: Orbis Books, 1985).

61. See Clarence E. Hardy III, *James Baldwin's God*. See also Anthony B. Pinn and Dwight N. Hopkins, eds, *Loving the Body: Black Religious Studies and The Erotic* (New York: Palgrave Macmillan, 2004).

62. See Beckford, *Jesus is Dread*, 61–78.

63. See Pinn and Hopkins, *Loving the Body*.

64. Beckford, *Jesus is Dread*, 61–95.

65. Beckford, *Jesus is Dread*, 147–50.

66. See note 6.

Chapter 5

1. See Anthony G. Reddie, "The Christian Education of African Caribbean Children in Britain: Creating a New Paradigm Through Developing Better Praxis" (unpublished PhD thesis, University of Birmingham, 2000).

2. This research project, which was given the title of the *Birmingham Initiative*, was the brainchild of Revd Christopher Hughes Smith, the then General Secretary of the Division of Education and Youth. Having formerly been a minister and District Chairman in Birmingham, he was aware of the deficiencies in the existing Christian education work with Black children sponsored by the Methodist church. In order to assess the effectiveness of the existing work and to create a mechanism that might attempt to develop a hypothesis for the Christian education of Black children in Britain, funds were obtained to create a research project to that end.

3. See Anthony G. Reddie, *Nobodies to Somebodies: A Practical Theology for Education and Liberation* (Peterborough: Epworth Press, 2003).

4. See Reddie, *Nobodies to Somebodies*.

5. See Reddie, *Growing into Hope*, 2 vols (Peterborough: The Methodist Publishing House, 1998).

6. See Anthony G. Reddie, *Faith, Stories and the Experience of Black Elders: Singing the Lord's Song in a Strange Land* (London: Jessica Kingsley, 2001).

7. See Paul Ballard and John Pritchard, *Practical Theology in Action: Christian Thinking in the Service of the Church and Society* (London: SPCK, 1996).

8. See Duncan B. Forrester, *Truthful Action: Explorations in Practical Theology* (Edinburgh: T & T Clark, 2000).

9. Elaine L. Graham, *Transforming Practice: Pastoral Theology in an Age of Uncertainty* (Eugene, OR: Wipf and Stock, 2002).

10. See Anthony G. Reddie, *Acting in Solidarity: Reflections in Critical Christianity* (London: Darton, Longman and Todd, 2005).

11. See Anthony G. Reddie, *Dramatizing Theologies: A Participative Approach to Black God-Talk* (London: Equinox, 2006).

12. Six such events took place over a three-month period. Prior to each session, participants were given selected extracts from "set texts" to read and were also encouraged to "read around" the bibliography on Black theology that I had constructed for the purpose.

13. See James H. Cone, *God of the Oppressed* (San Francisco: Harper, 1975); James H. Cone, *A Black Theology of Liberation* (New York: Orbis Books, 1986); Gayraud S. Wilmore and James H. Cone, eds, *Black Theology: A Documentary History, 1966–1979* (New York: Orbis Books, 1979) and Gayraud S. Wilmore and James H. Cone, eds, *Black Theology: A Documentary History, 1980–1992* (New York: Orbis Books, 1993).

14. See Jacquelyn Grant, *White Women's Christ and Black Women's Jesus* (Atlanta: Scholar's Press, 1989).

15. See Delores Williams, *Sisters in the Wilderness* (Maryknoll, NY: Orbis Books, 1993).

16. See Kelly Brown Douglas, *The Black Christ* (Maryknoll, NY: Orbis Books, 1994) and *What's Faith Got to Do With It?* (Maryknoll, NY: Orbis Books, 2005).

17. See Dwight N. Hopkins, *(Introducing) Black Theology of Liberation* (Maryknoll, NY: Orbis Books, 1999) and *Down, Up and Over: Slave Religion and Black Theology* (Minneapolis: Fortress Press, 2000).

18. See Katie G. Cannon, *Black Womanist Ethics* (Atlanta: Scholar's Press, 1988).

19. See Linda E. Thomas, "Womanist Theology, Epistemology, and a New Anthropological Paradigm," in *Living Stones in the Household of God: The Legacy and Future of Black Theology*, ed. Linda E. Thomas (Minneapolis: Fortress Press, 2004), 37–48.

20. See Robert Beckford, *Jesus is Dread* (London: Darton, Longman and Todd, 1998). See also Robert Beckford, *Dread and Pentecostal* (London: SPCK, 2000), and Robert Beckford, *God of the Rahtid* (London: Darton, Longman and Todd, 2001).

21. I have returned to this method for a later piece of work, which is described in final chapter "Making the Difference."

22. See Cone, *God of the Oppressed*, 62–83.

23. See Reddie, *Nobodies to Somebodies*, 53–57.

24. See Anthony G. Reddie, "An Interactive Odyssey," in Geoffrey Stevenson, ed., *Pulpit Journeys* (London: Darton, Longman and Todd, 2006), 149–65 for a more detailed exploration for how Black story and God's story works in a dialectical exchange in order to affect a form of existential self-recognition and identification, which is the starting point for being enabled to re-envision the Christian faith for the purposes of Black

Liberation. See also my earlier *Growing into Hope*, vols. 1 and 2 (Peterborough: Methodist Publishing House, 1998).

25. See Anthony G. Reddie, "Editorial," *Black Theology: An International Journal* 4, no. 2 (2006) where I talk about the importance of asking the "why questions."

26. See Cone, *God of the Oppressed*.

27. Michael Joseph Brown, *The Blackening of the Bible: The Aims of African American Biblical Scholarship* (Harrisburg, PA: Trinity Press International, 2004), 18.

28. Frederick L. Ware, *Methodologies of Black Theology* (Cleveland, OH: The Pilgrim Press, 2002), 28–56.

29. I shall say a little more about this in a short while when I discuss the dialectical relationship between Black experience and the Bible.

30. Gayraud S. Wilmore, *Pragmatic Spirituality: The Christian Faith through an Africentric Lens* (New York: New York University Press, 2004), 1–12.

31. Wilmore, *Pragmatic Spirituality*, 6.

32. Anthony G. Reddie, "Editorial," *Black Theology: An International Journal* 4, no. 1 (2006): 9.

33. In using this term I am referring to accepted social scientific methodology such as "sampling" and other means of ensuring that the group with which one is working is representative of the wider population from which that group is drawn. For more information see Tim May, *Social Research: Issues, Methods and Process* (Buckingham: Open University Press, 1997).

34. Cone, *God of the Oppressed*, 58.

35. See Reddie, *Dramatizing Theologies*.

36. Olivia P. Stokes, "Black Theology: A Challenge to Religious Education," in *Religious Education and Theology*, ed. Norma H. Thompson (Birmingham, AL: Religious Education Press, 1982), 97–98.

37. Stokes, "Black Theology," 97–98.

38. Cone, *God of the Oppressed*, 18.

39. See Reddie, *Acting in Solidarity* and Reddie, *Dramatizing Theologies*.

40. See Reddie, *Black Theology in Transatlantic Dialogue*.

41. See Anthony B. Pinn, *Terror and Triumph: The Nature of Black Religion* (Minneapolis: Fortress Press, 2003).

42. See Gayraud S. Wilmore, *Black Religion, Black Radicalism* (New York: Doubleday, 1973).

43. Beckford, *Dread and Pentecostal*, 144–56.

44. Robert Beckford, *God and the Gangs* (London: Darton, Longman and Todd, 2004), 85–86.

Chapter 6

1. There is a rich literature on the development, nature and intent of the "Black Church" in the African American context. The following are the mere tip of a growing and impressive iceberg. For further details see C. Eric Lincoln and Lawrence H. Mamiya, *The Black Church in the African American Experience* (Durham and London: Duke University Press, 1990); Anne H. Pinn and Anthony B. Pinn *(Fortress Introduction to)*

Black Church History (Minneapolis: Fortress Press, 2002); Henry H. Mitchell, *Black Church Beginnings* (Grand Rapids: Eerdmans, 2004); Iva E. Carruthers, Frederick D. Haynes III and Jeremiah A. Wright Jr, eds, *Blow the Trumpet in Zion* (Minneapolis: Fortress Press, 2005); Michael Battle, *The Black Church in America* (Oxford: Blackwell, 2006); Stacey Floyd-Thomas, Juan Floyd-Thomas, Carol B. Duncan, Stephen G. Ray Jr, and Nancy Lynne Westfield, *Black Church Studies: An Introduction* (Nashville, TN: Abingdon Press, 2007).

2. See Dwight N. Hopkins, *Introducing Black Theology of Liberation* (Maryknoll, NY: Orbis Books, 1999), 43–44. See also C. Eric Lincoln and Lawrence H. Mamiya, *The Black Church in the African American Experience* (Durham and London: Duke University Press, 1990) and Peter J. Paris, *The Social Teaching of the Black Churches* (Minneapolis: Fortress Press, 1985). See also Pinn and Pinn, *Black Church History*.

3. See Robert Beckford, *Dread and Pentecostal* (London: SPCK, 2000). See also Nicole Rodriguez Toulis, *Believing Identity* (Oxford and New York: Berg, 1997).

4. See James H. Harris, *Pastoral Theology: A Black-Church Perspective* (Minneapolis: Fortress Press, 1991). See also Dale P. Andrews, *Practical Theology for Black Churches: Bridging Black Theology and African American Folk Religion* (Louisville, KY: John Knox Press, 2002).

5. See Dwight N. Hopkins, *Down, Up and Over: Slave Religion and Black Theology* (Minneapolis: Fortress Press, 2000), 11–36.

6. See Emmanuel C. Eze, *Race and the Enlightenment* (Massachusetts: Blackwell, 1997).

7. See Robert E. Hood, *Begrimed and Black: Christian Traditions on Blacks and Blackness* (Minneapolis: Fortress Press, 1994), 23–43.

8. See Dwight N. Hopkins, *Being Human: Race, Culture and Religion* (Minneapolis: Fortress Press, 2005), 113–60.

9. See Anthony B. Pinn, *Terror and Triumph: The Nature of Black Religion* (Minneapolis: Fortress Press, 2003), 1–25.

10. Since this chapter was first conceived, Delroy Reid-Salmon, a highly promising and emerging Black theologian of Caribbean roots, has challenged me to reflect upon my Caribbean identity in the development of my perspectives on the "Black Church." I am mindful that the Caribbean has had a long and profound history in the development of "Black Church" and Black theology, some of which is detailed, in part, in this essay. Greater details on the development of Caribbean Black ecclesiologies can be found in Delroy A. Reid-Salmon, *Home Away From Home: The Caribbean Diasporan Church in the Black Atlantic Tradition* (London and Philadelphia: Equinox, 2008). I have continued to engage primarily with African American material in this chapter because of its unabashed declaration and intentionality in engaging with the semantic meaning of Blackness. The Caribbean literature on the Church (see, for example, Devon Dick, *Rebellion to Riot: The Jamaican Church in Nation Building* [Kingston, Jamaica: Ian Randle, 2004]) prefers to talk about "Caribbean" rather than "Black." I am clear, as I have outlined in the first chapter, that my scholarly gaze is concerned with the unapologetic rhetoric of Liberation and not the contextual theological identity of Caribbean (which may or may not be committed to Liberation). So whilst I acknowledge Reid-Salmon's critique of my American centred work, as a dialogue partner in this work, I still want to press for the sense of identity that arises from being Black people in the minority in numerically White dominated contexts (the experience of Black people in Britain and the US), where the

sense of political and theological charge around the term "Black" is unambiguous and deeply intentional. I have not gained a sense of that perspective in literature on the Caribbean church, Reid-Salmon's work notwithstanding.

11. Pinn, *Terror and Triumph*, 82–107.

12. Pinn, *Terror and Triumph*, 82–107.

13. Henry H. Mitchell, *Black Church Beginnings: The Long-Hidden Realities of the First Years* (Grand Rapids, MI; Cambridge: Eerdmans, 2004), 24–45.

14. See Pinn and Pinn, *Black Church History*, 6–8.

15. Mitchell, *Black Church Beginnings*, 8–45.

16. Noel L. Erskine, *Decolonizing Theology: A Caribbean Perspective* (Maryknoll, NY: Orbis Books, 1983), 41–45.

17. Pinn and Pinn, *Black Church History*, 32–43.

18. Pinn, *Terror and Triumph*, 90–93.

19. Pinn, *Terror and Triumph*, 93.

20. Harold Dean Trulear, "African American Religious Education," in *Multicultural Religious Education*, ed. Barbara Wilkerson (Birmingham, AL: Religious Education Press, 1997), 162.

21. Pinn, *Terror and Triumph*, 52–77.

22. See Pinn and Pinn, *Black Church History*.

23. For further details see Joe Aldred, *Respect: A Caribbean British Contextual Theology* (Peterborough: Epworth Press, 2006).

24. For further information see John L. Wilkinson, *Church in Black and White: The Black Christian Tradition in "Mainstream" Churches in England: A White Response and Testimony* (Edinburgh: St. Andrews Press, 1993).

25. See C. Eric Lincoln and Lawrence H. Mamiya, *The Black Church in the African American Experience* (Durham and London: Duke University Press, 1990) and Peter J. Paris, *The Social Teaching of the Black Churches* (Minneapolis: Fortress Press, 1985). See also Pinn and Pinn, *Black Church History* for a brief selection of an extensive literature in this area of Black theological work.

26. See John L. Wilkinson, *Church in Black and White: The Black Christian Tradition in "Mainstream" Churches in England: A White Response and Testimony* (Edinburgh: St. Andrews Press, 1993).

27. See Aldred, *Respect*.

28. See Roy Kerridge, *The Storm is Passing Over: A Look at Black Churches in Britain* (London: Thomas and Hudson, 1995). See also B.A. Miles, *When the Church of God Arises* (Studley, Warwickshire: History into Print, 2006).

29. See also Aldred, *Respect*.

30. See Aldred, *Respect* and Mark Sturge, *Look What The Lord Has Done!: An Exploration of Black Christian Faith in Britain* (London: Scripture Union, 2005).

31. See also Doreen McCalla, "Black Churches and Voluntary Action: Their Social Engagement with the Wider Society," *Black Theology: An International Journal* 3, no. 2 (July 2004).

32. Arlington Trotman, "Black, Black-Led or What?" in *"Let's Praise Him Again": An African Caribbean Perspective on Worship*, ed. Joel Edwards (Eastbourne: Kingsway Publications, 1992), 12–35.

33. Beckford, *Dread and Pentecostal*, 176–82.

34. See Sturge, *Look What The Lord Has Done!*, 123–25. See also Beckford, *Jesus is Dread* (London: Darton, Longman and Todd, 1998), 103–107.

35. For further details see *Black Majority Churches UK Directory* (London: African Caribbean Evangelical Alliance and Churches Together in Britain and Ireland, 2003), 67.

36. *Black Majority Churches UK Directory*, 59.

37. *Black Majority Churches UK Directory*, 112.

38. See Beckford, *Dread and Pentecostal*, 178–82.

39. See *Focus: The African Caribbean Evangelical Alliance Magazine* (May–August 2005): 8–9.

40. For more information see the "Minority Ethnic Christian Affairs" page of *Churches Together in Britain and Ireland* at http://www.ctbi.org.uk

41. See Beckford, *Dread and Pentecostal*, 119–20.

42. See Beckford, *Jesus is Dread*, 42–58. See also Roswith I.H. Gerloff, "A Plea for British Black Theologies: The Black Church Movement in Britain – Vol.1. and Vol.2" (unpublished PhD thesis, University of Birmingham, 1991).

43. See M. Byron, *Post War Caribbean Migration to Britain: The Unfinished Cycle* (Aldershot: Averbury, 1994). See also R.B. Davidson, *West Indian Migrants* (London: Oxford University Press, 1962) and R. Glass, *Newcomers: The West Indians in London* (London: George Allen and Unwin, 1960) for a historical analysis for the presence of disproportionate numbers of Black people living in inner-city conurbations in Britain.

44. Peter Brierley, *The Tide is Running Out: What the English Church Attendance Survey Reveals* (London: Christian Research, 2000), 136.

45. David Isiorho "Black Theology in Urban Shadow: Combating Racism in the Church of England," *Black Theology: An International Journal* 1, no.1 (November 2002): 29–48.

46. Isiorho, "Black Theology in Urban Shadow," 47.

47. See Robert E. Hood, *Must God Remain Greek?: Afro-Cultures and God-Talk* (Minneapolis: Fortress Press, 1990). See also Gay L. Byron, *Symbolic Blackness and Ethnic Difference in Early Christian Literature* (New York: Routledge, 2002).

48. See Sturge, *Look What The Lord Has Done!*, 134–35.

49. See Kelly Brown Douglas, *The Black Christ* (Maryknoll, NY: Orbis Books, 1993).

50. James H. Cone, *God of the Oppressed* (San Francisco: Harper San Francisco, 1975), 108–95.

51. JoAnne Marie Terrell, *Power in the Blood?: The Cross in the African American Experience* (Maryknoll, NY: Orbis Books, 1998).

52. Terrell, *Power in the Blood?*, 34; original italics.

53. See Beckford, *Jesus is Dread* and Riggins R. Earl Jr., *Dark Salutations* (Harrisburg, PA: Trinity Press International, 2001), 1–16.

54. See Karen Baker Fletcher, *Dancing with God: The Trinity from a Womanist Perspective* (St. Louis, MO: Chalice Press, 2006).

55. Gayraud S. Wilmore, *Black Religion and Black Radicalism* (Maryknoll, NY: Orbis Books, 1983), 103–35.

56. Vincent L. Wimbush, *The Bible and African Americans: A Brief History* (Minneapolis: Fortress Press, 2003), 63–67.

57. One of the churches was located in London, the other in Leeds (in West Yorkshire). One was a Methodist Church, the other, a Pentecostal. In the interests of

anonymity, (as promised) I will not reveal the identities of the two churches who contributed to this essay by taking part in this exercise.

58. In total, I undertook around 100 such conversations over a six-month period. The process was not a scientific one in that I did not create a representative sample or seek to correlate that sample with the broader population of Black (Christian?) people of faith in Britain. Rather, I simply wanted to have a reasonably large range of comments from which I could then make some tentative remarks on how "some" Black people feel and then reflect theologically on what this might mean for the missiological praxis of some Black churches in Britain.

59. See the texts cited in the first endnote in this chapter. These texts helped me to conceptualize the existential comments of the Black participants in their reflections on the imagined, missiological intentionality of Black churches in Britain in the 21st century.

60. See Victor Anderson, *Beyond Ontological Blackness* (New York: Continuum, 1995).

61. See James W. Fowler, *Stages of Faith* (San Francisco: HarperCollins, 1995).

62. "Faith development theory" is a developmental framework for assessing the ways in which people's faith progresses across a series of stages, as a product of and a response to the contingency of human life. Fowler is more concerned with the "how of faith" as opposed to the "what of faith," i.e. his theoretical and practical framework is concerned with how faith is constructed as a meaning-making device in people's lives rather than the exact subject/content of that faith.

63. See Jeff Astley, ed., *Learning in the Way: Research and Reflection on Adult Christian Education* (Leominster: Gracewing, 2000), 124–42.

64. See my exercise entitled "Re-defining the Norm" in Anthony G. Reddie, *Nobodies to Somebodies* (Peterborough: Epworth Press, 2003), 132–40.

65. Michael N. Jagessar and Anthony G. Reddie, eds, *Black Theology in Britain: A Reader* (London: Equinox, 2007), 305–306.

66. The title is derived from a popular film by African American director Spike Lee entitled *Get On The Bus*, which uses the journey of a group of African American men travelling on a bus to hear Louis Farrakhan speak at the "Million Man March" in Washington DC, as a means of exploring notions of identity and positionality in Black life in the US. See *Get On The Bus*, dir. Spike Lee (Forty Acres and A Mule Productions, 1996).

67. See Lewis V. Baldwin, *Toward the Beloved Community* (Cleveland, OH: The Pilgrim Press, 1995).

68. Thomas Groome, *Sharing Faith* (San Francisco: Harper, 1991).

69. Groome, *Sharing Faith*, 135.

70. In the Christian tradition this is primarily the Bible and the sacred narratives that are contained within it, identified as "Holy Scripture."

71. Groome, *Sharing Faith*, 138–51.

72. I resisted using the Body analogy of 1 Corinthians chapter 12, as I (a) felt it has been over used to the point of cliché and (b) its functionality has to be called into question, as the fixed nature of the various limbs cannot leave the body without that body being harmed, perhaps even fatally. Whilst there may be an essential theological truth in all the members being interconnected and none being able to leave without the whole being damaged, as a participative Practical theologian, I want to press this metaphor in light of the historical and contemporaneous experiences of those who are marginalized

and oppressed and who need to leave in order to preserve their very existence. The utility of the body metaphor as a dominant image for conceiving the "Body of Christ" can be sustained in terms of a more cosmic and trans-historical sense of the church as the "Body of Christ"; but when applied to more contextual settings, it can become a repressive means of maintaining unity in diversity (which is commendable), whilst still adhering to normative notions of hierarchy. It is not true that a foot is as important as the head in a body. We may amputate feet, but never a head. The author of this text is not being entirely honest in terms of the positionality of power within the ecclesia. Which then begs the question, who or what "sorts of people" are represented by the head and who are the feet? Who are the ones it is important to have as part of the body, but should a metaphorical case of gangrene emerge, we are only too happy to cut off that limb in order that the rest of the body can function? To what extent are Black people, women, gay, lesbian, bi-sexual and transgendered people actually expendable like a "gangrenous" foot? These reflections owe much to the reflections of Carol Troupe. See Carol Troupe, "One Body, Many Parts: A Re-reading of 1st Corinthians 12:12-27," *Black Theology: An International Journal* 6, no. 2 (2008).

73. See Robert Beckford, *Jesus Dub* (London: Routledge, 2006) for an exploration of the differing ways in which "dancehall culture" gave rise to multiple ways of "being community" amongst African Caribbean people in Britain. See also William David Spencer who charts the interplay between "traditional Christianity" and Rasta belief systems in other forms of faithful community construction across the African Diaspora. See William David Spencer, *Dread Jesus* (London: SPCK, 1999).

74. Lorraine Dixon and I have been friends for over ten years and we meet on a regular basis to catch up, and to share stories on our reflections on faith, work and ministry. Lorraine is one of the stalwarts of the Black theology movement in Britain and is one of the most gifted women authors and theological thinkers. See Lorraine Dixon's various contributions in Reddie and Jagessar, *Black Theology in Britain: A Reader*. See also her website in which details of her DJ identity – DJ Ayo – and her respective activities are revealed. See http://www.myspace.com/djayo05

75. The term "faithful community" has been adapted from the comparatively recent ecumenical report produced in Britain, which is entitled "Faithful Cities." See *Faithful Cities: A Call for Celebration, Vision and Justice* (Peterborough and London: The Methodist Publishing House and Church House Publishing, 2006). This report is a sequel to the landmark 1985 report *Faith in the City* (see *Faith in the City: Archbishop's Commission on Urban Priority Areas* [London: Church House Publishing, 1985]), and which sought to outline a vision for urban mission in the UK and the role of the church in offering hope to urban deprived conurbations in Britain, often in opposition to the right-wing Thatcherite government at the time. The "Faithful Cities" report is an updating of that report, seeking to provide a more contextually nuanced vision for British cities and the wider urban landscape as one that can be efficacious for a form of human flourishing that is both informed by and nourished by religious faith.

76. "Fresh Expression" is an Anglican inspired, ecumenical movement seeking to explore and give rise to new forms of ecclesial practice that are not constricted by the traditional patterns of Church that have been a product of Christendom. See *Fresh Expressions: Renewing Vision, Gathering News, Resourcing Growth, Developing Training* (London: Fresh Expressions, 2005). See also Ian J. Mobsby, *Emerging and Fresh Expressions*

of Church: How are they Authentically Church and Anglican? (London: Moot Community, 2007).

77. See Pinn and Pinn, *Black Church History*.

78. See "Psalm 23: A Modern Version for 21st Century Sceptics," in Anthony G. Reddie, *Acting in Solidarity* (London: Darton, Longman and Todd, 2005), 31–37.

79. Beckford, *Dread and Pentecostal*, 204.

80. Gayraud S. Wilmore, *Black Religion and Black Radicalism* (Maryknoll, NY: Orbis Books, 1983), 187–227.

81. This event and memory of it remains hugely significant in my Christian development. From my mother, I have learnt the importance of prayer and the need to see this as a literal resource in my Christian discipleship.

82. See James Fowler, *Stages of Faith* (SanFrancisco: Harper Collins, 1981).

83. See Riggins R. Earl Jr., *Dark Salutations* (Harrisburg, PA: Trinity Press International, 2001), 1–16.

84. Anthony G. Reddie, "Jesus Lives in the Spaces in my Life," in *Wrestling and Resting: Exploring Stories of Spirituality from Britain and Ireland*, ed. Ruth Harvey (London: CTBI, 1999), 72–74.

85. *The Contemporary English (Version) Bible* (Nashville, TN: Thomas Nelson Publishers, 1995), 1363.

86. See my post sketch reflections to "It Could Have Happened Like This?" in Reddie, *Acting in Solidarity*, 45–53.

87. See Kelly Brown Douglas, *Sexuality and the Black Church: A Womanist Perspective* (Maryknoll, NY: Orbis Books, 1999).

88. Beckford, *Jesus is Dread*, 61–78.

89. Jacquelyn Grant, "Freeing the Captives: The Imperative of Womanist Theology," in *Blow the Trumpet in Zion: Global Vision and Action for the 21st Century Black Church*, eds Iva Carruthers, Frederick D. Haynes III and Jeremiah A. Wright Jr (Minneapolis: Fortress Press, 2005).

90. See my dramatic sketch entitled "Black Voices" in Reddie, *Acting in Solidarity*, 109–19.

91. Janice Hale, "The Transmission of Faith to Young African American Children," in *The Recovery of Black Presence*, eds Randall C. Bailey and Jacquelyn Grant (Nashville, TN: Abingdon Press, 1995), 207.

92. Paulo Freire, *Pedagogy of the Oppressed* (New York: Herder and Herder, 1972), 68.

Chapter 7

1. I was very tempted to name the school and the young boy who saved me from a fate I would rather not consider; but in the interests of anonymity, I think it better that neither is revealed.

2. See Anthony G. Reddie, "An Unbroken Thread of Experience," in *Family and All that Stuff*, ed. Joan King (Birmingham: National Christian Education Council [NCEC], 1998), 153–60.

3. See Anthony Reddie, *Growing into Hope: Christian Education in Multi-ethnic Churches. Vol. 1: Believing and Expecting* (Peterborough: Methodist Publishing House, 1998), 8. This training exercise was constructed (using data from the 1991 census) to assist predominantly White leaders who work with Black children to understand both the context in which Black people live in Britain, and the psychological and emotional effects of being a minority in a White dominated country. Black people who predominantly live in inner-city areas have divided their existence in this country into areas of familiarity. Black children move interchangeably, from areas of great familiarity (where Black people although a minority are suddenly in the majority) to other situations where they become seemingly insignificant. This pattern has not changed appreciably since the post war wave of mass African Caribbean migration to this country. This interchangeability of African Caribbean life, which is centred on differing contexts, has given rise to issues of cultural dissonance. This issue is dealt with in greater detail in one of my previous books. See Anthony G. Reddie, *Nobodies to Somebodies: A Practical Theology for Education and Liberation* (Peterborough: Epworth Press, 2003).

4. See Robert E. Hood, *Must God Remain Greek?: Afro-cultures and God-Talk* (Minneapolis: Fortress Press, 1990).

5. It is interesting to note that two major sources for gaining some sense of the overarching development of Christian theology largely minimize or even ignore any substantive contribution of Black African thought to the development of Christianity. The more evangelical perspectives of Alistair McGrath make mention of such figures of Tertullian and St. Augustine of Hippo, but do not centre their African identity as offering any significant influence on their constructive theological thought or how their Africanness shaped the corporate identity of the faith. See Alistair E. McGrath, *Christian Theology: An Introduction* (Oxford: Blackwell, 1999). A more liberationist approach to reflecting on the flow and shape of Christian theology across several centuries is undertaken by Elaine Graham, Heather Walton and Frances Ward. In their twin volumes on theological reflection, the Black contribution is reduced to the work of Robert Beckford. In using Beckford, the impact of Black theological work on the shape of Christian theology is collapsed into "Vernacular theologies" of culture. See Elaine Graham, Heather Walton and Frances Ward, *Theological Reflection: Methods* (London: SCM Press, 2005) and Elaine Graham, Heather Walton and Frances Ward, *Theological Reflection: Sources* (London: SCM Press, 2007).

6. See Paul Gilroy, *There Ain't No Black in the Union Jack* (London: Hutchinson, 1987).

7. JoAnne M. Terrell, *Power in the Blood?* (Maryknoll, NY: Orbis Books, 1998), 99–119.

8. Gay Byron, *Symbolic Blackness and Ethnic Difference in Early Christian Literature* (New York: Routledge, 2002).

9. See Anne Hope and Sally Timmel, *Training for Transformation* (Gweru, Zimbabwe: Intermediate Technology Publications, 1999), 76–185.

10. Terrell, *Power in the Blood?*, 99–119.

11. See Delores Williams, *Sisters in the Wilderness: The Challenge of Womanist God-Talk* (Maryknoll, NY: Orbis Books, 1993), 60–83.

12. See http://ingeb.org/spiritua/henevers.html.

13. See Kelly Brown Douglas, *The Black Christ* (Maryknoll, NY: Orbis Books, 1993).

14. James H. Cone, *God of the Oppressed* (San Francisco: HarperSanFrancisco, 1975), 108–95.

15. Terrell, *Power in the Blood?*

16. See Andrew Walker, *Telling the Story: Gospel, Mission and Culture* (London: SPCK, 1996).

17. See John M. Hull, "Christian Theology and Educational Theory: Can there be Connections?" In *Critical Perspectives on Christian Education*, ed. Jeff Astley and Leslie J. Francis (Leominster: Gracewings, 1994), 314–30.

18. See Grace Davie, *Europe: The Exceptional Case: Parameters of Faith in the Modern World* (London: Darton, Longman and Todd, 2002).

19. See Rudolf Otto, *The Idea of the Holy* (Harmondsworth, Middlesex: Penguin, 1959). I am at pains to add that this is a particular reading of Otto. It would be wrong, for example, to assume that Otto's evocation of the numinous can be seen only in terms of dread and violence. I am at pains to explore the violent outcomes of religious experience, particularly as they affect Black people.

20. William James, *The Varieties of Religious Experience* (New York: Collier, 1961). See also Adam Hood, *Baillie, Oman and Macmurray: Experience and Religious Belief* (Aldershot: Ashgate, 2003).

21. See Canaan S. Banana, "The Case for a New Bible," in *Voices from the Margin: Interpreting the Bible in the Third World*, ed. R.S. Sugirtharajah (London: SPCK; New York: Orbis, 1997), 69–82. See also Timothy J. Gorringe, *Furthering Humanity: A Theology of Culture* (Aldershot: Ashgate, 2004), 177–93.

22. See Mark Lewis Taylor, *The Executed God: The Way of the Cross in Lockdown America* (Minneapolis: Fortress Press, 2001), 70–98.

23. See René Girard, *The Scapegoat*, trans. Yvonne Freccero (London: Athlone, 1986). See also Rene Girard, *Violence and the Sacred*, trans. Patrick Gregory (London: Athlone, 1988).

24. Kelly Brown Douglas, *What's Faith Got To Do With It?: Black Bodies/Christian Souls* (Maryknoll, NY: Orbis Books, 2005).

25. Douglas, *What's Faith Got To Do With It?*, 10–38.

26. Douglas, *What's Faith Got To Do With It?*, 39–70.

27. See Traci West's excellent treatment of Christian ethics as a form of disruptive practice, in which the embodied nature of Christian praxis becomes an ethical response to the actuality of racism and marginalization of Black people (Black women in particular) in history. This form of Christian ethics is one whose modus operandi is reflective of the challenge to abstract and contextless theorizing around absolute moral categories of right and wrong. Rather, it is a form of ethical praxis that arises from the necessity of attempting to respond to the messiness of one's oppressive realities in light of the central tenets of the Gospel. See Traci C. West, *Disruptive Christian Ethics: When Racism and Women's Lives Matter* (Louisville, KY: Westminster John Knox Press, 2006).

28. Douglas, *What's Faith Got To Do With It?*, 39–70.

29. Douglas, *What's Faith Got To Do With It?*, xi.

30. At the major international conference on Black theology and slavery, entitled "Freedom is for Freeing" (July 13–15, 2007), Randall Bailey (Andrew W. Mellon Professor of Hebrew Bible at the Interdenominational Theological Center in Atlanta, Georgia) in his plenary address reminded the audience of the ways in which many Black Christians have colluded with the oppressive nature of Christianity and its often violent treatment

of the other, often sanctioned in many instances from the rhetoric of violence in Hebrew narratives. Black Christians accomplish this feat by siding with the "winners in history." We read against our own experiential realities by ignoring the role played by those who are "othered" in the text – the ones who are often pathologized as being beyond the orbit of God's love. To what extent do Black Christians attempt this experiential and ideological "sleight of hand" in order to assure ourselves that we are on the side of the winners?

31. See Michael N. Jagessar and Anthony G. Reddie, eds, *Black Theology in Britain: A Reader* (London: Equinox, 2007).

32. See Jagessar and Reddie, *Black Theology in Britain*, 303.

33. See David Isiorho, "Black Theology in Urban Shadow: Combating Racism in the Church of England," *Black Theology: An International Journal* 1, no. 1 (November 2002): 29–48.

34. Isiorho, "Black Theology in Urban Shadow," 29–48.

35. See *The Methodist Recorder* – front page story, March 16, 2006. It is interesting to note that the continued rise of Black Christianity in Britain has not informed the collapsing of Whiteness with Christianity in the eyes of the right-wing British National Party.

36. This aside was made by Professor Randall C. Bailey in his plenary address at the Black theology and the slave trade conference, "Freedom is for Freeing," at the Queen's Foundation, Edgbaston, Birmingham, UK, July 14, 2007. His presentation was entitled "But it's in the Text."

37. See Naim S. Ateek, "A Palestinian Perspective: Biblical Perspectives on the Land," in *Voices from the Margin*, ed. R.S. Sugirtharajah, 267–76.

38. See Robert Allen Warrior, "A Native American Perspective: Canaanites, Cowboys, and Indians," in *Voices from the Margin*, ed. R.S. Sugirtharajah, 277–85.

39. Warrior, "A Native American Perspective," 279.

40. See R.S. Sugirtharajah, *The Bible and the Third World* (Cambridge: Cambridge University Press, 2001).

41. Sugirtharajah, *The Bible and the Third World*, 113–32.

42. R.S. Sugirtharajah, *Postcolonial Criticism and Biblical Interpretation* (Oxford: Oxford University Press, 2002).

43. Sugirtharajah, *Postcolonial Criticism and Biblical Interpretation*, 112–15.

44. Raul Vidales cited in Sugirtharajah, *Postcolonial Criticism and Biblical Interpretation*, 114.

45. Sugirtharajah, *Postcolonial Criticism and Biblical Interpretation*, 117.

46. Frederick L. Ware, *Methodologies of Black Theology* (Cleveland, OH: Pilgrim Press, 2002), 28–65.

47. See Jagessar and Reddie, *Black Theology in Britain*, 305.

48. Jagessar and Reddie, *Black Theology in Britain*, 305–306.

49. Robert Beckford, *God of the Rahtid* (London: Darton, Longman and Todd, 2001).

50. Beckford, *God of the Rahtid*, 1–10.

51. Beckford, *God of the Rahtid*, 11–30.

52. Beckford, *God of the Rahtid*, 8.

53. See chapter 2 on a Black theological approach to reconciliation.

54. See Robert E. Hood, *Begrimed and Black: Christian Traditions on Blacks and Blackness* (Minneapolis: Fortress Press, 1994). See also Byron, *Symbolic Blackness*.

55. See William R. Hertzog II, *Jesus, Justice and the Reign of God: A Ministry of Liberation* (Louisville, KY: Westminster John Knox Press, 2000).

56. See Taylor, *The Executed God*.

57. See Chapter 2 on reconciliation.

58. This issue has been addressed in the American context with great skill by Mark Lewis Taylor in *The Executed God*.

59. See Roxy Harris and Sarah White, eds, *Changing Britannia: Life Experience with Britain* (London: New Beacon Books), 193–225.

60. See A. Sivanandan, *A Different Hunger: Writings on Black Resistance* (London: Pluto Press, 1982). See also A. Sivanandan, *Communities of Resistance: Writings on Black Struggles for Socialism* (London: Verso, 1990).

61. See Bob Carter, Clive Harris and Shirley Joshi, "The 1951–1955 Conservative Government and the Racialization of Black Immigration," in *Black British Culture and Society: A Text Reader*, ed. Kwesi Owusu (London: Routledge, 2000), 21–36.

62. Anthony B. Pinn, *Terror and Triumph: The Nature of Black Religion* (Minneapolis: Fortress Press, 2002), 12–77.

63. Whilst there is no empirical evidence to articulate the extent to which the broader public did identify with Walker's protestations of forgiveness as opposed to systemic justice against racialized violence in Britain, it is worth noting the ease with which the media reported this aspect of the story. There was a greater concentration around the emollient language of forgiveness from the Walker family in the media than the trenchant calls for justice and systemic anti-racist action from the more militant sections of the Black community in Liverpool in the subsequent reporting. See http://news.bbc.co.uk/1/hi/england/merseyside/4471440.stm and http://www.indymedia.org.uk/en/regions/liverpool/2005/10/326246.html

64. See Chapter 11, which addresses HIV/AIDS from a Black theological perspective.

65. Ligali, the African campaigning group based in the UK, are claiming that racial violence directed at people of African descent is on the increase. In a report from September 12, 2007, they claim that "A mob of violent racists who have been responsible for a number of attacks on African people are being sought by police in Tilbury, Essex. Essex Police have increased their presence in the Tilbury area, particularly around the railway station and business areas, following a number of verbal and physical assaults targeted at the local African community. Three attacks have been reported this month alone although the spate of attacks has been occurring at a rate of one every week since July 2007." Taken from "Crime and Justice News" at http://www.ligali.org/index.php.

66. Explanation of educative method for undertaking participative Black theology with Black people has been detailed in a number of my previous publications. See Reddie, *Nobodies to Somebodies*; *Acting in Solidarity* (London: Darton, Longman and Todd, 2005), Anthony G. Reddie, *Dramatizing Theologies* (London: Equinox, 2006).

67. The exercise in question is entitled "Who's Invited to the Party" and is taken from Reddie, *Nobodies to Somebodies*, 161–71.

68. I met with the group on one occasion, for a session lasting three hours. We met in a large Anglican church in North London. The group consisted of five Black members (of whom three were women and two were men) and five White members (again, three women and two men). Their reactions to the exercise were flip-charted and follow-up

interviews were undertaken with three of the ten respondents, of whom two were female and one male; two being White and one Black.

69. A former heavyweight boxing champion of the world.

70. This term was used in the exercise to denote a form of White controlled, top-down patrician model of Christianity into which all people, but especially Black people, were expected to conform. Black Christianity, particularly through the guise of the Black Church, has largely sought to replicate this framework and not deconstruct it. I have touched upon this phenomenon in a previous piece of work. See "Black Voices" in Reddie, *Acting in Solidarity*, 109–19.

71. Black is used in the politicized sense that has been common occurrence in the UK, to mean those who are perceived as the socially constructed other in the body politic of postcolonial Britain. In short-hand terms, all who are not White can be understood to be Black. Amplification of this term, in the context of Black theological work in Britain, can be found in Michael N. Jagessar and Anthony G. Reddie, eds, *Postcolonial Black British Theology* (Peterborough: Epworth Press, 2007), xiii–xv.

72. This exercise was not a scientifically controlled one, nor were the numbers anywhere near statistically relevant in order to make any generalized deductions about the comparative perceptions of Black people and White towards viewing Black bodies in the popular imagination. The purpose of the exercise was to act as a form of experiential heuristic in assisting me to reflect theologically on the nature of Black bodies in the popular imagination of Black and White people in Christian-inspired settings.

73. See "Black Voices" in Reddie, *Acting in Solidarity*, 109–19.

74. See Pinn, *Terror and Triumph*.

75. See my exercise entitled "The Quest for Racial Justice" in Reddie, *Acting in Solidarity*, 109–19.

76. See Gretchen Gerzina, *Black England: Life Before Emancipation* (London: John Murray, 1995) and Ron Ramdin, *Reimaging Britain: 500 Years of Black and Asian History* (London: Pluto Press, 1999).

77. See Isiorho, "Black Theology in Urban Shadow," 11–28.

78. See the dramatic sketch "Black Voices" in Reddie, *Acting in Solidarity*, 109–19 for a comedic look at aspects of African Caribbean culture in Britain and the extent to which these facets are often beyond the immediate comprehension of many White people.

79. See Reddie, *Nobodies to Somebodies*, 49–51.

80. Bhikhu Parekh, *Rethinking Multiculturalism* (Basingstoke, Hampshire: Macmillan, 2000), 142–78.

Chapter 8

1. The Clapham Sect was a group of predominantly (although not exclusively) evangelical Anglicans who, through their base at Holy Trinity Clapham, were active in the anti-slavery abolition movement in Britain in the 18th and early 19th centuries. The most famous member of this group was William Wilberforce, the parliamentary MP for Kingston-upon-Hull and the chief architect of the parliamentary bill ending the slave

trade in Britain (March 25, 1807). See Stephen Tomkins, *William Wilberforce: A Biography* (Grand Rapids: Eerdmans, 2007).

2. See *The Longman Dictionary of the English Language* (London: Penguin, 1994), 1363.

3. I was invited by my brother, Richard S. Reddie, to undertake the informal role as "Black Theological Advisor" to *set all free*. SAF was an initiative of "Churches Together in England" to mark the bicentenary of the abolition of the slave trade in Britain. Richard Reddie was the project director of SAF, until the project came to an end in April 2008. In my informal capacity as theological advisor, I have written materials and given talks around how Britain should mark the bicentenary. For further details on SAF see Richard S. Reddie, 'set all free – Meeting the Challenge of Marking the Bicentenary of the Abolition of the Slave Trade in 1807: A Personal Credo," *Black Theology: An International Journal* 5, no.2 (2007): 244-49. See also Richard S. Reddie, *Abolition: The Struggle to Abolish Slavery in the British Colonies* (London: Lion Books, 2007).

4. Whilst in the process of researching and writing this chapter I was amazed to read the content of *Anvil: An Evangelical Journal for Theology and Mission*, 24, no.2 (2007), where the treatment of Britain's involvement in the transatlantic slave trade was still filtered through a conservative biblical White patrician and paternalistic framework. This approach is one that seeks to relativize the economic greed and moral debasement of White Christian religio-cultural mores by implicating Africans as culpable and complicit in their own oppression. This work compares poorly (to my mind) with the treatment of this subject by *Black Theology: An International Journal* 5, no.2 (2007). The latter publication approaches the legacy of Britain's involvement in the slave trade from a Black theological perspective in which the blandishments of White patrician control of the discourse of Black suffering is exorcised.

5. Within British theological education, it is now *de rigueur* for all persons undertaking training for ordained ministry to undertake some "racism awareness training." The rationale for this training is to sensitize and challenge (predominantly) White ordinands on the continued existence of racism, and to offer them tools by which they might seek to undertake their future ministries, within a framework of anti-racist and anti-oppressive practice. For many years, the leading exponents of this work were MELRAW – Methodist and Ecumenical Leadership in Racism Awareness. MELRAW was founded in the late 1980s following the initial urban riots or racialized disturbances in many inner-city communities across Britain. For a number of years they were the central agency for the delivery of racism awareness training in British theological education. MELRAW was discontinued as a unit within the British Methodist Church in 2004.

6. At the time of writing, not one single representative of the British Government has apologized for the evils of the slave trade. The former Prime Minister, Tony Blair, offered "deep regret" but stopped short of apologizing. One of the few, if not the only exception in terms of a British politician has been Ken Livingstone, the former Mayor of London. Speaking at London's first annual Slavery Memorial Day (August 23, 2007 at City Hall), organized to mark the rebellion in Haiti on August 23, 1791, Livingstone apologized for Britain's involvement in the slave trade. At the time of writing, the Archbishop of Canterbury, Rowan Williams, has apologized on behalf of the Church of England and the City of Liverpool has also issued an apology. Elsewhere, I have argued that "apologetic rhetoric" can be an expedient tactic or ruse adopted by some cynical White people in power to avoid engaging with the systemic and debilitating effects of

racism on the psycho-social well-being of Black people. I have termed this concept "a theology of good intentions." In this concept, White people with power invoke the seemingly magical words of "I'm sorry" as a basis for not engaging in any constructive forms of systemic analysis in order to assess the underlying reasons that made the apology necessary in the first instance. See Anthony G. Reddie, *Nobodies to Somebodies* (London: Epworth Press, 2003), 152–71. In the case of reparations for Black people, White hegemony in Britain is unwilling to even say sorry.

7. Taken from the *Contemporary English Version* (Atlanta: Thomas Nelson Publishers, 1995).

8. This issue is addressed with great alacrity by the South African scholar Itumeleng Mosala in his Marxist inspired critique of biblical texts, which are produced by the conflation of cultural production arising out of political self-interests and hegemony within the ancient world. See Itumeleng J. Mosala, *Biblical Hermeneutics and Black Theology in South Africa* (Grand Rapids, MI: Eerdmans, 1989).

9. See Michael N. Jagessar and Anthony G. Reddie, eds, *Black Theology in Britain: A Reader* (London: Equinox, 2007), 300–302.

10. See Chapter 2 on reconciliation where a similar point is made.

11. William R. Hertzog II, *Jesus, Justice and the Reign of God: A Ministry of Liberation* (Louisville, KY: Westminster John Knox Press, 2000).

12. Mark Lewis Taylor, *The Executed God: The Way of the Cross in Lockdown America* (Minneapolis: Fortress Press, 2001).

13. Musa W. Dube, *Postcolonial Feminist Interpretation of the Bible* (St. Louis: Chalice Press, 2000).

14. Catherine Keller, Michael Nausner and Mayra Rivera, eds, *Postcolonial Theologies: Divinity and Empire* (St. Louis: Chalice Press, 2004).

15. See Mosala, *Biblical Hermeneutics*, 154–89.

16. Mosala, *Biblical Hermeneutics*, 154–89.

17. Postcolonial Indian scholar David Joy examines the exploitative nature of Temple economics and power in his fascinating study on the Markan narratives and the use of the crowd as a postcolonial lens for unlocking this, the earliest of the Gospel accounts. See David Joy, *Mark and its Subalterns: A Hermeneutical Paradigm for a Postcolonial Context* (London: Equinox, 2008).

18. I am not assuming that this meal can necessarily be understood as a Eucharistic one in the strict sense of that term; but even if this is not the case, it still represents Christ's healing presence with an estranged individual.

19. See Anthony Reddie, "A Black Theological Approach to Reparations," *Black Theology: An International Journal* 5, no.2 (2007): 184–202 .

20. See the work of such organizations as "Ligali" who describe themselves thus: "Ligali (*pronounced lee-ga-lee*) is the African British Equality Authority. We are a Pan African Human Rights Organization that challenge the misrepresentation of African people and culture in the British media. Our remit is to actively campaign for cultural, economic, political and social justice on behalf of the African community." For further information go to http://www.ligali.org/

21. See James Walvin, *Black Ivory*, rev. ed. (Oxford: Blackwell, 2006).

22. See Eric Williams, *Capitalism and Slavery* (London: Andre Deutsch, 1990).

23. See http://www.robertbeckford.co.uk.

24. See Emmanuel C. Eze, ed., *Race and the Enlightenment: A Reader* (Oxford: Blackwell, 1997), 97–108.

25. The 2005 G8 summit met at the Gleneagles Hotel, in Perthshire, Scotland, July 6–8, 2005.

26. R. Reddie, *Abolition*, 234.

27. This statement was made in his Leader's address at the annual Labour party conference in Brighton, October 2, 2001.

28. The Africa Commission was the brainchild of the British Prime Minister, Tony Blair. "The Commission established the Commission for Africa. The 17 members of the Commission, 9 from Africa and all working in their individual and personal capacities, published their report 'Our Common Interest' on 11 March 2005." (See http://www.commissionforafrica.org/english/home/newsstories.html, accessed October 15, 2007.) The commission's first report was published in March 2005. See *Our Common Interest: Report of the Commission for Africa* (London: Penguin Books, 2005).

29. See Walter Rodney, *How Europe Underdeveloped Africa* (London: Bogle-L'Ouverture Publications, 1972).

30. R. Reddie, *Abolition*, 224.

31. Talk by Richard Reddie at Solihull Central Library as a part of Solihull Council's celebration of "Black History Month," October 12, 2007.

32. Ibid.

33. See Tissa Balasuriya, "Liberation of the Affluent," *Black Theology: An International Journal* 1, no.1 (November 2002): 83–113.

34. See Dietrich Bonhoeffer, *The Cost of Discipleship* (London: Touchstone, 1995).

35. See James H. Cone, *A Black Theology of Liberation* (Maryknoll, NY: Orbis Books, 1986). See also *God of the Oppressed* (San Francisco: Harper, 1975).

36. See James H. Cone, "Theology's Great Sin: Silence in the Face of White Supremacy," *Black Theology: An International Journal* 2, no.2 (July 2004): 139–52.

37. See Reddie, *Nobodies to Somebodies*, 153–71.

38. Reddie, *Nobodies to Somebodies*, 153–71.

39. See Robert Beckford, *God and the Gangs* (London: Darton, Longman and Todd, 2004), 72–84. See also James W. Perkinson, *White Theology: Outing Supremacy in Modernity* (New York: Palgrave, 2004).

40. See Anthony G. Reddie, *Acting in Solidarity: Reflections in Critical Christianity* (London: Darton, Longman and Todd, 2005), 123–26.

41. See Anthony G. Reddie, *Dramatizing Theologies: A Participative Approach to Black God-Talk* (London: Equinox, 2006), 103–27.

42. Some of this work has already taken place, initiated by the Committee for Minority Ethnic Anglican Concerns (CMEAC), where through a series of "hearings" White Christians have been invited to hear the pain of Black African Caribbean Christians, in very controlled and carefully modulated arenas. These events began in early 2007, prior to the bicentenary of the abolition of the slave trade in Britain (March 25, 2007).

43. See R. Reddie, *Abolition*, 87–109.

44. See Lewis V. Baldwin, *Toward the Beloved Community* (Cleveland, OH: Pilgrim Press, 1995) for an excellent treatment of the internal and external struggle to overthrow apartheid in South Africa.

45. See Iain Whyte, *Scotland and the Abolition of Black Slavery, 1756–1838* (Edinburgh: Edinburgh University Press, 2006), 117–40 for the plethora of arguments

and counter-arguments for the abolition or retention of slavery. In particular note the ways in which notions of natural law and the rights of man were invoked as proof for the iniquitous state of the institution of slavery in Britain in the late 18th and early 19th centuries.

46. See Wale Babatunde, *Great Britain has Fallen: How to Restore Britain's Greatness as a Nation* (London: New Wine Publishing, 2002). See also "A Call to Prayer and Action from Dr Jonathan Oloyede," *Keep the Faith* magazine (Bury St. Edmonds: Black UK Publications, October 2007): 16.

Chapter 9

1. In terms of the latter, as editor of *Black Theology: An International Journal* I compiled a special themed issue to mark the bicentenary of the abolition of the slave trade in Britain. I contributed an essay to that particular issue entitled "A Black Theological Approach to Reconciliation: Responding to the 200th Anniversary of the Abolition of the Slave Trade in Britain," *Black Theology: An International Journal* 5, no.2 (2007): 184–202, which is reproduced in this book (Chapter 2). The other major scholarly contribution to the myriad issues and debate concerning the slave trade in its legacy in Britain was the first ever reader in Black Theology in Britain, co-edited with my colleague Michael Jagessar. See Michael N. Jagessar and Anthony G. Reddie, eds, *Black Theology in Britain: A Reader* (London: Equinox, 2007).

2. Two excellent treatments on this issue can be found in James W. Perkinson, *White Theology: Outing Supremacy in Modernity* (New York: Palgrave Macmillan, 2004) and James W. Perkinson, *Shamanism, Racism and Hip Hop Culture: Essays on White Supremacy and Black Subversion* (New York: Palgrave Macmillan, 2005).

3. It is interesting to note the number of texts written on William Wilberforce. See Stephen Tomkins, *William Wilberforce: A Biography* (Grand Rapids, MI: Eerdmans, 2007) and William Hague, *William Wilberforce: The Life of the Great Anti-Slave Trade Campaigner* (London: Harper Press, 2007) for two of a growing number of texts on his life.

4. In terms of these four pivotal African men and their political activism and theological legacy, see Chigor Chike, *Voices from Slavery: The Life and Beliefs of African Slaves in Britain* (Milton Keynes: AuthorHouse, 2007). See also the excellent resource material created by my colleague at the Queen's Foundation, Carol Troupe, on Black abolitionists of the 18th century in Britain. See her website http://www.livingoutfaith.org for further details.

5. See Eric Williams, *Capitalism and Slavery* (London: Andre Deutsch, 1984).

6. See the work of Ligali (reference has been made to them in previous chapters). See also Robert Beckford's influential television documentary *The Empire Pays Back*, Channel 4 television (August 15, 2005). In the promotional literature for this documentary, Beckford writes "I believe African slaves were ripped off by the British Empire… I want to know who bankrolled it, who insured it and who made a mint from it." See http://robertbeckford.co.uk/taxonomy/term/2%2B3 (accessed October 12, 2007).

7. The term "dibby dibby" is from Jamaican vernacular and its approximate meaning relates to something or someone who is considered "second rate" or inferior in quality.

8. *Holy Bible – New Revised Standard Version* (London: HarperCollins, 1989).

9. James H. Cone, *The Spirituals and the Blues* (Maryknoll, NY: Orbis Books, 1992), 30.

10. See Cheryl A. Kirk-Duggan, *Exorcizing Evil: A Womanist Perspective on the Spirituals* (Maryknoll, NY: Orbis Books, 1997).

11. See Yolanda Y. Smith, *Reclaiming the Spirituals: New Possibilities for African American Christian Education* (Cleveland, OH: Pilgrim Press, 2004).

12. Smith, *Reclaiming the Spirituals*, 71–72.

13. See Anthony G. Reddie, "A Run of Bad Luck," in *Acting in Solidarity* (London: Darton, Longman and Todd, 1995), 22–30.

14. I am at pains to add that this is not to suggest that all Black British Pentecostals do not possess any sense of lament and "theological struggle" in their spirituality and reflective practices. At the international conference on Black Theology in Britain held at the Queen's Foundation, to mark the bicentenary of the abolition of the slave trade, entitled *Freedom is for Freeing* (July 13-15, 2007), Bishop Delroy Hall of the Church of God of Prophecy presented a paper entitled "The Middle Passage as Existential Crucifixion." The paper was a theological and historical meditation on the Middle Passage as a period that can be likened to "Low Saturday," the day between "Good Friday" and Easter Sunday. Hall argues that the ongoing psycho-social travails of Black people in Britain as evinced in high numbers of Black males incarcerated in prisons, and disproportionately high levels of Black people also incarcerated or over medicated on drugs for mental ill health, all point to a collective sense of continuing existential crucifixion. Hall argues that Black people in Britain are still collectively in a state of "Low Saturday," where our prevailing memories of the immediate past are of "Good Friday" and suffering and struggle and where Easter Sunday is an eschatological promise that has yet to be realized. See Anthony G. Reddie, ed., *Black Theology, Slavery, and Contemporary Christianity: 200 Years and No Apology* (Aldershot: Ashgate c.2009), forthcoming.

15. 2007 was the year of marking the 200th anniversary of the abolition of the slave trade on March 25, 1807.

16. It is interesting to note the activity of the major academic conference for theology and religious studies in Britain – the Society for the Study of Theology (SST), which meets every spring in a setting of higher education. In the year in which Britain marked the bicentenary of the abolition of the slave trade, 2007, the conference theme for the SST conference was "Celebration and Accountability: Theology in the World" (March 26-29, 2007). From a casual perusal of the plenary speakers there was no mention of the bicentenary in the titles of the papers. There may have been some reference to the events of the year in the content, but as I did not attend the conference, I do not have access to the substantive content of these presentations. What is interesting to note is the extent to which the "theological mainstream" in Britain has largely ignored the commemoration of the bicentenary.

17. These settings included in churches; informal learning contexts such as Sunday Schools, weekly Fellowship and Bible studies; meetings in the wider Black communities with activists and in Black cultural discussion groups.

18. This exercise was first developed for a previous study. See the introduction to "The Plain Old Honest Truth" in Reddie, *Acting in Solidarity*, 144–45.

19. Frederick Ware outlines some of the opposition mounted by a number of Black theologians to the notion of God being on the side of oppressed Black peoples. Some of these scholars argue that there is no evidence to suggest that God does take sides, and if God does not choose to side with the oppressed, then what is the point of the oppressed believing in God? See Frederick L. Ware, *Methodologies of Black Theology* (Cleveland, OH: Pilgrim Press, 2002), 66–114. See also William R. Jones, *Is God a White Racist?: A Preamble to Black Theology* (Boston: Beacon Press, 1998).

20. In a previous piece of work I created a piece of drama entitled "My God," in which God appears as a Black woman to four men, in response to their prayers, as the words "My God!" are uttered by the praying supplicants. The men are naturally shocked and in some cases scandalized at the sight of God as a Black woman. When I have used this section of the study with a number of students, a few have been known to remark that although I acknowledge the critique of Black Christian theism by the likes of William Jones and Anthony Pinn (to whom reference is made at a later point in this chapter), I nevertheless assume a normative stance for God's engagement with humankind, by the sheer fact that God reveals Godself when the four pray. This is itself a faith-based presupposition of a Christian Black theologian. In this respect, I was guilty as charged. See Anthony G. Reddie, *Dramatizing Theologies* (London: Equinox, 2006), 64–80.

21. As demonstrated in the previous reference.

22. This exercise, like many others in this book, was not a scientific piece of work and so I cannot offer any empirical proof for my "findings" nor can I claim them to be statistically significant for the wider population (Black people in Britain) from which it is extracted.

23. Many of these exercises are detailed in this book. A fuller explication of this method for undertaking Black theology can be found in chapter one of a forthcoming piece of work. See Anthony G. Reddie, *Transformative Worship: Black Theology, Racial Justice and Christian Ministry* (London: SPCK, c.2009/10).

24. See William R. Jones, *Is God a White Racist?* (Boston: Beacon Books, 1998).

25. This term comes from Jones, *Is God a White Racist?*, 185–202.

26. Jones, *Is God a White Racist?*, 195.

27. Jones, *Is God a White Racist?*, 196.

28. This term is derived from the work of Orlando Patterson. See Orlando Patterson, *Slavery and Social Death: A Comparative Study* (Cambridge, MA: Harvard University Press, 1982).

29. A. Elaine Brown Crawford, *Hope in the Holler: A Womanist Theology* (Louisville, KY: Westminster John Knox Press, 2002).

30. Crawford, *Hope in the Holler*, 4–5.

31. See Jurgen Moltmann, *Theology of Hope: On the Ground and the Implications of a Christian Eschatology* (London: SCM Press, 1967).

32. See Crawford, *Hope in the Holler*, ix–xvii.

33. See Kelly Brown Douglas, *The Black Christ* (Maryknoll, NY: Orbis Books, 1993).

34. James H. Cone, *God of the Oppressed* (San Francisco: HarperSanFrancisco, 1975), 108–95.

35. JoAnne Marie Terrell, *Power in the Blood?: The Cross in the African American Experience* (Maryknoll, NY: Orbis Books, 1998).

36. Terrell, *Power in the Blood?*, 34.

37. See Robert Beckford, *Jesus is Dread* (London: Darton, Longman and Todd, 1998), 130–52 and Riggins R. Earl Jr., *Dark Salutations* (Harrisburg, PA: Trinity Press International, 2001), 1–16.

38. See Valentina Alexander, "Passive and Active Radicalism in Black-Led Churches," in Jagessar and Reddie, eds, *Black Theology in Britain: A Reader*, 52–69.

39. See Robert Beckford, *Dread and Pentecostal* (London: SPCK, 2000), 46–48.

40. Beckford, *Dread and Pentecostal*, 95–130.

41. Beckford, *Dread and Pentecostal*, 101.

42. My work is sponsored by the British Methodist Church.

Chapter 10

1. Olivia Pearl Stokes, "Black Theology: A Challenge to Religious Education," in Norma H. Thompson, ed., *Religious Education and Theology* (Birmingham, AL: Religious Education Press, 1982), 71–92 (71).

2. Albert Raboteau, *Slave Religion* (Oxford: Oxford University Press, 1978), 44–150.

3. Eric Williams, *Capitalism and Slavery* (London: Andre Deutsch, 1964), 30–168.

4. W.E.B. Dubois, "The African Slave Roots of War" (1915), in Meyer Weinburg, ed., *W.E.B. Dubois: A Reader* (New York: Harper and Row, 1970), 360–71.

5. Bob Marley, "Redemption Song," from the album *Uprising* (copyright Bob Marley Music; Island Records, 1980).

6. Franz Fannon, *The Wretched of the Earth* (London: Penguin Books, 1967), 52.

7. Erik Erikson, *Identity: Youth arid Crisis* (London: Faber & Faber, 1968), 59.

8. Jocelyn Maxime, "The Importance of Racial Identity for the Psychological Well Being of Black Children and Young Black People," in Hewlet Andrew, ed., *To Overcome is to Undertake: First Connexional Conference of Young Black Methodists* (London: The Methodist Church, 1990), 9–13 (9).

9. Winston James, "Migration, Racism and Identity," in W. James and C. Harris, eds, *Inside Babylon* (London: Verso, 1993), 9–20 (9).

10. G. Lewis, "Race Relations in Britain: A View from the Caribbean," *Race Today* 1, no. 3 (1969): 9–19 (9).

11. A child of a "negro" mother and a "negro" father.

12. A child of a mother who is one-fifth Black and a White father (B. Higman, *Slave Populations and Economy in Jamaica: 1807–1834* [Cambridge: Cambridge University Press, 1976), 139.

13. James, "Migration, Racism and Identity," 234.

14. James, "Migration, Racism and Identity," 234.

15. Walter Rodney, *The Groundings with my Brothers* (London: Bogle-L'Ouverture, 1969), 33.

16. Rodney, *The Groundings*, 33.

17. Caryl Phillips *The European Tribe* (London: Faber & Faber, 1987).

18. Phillips, *The European Tribe*, 2.

19. See Vanessa Howard, "A Report on Afro-Caribbean Christianity in Britain," in *Community Relations Project* (Leeds: University of Leeds, 1987), 23. According to

Howard, 52 per cent of the African-Caribbean population in the United Kingdom are British born.

20. Cornel West, *Race Matters* (Boston: Beacon Press, 1993), 11–15.

21. See Jawanza Kunjufu, *Countering the Conspiracy to Destroy Black Boys*, I (Chicago: Afro-Am, 1982); Jawanza Kunjufu, *Countering the Conspiracy to Destroy Black Boys*, II (Chicago: Afro-Am, 1986); Jawanza Kunjufu, *Countering the Conspiracy to Destroy Black Boys*, III (Chicago: Afro-Am, 1990).

22. Tony Sewell, *Black Masculinities and Schooling* (Stoke-on-Trent: Trentham, 1997).

23. Michael Ross, *Building Positive Images in African American Males through the Sunday School from a Black Perspective* (unpublished DMin thesis; United Theological Seminary, 1993).

24. Grant Shockley, "Historical Perspectives," in Charles R. Foster and Grant. S. Shockley, eds, *Working with Black Youth* (Nashville, TN: Abingdon Press, 1989), 21–26.

25. Jacquelyn Grant, "A Theological Framework," in Foster and Shockley, eds, *Working with Black Youth*, 60–74.

26. Grant, "A Theological Framework," 71–74.

27. Romney M. Moseley, "Retrieving Intergenerational and Intercultural Faith," in Foster and Shockley, eds, *Working with Black Youth*, 95–96.

28. Moseley, "Retrieving Intergenerational and Intercultural Faith," 91–92.

29. Evelyn L. Parker, "Twenty Seeds of Hope: Religious Moral Values in African-American Adolescents in Chicago and Implications for Christian Education in the Black Church" (unpublished PhD thesis; Garrett/Northwestern program in Religious and Theological Studies, 1996), 1–74. See the more recent *Trouble Don't Last Always* (Cleveland, OH: Pilgrim Press, 2003).

30. See Parker, "Twenty Seeds of Hope," 147.

31. Parker, *Trouble Don't Last Always*.

32. Helen A. Archibald, "Notes on the Culture of the Urban Negro Child," *Religious Education* 62, no. 4 (July–August 1967): 321-27 (324).

33. Archibald, "Notes," 325.

34. Andrew White, "Why Should the Church Evangelise Black Youth?" *Religious Education* 64, no. 6 (November–December 1969): 446–50 (447–48).

35. White, Why Should the Church Evangelise Black Youth?" 449.

36. Nelson E. Copeland Jr, *The Heroic Revolution: A New Agenda for Urban Youth Work* (Nashville, TN: James C. Winston Publishing Co., 1995), 27–31.

37. Copeland, *The Heroic Revolution*, 83–85.

38. Copeland, *The Heroic Revolution*, 85.

39. Na'im Akbar, *Chains and Images of Psychological Slavery* (Jersey City: New Mind Publications, 1984), 20–23.

40. Copeland, *The Heroic Revolution*, 110.

41. Paulo Freire, *Pedagogy of the Oppressed* (New York: Herder & Herder, 1972), 31.

42. Freire, *Pedagogy of the Oppressed*, 32.

43. Paulo Freire, *Education for Critical Consciousness* (New York: Continuum, 1973), 18–20.

44. Freire, *Pedagogy of the Oppressed*, 33.

45. Grant S. Shockley, "Black Theology and Religious Education," in Randolph Crump Miller, ed., *Theologies of Religious Education* (Birmingham, AL: Religious Education Press, 1995), 323.

46. Grant S. Shockley, "Christian Education and the Black Religious Experience," in Charles R. Foster, ed., *Ethnicity in the Education of the Church* (Nashville, TN: Scarritt Press, 1987), 31.

47. Shockley, "Christian Education and the Black Religious Experience," 31.

48. See Anthony G. Reddie, *Growing into Hope*, 2 vols. (Peterborough: Methodist Publishing House, 1998).

49. See Reddie, *Growing into Hope*, I, 29–32.

50. The development of this exercise and the many others in *Growing into Hope* were influenced by the work of Hope and Timmel.

51. See Shockley, "Black Theology and Religious Education."

52. James Cone, "Black Theology and the Black Church: Where Do We Go From Here?" in Gayraud Wilmore and James H. Cone, eds, *Black Theology: A Documentary History, 1966–1979* (Maryknoll, NY: Orbis Books, 1979), 350–59.

53. See *Growing into Hope*, I, 29–32. Note the Bible passages that are highlighted from Matthew's Gospel and how these are linked to the exercise and the overall theme for that Sunday's lesson.

54. See Daniel S. Schipani, "Liberation Theology and Religious Education," in Randolph Crump Miller, ed., *Theologies of Religious Education* (Birmingham, AL: Religious Education Press, 1995), 286–313.

55. See Gustavo Gutierrez, *A Theology of Liberation* (Maryknoll, NY: Orbis Books, 1973).

56. Schipani, "Liberation Theology and Religious Education," 288–89.

57. Schipani, "Liberation Theology and Religious Education," 290–91.

58. Schipani, "Liberation Theology and Religious Education," 294.

59. Delores H. Carpenter, "A Response to Brian Tippen," *Religious Education* 88, no. 4 (Fall 1993): 622–26.

60. Olivia Pearl Stokes, "Education in the Black Church: Design for Change," *Religious Education* 69, no. 4 (January–February 1974): 433-45 (438).

61. Stokes, "Education in the Black Church," 438.

Chapter 11

1. See Anthony G. Reddie, *Acting in Solidarity: Reflections in Critical Christianity* (London: Darton, Longman and Todd, 2005), 127–35.

2. The first significant positive sense of my own self-worth within the Methodist Church came with the publication of Heather Walton's *A Tree God Planted: Black People in British Methodism* (London: The Methodist Church, 1985).

3. See Lee N. June, ed., *The Black Family* (Grand Rapids, MI: Zondervan, 1991).

4. See Franz Fannon, *The Wretched of the Earth* (New York: Grove Books, 1984).

5. See Isaac Julien, "Black Is, Black Ain't: Notes on De-Essentializing Black Identities," in Gina Dent, ed., *Black Popular Culture* (Seattle: Bay Press, 1992), 255–63.

6. Victor Anderson, *Beyond Ontological Blackness* (New York: Continuum, 1995).

7. See Edward P. Wimberly, *Moving from Shame to Self Worth: Preaching and Pastoral Care* (Nashville, TN: Abingdon Press, 1999).

8. In this regard the work of the British Empirical Practical theologian Leslie Francis is particularly apposite. His theological work is explored through the framework of quantitative social science methodologies. See Leslie J. Francis, *Faith and Psychology: Personality, Religion and the Individual* (London: Darton, Longman and Todd, 2005).

9. See Anthony G. Reddie, *Dramatizing Theologies: A Participative Approach to Black God-talk* (London: Equinox, 2006).

10. The fact that the group was older was very much in keeping with the age demographics of most inner-city Black, African Caribbean congregations in Britain. Many inner-city churches are, in effect, ageing congregations.

11. Robert S. Beckford, "Theology in the Age of Crack: Crack Age, Prosperity Doctrine and 'Being There'," *Black Theology in Britain: A Journal of Contextual Praxis* 4, no.1 (November 2001): 9–24.

12. Robert Beckford, *Dread and Pentecostal* (London: SPCK, 2000), 204.

13. See Anthony G. Reddie, *Nobodies to Somebodies* (Peterborough: Epworth Press, 2003), 3–36.

14. See Gary Gunderson, *Deeply Woven Roots: Improving the Quality of Life in Your Community* (Minneapolis: Fortress Press, 1997).

15. Gunderson, *Deeply Woven Roots*, 83–92.

16. *Unfinished Business: Children and the Churches* [Commissioned by the Consultative Group on Ministry among Children – CGMC] (London: CCBI Publications, 1995).

17. See Charles R. Foster, *Educating Congregations: The Future of Christian Education* (Nashville, TN: Abingdon, 1994).

18. See Charles R. Foster and Theodore Brelsford, *We are the Church Together: Cultural Diversity in Congregational Life* (Valley Forge, PA: Trinity Press International, 1996).

19. Charles R. Foster, *Embracing Diversity: Leadership in Multicultural Congregations* (Herndon, VA: The Alban Institute, 1998), 57.

20. See Anthony G. Reddie, "Editorial," *Black Theology: An International Journal* 4, no.1 (London: Equinox, 2006): 8–9.

21. I have attempted something of this sort in terms of my previous work. See Anthony G. Reddie, *Growing into Hope*, 2 vols. (Peterborough: The Methodist Publishing House, 1998). See also Reddie, *Nobodies to Somebodies*, 53–57.

22. See Beckford, "Theology in the Age of Crack," 9–24.

23. See http://www.creflodollarministries.org/ for further details of his ministry.

24. See http://www.kicc.org.uk/ for further details of his ministry.

25. See Beckford, "Theology in the Age of Crack," 9–24.

26. I have addressed elements of this phenomenon in a previous piece of work. See Reddie, *Acting in Solidarity*, 45–53.

27. See Harry H. Singleton III, *Black Theology and Ideology* (Collegeville, MN: The Liturgical Press, 2002), 47–67. See also Anthony B. Pinn and Dwight N. Hopkins, eds, *Loving the Body* (New York: Palgrave Macmillan, 2006) for an excellent exploration of the limits placed on Black people by the Black Church in terms of its prohibitions around same-gender sexual relationships and sexuality as a whole.

28. This form of reading has been inspired by Kelly Brown Douglas' recent book *What's Faith Got to Do With It?* (Maryknoll, NY: Orbis Books, 2005), where Brown

challenges the traditional Christian imperial hegemony that is built on an adversarial closed monotheism.

29. This has been the central task of Black theologians such as James Cone and Womanists like Jacquelyn, both of whom have a strong Christological focus to their theological method. See James H. Cone, *God of the Oppressed* (San Francisco: HarperSanFrancisco, 1975), 108–95. See also Jacquelyn Grant, *White Women's Christ and Black Women's Jesus* (Atlanta: Scholars Press, 1989).

Chapter 12

1. Although I developed five case studies in the development of this chapter, only one of them is explored in greater depth as a means of outlining a model for how Black theology can begin to make a difference. This case study is explored in greater detail at a later juncture in this chapter.

2. See Joe D. Aldred, *Respect: Understanding Caribbean British Christianity* (Peterborough: Epworth Press, 2005). See also R. David Muir, "Black Theology, Pentecostalism, and Racial Struggles in the Church of God" (unpublished PhD thesis, King's College London, 2004).

3. See Anthony G. Reddie, *Black Theology in Transatlantic Dialogue* (New York: Palgrave Macmillan, 2006), 126–41. This work also builds on the thoughts and reflections of Robert Beckford, who has created a Pentecostal-centred approach to a Black political pneumatology for the British context. See Robert Beckford, *Dread and Pentecostal* (London: SPCK, 2000).

4. See Chapter 2.

5. See Chapter 8.

6. See Beckford, *Dread and Pentecostal*. See also Anthony G. Reddie, *Dramatizing Theologies: A Participative Approach to Black God-talk* (London: Equinox, 2006); Dwight N. Hopkins, *Being Human: Race, Culture and Religion* (Minneapolis: Fortress Press, 2005) and Kelly Brown Douglas, *What's Faith Got to Do With It?: Black Bodies/Christian Souls* (Maryknoll, NY: Orbis Books, 2005).

7. See Charles R. Foster and Fred Smith, *Black Religious Experience: Conversations of Double Consciousness and the Work of Grant Shockley* (Nashville, TN: Abingdon Press, 2003).

8. See Chapter 4.

9. See Anthony G. Reddie, *Nobodies to Somebodies: A Practical Theology for Education and Liberation* (Peterborough: Epworth Press, 2003), 22–29.

10. See Anthony B. Pinn, *Terror and Triumph: The Nature of Black Religion* (Minneapolis: Fortress Press, 2003), 52–80.

11. See Dwight N. Hopkins, "The Religion of Globalization," in Dwight N. Hopkins, Lois Ann Lorentzen, Eduardo Mendieta and David Batstone, eds, *Religions/Globalizations: Theories and Cases* (Durham and London: Duke University Press, 2001), 7–32.

12. James H. Cone, "Theology's Great Sin: Silence in the Face of White Supremacy," *Black Theology: An International Journal* 2, no.2 (2004): 139–52.

13. In this regard, James H. Harris, *Pastoral Theology: A Black Church Perspective* (Minneapolis: Augsburg Press, 1991) remains the classic text. See also Dale P. Andrews,

Practical Theology for Black Churches: Bridging Black Theology and African American Folk Religion (Louisville, KY: Westminster John Knox Press, 2002).

14. To the best of my knowledge no authoritative figures exist for the ratio of Black women to Black men in Black majority churches in Britain.

15. I say "numerical terms" because, as the highly influential study by Elaine Foster attests, whilst Black women are numerically in the ascendancy in the Black Church in Britain (and do most of the work), Black men continue to hold and exercise power. See Elaine Foster, "Black Women in Black Led Churches: A Study of Black Women's Contribution to the Growth and Development of Black Led Churches in Britain" (unpublished M.Phil thesis, University of Birmingham, 1990).

16. Recent excellent work has been undertaken in the US that seeks, in part, to address this question. See Stephen C. Finley, "Homoeroticism and the African-American Heterosexual Male: Quest for Meaning in the Black Church," *Black Theology: An International Journal* 5, no.3 (November 2007): 305–26.

17. See the beginning of Chapter 7.

18. See Anthony G. Reddie, *Nobodies to Somebodies: A Practical Theology for Education and Liberation* (Peterborough: Epworth Press, 2003), 67–70.

19. See Reddie, *Black Theology in Transatlantic Dialogue*.

20. Reddie, *Black Theology in Transatlantic Dialogue*, 202.

21. See Bruce J. Malina, *The Social Gospel of Jesus: The Kingdom of God in Mediterranean Perspective* (Minneapolis: Fortress Press, 2001).

22. The Black British woman theologian Kate Coleman has explored the notion of hybridity and multiple and intersectional subjectivities of Black Christian women in Britain in her more recent work. Although I am clearly not a Black woman, and recognize that Coleman is not writing about me, I nonetheless accept that aspects of her conceptual and empirical work resonate with my own postcolonial subjectivity as a Black Christian male in Britain. See Kate Coleman, "Being Human: A Black British Christian Woman's Perspective," in Michael N. Jagessar and Anthony G. Reddie, eds, *Black Theology in Britain: A Reader* (London: Equinox, 2007), 160–66. See also Kate Coleman, "Another Kind of Black," *Black Theology: An International Journal* 5, no.3 (2007): 279–304.

23. These terms are notoriously slippery entities, requiring a great deal of nuanced thinking and reflection, for they strike at the heart of postmodern, post-structuralist discourse. What do we mean by "Black" in order to speak of "Black majority" or "Black led" churches? A number of Black British religious scholars have addressed these questions in their recent work. For further information see Mark Sturge, *Look What the Lord Has Done!* (London: Scripture Union, 2005), Joe Aldred, *Respect* (Peterborough: Epworth, 2005) and Reddie, *Dramatizing Theologies* and *Black Theology in Transatlantic Dialogue*.

24. See Beckford, *Dread and Pentecostal*, 194.

25. Modern theologians such as Stanley Grenz have argued that "Trinitarian Theology" (Three-in-one dynamics of the Godhead – Father, Son and Holy Spirit) provides the most compelling Christian theological anthropology for a communitarian human ethic. The relationship between the three persons of the Godhead mirror the way in which human beings should relate to one another in community. For further thoughts on this point see Stanley J. Grenz, *Rediscovering the Triune God: The Trinity in Contemporary Theology* (Minneapolis: Fortress Press, 2004). For a Womanist treatment

see Karen Baker-Fletcher, *Dancing with God: The Trinity from a Womanist Perspective* (St. Louis: Chalice Press, 2007).

26. I should note that there are innumerable reasons why the men did not accept my invitation. Due to my very busy schedule I was only able to offer one date for our prospective meeting, which was a Saturday. Many could have had other pressing commitments on that day. Many of the men would not necessarily have known me (only of me) and so might have had an element of trepidation about volunteering. In short, there could be myriad reasons for the non-appearance of the men.

27. See the Interactive Bible study entitled "Offering what we are and can be to God – a critical assessment of selfhood," in Anthony G. Reddie, *Dramatizing Theologies* (London: Equinox, 2006), 134–40 and 191.

28. Matthew 25:14–30. Reddie, *Dramatizing Theologies*, 134–40.

29. James Fowler, *Stages of Faith* (San Francisco: HarperSanFrancisco, 1995).

30. K.E. Nipkow and Friedrich Schweitzer, eds, *Stages of Faith and Religious Development: Implications for Church, Education and Society* (London: SCM Press, 1992).

31. John Westerhoff III, *Living the Faith Community* (San Francisco: HarperCollins, 1985).

32. See Romney Moseley, *Becoming a Self Before God* (Nashville: Abingdon, 1991).

33. See Reddie, *Nobodies to Somebodies.*

34. Thomas Groome, *Christian Religious Education* (San Francisco: Harper & Row, 1980), 49–51.

35. Thomas Groome, *Sharing Faith* (San Francisco: Harper San Francisco, 1991).

36. Groome, *Sharing Faith*, 135.

37. In the Christian tradition this is primarily the Bible and the sacred narratives that are contained within it, identified as "Holy Scripture."

38. Groome, *Sharing Faith*, 138–51.

39. Groome, *Sharing Faith*, 266–92.

40. See volume 2 of Reddie, *Growing into Hope: Liberation and Change*, 7–8.

41. See Reddie, *Growing into Hope: Liberation and Change*, 8–9.

42. As in my previous examples of participative Black theology, I am not making any claims to be unearthing conclusive knowledge about the religious consciousness of all Black people in Britain. This participative exercise makes no claim to be a scientifically valid and generalized, replicable piece of work. Rather, like the other pieces, it is constructed as a diagnostic heuristic, which is used in order to gain some sense of the feelings and attitudes of "some" ordinary Black people in Britain.

43. The reflections of a number of members of the group on the relationship between a humble and accessible Jesus of History when juxtaposed with a mighty, proud, imperial church echoes some of the thoughts of Albert Nolan in his landmark book *Jesus Before Christianity: The Gospel of Liberation* (London: Darton, Longman and Todd, 1991).

44. See David Isiorho, "Black Theology in Urban Shadow: Combating Racism in the Church of England," *Black Theology: An International Journal* 1, no.1 (November 2002): 29–48. See also Lorraine Dixon, "Response to David Isiorho," *Black Theology: An International Journal* 1, no.1 (November 2002): 49–51. See also David Isiorho, "Black Theology, Englishness and the Church of England," in Michael N. Jagessar and Anthony

G. Reddie, eds, *Postcolonial Black British Theology* (Peterborough: Epworth Press, 2007), 62–72.

    45. Groome, *Sharing Faith*, 151–53.

    46. Groome *Sharing Faith*, 153.

    47. It is interesting to note the relatively little work that has been done on the Trinity in Black theology. There is nothing to the best of my knowledge in Britain and only the odd text in the US: for example, see Karen Baker-Fletcher, *Dancing with God: The Trinity from a Womanist Perspective* (St. Louis: Chalice Press, 2007). There may be a variety of reasons for this. In the UK as in the Caribbean and the US, significant numbers of Black Christians belong to the "Oneness Tradition," which eschews any notion of the Trinity as having any probative functionality within the Bible. In the Black British tradition one should note the pioneering work of Roswith Gerloff. See Roswith I.H. Gerloff, "A Plea for British Black Theologies: The Black Church Movement in Britain," 2 vols. (unpublished PhD thesis, University of Birmingham, 1991). See also Mark Sturge, *Look What The Lord Has Done!* (Milton Keynes: Scripture Union, 2005), 134–36. Given the intense metaphysical and philosophical *modus operandi* demanded of those seeking to explore the complexities of the "Immanent" and "Economic" Trinity, I wonder whether, for many Black theological scholars, there has been a preference for undertaking more contextually based and embodied forms of discourse around which most Black people can cohere, as opposed to more speculative forms of scholarship that might divide us even further? Given that, for the most part, Black theology has not always sought to work within the prescribed frameworks as those often found in "systematic Theology," in-depth reflections on the Trinity are in relative short supply. Exceptions can be found in James Cone, *A Black Theology of Liberation* (Maryknoll, NY: Orbis Books, 1990), James H. Evans Jr., *We Have Been Believers: An African American Systematic Theology* (Minneapolis: Fortress Press, 1992) and Lewin Williams, *Caribbean Theology* (New York: Peter Lang, 1994).

    48. See Anne Hope, Sally Timmel and Chris Hodzi, *Teaching for Transformation: A Handbook for Community Workers* – Books 1–3 (Gweru, Zimbabwe: Mambo Press, 1994), and Anne Hope, Sally Timmel and Chris Hodzi, *Teaching for Transformation: A Handbook for Community Workers* – Book 4 (London: Intermediate Technology Publication, 1999).

    49. Paulo Freire, *Pedagogy of the Oppressed* (New York: Herder and Herder, 1968), 62.

    50. Hope, Timmel and Hodzi, *Teaching for Transformation*, Book 2, p. 4.

    51. See Anthony G. Reddie, *Nobodies to Somebodies: A Practical Theology for Education and Liberation* (Peterborough: Epworth Press, 2003), 142–47.

    52. For many of them, the two – the Bible and God – are actually synonymous. Often the Bible becomes a synonym for God.

    53. Some of my initial thinking has been inspired by Jose Irizarry and his notion of theology as "Performative Action." Irizarry argues for a dramatic process of doing theology in which participants and the educator enter into a process of performance in which there is an inherent dialectic and from which new truths can be discerned. See Jose R. Irizarry, "The Religious Educator as Cultural Spec-Actor: Researching Self in Intercultural Pedagogy," *Religious Education* 98, no.3 (Summer 2003): 365–81.

    54. The two principal Black theologians in Britain outline their differing but complementary practical approaches to reading the Bible with ordinary Black people

which utilizes a "reader-response" approach to the text. This is a particular reading strategy in which the experience of the reader and their ideological presuppositions (that arise from an analysis of their material realities) are used to "unlock" the text. See Robert Beckford, *God and the Gangs* (London: Darton, Longman and Todd, 2004), 96–100. I attempt something to this effect in a previous piece of work, but offer a more interactive and participative approach, by means of drama. In one particular piece of drama, I use the regulative features of "shame" and "conformity" in African Caribbean life as hermeneutical tools for re-imagining Paul's encounter with Eutychus as depicted in Acts 20:7–11. See "It Could Have Happened Like This?" in Anthony G. Reddie, *Acting in Solidarity* (London: Darton, Longman and Todd, 2005), 45–53.

55. See Chapter 3.

56. See James W. Perkinson, *White Theology: Outing Whiteness in Modernity* (New York: Palgrave Macmillan, 2004).

57. See Beckford, *God and the Gangs*, 72–84.

58. I address aspects of this phenomena in a previous piece of work. See Reddie, *Dramatizing Theologies*, 86–91.

59. See Hope, Timmel and Hodzi, *Teaching for Transformation*, Book 2, pp. 1–3.

60. See Freire, *Pedagogy of the Oppressed*, 62.

Index

Printed in the United States
208636BV00001B/1-57/P

9 781845 533861